CENTRED IN TRUTH
The Story of Swami Nitya-swarup-ananda

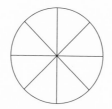

CENTRED IN TRUTH

The Story of

SWAMI NITYA-SWARUP-ANANDA

VOLUME 2

Selected Writings

Reminiscences

Memorial Lecture Programmes

SHELLEY BROWN, M.D.

Kalpa Tree Press

New York

Kalpa Tree Press
65 East 96th Street, Suite 12D
New York, NY 10128

First edition

Designed by Thomas Whitridge
Set in Monotype Fournier by Ink, Inc., New York, New York
Printed in the United States of America

Library of Congress Catalog Card Number: 00-193244

Publisher's Cataloging-in-Publication Data

Brown, Shelley.
  Centred in truth: the story of Swami
Nitya-swarup-ananda / Shelley Brown. —New
York: Kalpa Tree Press, 2001.
    p. ; cm.
Includes bibliographical references and index.
  CONTENTS: v. 1. Visionary monk of the
Ramakrishna Order, founder of the Institute
of Culture in Calcutta, and apostle of
human unity — v. 2. Selected writings,
reminiscences, memorial lecture programmes.

    ISBN 0-9706368-0-6
      1. Nityaswarupananda, Swami. 2. Ramakrishna
Mission—Biography. 3. Hindus—India. 4. Hinduism
Missions—Biography. 5. Nityaswarupananda,
Swami—Correspondence. I. Title. II. Centered in Truth.
  III. Story of Swami Nitya-swarup-ananda.

BL1280 . 292 . N58 B76 2001   00-193244
294 . 555 / 092 B—dc21   CIP

CONTENTS

Volume 2

Selected Writings

Swami Nitya-swarup-ananda writing at his desk at the Institute of Culture, 1992

INTRODUCTION

AT THE AGE OF NINETY-THREE, Swami Nitya-swarup-ananda could still be seen bent daily over his desk with total concentration, pen in hand, writing and rewriting in his own neat script the latest proofs from a book-in-progress. This scene epitomized a lifetime of putting his thoughts on paper and his visions in print, surrounded by his dictionaries and the ever-present, dog-eared early hardbound edition of *The Complete Works of Swami Vivekananda*. Writing was an act of service, no less than building the grand edifice of the Institute of Culture in which he spent, in a small room, his final days.

As a result, we have been gifted with a literary legacy spanning more than a half century, from his work as a young monk in the early 1930s to his last book in 1992. Choosing for this brief anthology was a challenge, for his writings are brimful of stimulating ideas. A piecemeal selection doesn't do justice to the subtle and complex scheme for worldwide education that he developed over a lifetime, nor to his broad range of related topics. The final offering is an exciting glimpse (but merely a glimpse) of his deep commitments and encyclopaedic interests.

Four major groupings of his work are presented. The first is a small sampling from what might be called his master theme, "education for human unity and world civilization," already discussed at length in Volume 1. Secondly, selections of his published "Observations" from the 1950s and early 1970s show the truly amazing diversity of subjects that he essayed over the years. Thirdly, his monograph *How I Came to the Feet of Sri Ramakrishna* lends a personal note and gives the reader a privileged view of his most sacred memories. Fourthly, *Divine Rights of the Sangha* presents the culmination of his thought and his final testament to his Order.

FOR THE FIRST GROUP of selections, a preliminary explanation of how Swami Nitya-swarup-ananda's writings flowered into his master theme may be helpful. The main body of his published work was devoted to various aspects of a new kind of cultural education, spiritually based, to bring about a harmonious world civilization. A steely purpose united all these writings. From one decade to the next, his conviction about the *modus operandi* never faltered. There was naturally some repetition, but what evolved over the course of time was an enrichment as well as a reinforcement of his blueprint for education, becoming ever more detailed as it expanded to fulfil a global agenda.

These core writings testify not only why, but how, the human race must ultimately broaden its perspective, deepen its awareness of wholeness, and become spiritualized—at which point true civilization will begin. If this seems utopian in a world emotionally crippled by selfish materialism, Swami Nitya-swarup-ananda had faith in the words of his source, Swami Vivekananda, a prophet of our own age whose predictions carry the inevitability of their eventual fulfilment and who declared that consciously or unconsciously all of mankind was headed towards "harmony of Oneness," which will eventually unite the whole world. This grand vision was Swami Nitya-swarup-ananda's life's work; with eyes unveiled, he became its impassioned apostle.

A long succession of publications on the master theme emerged over the years in step with the growth of the Institute of Culture as he guided it towards new frontiers of education and an ever-widening global outreach—beginning with his earliest reports and articles and extending later to his monographs and books: *The Threefold Cord* (1959, 1962), *School of World Civilization* (1964, 1967), *Education for World Civilization* (1970), *Human Unity and Education for World Civilization* (1978), *The World Civilization Centre* (1978, 1983), *India's Message to Herself and to the World* (1983), and *Education for Human Unity and World Civilization* (1986). The reader is referred to the 1986 book for the most comprehensive review of his master theme, and to the biography in Volume 1 for a detailed discussion of its components and development.

The two selections in the first grouping have been chosen mainly for their concise summary of his major objectives. The preface to the second edition of *The Threefold Cord* (January 1962) is his classic statement about the role of the Institute of Culture in promoting a remedy for the world's disunity and strife. Oft quoted, and reproduced entirely in Irene Ray's 1962 monograph, *Will Towards Mankind,* the preface embodies Swami Nitya-swarup-ananda's credo: a new kind of cultural education to create an allegiance to mankind-as-a-whole and to "ensure to coming generations a worldwide union of minds and hearts." A few months later, when Swami Nitya-swarup-ananda was addressing a tearful audience at the Institute who had come to bid him farewell, his final words spoke of this credo, and of how it had developed from the teachings of Swami Vivekananda, at whose feet he laid the Institute's past, present, and future endeavours (see Appendix 4).

The second selection was written eight years later, after Swami Nitya-swarup-ananda had completed a world tour and had returned to the Institute as its Secretary. The "Rationale" that opens *Education for World Civilization,* his 1970 monograph, neatly outlines his key concepts for a global agenda: the psychological changes needed for a new world order, the roles of science and philosophy, and a new teaching strategy called "cultural confrontation."

THE SECOND GROUPING is a selection of Swami Nitya-swarup-ananda's short essays published in the *Bulletin,* the monthly journal of the Ramakrishna Mission Institute of Culture, during the years he was Secretary. The discovery of these long-forgotten and highly readable "Observations" unearthed a treasure trove.

As befits the nature of what are truly "observations," Swami Nitya-swarup-ananda takes care to introduce the topic under discussion and to place it in context. But before our eyes he is also deepening and heightening its perspective, distilling the essence while hoisting it aloft to examine it in the light of truth. Remaining hidden, as it were, within the discussion, and bearing his own vast erudition lightly, he makes even the most difficult subject seem within reach of our understanding.

Varying in length from one to seven pages at the beginning of each issue of the *Bulletin,* the essays contain piercing insights into the arts, literature, social commentary, cultural life, current world events, and whatever else of importance was swirling in the enlightened vortex of the Institute. Little seems to have escaped his keen eye. A perennial learner and prodigious reader, he culled the world's finest journals, magazines, and books for challenging articles and reports.

The "Observations," while bonded to the goals of the Institute, are innovative explorations of widely diverse subjects. Some offer a gentle corrective to Western misconceptions of Indian metaphysical thought, which otherwise tend to become embedded as obstacles to the flow of genuine Indian ideals into the world view. Typical of this mode are "On the Misuse of Indian Philosophical Terms" (August 1952) and "Schweitzer and Indian Philosophy" (January 1954). Swami Nitya-swarup-ananda not only takes on Dr. Schweitzer's negative misconceptions, but goes further to apply the positive view of Indian philosophy to every facet of life, to individuals and to society at large, showing how the concept of unity can be worked out in each sphere, be it moral, ethical, or material.

His commentaries on life's personal problems and spiritual growth are the subject of such helpful essays as "Spiritual Understanding" (September 1951; see Chapter 3 in Volume 1), "Who Can Be a Leader of Souls?" (May 1952), and "The Desire to Escape from Everyday Consciousness" (November 1952). These no-nonsense reflections on the harsh realities of life expose our clever self-delusions in avoiding them and explain the conscious disciplines that are needed to bring us back on course.

Other "Observations" bring our modern civilization under scrutiny, its soulless quality and its malaise, more than ever in need of conscience, refinement, and spiritual intuition. "Head or Heart?" (February 1953), for example, questions the individual's satisfaction in an increasingly mechanized and depersonalized society without laying the finger of blame on the achievements of science and technology. Science is not harmful in itself, he argues, but we must engage the power of the human spirit by cultivating "heart" (our finer feelings) to balance the intellectual accomplishments of the modern age. This alone can nourish the world soul, which we neglect at our peril.

Today's reader will be struck by his foresight, his ability to grasp future paradigms years or even decades before others could catch up to stake their claims. His discussion of the mysteries of matter and spirit as viewed by quantum theory and monistic philosophy in "Some Implications of Modern Physics" (July 1953) anticipated the current writings on this theme, such as *Belonging to the Universe: Explorations on the Frontiers of Science and Spirituality* (1991), by Fritjof Capra, David Steindl-Rast, and Thomas Matus. "Gone is the solid world," the Swami states, as he relates the discoveries of modern physics to the basic conceptions of Vedantic thought, requiring in each case a basic change in our perception of what "is and is not." These complementary definitions of "reality," he points out, are poised jointly to influence the way we will think and live in future, and are equally relevant to East and West.

The Vedantic view of reality comes into subtle focus in his essay on the sacred symbol *Om*, "A Universal Symbol" (February 1954). While praising the rational approach of the scientific age for opening the door to the knowledge of the true nature of the universe, he stresses the suprarational training needed for deep spiritual discovery. The universe is revealed as pure spirit to the seeker only when the mind is intuitively sharpened to the point of "breaking through the outer crusts of forms and names." And only then is the seeker prepared to understand the symbol *Om*. The metaphysical discussion of sound, symbol, and thought that ensues plumbs the very depths of serious spiritual study.

Advancing age did not dim his avant-garde mentality. Examples of it abound in his later essays, such as "India and the Coming of TV" (March 1972), which relates the ideas of the celebrated Canadian scholar and media prophet, Marshall McLuhan, to the aims and methods of

Upanishadic education. Will the new medium of television have a positive impact on Indian civilization?—only, the Swami argues, if it is consciously applied.

In such manifold ways, Swami Nitya-swarup-ananda's "Observations" call for our personal engagement in developing a spiritualized world culture through a synthesis of lofty thought and action. These essays, cosmopolitan as they are, go far beyond intellectual discourse for its own sake. Their hallmark is his visionary yet practical approach to all kinds of serious ideas, from all parts of the globe, that he felt could broaden or deepen our cultural and spiritual commitment.

THE THIRD GROUP consists of two lectures that present a rare glimpse of Swami Nitya-swarup-ananda's personal reflections on Sri Ramakrishna and the direct disciples. As is well known, he was almost never heard to speak in this personal fashion. Nor did he himself write any of the articles on Sri Ramakrishna that appeared in the *Bulletin*, relying on guest contributors for this task. Thus to have captured, as it were, his few remarks in the two lectures that constitute his monograph *How I Came to the Feet of Sri Ramakrishna* is a rare treat. After many decades of being requested to put down his reminiscences of the direct disciples of Sri Ramakrishna, and of the Holy Mother who initiated him into spiritual life, he finally did so at the age of eighty-nine. The reader has thus gained the advantage of Swami Nitya-swarup-ananda's own poignant story of his earliest years, to which the author's remarks in the biography are an embellishment.

THE FOURTH SELECTION, *Divine Rights of the Sangha* (1992), is offered unabridged. This final testament of Swami Nitya-swarup-ananda is an epiphany. The true meaning of the advent of Sri Rama-krishna as an Avatar, and Swami Vivekananda as the Prophet of our age, strikes his deepest sensitivity. A lifetime of striving to bring the world closer to Swami Vivekananda's vision of human unity now finds its culmination for Swami Nitya-swarup-ananda in this most sacred revelation of their teachings. In his final monograph he sets forth how humanity will find its unity, its harmony, becoming One with Their Universal Form when the ideal is realized—and how it is that the polestar shines on Swami Vivekananda's own Order, the Ramakrishna Sangha, as the vehicle of its fulfilment.

THE THREEFOLD CORD

Preface to the Second Edition (1962)

This is the second edition of *The Threefold Cord* which was first published in 1959. It has been revised and in parts rewritten to make it more clearly expressive of the ideology underlying the work of this Institute of Culture.

Today, among those in all nations who ponder upon the problems confronting the modern world, there is discernible a strong current of agreement that the way forward for mankind is the development of a basic world viewpoint which will provide for the individual viewpoint, whether cultural, national, or personal, a sense of completion and fulfilment. The cultivation of this basic world viewpoint, it is agreed, is the one sure means of ridding the world of its present fissiparous tendencies which now assume such a proportion as to render into mere mockery all man's achievements in social and individual welfare.

Two forces engage the world today, one making for provincial fragmentation, isolationism, disunity, and strife, the other making for the acceptance of global consciousness and global organization. The former force is fed by ignorance and fear, and by long-sustained habitual attitudes of superiority and exclusivism, while the latter is mainly a force of circumstance, unconsciously produced by the coming together of nations made possible by modern methods of communication. But it is also fostered consciously, by some who are visionaries, those few who actually perceive global unity as a fact, and by others who formulate political and economic plans on a world scale and try to administer them through world agencies. Although a strong body of opinion is thus created, conscious fostering of the world viewpoint lacks, so far, effective planned organization. The need to create the psychological background, the social and cultural atmosphere, required for global political and economic administration has not yet been widely conceded. Consequently the conscious efforts towards this goal that do exist, the political and economic plans, and the efforts of such organizations as UNESCO, are largely frustrated. Seeds are sown, but the ground has not been prepared; the new pattern of life designed for a cosmopolitan citizen is offered to the citizen who is still immersed in provincialism and exclusivism. This new pattern of life, being largely presented in political and economic terms, is unable to touch the finer responses in those to whom it is offered.

The immediate need in the world today may thus be seen to be cultural education which will ensure the development of global consciousness, a basic world viewpoint, as the next forward step in the thought of man. The need for this forward step in thought is clearly fundamental to all other needs, for, urgent and imperative as physical needs undisputedly are, the fulfilment of those needs cannot by itself bring to man the well-being that is its aim, a fact which finds ready proof in the modern world.

The happiness, even the very existence, of the human race is thus seen to be dependent upon social, cultural, and psychological education which will ensure the development of a world community. Before such a community can develop there must be implanted in the minds and hearts of men everywhere an appreciation of the fact of the solidarity of mankind. The loyalty of every individual will be broadened out to embrace the world as a whole; and every man's heritage will be the human heritage which is common to all. Through cultural education based on the world viewpoint, a world civilization will be brought into existence which will absorb and integrate the contributions of every nation in every age.

The role of cultural education is of immense significance today in creating a new allegiance which is the prerequisite to global harmony. In working towards this new allegiance to mankind-as-a-whole, cultural education of a new type is called for. The limited perspectives which have so far prevailed, and have been found acceptable in assessing standards of education and culture, will no longer suffice. The function of education will now be conceived as the building of an individual strengthened and supported by the cultural heritage of the whole of humanity. The creative mind will draw upon the achievements, the highest attainments, not of one culture only, but of all cultures combined into a single store of multitudinous wealth. The future world citizen will acknowledge as his cultural forebears Plato and the Buddha, Isaiah and Lao Tse, Cicero and Shankara, Kalidasa and Shakespeare, lifting each one of these great minds out of the narrow confines of the single culture that has so far claimed him as its own. This does not imply a mere superficial acquaintance with the cultures of the world, but, on the contrary, it calls for a deep understanding of each culture to reveal its universal dimension, its unique contribution to the over-all thought of humanity.

   This Institute of Culture exists to play its part in promoting cultural education of this type—education at the academic level, at the level of practical research, and at the popular level. The aim of this education is to ensure to coming generations a world-wide union of minds and hearts, springing from the integration of all the essential insights now carried within the various cultures of the world.

In the third presentation of his master theme of "education for world civilization," in 1970, Swami Nitya-swarup-ananda added an elegantly written rationale, explaining in a few paragraphs the basic building blocks for creating a new type of personality—a global citizen—for a new world order.

EDUCATION FOR WORLD CIVILIZATION

The Rationale

OLD ATTITUDES VERSUS NEW ATTITUDES

Every thinking individual feels concern about the tensions of the modern world and the direction in which the world is moving.

The basic cause of tension may be seen in the lack of adjustment between old attitudes and habits of thought and new ways of life which advances in science and technology have enforced.

The old attitudes are based on the idea of separateness, whether of individuals or of nations. They are rooted in a psychological attitude that may be called "fragmented," the assumption that man stands against man, nation against nation; that thoughts and ideas and ways of life different from our own can only be regarded with suspicion and mistrust. The individual regards himself as a separate entity confronting an alien world and it is this idea of separateness that gives rise to such attitudes as superiority, exclusivism, hostility, fear, callous indifference, and sheer uncomprehending ignorance.

The new way of life, springing from ease of communications, exposes these attitudes to new situations which reveal interdependence as a basic fact of existence.

SCIENCE AND TECHNOLOGY: FRAMEWORK FOR GLOBAL UNITY

Thus science and technology are today helping forward the natural process of life, which is interdependence. Since the world is, in fact, an indivisible whole, of which each individual part is an expression, those parts are interrelated and interdependent.

Now, for the first time in history, this interrelation has been made obvious to man by political and economic factors. Man can now see for himself that what happens to one part of the world ultimately affects the whole; and that progress in one part cannot succeed unless it ultimately spells progress for the whole. Man can now see that in all its aspects and activities, humanity is a unity.

Seeing these facts for himself, however, does not release man from his old attitudes. It does not help him to achieve a psychological change; it does not touch his feelings, broaden his loyalties, deepen his character. His old attitudes and feelings still find support and justification in laws and social institutions and in ingrained habits of thought and speech.

Science and technology, therefore, have provided merely a framework for global unity. The true foundation has yet to be laid.

ONE EXISTENCE: FOUNDATION OF GLOBAL UNITY

The true foundation of global unity rests in the consciousness of an underlying spiritual oneness; it rests in the realization that every separate group or community, every individual, although unique, is yet an expression of that spiritual unity.

The highest teachings of every system of thought converge on one point—that the life of man finds fulfilment in the knowledge of his own spiritual nature, his real nature. Today, throughout the world, youth is engaged in a search for "reality." This search is conducted through sex, music, and drugs, yet it is leading to the discovery that neither the body, nor the mind, nor the senses constitutes man's real and basic nature. The way is therefore open to the discovery that the real nature of man rests in existence itself, the spirit that lies beyond body, mind, and senses, while these merely provide a very limited view of that real existence.

Youth's search for the knowledge of "reality" can therefore lead to a forward step in man's progress, for if it leads to the knowledge that man's real nature rests in existence itself, the concept of spiritual oneness must follow. Existence is universal; it is infinite, one, not many. Humanity is thus essentially one.

It is only by grasping this fact of the spiritual oneness of mankind that the psychology of fragmentation can be overcome. The idea of separateness springs directly from ignorance of the fact that man's real nature rests in existence itself. True human relationships must therefore be grounded in the knowledge of man's real nature and the underlying oneness of existence. This knowledge alone can provide the real basis of human understanding and unity.

PSYCHOLOGICAL CHANGE BASED ON KNOWLEDGE OF UNITY OF EXISTENCE

Knowledge of the unity of existence will change man's attitude to himself. The way man looks at himself, his conception of his own nature, governs all his other concepts. Thus a profound sense of unity, within himself and within the world around him, will lead man forward to the understanding that, in spite of outward appearances, every individual, every nation, is interrelated and interdependent. Then he will see that differences in thought and ideas and ways of life can be accepted because varying ideas are but varying expressions of the same basic reality and are therefore enriching experiences. It is then that man will acquire a sense of human community and release himself from his old narrow attitudes and feelings.

What is needed therefore is a reorientation of man's view of himself. He must be given a new psychology. Science and technology, as we have seen, have paved the way to this by opening his eyes to the fact of the world's interdependence and interrelation. Now the time is ripe for a planned, full-scale attack upon the psychology of modern man to prove to him that wherever there is expansion in love or progress in well-being, individually or collectively, it springs from the perception, the realization, and the putting into practice of the eternal truth—the oneness of all beings.

EDUCATION THROUGH CULTURAL CONFRONTATION

Such a full-scale attack upon man's psychology can only be made through a new type of education which embraces and makes detailed use of mankind's various cultures. Each culture of the world has its own basic idea which is its genius or life-force, and to which it gives particular emphasis in the course of its expression through various fields. This basic idea is a universal truth and thus becomes that culture's contribution to the thought of mankind.

The new type of education envisaged calls for a carefully planned confrontation of cultures. This confrontation will take the form of an educational programme in which scholars and students from all parts of the world will participate. The outcome of the educational programme will be not skin-deep knowledge imparted from teacher to student, but a living experience, enjoyed by teachers and students alike. Through an active process, in which everyone present is engaged, each individual will enter into ways of thinking, feeling, and living different from his own.

Now, having viewed each culture from its own standpoint, the standpoint of its own special genius, the participant will experience a deep change in his mentality. His prejudices, his narrow attitudes and feelings will be swept away and he will begin to think in a new way. A vital reorientation of his mind and personality will have taken place.

This confrontation of the genius or life-force in each culture, and of the universal elements contained in its various fields of activity, will also reveal to him the fact that all the cultures are complementary to each other, each making a valuable contribution to the overall thought of man and the process of civilization. It is then that the meaning of world civilization will be made clear to him, for he will see that world civilization is, in fact, the sum total of all the achievements of the human race, in whatever age and in whatever field.

EDITORIAL "OBSERVATIONS"
From the *Bulletin*

April 1951, pp. 51–52
TRAGEDY

One of the Western speakers at the symposium on "The Western View of Life" held recently at the Institute made, in passing, an interesting observation. "India," he said, "has no sense of tragedy and Indian literature has not produced great tragedies such as were produced by the Greeks." The speaker presented his observation not as a criticism but as a plain statement of fact. The reply given to this by a subsequent speaker was that in the life of the Buddha we have a very great example of the Indian sense of tragedy, for it was tragedy which impelled him to seek Enlightenment.

This reply, we feel, epitomizes all that may be said in answer to the Western speaker's observation. Tragedy, as Western drama shows, can only exist when problems remain unsolved. Death and destruction and affliction are not in themselves tragedy. They become tragic when not resolved in some system of thought large enough to embrace them.

Tragedy exists in the Indian mind—but it cannot stay there long enough to provide a basis for great literature. The Indian mind must resolve its tragedy, and the greatness of Indian literature lies always in the presentation of that solution and not, as the Western speaker rightly said, in the tragedy itself. This great urge towards solution reflects the keenness and depth of the Indian sense of tragedy. It must not be supposed that the solution is independent of tragedy as the cause, for the solution presented is not a facile divorcement from life. It was tragedy as a great impelling force that led to the solid practical search for "That, knowing which all things are known."

"One thing only do I teach," said the Buddha, "sorrow—and the uprooting of sorrow." This is the fundamental message of Indian teaching. The individual, aware of tragedy, is provided with innumerable ways and means of resolving his tragedy. This is the search which every individual must undertake and achieve for himself. There is no vicarious solution to tragedy.

May 1952, pp. 83–84

WHO CAN BE A LEADER OF SOULS?

An outstanding, and hitherto unpublished, essay by the late Swami Gnaneswarananda appears in the bi-monthly *Vedanta and the West* (Los Angeles) in the first issue for 1952. "Who can be a leader of souls?" asks the Swami—a perennial question, no doubt, in this world where guidance is constantly sought and constantly offered, for there are plenty who are willing to lead. And yet the question remains, for such leadership fails and in the end the individual is left to his own resources. Thus it is that in giving his reply the Swami concentrates on the individual. He recalls that in the Katha Upanishad the journey of life is compared to a ride in a chariot. The faculty symbolized by the driver of this chariot is the buddhi, "a determined will" or "a part of human consciousness which registers determination." Thus none other than the buddhi can be the leader of souls, and the secret of a successful journey is the development of the buddhi. This means overcoming the swing between the two poles of certainty and doubt. It is a common experience that doubt means powerlessness, whereas decision is at once reflected in action. All religious practice therefore has this one end in view—the attainment of a large supply of certainty in the buddhi. For the unfoldment of spiritual perfection we must arrive at the single conviction that we are divine, and then gradually regulate our life's course accordingly. If this one proposition is accepted with strength and tenacity, and if this one certainty is reflected in and through life's actions, life will be entirely revolutionized and spirituality will unfold as naturally as a flower. Thus the soul can only find leadership within, and aspiring leaders who want to help the world can only do so by the power of their own inner light. Leadership consists in the power that silently illumines.

May 1952, p. 84
THE RIVER COMES TO CALCUTTA

The well known film *The River*, which was made near Calcutta, was shown locally last month. Those in other countries who have already seen it will be interested to know the reactions of the Calcutta audience since they, in this case, hold a unique position as critics. The story deals with an English family who, living beside Bengal's great river and deriving their income from jute, conduct their affairs in full harmony with their Indian background. Every opportunity is taken in the film to show, describe and explain that background, even including such charming details as the young boatman grinding the "mosala" for his curry. It is this that has led the film to be described in some quarters as a documentary and this verdict is supported by local opinion, for no fault has been found with the interpretation of Indian life. But there local interest in the film apparently ended. It ran for three weeks.

Mr. Harper, in his "After Hours" comments in *Harper's Magazine*, November, 1951, devoted over three columns to a severe criticism of this film and of the reviewers who had praised it. Although he concedes that "the Ganges is a handsome stream and that it is interesting to know that along its banks the smokestack is as much a feature of the landscape as on the Delaware," Mr. Harper is obviously only concerned with the film as entertainment and he judges it according to conventional standards. We feel, however, that other aspects of this pioneer effort are far more important. From country to country mutual ignorance and misrepresentation flourish, and conventional entertainment either trades on this fact or ignores it. *The River* is a sincere and successful attempt to present Bengali life to the world, and in doing this in the name of entertainment it is an attempt ennobling to the industry.

August 1952, pp. 143–45
ON THE MISUSE
OF INDIAN PHILOSOPHICAL TERMS

The simplicity of an idea is no guarantee of its being easily under-stood. Indian traditional thought is in its essence simple; it is composed of simple ideas clothed in simple words. These simple ideas, however, being simple in the sense of Lao Tse's "Simple Way," and easy in the sense in which Jesus said "My yoke is easy," lend themselves, equally with these, to misunderstanding and sheer incomprehension. The rea-son for this is not far to seek. The ideas of philosophy and religion are nothing less than expressions of spiritual experience. To be grasped therefore they must be experienced spiritually, and by those who have prepared themselves for the experience. "Who can explain sex to a child?" said Sri Ramakrishna when asked to describe samadhi.

Many of the terms which express Indian philosophical thought are nowadays rapidly being adopted by Western intellectuals. And if these terms are misunderstood in this country, there is evidence to show that they are equally, if not more, misunderstood in the West. It is quite natural that this should be so for, in this preliminary stage of under-standing between East and West, books move more freely than indi-viduals; but the study of books, even the greatest of them, needs to be backed by the living touch of a teacher if the necessary reorientation of the mind is to be achieved. There should be no thought therefore of condemning the misuse of Indian philosophical terms. Rather may it be regarded as an opportunity for a simple and constructive exchange of ideas, such as is always aimed at in these "Observations."

Non-attachment

Among the terms which are most commonly misunderstood, in both East and West, is "non-attachment" which is used to translate the San-skrit "anasakti." Professor J. B. S. Haldane, scientist and friend of India, writing in *The Visva-Bharati Quarterly* (Feb.–April) has devoted several paragraphs to this subject, and if we now base our remarks on his we feel sure that he will be interested in what we have to say. The article to which we refer, entitled "A Biologist Looks at India," was written following a recent visit to this country. It is noteworthy in many respects; it is charming and instructive, and contains several very interesting and important suggestions which will be of value to artists and scientists.

It so happens that, having used a number of Sanskrit terms, Professor Haldane graciously remarks, "and I have little doubt that I misuse them." This does not however appear to refer to what he has to say on the subject of non-attachment. We agree with him when he describes non-attachment as not only an ideal of Indian culture but a human ideal. But he seems to relate it largely with economics and at the same time to equate it with mere indifference to things material. "In a country where poverty is as widespread as in India non-attachment may quite literally mean death from starvation, and death for one's family as well as oneself.". . . "Non-attachment to possessions is only possible for ordinary people when the community is so organized that those who have worked hard are not going to starve.". . . "A scholar who is interested in abstract problems and is not concerned with the pursuit of wealth or fame is nearer to being completely non-attached than a person who is constantly seeking wealth, power, or sensual gratification."

Non-attachment is a characteristic of the liberated soul, and is therefore also a means to liberation. Liberation, which is the goal of all religious endeavour, whether recognized as such or not, implies freedom from the bondage of good as well as from the bondage of evil. How is this to be achieved? Bondage occurs when the mind identifies itself with its experiences. "Remember that great saying of the Sankhya," said Swami Vivekananda, "'The whole of nature is for the soul, not the soul for nature.' The very reason of nature's existence is for the education of the soul; it has no other meaning; it is there because the soul must have knowledge, and through knowledge free itself. If we remember this always we shall never be attached to nature; we shall know that nature is a book in which we are to read, and that when we have gained the required knowledge the book is of no more value to us. Instead of that, however, we are identifying ourselves with nature, we are thinking that the soul is for nature, that the spirit is for the flesh, and, as the common saying has it, we think that man 'lives to eat' and not 'eats to live'; we are continually making this mistake; we are regarding nature as ourselves and are becoming attached to it; and as soon as this attachment comes, there is the deep impression on the soul which binds us down and makes us work not from freedom but like slaves."

The Test of Non-attachment

Slaves work under compulsion; he who is attached lives, thinks and acts under the compulsion of selfishness. An action is not unselfish or unattached merely because it is philanthropic or concerned with abstract problems. This is not the test. The test lies in the peace and happiness it brings. Attachment brings, sooner or later, misery and a reaction of pain. Any happiness it brings is only temporary. But non-attachment brings the love which can only be known through freedom. He who can love and act and serve without a painful reaction works like a master, not like a slave, and is fit to achieve non-attachment.

The secret of working and acting thus without a painful reaction is to look for no selfish return. Not that there will be no results, no return. Results must come, but they will not be appropriated to the individual; the individual will not identify himself with them. Nor does this imply an attitude of indifference, or of half-hearted endeavour. There must be as much power of attachment as of detachment. Externally, the unattached man appears the same as the attached man. The difference lies within, in his attitude and in his ability to withdraw his mind whenever he should do so. Perhaps St. Paul had just this in view when he used the words, "Having nothing, and yet possessing all things."

These few remarks on the subject of non-attachment are by no means an adequate explanation. The lectures of Swami Vivekananda will be of immense help to the earnest seeker who wishes for real understanding but in the end that can only be achieved by spiritual perception.

November 1952, pp. 203–4
THE DESIRE TO ESCAPE
FROM EVERYDAY CONSCIOUSNESS

Life is a burden and the burden of life comes as a problem, sooner or later, to every individual. It does not imply only the major trials and tragedies of life; it does not imply only the physical ills that beset the elderly or the chronic invalid; it does not imply only the constant vexations of daily life. More than these, it implies the desire to escape from everyday consciousness. This desire is felt by every healthy adult. There is an indefinable sense of the need to go beyond the limitations imposed by the fact of being an individual. Those who, by training or by insight, are able to recognize this feeling as one arising from man's own inner nature are able to use it wisely as a means of progress on the spiritual path. But the majority of people are unable to recognize the feeling, nor are they able to act upon it with control. They therefore respond to the urge to "get out of themselves" in ways both good and evil. This urge is one of the strongest motivating powers in the behaviour of the individual and, if consciously directed, can be of tremendous value in spiritual life. Unfortunately it is but rarely consciously directed and is all too often allowed either to pose as altruism or to be spent in mere indulgence.

Self-Transcendence

Aldous Huxley discusses this subject in an article entitled "Substitutes for Liberation" published in *Vedanta and the West* (Los Angeles) in its July–August, 1952, issue. In his article, which is a chapter from his forthcoming book *The Devil of Loudun,* he shows that "self-transcendence is by no means invariably upwards. Indeed, in most cases it is an escape either downwards into a state lower than that of personality, or else horizontally into something wider than ego, but not higher, not essentially other.... Without an understanding of man's deep-seated urge to self-transcendence, of his very natural reluctance to take the hard, ascending way, and of his search for some bogus liberation either below or to one side of his personality, we cannot hope to make sense of the observed and recorded facts of history, of individual and social psychology."

In describing a few of the more common "grace-substitutes, into which and by means of which men and women have tried to escape from the tormenting consciousness of being themselves," Aldous Huxley gives three examples of the most popular avenues of downward self-transcendence. These are drugs, including alcohol, elementary sexuality indulged in for its own sake, and crowd-delirium. "Being in a crowd is the best-known antidote to independent thought." In each of these, "what matters is the awareness, if only for an hour or two, if only for a few minutes, of being someone, or more often something, other than the insulated self."

But most men and women choose to go neither up nor down, but sideways. "They identify themselves with some cause wider than their own immediate interests, but not degradingly lower and, if higher, higher only within the range of current social values. This horizontal, or nearly horizontal, self-transcendence may be into something as trivial as a hobby, or as precious as married love. It can be brought about through self-identification with any human activity. . . ."

This urge to self-transcendence, expressed in such varied ways, arises because "we know (or to be more accurate, something within us knows) that the ground of our individual knowing is identical with the Ground of all knowing and all being." If this were properly and widely understood, what an impetus would be given to human endeavour for good. Civilization demands from the individual self-identification with the highest of human causes. When that self-identification is accompanied by self-identification with the Ground of all being, then will the individual achieve true self-transcendence.

February 1953, pp. 31–33
HEAD OR HEART?

The supporting framework of modern civilization is the intellect of man. With just pride man can survey what he has achieved in penetrating the secrets of nature and in overcoming natural limitations. Whatever is great and good in Western civilization today has been earned not merely by toil and effort, but by thought and the power of man's will. It is commonplace today to speak of these great achievements and of the good to humanity that can accrue if the blessings of modern civilization are allowed to spread throughout the world and change the way of life of even the humblest in every land.

Occasionally, however, a voice is raised to point out that in the midst of all these blessings danger lurks. Evil follows good as shadows follow the sun, and the dangers inherent in modern civilization are no less great than the blessings. The Pope, in his broadcast last Christmas Eve, gave the world such a reminder. He spoke of the "mechanized society" of the present day, of "the demon of organization" that was robbing man of his personality. These are dangers which have arisen by a process of insidious growth, but the development of atomic weapons presented a sudden danger. The suddenness, coupled with the realization of what these and greater weapons can do, has served to jolt the modern mind into an awareness of the need to study critically the trends and the foundations of civilization. President Truman, in an address outspoken to a degree only possible for an outgoing President unlikely again to hold high office, pointed out last January that something profound has happened which has entirely altered the "preatomic" view of society and history. "The war of the future would be one in which man could extinguish millions of lives at one blow, demolish cities, wipe out the cultural achievements of the past, and destroy the very structure of civilization."

Thus having arrived at a level of civilization that is not merely mechanized and soulless, organized and de-personalized, but is also capable of self-destruction, it is necessary for man now to discover what is lacking in his approach to life. It is necessary to discover the effects on human beings of the growth of an industrial civilization. This problem is, in fact, being studied, not merely by sociologists but by industrialists in conference with representatives of the arts, the professions, science, and humanistic studies, as at the conference held at Cornell, New York, in 1951, sponsored by the American Council of Learned Societies and the Corning Glass Works. In spite of all the amenities provided by industrial and State welfare, it is obvious that other problems still remain untouched; and these are problems of the mind, of the heart, of the spirit. The amount of satisfaction the individual derives from his work, his use of leisure, his part in community life, the extent of his confidence in life, his faith, security, and peace of mind—these are all aspects of that one basic problem of the effect of mechanization and organization upon man's spiritual development.

Looking Within

There is further significance in stating these problems. To raise them is to recognize that human progress means spiritual progress; without it all other progress loses meaning and value. It is to recognize that it is, after all, the cultivation of the heart and not only of the intellect and the body that can carry man forward. The exclusive cultivation of the intellect results in external changes, in wonderful inventions bringing wonderful improvements. But, as is so obvious today, these improvements are not enough; without internal changes to hold the balance all the refinements of civilization must come to nothing—and, worse than nothing, to disaster.

"The real question before humanity," said President Prasad recently, "is how to make the heart of man big and strong, instead of concentrating only on the brain." It is by training that the heart can be made big and strong. Education today means intellectual education which provides mental and physical training; the training of the emotions is a discipline unheard of. In every other sphere great emphasis is placed upon the need for training, and an untrained practitioner in any field is a quack. But feelings and emotions are left either to run wild or to remain stunted and undeveloped, with the greatly unfortunate results that we see around us.

Let Head and Heart Combine

An immediate remedy which can be put into effect by every thoughtful person is, then, to promote the proper cultivation and guidance of the faculty of feeling. If there is anywhere a rich field of research, it is here—and one of the utmost practical significance. Man is in search of power. His greatest source of power until today he thought was in the pursuit of science. But the truth is now forcefully brought home to him that science is not enough. It has led him to great achievements, but it cannot save him from the dangers inherent in those achievements. And so, to save himself he will be forced to search for that which is greater than the power attained by the intellect through science—that other power which lies within him, the power of the heart.

In order to discover this power it is necessary for man to cultivate all fine feelings, all the noble aspirations that lie dormant and neglected within. He must cultivate faith; not so-called blind faith which attempts to believe in what cannot be proved, but a grasp upon the ultimate reality behind all things; the faith of a student who, setting out to master a subject, visualizes the end in view and knows that he can achieve it; or the faith of an artist who, embarking on a work of art, first visualizes the work completed and knows that he can achieve it. Faith, far from being blind, is the vision of truth and the conviction that it can be attained. And with the cultivation of faith it is necessary for man to cultivate the habit of seeing all things constantly in the light of that wider vision until at last he can perceive the reality behind all things. He will then realize that in essence he is one with this ultimate reality which is expressed in the divers forms of the universe. The universe will become one to him. Thus will be born the forbearance, the compassion, the love for all humanity, for all creation, that is now too often regarded as an idle dream. For when man can see the unity behind the universe expressed in all things he will know that to injure others, in thought or in deed, is to injure himself, but to serve others, to love others, is to attain the wholeness for which he longs.

It is this cultivation of subtle, finer feelings that can give to man the perspective and the balanced outlook that now he lacks. To discover the power of his own spirit would be his greatest scientific achievement—for the proper cultivation of love is a science no less than the pursuit of knowledge. This discovery would immediately assign all other discoveries to their proper place. Atomic energy is not in itself dangerous; it is the use to which it is put that spells danger or otherwise. And this is true of every power man holds within his grasp. The power he wields through science must be harnessed, as a river is harnessed, and guided into proper channels for the good of mankind.

The pursuit of science is not in itself evil or wrong, and a mechanized civilization need not kill the soul of man. But heart must keep pace with head and both must combine in the service of humanity, "for the good of the many, for the happiness of the many."

July 1953, pp. 151–56

SOME IMPLICATIONS OF MODERN PHYSICS

[Abridged]

The relationship between matter and spirit, what Lao Tze described as "the profound, the great deep, the open door of bewilderment," has always exercised the greatest fascination over man. In East and West he has ever sought to penetrate the mystery of life, to understand its meaning. Either through the study of the world around him, or through the study of the world within his own mind, the search has continued for the answers to those questions that will reveal the nature of the universe, the nature of man himself. These are questions of equal importance to the scientist and the philosopher. Indeed it is in seeking solutions to them that science and philosophy meet. Fundamentally the problem is one, and the solution must therefore be one.

It has been generally accepted that whatever solution to these mysteries might be found it would be a solution which, as seen through time and space, would fall within the scope of the law of cause and effect.... In the Western world, science, based on Galileo and Newton, has led to a wide acceptance of a mechanistic explanation of the universe; everything is governed by law and all that is required to understand the universe is to understand the complicated functioning of those laws.... In the Eastern world, the law of Karma based on the principle of cause and effect, has dominated man's attitude to life.... The present is determined by past actions, and the future by the present. Even the mind of man, which to all appearances is free, is bound by law....

The law of causality thus accepted throughout the world as unassailable has recently, however, been held up to question. In a B.B.C. broadcast talk entitled "Causality in Modern Physics" (*The Listener*, 22nd January 1953), Professor O. R. Frisch, of Cambridge University, described how "in quantum theory, which in the past twenty-five years has become an important branch of modern physics, it is asserted that atomic events do happen without cause." Radioactive nuclei, for example, do not grow old; they just die one day....

Professor Frisch anticipates the two reasons that come readily to mind for not accepting the contention that these events happen without cause. Firstly, it may be waved aside by saying that the causes for the unexplained behaviour of molecules and atoms are too complex to be completely analysed; as in the case of weather predictions. Secondly, it may be waved aside by saying that the causes are inaccessible, not in principle, but only for the time being. He shows these two arguments to be insufficient and leaves us—at the open door of bewilderment!

Gone Is the Solid World

Now these things that happen without cause are all in the atomic domain, and while Professor Frisch impresses upon us their far-reaching consequences, for "the behaviour of an entire living organism is significantly influenced by what happens to individual molecules," he does at the same time attempt to reassure us. "Much of an organism

does consist of dead matter, of chemicals which interact in a predictable manner, of bones and muscles which are subject to the laws of
classical mechanics. This must be so, or there could be no science of
physiology or biochemistry, and indeed our own bodies would be
unpredictable and uncontrollable. In the same way, the world around
us is essentially real and predictable, and if we are not physicists we
have no need to worry about its roots which reach into the atomic
domain, into the quicksands of quantum theory where things happen
without cause."

But can we be so easily reassured? The world around us may still
appear to be "essentially real" and "dead matter" may still be subject to
the laws of classical mechanics, but Professor Frisch himself has warned
us against "belief in an outside world independent of our observations
and subject to strict causality; the kind of world that is solid and reassuring like a Victorian home."

We have now to give up "the solid, scientific world of the nineteenth century," for quantum theory has revolutionized the scientific
approach, it has "revealed the spark of life which glows even in atoms
and molecules." More than this even, it has taught us "that there is no
sharp distinction between doing and watching. There is no mere
watching, no one-way action of the object on the observer.... It is a
mutual interaction between observer and object. Once that is fully
accepted, we can no longer make a clean cut between ourselves, the
observers, and the passive outside world, waiting to be observed by us.
The outside world is a construction of our mind, designed to fit the
network of actions and observations which constitute our life; that fit
can be made very close when we are concerned with large objects, but
not when objects of atomic size are involved."

Modern physics has yet another shock for those who would cling to
the assumption of a solid world. Professor Leon Rosenfeld, of Man-
chester University, in a B.B.C. broadcast talk on "The Philosophy of
Atomic Physics" (*The Listener,* 5th February 1953) shatters at once the
old idea of the dualism of matter and force. "After years of strenuous

effort, a new picture has emerged, from which the long familiar dualism of matter and force has disappeared. It has been replaced by a synthesis of these two apparently contrasting conceptions.... We must now think of every physical agency as partaking of the two aspects of matter and force.... If we submit them to appropriate tests, each will reveal its double nature. Thus, the exploration of the world of atoms has opened to us a profound unity underlying an apparent duality."

The Interchange of Knowledge

"A profound unity underlying an apparent duality"—familiar words to one who has even a nodding acquaintance with Indian thought. Let us not, however, equate similarities too easily. Let us not take anything for granted, nor assume that the unity visualized by the modern physicist is the same unity perceived by the ancient sages. That the two systems of thought have points in common is already evident, and equally acceptable is the fact that in endeavouring to penetrate the secrets of nature they are moving towards the same goal.

What is required, and what can be of the utmost value to world thought, is the interchange of knowledge between the old world and the new. Indian philosophers knew centuries ago that atoms are not the primal state. Step by step the process of the transformation of the subtle into the gross universe is set out and each stage in the process is carefully named. This knowledge was not gained in the physics laboratory, but by processes purely mental. Let the modern philosophers therefore be acquainted with modern physics, let them see their theories proved by mathematics....

... Quantum theory has revealed, as Professor Frisch explains, that "even looking at a molecule is apt to alter its course." Research into such subtle influences upon action in their relation to the law of Karma would seem to hold out great possibilities. The power of the subtle over the gross is the keynote of ancient philosophy; modern physics confirms that....

Also, then, let the modern physicists be acquainted with ancient thought. The new era in physics has opened up avenues of approach, and introduced perspectives and conceptions which until now have been quite foreign to Western science. And since they happen to be perspectives and conceptions which are fundamental to Eastern thought, surely some help, some inspiration, could be derived, at least in the world of ideas, from an understanding of the older system.

... Modern physics will in its turn influence popular thought and the scientist has the responsibility now of endeavouring to make that influence of the highest possible order.

The Vedantic View

The breaking down of the solid universe of the nineteenth century implies a change in perception.... The paradox can now be admitted of the universe being at once real and unreal. Professor Frisch emphasized the undesirability of accepting poetic and imaginative explanations, such as Plato's idea that what our senses show us are mere shadows of a true and real world which is for ever closed to us; such explanations are unscientific for "it is outside the province of science to ponder over the features of a world that is for ever inaccessible." The way is now open therefore to an understanding of *maya*, the Vedantic explanation which, since it posits a reality fully accessible to all who seek it, is fully scientific.

Vedanta says that whatever can be sensed by the senses or conceived by the mind, whatever, in other words, has name and form, has the dual characteristic of "is and is not." *Maya* is thus more than an explanation, it is the description of a fact. A solid *is* solid, we know it and feel it and use it as such; but a solid is at the same time merely the temporary form of something that by its nature is formless. It is through a process of causation, through a chain of protons, electrons, atoms, and molecules that the formless has taken form, but the whole process is not known; and it may be that the discovery in modern physics of a stage in that process that is apparently "without cause" will prove to be the first step on the road that will bridge the gulf and somehow bring us nearer to an understanding of how pure being comes under the thraldom of matter.

The "is and is not" of *maya* will be understood by recognizing the form and formless aspects of an object. Its form is ever subject to change and cannot therefore be termed the reality of that object. Its formless aspect does not change, it merely adopts different forms; and this therefore is the reality of that object. So while an object "is" in the sense that it has form, it also "is not" in that that form is not the reality of the object. Its reality is formlessness, and that formlessness is the infinite Reality of the universe....

As in the external world, in the internal world also such paradoxes may be seen. Nothing either physical or mental has absolute existence. There is, for example, the paradox of happiness and suffering. Every sentient being is capable of happiness; but the senses which make happiness possible make at the same time suffering possible. Thus we find that the greater the sense of pleasure the greater also the sense of suffering. And the more subtle the pleasure, the more exquisite the pain. We are all constantly struggling to attain happiness and to overcome suffering. But how many of us begin our struggle by admitting the paradox that where there is happiness there also sorrow must be? ...

And likewise good and evil are two sides of the same medal. They do not exist independently; that which makes good possible makes possible evil also. So wherever there is good there is evil, and wherever there is evil there must be some good. The same thing may appear as good at one time and evil at another; what one man regards as good another may regard as evil. "One man's meat is another man's poison" is a proverb that carries a far deeper meaning than a reference to individual tastes. And here again is a fact of the nature of the universe that must be borne in mind by all who seek to increase the good in the world and eliminate evil.

Facing facts is no easy task, and really to look life in the face is a terrible experience. But our feet are in the path, we are truth-seekers, bold scientists, and there is no turning back. So following through our line of thought we are forced to the conclusion that the world as we see it has no absolute existence. It exists only in relation to the mind. We see it with our five senses, and if we had more senses it would be an entirely different world. It is, as Professor Frisch said, "a construction of our mind, designed to fit the network of actions and observations which constitute our life." But at the same time the world does exist, and we have to work in and through it. It is a mixture of existence and non-existence. It is *maya*.

Into Freedom

Then the question arises, Can we go beyond *maya*? Can we go beyond the pairs of opposites, existence and non-existence, happiness and sorrow, good and evil? ...

Freedom lies beyond name and form. It is the formless, the real, aspect of nature, that which never changes.... All that is required of us is to open our eyes and recognize it. As soon as we see the world in the positive aspect of its real nature, we have freedom. For then we cease to identify ourselves with the changing world of name and form, and identify ourselves instead with the changeless spirit behind. Of vital importance therefore is our attitude to the universe, the way we view it. There are poetic and imaginative ways of viewing the facts we have here described. But a scientific age will take a scientific view and modern physicists have this great contribution to make to the thought of their generation....

Modern physics leads directly to this conception of oneness. The recognition of the oneness of matter and force, as explained by Professor Rosenfeld, brings nearer the conception of the spiritual oneness of the universe. The way has been opened, and the conception of spiritual unity can now be appreciated; and this is something that was quite impossible for the nineteenth century scientist. The importance and the full significance of this will be felt when it is realized that it must in time completely reorientate the Western view of the essential nature of man. Now man regards himself as a weak and fearful human being, a sinner to be saved. When Reality is seen as one, then will man recognize himself as all-pervading, indivisible, strong, and fearless; his whole life will be transformed.

These, then, are some of the implications behind the trend of modern physics. Sooner or later physicists must arrive at an understanding of the true nature of the universe. Since truth is one, the findings of those who conduct their search through matter must tally with the findings of those who conduct their search through the mind. Already confirmation of this is visible... no longer foreigners to each other, no longer rivals, but exponents of complementary systems.

Einstein's New Theory
[Addendum on page 172]

The Princeton University Press recently published Dr. Einstein's latest concepts of the fundamental laws governing the universe. These form an appendix, headed *Generalization of Gravitation Theory*, to the fourth edition of his book, *The Meaning of Relativity*, originally published in 1922. Calling his new theory a "unified field theory," Dr. Einstein believes that these laws reduce the physical universe in its totality to a few simple, fundamental concepts that will unify all its multifarious and seemingly unrelated manifestations into one all-embracing intellectual synthesis.

In our "Observations" in this issue we have related the trend in modern physics, the revolutionary changes in conception which have occurred during this century, to the basic conceptions of Vedantic thought. Quantum theory, of which Dr. Einstein himself was one of the principal founders, and his theories which united matter and energy, space and time, gravitation and inertia, are the foundations upon which the new physics rests. Dr. Einstein found it necessary to go beyond quantum theory because he could not accept the idea that what holds good for the outer universe does not hold good for the atom, and quantum theory says there is no certainty within the atom.

His latest work now bridges that gulf. Commenting on this the *New York Times* (31st March 1953) said, "... We have learned from him that space and matter are inseparable constituents of one 'continuum.' If he has at last found his unified field theory we shall have to regard light and other electromagnetic effects as part of that continuum. He himself points out how hard it will be to prove this prediction by observation and experience. As it is, the majority of physicists are pitted against him. He sees uniformity, perfection and continuity in the universe from galaxy to atom, his opponents nothing but chance and discontinuity.... If he proves to be right, his unified field theory will be a supreme achievement of the human intellect. There is much more than mathematical genius in all this. The equations (published)... must be regarded as a kind of sublime mathematical poetry—an expression of a deep, almost mystical conviction that if we can only disentangle our confused sense impressions we shall come a little nearer to what we call 'reality.'"

January 1954, pp. 1–6

SCHWEITZER AND INDIAN PHILOSOPHY

[Abridged]

The *Saturday Review* of New York, in its issue of the 13th June 1953, published an article by Dr. Albert Schweitzer entitled "The Problem of Ethics for Twentieth Century Man." Dr. Schweitzer, now seventy-eight years old, was awarded the Nobel Peace Prize for 1952. This author of a dozen books, a doctor, musician, and philosopher, lives, as is well known, in a village in French Equatorial Africa. Here he runs his own hospital and serves the villagers for many miles around, "atoning," as he has said, "in an infinitesimal degree, for all the wrongs inflicted by white men on the black." Dr. Schweitzer is a man with a philosophy and his whole life has been spent in an endeavour to put that philosophy into practice. Above all, he is a man of ethics and none can study the story of his life without being deeply moved at his determination to live out his conviction that a life based on ethics must be a life full of compassion and service to his fellowmen and to all creatures.

    The position of Dr. Schweitzer as a world-famous philosopher, together with the background of his austerely simple life of earnest ethical endeavour, makes his thought-provoking article in the *Saturday Review* all the more interesting to those who are tired of the blatantly materialistic trend of the modern world.

With all respect to his personality, however, we are obliged to say that we cannot agree with several of his statements regarding Indian philosophy and ethics. But they do not come as a surprise to us for they are a part of a persistent misunderstanding that exists outside India regarding her philosophy of Advaita. This is firstly due to a confusion of thought which wrongly attributes the political, social, and economic condition of this country [India] to the Indian philosophy of life. The second cause of misunderstanding may best be stated in the words of Swami Vivekananda who commented on the world's startling ignorance of Indian thought. He said: "The Hindus were bold, to their credit be it said, bold thinkers in all their ideas, so bold that one spark of their thought frightens the so-called bold thinkers of the West. Well has it been said by Professor Max Müller about these thinkers, that they climbed up to heights where their lungs only could breathe, and where those of other beings would have burst." We take Dr. Schweitzer's thoughts to be representative of the West, and in dealing now with some of the issues raised by him, we hope also to remove some of the widespread misconceptions about Indian philosophy that prevail there.

Opening his discussion by observing that ethics is invariably influenced by "the particular conception of the world to which it is related," Dr. Schweitzer divides such conceptions into two categories, one of which he calls the affirmative attitude, and the other the negative attitude of the individual to the world. "Among the thinkers of India," he says, "this negative conception of the world is the consequence of their conviction that true existence is immaterial, immutable, and eternal, and that the existence of the material world is unreal, deceptive, and transitory."

According to Indian philosophy, this description of the nature of Reality is perfectly correct, not only intellectually and theoretically, but also practically and intuitively through the highest spiritual experience of both ancient and modern sages and seers. To the layman or novitiate, God, Reality, or Brahman at first appears different from the world he sees around him; but as his insight is awakened he sees the universe pervaded by It in both the immanent and the transcendental sense. Then, as he nears his journey's end and completes his quest in the realm of the spirit, he finds that *"Sarvam khalvidam Brahma,"* all that exists is Brahman.... The Upanishads, which embody these three forms of thought, allow the disciple to choose his way of life, and this he does according to the evolution of his own mind. At the same time, he must always keep in view the ideal of Advaita or non-dualism as the final goal which he has ultimately to reach....

The complete identification of the individual self with the cosmic Self is the doctrine of Advaita. It is difficult to experience through mystic intuition, but even in theory it is fully satisfying to the intellect and uplifting to the heart of the common man. Throughout the religious and philosophical literature of India gems of this most wonderful oneness of life may be found in profusion. Many beautiful verses may be quoted in illustration, but the following from the *Svetashvataropanishad* will serve our present purpose: "Thou art the woman, Thou art the man, Thou art the youth and the maiden too. Thou art the old man who totters along, leaning on the staff. Thou art born with faces turned in all directions. Thou art the dark blue butterfly, and the green parrot with red eyes. Thou art the thunder-cloud, the seasons, and the oceans. Thou art without beginning, and beyond all time and space. Thou art He from whom all the worlds are born" (IV. 3, 4).

The Ethical Implications of Advaita

It will be seen that the so-called world-negating doctrine of Indian thought is no more than the admission of a fact, a universal truth; this is that the phenomenal world of change, decay, and destruction which we see around us cannot be in itself Reality.... There is a positive aspect of the same doctrine, and without this positive aspect the negative aspect is incomplete. It is misleading and confusing to speak of one aspect only. The positive aspect affirms the Oneness, and, from another point of view, the Reality, of life, nature, and the world. This is the central theme of the Advaita philosophy; and far from being negative it is the most positive thought in the annals of the world's history. It contains, however, as we have indicated, a paradox within itself, a paradox which must be spiritually perceived to be understood. It is this: the world is unreal for the man who takes the manifestation to be the reality, but it is real for him who says that all is Brahman. Thus, to the worldly man life indeed ends in negation, but to the wise it is ever throbbing and pulsating with eternal life. As the *Ishavasyopanishad* says in its opening verse, "Whatever there is changeful in this ephemeral world—all that must be enveloped by the Lord." ...

Thus the deification of the universe is the supreme truth of the Vedanta philosophy, and its implications in the realm of ethics, religion, and all human sciences are far reaching. Swami Vivekananda devoted his life to preaching this philosophy and all its implications. He said: "In injuring another, I am injuring myself; in loving another, I am loving myself. From this also springs that principle of Advaita morality which has been summed up in one word—self-abnegation. The Advaitist says, this little personalized self is the cause of all my misery. This individualized self, which makes me different from all other beings, brings hatred and jealousy and misery, struggles, and all other evils. And when this idea has been got rid of, all struggle will cease, all misery vanish. . . . We must always hold ourselves ready even to give up our lives for the lowest beings. When a man has become ready even to give up his life for a little insect, he has reached the perfection which the Advaitist wants to attain; and at that moment, when he has become thus ready, the veil of ignorance falls away from him, and he will feel his own nature. Even in this life, he will feel that he is one with the universe."

This brings us to the famous injunction *"Ahimsa paramo dharmah,"* the highest duty is non-violence. Dr. Schweitzer most strangely equates *ahimsa* with non-activity which "preserves man from the danger of doing harm to others by acts of violence . . . it demands only abstention from evil and not the activity which is inspired by the notion of good." Dr. Schweitzer's interpretation is quite wrong. The Sanskrit language often employs a negative term to express a positive thought. *Ahimsa* although most easily translated into English as "non-violence," carries the positive implications of love, service, and sacrifice which Swami Vivekananda so vividly describes in the passage quoted above. *Ahimsa* does not, as Dr. Schweitzer supposes, stem from a negative approach to the world, nor from a doctrine of inactivity, for neither of these exists in Indian philosophy. As we have tried to show, Indian thought is based upon an intensely positive attitude to the world. "Inactivity," as used in Indian philosophy, means not idleness, but unattachment. Dr. Schweitzer talks of the *Bhagavad-Gita*. If he would study it not through English or German, but with his "spiritual eye," we do not doubt that he will see that non-attachment is its central teaching. He who sees the Lord in all things is "non-attached" to their external forms. Then alone is one enabled to act with fearlessness and calm.... This is the ideal of the *Gita*.

Ethics and Social Life

Dr. Schweitzer remarks that while for the great thinkers of India the idea of the brotherhood of human beings is contained in their metaphysical notion of existence, they encounter difficulties in incorporating it in their ethics. "They are unable, in fact, to abolish the dividing walls between men erected by the existence of different castes and sanctioned by tradition." There is, we admit, every excuse for the observer of modern India who falls into the error upon which this thought is based. For the dividing walls of caste are a fact which modern India is herself now in the process of removing. And, indeed, modern India is concerned not alone with the present aberrations of the caste system, but with innumerable other social manifestations of the need to build up national practical ethics. It is quite wrong, however, to assume that the gap between "metaphysical notions" and ethical practice remains unbridged. The "metaphysical notions" of Indian thought are more than mere metaphysical abstractions, as has already been explained; they are the ideal held up before every individual. Whoever attains the ideal attains all else besides, wisdom and the most loving heart, the most ethical life. But there is no half-way house, there is no compromise. There are no ethics apart from the fulfilment of the ideal.... It is the ideal, the "metaphysical notions" which tell us why we are to do these things....

There is a fundamental difference between the Indian conception of ethics, the ethical implications of Advaita, and the Christian or Western ethic. Dr. Schweitzer explains how the Christian ethic is rooted in the affirmation of the world, the attempt to transform the world into the perfect world of the Kingdom of God. It is, above all, he explains, a matter of compassion or, as Hume said, a matter of sympathy "which leads us to devote ourselves to others and to wish to contribute to their well-being and to that of society." To the Indian mind, ethics can never be limited to the conception of compassion, nor can compassion be held to be an end in itself. Compassion and sympathy are seen as corollaries of the one basic ideal of the spiritual oneness of existence, the divinity of all things, but to ask them to stand alone, and to give to them the status of the ground of ethics is to make a mockery of divinity.

There is one basic problem which Christian or Western thought has not yet solved, nor, it seems to us, faced boldly. The problem of evil remains to confuse and confound the average Western seeker after truth; and many are the anomalies which stem from the failure to solve this problem. The need for compassion, for example, from the Western viewpoint rests upon the conception of evil as a separate entity or reality; and the need for compassion therefore has yet to be reconciled with the Christian conception of an all-wise, all-loving God.

...In spite of the title of his article, Dr. Schweitzer appears to ignore the light which may be thrown upon this problem by twentieth century science which has itself opened the way to the resolution of all such contradictions within the all-embracing grasp of a fundamental unity. The Advaita philosophy, which has proceeded further than modern science, preaches the divinity of the universe and all that it contains. Relegating good and evil alike to the sphere of the transitory, it shows that everything is to be gained by a true knowledge of the world. All anomalies and contradictions lose their sting; it provides, as we have said, the one ground of all ethics.

This comparison between the Eastern and Western conception of ethics deserves to be carried further, for it is a matter of vital interest to the modern world. It is perhaps the most fundamental level at which... benefit could be derived from mutual understanding and the mutual exchange of ideas. The world is well aware of the vivid contrast now to be seen between social life in the West and in the East. The West presents above all a picture of a polished, ethical society... a society based consciously on ethics. The latest, most obvious, expression of this is the Welfare State; but there are other, less obvious, expressions of it also, such as the whole code of etiquette, the cultivation of the team spirit, and such innovations as queuing and the rationing of food-stuffs, all of which are based upon a conscious endeavour towards fair play and thought for others. Social life in most Eastern countries, on the other hand, presents a strong contrast to the polished maturity of the West. Those everyday expressions of thought for others are either entirely lacking or are cultivated within limited spheres....

In this picture... it appears that good is all on the Western side, while the East is far inferior. But true understanding has to penetrate deeper than this surface view. The forms of society constantly undergo change; it is the basic thought, the "metaphysical notions" which, in the long run, decide the fate of that society. Of what use are Western polish and the Western ethical society if, being based on faulty premises, they collapse and sink into the new barbarities that modern science has now made possible? At the same time, of what use is the fact that India has a highly developed philosophical code if its principles find no expression in social and individual life?

What is required therefore is a synthesis; let Western ethics recognize their true ground in the universal principles expressed in India's "metaphysical notions"; but let India learn to give practical expression to her ideals by developing in her social life the polish and maturity of thought for others wherever these may be lacking.

February 1954, pp. 25–30
A UNIVERSAL SYMBOL
[Abridged]

There can be no doubt that for the majority of people in this age of science, the approach to religion is primarily an intellectual one. The Westerner, in particular, is becoming increasingly wary of giving rein to his emotions in regions where his reason finds no satisfaction.... In the West, as in the East, the search for true religion continues. By taking its stand now upon the rational approach the way has been opened to the universal recognition and acceptance of certain fundamental spiritual truths. One way in which this process can be hastened is by the study and understanding of the symbol *Om*, which is an embodiment of those fundamental spiritual truths. Prayer, study, and deep spiritual understanding all demand as a prerequisite a certain mental attitude or frame of mind; and often this implies a complete reorientation of mind and outlook. By the study and understanding of the meaning of the word *Om* that reorientation of mind can be acquired....

The First Step

The reorientation of mind required of the spiritual seeker implies the development of the ability to understand the true nature of the world and everything in it. Sooner or later to all of us must come the conviction that the happiness we seek does not lie in the direction in which we normally seek it. We spend our lives striving that the time may come when we shall be established in happiness. Hoping against hope, we still believe that all our difficulties can eventually be overcome and that all hindrances to happiness will be removed. Then at last, we claim, we shall relax and enjoy life, and peace and contentment will be ours. This is our dream, but over and over again the dream is shattered. Always something comes to withhold that peace from us.

This is not pessimism, but a statement of fact. There is no happiness in this world that does not hold within itself the seeds of sorrow. The attitude adopted by most people is that we should make the best of a bad job. Life may be full of suffering, but it is full of joy too; so let us not think of the dark side, but make the most of whatever joy we have. How wonderful it is to have lived, to have known the beauties of nature, to have experienced the joys of friendship, or of parenthood, or of work and achievement. If we have also suffered much—well, it is worth it! This is the attitude to life which is widely prevalent today. It is called optimism and is regarded as correct and courageous.

It is an attitude, however, which is fraught with danger, for it rarely proves sufficient to carry the individual over the roughest patches of life. It is an attitude which can only be maintained by turning a blind eye upon some of life's most fundamental problems. The problem of evil and the problem of death can never be solved by ignoring them or pretending that they do not exist. Sooner or later they have to be faced, and it is the man who has not prepared himself to face them who is in the end defeated by life and who dies embittered and disappointed.

"Where ignorance is bliss," said the poet, "'tis folly to be wise." But ignorance is never bliss. It is ignorance of the true nature of the world that leads us astray. We judge only from externals and pin our faith to things that by their very nature have no stability. It is stability that we seek, happiness that does not change, good that does not decay. But pleasures, sorrows, possessions, poverty, and even life itself are all evanescent; change and decay are ever present and we are left to wonder where reality lies.

At last, finding that unchanging happiness is not to be attained through sense perceptions, the understanding dawns that it is to be found in the spirit. It is in every case the spirit behind the form and not the form of itself that brings true happiness. It is in the spirit that reality lies.

Now comes the reorientation of mind that will reveal to the spiri-

tual seeker the direction in which he is to turn his search... what may
be termed the deification of the world. "Whatsoever moves in the
world is to be covered by the Lord," says the *Isha Upanishad*.... This
means seeing God in everything, breaking through the outer crusts of
forms and names. Since the real nature of the universe is spirit... we
have but to open our eyes and see Him. In good, in evil, in happiness,
in sorrow, in life, and in death God is equally present.

Seeing God in everything reveals the spiritual unity underlying all
things, and it is this consciousness of oneness that brings unchanging
happiness....

His Manifesting Word Is Om

Having arrived at this conception of the spiritual unity of the universe
and of the relationship between form and spirit, the spiritual seeker is
now ready to understand the significance of the symbol *Om*. The
human mind is so constructed that there cannot be a single wave in the
mind-stuff that is not conditioned by name and form.... Form is, as it
were, an outer crust encasing a kernel or inner essence which is *shabda*
(sound). In all beings with the power of speech, sound-symbols are
associated with name. In the individual man thought-waves rising in
the mind-stuff must manifest themselves first as words and then as
more concrete forms.

In the same way, it is held, the cosmic Mind first manifested Itself as
sound (name) and then as form, which is the universe we see. Behind
the physical universe of the senses is that which is eternal and inexpressible, the *sphota* which manifests as logos, or Word. The *sphota* is
the essential eternal material of all ideas or names. It is not only the
power through which the universal Spirit creates the universe, it is
itself the universal Spirit. The universal Spirit first becomes conditioned as *sphota* and then evolves Itself out as the yet more concrete
sensible universe.

The sound-symbol associated with the *sphota* is the word *Om*....
and *Om* may thus be held to be the holiest of all words, the mother of

all names and forms, and out of it the universe may be supposed to have been created.

The objection may be raised that although thought and word are inseparable, there are often various word-symbols for the same thought. It may therefore be contended that one particular word, *Om*, need not necessarily be the word representative of the thought out of which the universe has become manifested. The answer to this is that *Om* is the only possible symbol, because it is the only sound-symbol which covers the whole ground of sound. The *sphota* is the eternal, imperceptible, creative element of all words, yet it is not any definite word in its fully formed state. It is what remains when all the peculiarities which distinguish one word from another have been removed. Every word that is intended to express the inexpressible *sphota* must, of necessity, limit it in some degree.... That word which limits it the least, and at the same time most accurately expresses [it], will be the truest symbol of the *sphota*. That word is *Om* and no other.

The three sounds *a*, *u*, and *m*, when pronounced together give the word *Om*, and these three sounds are the basic or generalized symbol of all possible sounds. All articulate sounds are produced in the space within the mouth beginning with the root of the tongue and ending with the lips. The sound *a* is the least differentiated of all sounds, and it is also the throat sound; the sound *u* is made by the rolling forward of the impulse which begins at the root of the tongue and ends at the lips; *m* is the last lip sound.

Om, when properly pronounced, thus represents the whole phenomenon of sound production. No other word can do this and *Om* is therefore the fittest symbol of the *sphota*, and this is the real meaning of *Om*. Moreover, since a symbol can never be separated from the idea it signifies, *Om* and the *sphota* are one.... As Om symbolizes the sphota ... so also it symbolizes the universal Spirit....

Now the universal Spirit is what is conceived by man as God. Being coloured by the prevailing elements in man's own mind, the universal Spirit is seen from particular standpoints and associated with particular qualities. In the same way, the universe, which has been evolved, as it were, out of the universal Spirit, is also seen... in man's mind... as full of manifold forms. Each of these differentiated views of the universal Spirit and the universe has its own particular word-symbol, names which have been evolved out of the deepest spiritual perceptions of sages.... These symbols represent the differentiated views of the universal Spirit, but *Om* represents the undifferentiated universal Spirit.

...It belongs to all languages and to all people.... and it can therefore be accepted by all.

The Goal Is the Way

...When the meaning of *Om* has been studied and grasped, then *Om* must be used as a means to the end that it symbolizes.... "His manifesting word is *Om*. The repetition of this (*Om*) and meditating on its meaning (is the way)," says Patanjali in his *Yoga-Sutra* (Aphorisms). The reason why repetition of *Om* while meditating on its meaning is advocated is that mental repetition thoughtfully performed amounts to what may be called "keeping good company in the mind." The mind is coloured by the company it keeps.... So the repetition of *Om* while thinking of its meaning acts as a stimulus to the development of spiritual understanding and the growth of spirituality.

...*Om* can colour the mind with its meaning not only at the time of meditation but at all times. For if *Om* is remembered as the mother of all names and forms, and as the one sound-symbol which covers the whole ground of sound, the truest symbol of the *sphota*, then all names and forms and sounds will be immediately made holy, or deified. "The practice of the presence of God," as Brother Lawrence described this universal spiritual experience, is the aim of all spiritual discipline. Consciousness of the presence of God may be achieved through constantly thinking of *Om* and applying its meaning to the common experiences of daily living.... Through *Om*... [every] object can be linked immediately to the cosmic Mind; and in this way the fundamental spiritual unity of the universe can be established in the mind of the individual as a very real experience.

And as that experience develops and strengthens, the reorientation of mind which sees God in everything becomes more and more firmly established.... Ultimately this process must lead to the fullest development of the spiritual life, which is pure unselfishness. For as one's attitude to the world around undergoes these fundamental changes, so, too, must one's attitude to one's own self, as an individual, undergo a fundamental change.

...True individuality lies in the domain of things that do not change, and this is the life of the spirit.... This is the real nature of man; and this one, undivided, infinite Spirit is the real individual. So now we are only struggling towards individuality. Real, unchanging individuality will come when we can say, "I am in everything, in everybody, I am in all lives, I am the universe."

... This is the goal towards which we are all struggling, and various are the means we use to help us in our struggle. Meditation upon the symbol *Om* besides the study of its meaning is one of the means, for, as the *Brhadaranyaka Upanishad* says, "This Atman is first to be heard, then thought about, and then meditated upon."

March 1972, pp. 81–86

INDIA AND THE COMING OF TV

[Abridged]

A press announcement early in February stated that the proposed TV station in Calcutta, which is expected to go into operation in two years' time, will have two relay transmitters which will extend coverage to the neighbouring industrial areas. The total area covered by the Calcutta TV station will be about 40,000 sq. km., serving a population of about 16 million.

The addition of TV to the Calcutta scene will be a significant event, for its field of influence will ultimately extend far beyond the immediate population of Calcutta and its industrial belt. Calcutta's population is made up of segments drawn from the whole of India, and the influences radiating outwards from the city are not difficult to trace. To most of us in India, of course, TV is not yet a reality and it is pooh-poohed as something likely to be of interest only to the rich. It would be unwise, however, to dismiss TV as a toy for the wealthy, far beyond the reach of the poor, and therefore as something that need not concern us now. As may be seen in countries where "the telly" is now part of everyday life, TV, like the railway, the bicycle, the telegraph, the cinema, and the transistor, will sooner or later and in devious ways exert its influence over every individual. Technology is marching on, and the significance of the spread of TV in India lies mainly in the fact of the influence it will exert over minds, both educated and uneducated.

The influence of TV, however, reaches a level far deeper than the influence of the actual TV programme. The object of the Indian Government in extending TV coverage to Calcutta's industrial belt was stated to be the hope that it "could be utilized to provide some imaginative social education programmes to combat anti-social elements and unrest in these industrial pockets." There is nothing to suggest that in deciding upon this aim the Government has, at the same time, given any thought to or shown any awareness of the wider and deeper influences of TV upon the individual and upon society.

Man in the Electric Age

Some years ago a Canadian university professor named Marshall McLuhan startled the western world by proclaiming in a series of books and essays his contention that all the modern communication media were bringing about revolutionary changes in human perception. The changes were caused, he said, not by the content of what was communicated but by the nature of the communication media themselves, for technical media were extensions of human faculties and consciousness—as a chair was an extension of the body. He epitomized his contention into the slogan "the medium is the message." By the word "message" he meant the change of scale or pace or pattern that a given medium introduced into human affairs. "The railway did not introduce movement or transportation or wheel or road into human society, but it accelerated and enlarged the scale of previous human functions, creating totally new kinds of cities and new kinds of work and leisure. This happened whether the railway functioned in a tropical or a northern environment, and was quite independent of the freight or content of the railway medium...." (*Understanding Media*, New York, 1965, p. 8)

Language is a medium that well illustrates the influence of media on the perceptions. One's own mother tongue is a medium that is itself much more potent and effective than anything that is actually said. Even the most trivial remark invokes the totality of the language. Our mother tongues call for our total participation, and they control our perceptions.... The same is true of printing, radio, movies, and TV. McLuhan contends that they actually alter our organs of perception without our knowing it. We are never aware of these changes. It's like fish in water, he says. Fish know nothing about water! (*The Listener*, London, 26 March 1970)

... "Today, after more than a century of electric technology, we have extended our nervous system itself in a global embrace, abolishing both space and time as far as our planet is concerned. Rapidly, we approach the final phase of the extensions of man—the technological simulation of consciousness, when the creative process of knowing will be collectively and corporately extended to the whole of human society, much as we have already extended our senses and our nerves by the various media....

... In the electric age, when our central nervous system is technologically extended to involve us in the whole of mankind and to incorporate the whole of mankind in us, we necessarily participate, in depth, in the consequences of our every action. It is no longer possible to adopt the aloof and dissociated role of the literate Westerner." (*Understanding Media*, pp. 3–4)

TV Creates Involvement

McLuhan points out the great differences between radio and television in their demands upon those who use them. In its immediate aspect radio comes to the listener as a private [auditory] experience....

The demands of TV, however, are very different, for TV stresses participation, dialogue, and depth; it demands involvement in depth, and may be seen as an extension of the sense of touch. In closed-circuit instruction in surgery, for example, medical students reported a strange effect—that they seemed not to be watching an operation, but performing it. They felt that they were holding the scalpel.

...The child accustomed to TV has difficulty in adjusting to conventional education....

McLuhan shows how education by classified data, the method that has prevailed since Plato, is now being superseded by the method of "pattern recognition," the key phrase at IBM.... "The young student today grows up in an electrically configured world. It is a world not of wheels but of circuits, not of fragments but of integral patterns. The student today *lives* mythically and in depth. At school, however, he encounters a situation organized by means of classified information. The subjects are unrelated. They are visually conceived in terms of a blueprint. The student can find no possible means of involvement for himself, nor can he discover how the educational scene relates to the 'mythic' world of electronically processed data and experience that he takes for granted." (ibid. p. vii)

McLuhan emphasizes that the change of attitude brought about by TV has nothing to do with the content of the TV programme. It is the result of TV itself as a medium of experience, and will therefore occur whatever the content of the programme. The important thing, therefore, is to understand the change in attitude and use it in the making of the society of the future. "The TV child expects involvement and doesn't want a specialist *job* in the future. He does want a *role* and a deep commitment to his society...." (ibid. p. 335)

What are likely to be the social effects of TV now become a little clearer. McLuhan suggests that electric speed, in bringing all social and political functions together in a sudden implosion, has heightened human awareness of responsibility. As electrically contracted, the world is no more than a village, a global village, and "might not our current translation of our entire lives into the spiritual form of information seem to make of the entire globe, and of the human family, a single consciousness?" (ibid. p. 61)

Education by Involvement

The final message of the media of the electric age, as seen by McLuhan, is, then, a message of global, single consciousness. McLuhan's views have created a great deal of interest and have been very widely debated. Most people feel dimly aware that established ways of living and thinking have already undergone definite changes and they are therefore able to accept the contention that even greater changes are likely to take place in the future. Some idea of how revolutionary those changes will be has perhaps been provided by McLuhan's analysis of the effects upon the mind of the electric media in general and of TV in particular. Communication by satellite, which is regarded as one of the most important scientific events of the age, will ensure that people everywhere in the world participate in those changes. It seems possible that life seventy years from now will be as different from the present as the present is from life seventy years ago.

The introduction of TV into wider Calcutta is therefore of much greater significance than the provision of social education programmes to combat anti-social elements in the industrial belt. McLuhan has depicted the difference between education through literacy, which he describes as an extension of the visual sense, leading to non-involvement or fragmentation, and education through TV which he describes as an extension of the sense of touch, leading to involvement in depth. While western countries are now experiencing the results of a clash between these two systems, India is faced with the interesting question of what will result when an illiterate, or almost illiterate, population is provided with TV.

Bearing in mind the fact that it is not the TV programme that produces the sense of involvement but the TV method, it would appear that education by involvement will be of greater significance to India than literacy. At the present rate of progress of literacy and of TV, illiteracy will not be eradicated before TV takes over. This will not, of course, eliminate the need for literacy, but it will change entirely the role of literacy and therefore it will also change the course and the methods of education.

Education Towards Wholeness

This opportunity for revolution in education is India's greatest need today, particularly since it is a revolution that will embrace the whole population and not merely the "educated" segment. The tragedy of modern India lies in the fact of the great division between the "educated" and the "uneducated." Yet an even greater tragedy lies in the quality of the education which produces the "educated." The mere cramming of unrelated facts into the brain, which constitutes education in India today, and which is completely divorced from any approach to life which may be called Indian, is surely the worst possible use to which education by the classification of data could possibly be put. As McLuhan says, "TV is only one component of the electric environment of instant circuitry that has succeeded the old world of the wheel and nuts and bolts. We would be foolish not to ease our transition from the fragmented visual world of the existing educational establishment by every possible means." (ibid. p. ix) The fragmentary effects of education in India today are plain for all to see, and this "fragmented visual world" will have to be left behind if India is to live.

Given, then, TV as a medium that demands participation, involvement in depth of the whole being, and given also TV as a medium of education, the question finally arises as to what will be the content of that education. McLuhan sees the aspiration of our time for wholeness, empathy, and depth of awareness as a natural adjunct of electric technology. If the aspiration is there to provide the goal, and if electric technology is there to provide the means, what remains is the harnessing of man's will to ensure that the means will lead to the goal. The content of education will therefore be all that strengthens man's will towards wholeness.

India's education of the future will therefore find in TV the opportunity to carry forward her own ancient national ideal of education. Upanishadic education was education by involvement of the whole being. The student lived with the guru and was educated, not without books, but mainly by means of involvement with daily household tasks and the familiar world of nature around him. In practical ways, such as taking the cows out to graze, the student was led not only to an understanding of the inner nature of all that he saw around him, but also to an understanding of himself, seeing finally his own identity with all. Education was transformation. The world of separate beings and objects became transformed in the heart and mind of the student into one great and glorious unity in which individuality was preserved. The world of separate beings was known and understood through that unity and the student went forth with the light of knowledge and of love in his eyes.

The Individual's Place in the Universe

Writing of this method of education, Swami Vivekananda pointed out how those ancient teachers were never negative in their approach. Nothing that was meaningful to the students was destroyed, but they were led forward to broader and broader ideas. By this method ideas and concepts which were later expressed in the language of philosophy and logic were experienced by the students through their own internal perception. This education, as Swami Vivekananda said, "does not destroy the world, but it explains it; it does not destroy the person, but explains him; it does not destroy the individuality, but explains it, by showing the real individuality. It does not show that this world is vain and does not exist, but it says, 'Understand what this world is, so that it may not hurt you.'" (*Complete Works*, Vol. II, Calcutta, 1963, p. 312)

In modern times revolutionary changes in human perception have been, and will increasingly be, brought about by TV and other electric media. These newly awakened perceptions open up the possibility of reproducing in the world the results achieved by the Upanishadic education of the whole being. One of the problems pointed out by McLuhan as being a direct result of the influence of electric media is the question of the identity of the individual. In the issue of *The Listener* already referred to he said:

> ... There is no more audience in our world: on this planet the entire audience has become active and participant. Naturally religion undergoes tremendous changes under these conditions.... All forms of sham, all forms of irrelevance, all forms of routinised repetition, are swept aside, and going with that clean sweep is this wiping out of the old private identities of centuries of cultural heritage.... There is no longer such a thing as a private individual because of our electric culture of total involvement.... Individualism in the old 19th-century sense has been scrubbed right off our culture; and many people find themselves completely bewildered by this change.

Ancient Indian education, as we have shown, solved this ever-new problem of the relationship between the individual and the universe. Upanishadic education did not wipe out the individual; it gave him his true place within the universe by giving him that inner, superfine perception by which he could see the whole universe in himself.

The task before Indian education today will therefore be to use the perceptions awakened by TV and the electric media to give to everyone everywhere in the world that understanding of man and his place in the universe that is true education—understanding without which, as has been amply proved in today's world, the knowledge of data becomes not only useless but dangerous.

Two lectures given by Swami Nitya-swarup-ananda in 1988 at the Vedanta Society in New York were subsequently published as this two-part monograph in 1989.

HOW I CAME TO THE FEET OF SRI RAMAKRISHNA

Preface

In the following pages I have told the story of how I came to the feet of Sri Ramakrishna.

I visited America twice, once in 1962 as a State guest and lived there for one year. I made the second visit in 1987 and lived there for fourteen months solely as a guest of Jack Kelly and Erik Johns. During the second visit I told this story at the Vedanta Society in New York on June 12, 1988, but the whole story could not be delivered as contemplated. And this is now given, in two parts, in the present publication. With a view to elucidating certain aspects of the story, I have made herein some additions that have since occurred to me.

Belur Math   Nitya-swarup-ananda
June 1, 1989

PART ONE

Swami Tathagatananda, devotees, and friends:

I thank you, Swami, for kindly having asked me to say a few words to you all on the subject of how I came to the feet of Sri Ramakrishna.

Before I begin, let me tell you that I remember with much love and reverence Swami Pavitrananda with whom I had the pleasure and privilege of living and working at the Advaita Ashrama in Calcutta. I also remember with much love and joy my meeting with him again in New York in 1962, and how I used to spend time with him at this centre. I remember how, at his request, I spoke here from this pulpit and, on request from the audience, I said a few words about Sri Ramakrishna's photograph, and why at the Vedanta Societies all over America we keep his photograph on the altar although we do not belong to a sectarian organization.

Let me begin, then, with a few words about the photograph of Sri Ramakrishna, which will give us an idea of what it stands for.

Four photographs of Sri Ramakrishna

There are three photographs of Sri Ramakrishna which were taken during his lifetime, and with which we are all familiar. One is in the sitting posture, taken at Dakshineswar. The second was taken at a studio, with Sri Ramakrishna standing with his right arm resting on a pillar. The third was taken at the house of the Brahmo Samaj leader, Keshab Chandra Sen. In all these photographs he was completely immersed in the deepest *samadhi*. There is also a fourth photograph, which was taken after his *mahasamadhi*, but it is not publicized.

The only historical representation of God in human form

These three photographs are not photographs in the ordinary sense. They are unprecedented in the history of photography, unique in the spiritual life of humanity, and a phenomenon which has never happened in the recorded history of mankind. They are photographs of a human being fully and completely merged in God consciousness, transcending all consciousness of body, mind, senses, and the world outside. They are photographs of one who not only became united with God consciousness; for in reality he was nothing but God, or we may say, he became God Himself. Therefore, if we try to form a representation of God in human form, then this is the only historical figure we have ever had. The photograph of this figure is in reality not a photograph of a human being. It is a photograph of a human being who at the moment of being photographed was, in reality, in every sense of the term, God, and nothing but God. It is a photograph of God. In this sense, if we want to meditate on God in human form, this is the only historical form available to humanity. It is therefore essential that we bear in mind the fact that when we meditate on Sri Ramakrishna we meditate on God Himself.

Different aspects of Godhood are different stages of realization of the One Absolute Reality

This photograph immediately brings humanity in communion with Sri Ramakrishna's whole life—his different intense spiritual practices, realizations, and teachings.

This photograph reminds and enables humanity to visualize how Sri Ramakrishna worshipped, and realized, God as the Divine Mother, how he worshipped, and realized, the Universal, the Impersonal, the Formless Spirit in its different aspects—both with form and without form, through his varied spiritual practices. These spiritual practices he performed under the guidance of spiritual teachers who had themselves realized Godhood through those very practices. Ultimately, however, each of these spiritual realizations, which enabled him to realize a particular aspect of Godhood, culminated in his own realization of the One Absolute Ultimate Reality. This ultimate realization enabled him to realize that the different *aspects* of Godhood were but the different *stages* of realization of the One Absolute Ultimate Reality.

Each one's method is each one's way of realization

This photograph symbolizes Sri Ramakrishna's spiritual practices and realizations, and these enable humanity to move along spiritual paths according to each individual's taste and temperament, following the various methods of dualistic or qualified nondualistic or absolute nondualistic disciplines, and thus to realize each one's own chosen ideal in his own distinctive way.

Religions are varied expressions of Oneness

This photograph symbolizes Sri Ramakrishna's spiritual practices and realizations which enable humanity to understand, realize, and harmonize the different religions which appear to be conflicting and contradictory, but are not really so. The different religions, in reality, reflect and embody the different aspects and the varied expressions of *the* Religion which is Oneness. Religion is thus one in substance but many in forms which are meant for and suited to diverse types of spiritual aspirants at different stages of their gradual development. These forms vary from community to community, group to group, and person to person, according to every individual's constitutional mental make-up in his distinctive taste, temperament, and innate capacity.

Testimony to the unity and harmony of religions

This photograph symbolizes Sri Ramakrishna's realization of the unity and harmony of religions, and his testimony to this unity and harmony, which enable humanity to understand the true significance of the Vedas, the Bible, the Koran, and all other scriptures. Thus, through his realization and teaching the whole world is enabled to forget its disputes and disagreements and be united in a fraternal bond in religious and other matters and promote worldwide peace and progress.

Synthesis of Yogas

This photograph reveals that such a unique personality as Sri Ramakrishna—a synthesis of Jnana (knowledge), Yoga (psychic control), Bhakti (devotion), and Karma (action), in their utmost perfection—never before appeared in the human race, and that the formation of such a perfect character is the aim of this age, and everyone should strive for that alone with all his might.

Limiting the infinite aspect of God is blasphemy

This photograph is an emphatic reminder of the Master's repeatedly urging mankind to avoid limiting the infinite aspect of God.

Limiting the infinite aspect of God indeed is blasphemy—this teaching is of paramount importance for the present age.

Coexistence of width and depth

This photograph reveals to humanity that width and depth can coexist in a society. A narrow society has depth and intensity of spirituality. A narrow stream is more rapid. In a catholic society, along with the expansion of its ideas, their depth and intensity are seen to dwindle. But the wonder of it is that in this Ramakrishna Form there has been a combination of ideas deeper than the sea and vaster than the sky, transcending all records of history. This proves that vastness, catholicity, and intensity in the highest degree can coexist in a single individual, and that a society also can be built in the same pattern; for society is only an aggregate of individuals.

Universal historical symbol

This photograph, therefore, should not be regarded as the photograph of a saint or prophet of a particular creed or religion. It is the only universal symbol in a historical human form representing the infinite aspects of the One Absolute Impersonal Formless Spirit and enabling every human being to pursue any possible path according to his own distinctive taste and temperament in order to realize his own divine nature. Thus Sri Ramakrishna is the only historical human prototype for a future universal diversified global society.

The raison d'être

This, then, is the significance of the photograph of Sri Ramakrishna and the reason why he is worshipped in this form in the temples of the Ramakrishna order and may as well be worshipped in any place of worship irrespective of any creed—this will fulfil his own words: "This photograph will be worshipped in every home."

Ordination of Swami Vivekananda

Sri Ramakrishna's main disciple, Swami Vivekananda, was ordained by him to preach his message unto mankind. On one of his last days, Sri Ramakrishna wrote with his own hand on a piece of paper: "Naren will teach. While wandering he will give a clarion call abroad." Similarly, on another occasion, Sri Ramakrishna called Swami Vivekananda to his side and in a most extraordinary ecstatic mood transmitted into his soul his whole life's spiritual wealth of realization and charged him to bring to fulfilment through his work his own mission on earth. His words to Swami Vivekananda at the time of this event were: "Today I have emptied myself and bequeathed to you the treasury of my whole life's acquisition of spiritual realizations and made you heir to all of them and thus made myself a beggar. Now, however, the key to the door of your exit remains with me. There is no release for you until your task is fulfilled." Swami Vivekananda began his spiritual ministrations when he came to America and preached the message of Sri Ramakrishna. Swami Vivekananda's teaching therefore is Sri Ramakrishna's teaching in the garb as demanded by modern man, modern times, modern language, and similar other considerations. Sri Ramakrishna is the text and Swami Vivekananda the accredited commentary.

Crucial teaching of Sri Ramakrishna

Sri Ramakrishna's life is God realization itself. His teaching is: God alone is real. God is both with form and without form. And He is that which includes both form and formlessness. As the same one master of the house appears in various aspects, being father to one, brother to another, and husband to a third, so God is described and called in various ways according to the particular aspect in which He is perceived by a particular individual. He is like a chameleon, viewed sometimes as red, sometimes as green, sometimes as yellow, sometimes as blue, and so on, and sometimes as having no colour at all. God is thus one in substance, but many in relation to the particular aspect in which He is perceived by a particular individual.

Swami Vivekananda's teaching is based on Sri Ramakrishna's teaching

This teaching of Sri Ramakrishna made Swami Vivekananda the great preacher of Karma (action), not as divorced from but as an expression of Jnana (knowledge) and Bhakti (devotion). Swami Vivekananda based his teaching on Sri Ramakrishna's exhortation. Sri Ramakrishna said: "Standing on the bedrock of Advaita (nonduality), follow any path in any form suited to your taste and temperament as a means to realization." Sri Ramakrishna thus revealed to Swami Vivekananda a new dimension of the deepest intrinsic meaning of Advaita (nonduality) which includes that experience in which all is One without a second and Dvaita (duality), Vishishtadvaita (qualified nonduality), and Advaita (nonduality) are but three phases or stages in a single development, of which Advaita (nonduality) constitutes the ultimate goal.

No distinction between "sacred" and "secular"

This revelation opened up to Swami Vivekananda infinite vistas of the One Ultimate Reality and became the bedrock of his doctrine that the many and the One are the same Reality, perceived by the mind at different stages, in different attitudes, at different times, and in different circumstances. As the many and the One are the same Reality, it is not one particular form, mode, or medium alone, but equally all forms, modes, and media, which are paths of realization. It is not all modes of worship alone, but equally all modes of work, all modes of struggle, all modes of creation, which are paths of realization. There can be no distinction between "sacred" and "secular" nor any difference between service of man and worship of God. To labour is to pray. To conquer is to renounce. To have and to hold is as stern a trust as to quit and to avoid. Life itself is religion. The farmyard and the field, the workshop, the study, and the studio are as true and fit scenes for the meeting of God with man as the cell of the monk or the door of the temple. Art, science, and religion are but three different ways of expressing a single truth.

Every being is divine

To this unique teaching of Swami Vivekananda may be added his message of the divinity of man—the essence of all religions. Every being is divine, is God. Every soul is a sun covered over with clouds of ignorance. The apparent difference between soul and soul is due to the difference in density of these layers of clouds; the difference is in stages of manifestation, in degree not in kind. This eternal truth is the *conscious or unconscious* basis of all religions, and is the *explanation* of the whole history of human progress, either on the material, or on the intellectual, or on the spiritual plane—the same Divine Universal Spirit is manifesting itself through different planes.

Prophet of New Age and Messenger of Divinity of Man

Swami Vivekananda's teaching adds its crowning significance to his becoming the meeting-point not only of East and West, but also of past and future. To him life is itself religion and every being is divine. He thus becomes the Prophet of the New Age and the Messenger of the Divinity of Man, impressing upon all the need to manifest that divinity in every movement of life. He declared unto mankind that as long as he was on the face of the earth he would preach this message and even when he passed away from this world he would still continue to preach this message until every human being on earth realized that he was one with God. This, in essence, is the supreme message of Vedanta.

First impression on seeing Sri Ramakrishna's photograph

Now I wish to speak to you of how I first saw Sri Ramakrishna's photograph in the sitting posture. As far as I remember, I first saw this photograph in the *Udbodhan*, the Bengali journal of the Ramakrishna Order. I had not the least knowledge of who Sri Ramakrishna was, but his photograph was so enchanting to me that I was spontaneously struck by it and immediately felt that he was the God of my heart. I was unconsciously so deeply moved that since that day this figure remains indelibly impressed on my mind. Since that time I felt that he was my life's all-in-all. And since then never in my life have I had any God or Goddess other than Sri Ramakrishna. I instinctively made him my chosen ideal and the only object of my regular meditation and worship. My life has been inextricably linked with his feet from the very first day of my seeing that photograph.

First visit to Belur Math to attend Sri Ramakrishna's
birth anniversary celebrations

With this beginning, I would like now to share with you how I came in touch with the Ramakrishna Order, with the Belur Math, and with the disciples of Sri Ramakrishna, and then how I came to the feet of the Holy Mother. As I have said, I naturally became more and more interested to know about Sri Ramakrishna, and then, in 1914, one day I found in the almanac that the birthday anniversary of Sri Ramakrishna would be celebrated that year at the Belur Math on Sunday, March 1. I became eager to visit the Belur Math and see the celebrations, but our home was far away in a village in the district of Dacca, now in Bangladesh. It was indeed very far from the Belur Math. One had to go by road, then by steamer, then by rail to Calcutta, and from Calcutta one had to cross the Ganges and then travel further to reach the Belur Math.

Born on February 22, 1899, I then was only fifteen years old. I was reading in class IX in the high English school of our village and never travelled outside. Nevertheless, with one of my relatives I arranged to visit the Belur Math. As it was a place new to us, we wrote to one of our friends who was living at Salkia, not very far from the Math. When we reached the Railway Station in Calcutta our friend was there to receive us and he took us to his family's house. Next Sunday would be the celebration. We decided to go and pay a short visit to the Belur Math in the evening on Saturday. Accordingly my relative, my friend, and I went to the Belur Math. It was about three miles away. As soon as we entered the then main gate to the south of the monastery, I noticed an elderly monk (whose lifelong monastic name, I later came to know, was Jnan Maharaj) sitting near the Vivekananda Temple. At that time this temple was not as we see it now. It looked like a small tomb with the present marble relief sculpture of Swamiji inside. All other additions to the temple were made long afterwards. We approached the monk and he immediately inquired from where I came. I told him I came from a village named Sholaghar in the district of Dacca, and I also told him that I came only with the desire to visit the Math and to attend the celebration. He immediately asked me whether I was prepared to participate in the celebration and become a volunteer and help in the preparations for the celebration the next day. The very suggestion, that I participate in the celebration, made within moments of my entering the Math, transcended the domain of all my expectations and amply fulfilled the dream of my life. It indeed was a call from Sri Ramakrishna and the Divine Mother who beckoned me to come to their feet—my own eternal home. My whole being was thrilled, and I jumped at the suggestion. Jnan Maharaj asked me to begin work immediately. My relative and my friend left the Math and went back to Salkia to come again the next day.

First duty assigned by Belur Math on the first day of visit

This was a most memorable day in my life—the day of my first visit to the Belur Math. It was Saturday, February 28, 1914. The memory of the first day of my life at the Math has remained indelibly imprinted on my mind in letters of gold.

Of course, I did not know anything about the Math. It was a vast place, but the shed for preparing and storing food to be distributed the next day among the devotees stood near the gate. The duty assigned to me was to help in the work in the shed. A group was engaged in this work. I immediately joined the group and began to work. The whole night passed in preparing khichuri, curry, and sweets and storing them in an orderly manner to facilitate smooth distribution. The whole night I worked without seeing anything else. I did not know even where the temple was and what was going on elsewhere. My assigned duty, however, came to a happy close to my greatest delight. My joy knew no bounds.

Thus, the very first duty assigned to me by the Belur Math on the very first day of my visit taught me in an objective manner the very first lesson, nay, the greatest lesson I ever have learnt in my whole life. This lesson is: *To serve*, the quintessence of spiritual practice, at once the means and the end to fulfilment of life. I bow to Belur Math.

Day of all days of dreams

At last the day dawned—that day of all days of my dreams— Sunday, March 1, 1914.

I moved out and witnessed a small incident—small, but of tremendous impact on my juvenile mind. It was an instance of how the spirit of service transforms human activity into worship of God.

Makhan Sen, a veteran freedom fighter of early days and subsequently one of the founders of the great nationalist Bengali daily *Ananda Bazar Patrika*, was the chief in charge of the volunteers engaged for the orderly management of the various functions of the entire celebration. Very early in the morning it now was time for the volunteers to take up positions in different areas of the celebration as already decided upon. When, however, Makhan Sen began ordering the distribution of volunteers an elderly gentleman suddenly came and requested him to accept his service. Makhan Sen told him that an adequate number of volunteers had already been enlisted and no more were necessary. The gentleman, however, so very humbly begged him to give him this privilege that, moved by his extreme eagerness and repeated entreaties, he said: "Well, if you are so very eager I can give you the only work, which is sweeping and cleaning the places where people, irrespective of class or any other consideration, will be fed together." The immediate scene I saw startled me and touched me very deeply. The moment Makhan Sen gave him this permission, the gentleman lifted his arm and cried out: "Ah! Very well! Very well! Wonderful! Wonderful! Blessed am I! Blessed am I!" With these words he quietly moved to his place of service as directed. An extraordinary spiritual wave had permeated the entire atmosphere of the Math and manifested itself in diverse forms on the solemn occasion of that day. A feeling of worship through service had deeply captivated the gentleman and guided him to behave in the way he did. His outbursts of joy overwhelmed me and made me dumb and feel myself blessed. I am reciting this story today after seventy-three years with as much thrill as I felt so long ago.

With a glorious morning the celebration began. I felt I was in a dream-land. A big pandal had been erected and inside it a huge painting of Sri Ramakrishna was placed in a beautifully decorated setting. Streams of people began assembling and gradually filled the whole grounds. The congregation then became a solid mass. There were songs, music, religious stories, distribution of sweet drinks, and so on. All these created a vibrant religious atmosphere and the people were filled with great joy. It indeed was a most impressive scene of the highest order of spiritual elevation.

Thousands of all classes sitting and taking food together

Like an enchanted boy I unconsciously moved from place to place. I came across a scene which I never before saw in my life. Thousands of people of all classes, from the highest to the lowest and most downtrodden, all sat together and took food together. It seemed that all sense of discrimination had vanished from the minds of these people. This scene was a brilliant testimony to the natural eradication of all kinds of social distinction of caste and creed through the development of the consciousness of the spiritual unity of man as exemplified in the life and teachings of Sri Ramakrishna.

The Math building, Sri Ramakrishna temple, and the mango tree

As I spontaneously moved from one place to another being charmed by whatever I happened to see, I at last came to the mango tree in the courtyard of the Math building itself. This building stands on the east side of the mango tree and faces the Ganges to its east, flowing from north to south. It is situated on the northernmost side of the Math grounds. Here in this building lived Swami Vivekananda, Swami Brahmananda, Swami

Premananda, Swami Shivananda, and all other disciples of Sri Ramakrishna as well as the disciples of Swami Vivekananda and other monks of
the Order. Being then the main building it also was used for all other purposes of the Math except cooking and dining. To the north of the mango
tree is a two-storied building which accommodated the then Temple of
Sri Ramakrishna on the first floor and the kitchen, store room, dining hall,
etc. on the ground floor. At the time, however, when I came to the spot I
did not know anything about these buildings nor did anybody guide and
help me to know anything in any way.

Kali Kirtan of Andul

Under the mango tree I found a group of musicians with long mat-
ted hair singing songs in praise of God as *Kali* the Mother Divine. I
took them to be monks but later I came to know that they were not.
They were merely dressed like monks. The songs they were singing
are the compositions of different saints of Bengal at different times.
When sung collectively, they are called *Kali Kirtan.* They embody the
highest truths of spiritual realization of God as Divine Mother. These
songs were being sung in the prestigious traditional classical style specially developed by a group belonging to a village named Andul.
Hence the name *Kali Kirtan* of Andul. This *Kirtan* is still sung by the
traditional group of Andul every year under the same mango tree on
the occasion of the birthday anniversary of Sri Ramakrishna.

Failure to take prasad

From early morning I was so deeply absorbed and so full of joy
watching the various functions of the celebration that I had not the
time even to think of taking *prasad* (consecrated food) though it is considered a must—an essential religious ritual to be observed by every
devotee. When therefore I became conscious of my great failure and
felt that I must have a little *prasad,* I went to the store where I had
worked the whole night as a volunteer and found that it had been completely exhausted and that nothing was left. I however found a devotee

carrying home some *prasad;* so I asked him to give me a little, which he was happy to do. I was most delighted and felt myself fully blessed with the *prasad.* My long-felt desire was thus fulfilled to my heart's content. I indeed felt so happy.

Jnan Maharaj

This was my first visit to the Belur Math. I had never visited a place like this before and it still remains the same for me today. I did not know any monk of the Order before that time. It was Jnan Maharaj, a disciple of Swami Vivekananda, whom I first met on the very first day just after entering the gate of the Math as I mentioned before. I got to know him and I became very close to him and remained so from that time until the end of his life.

He was very fond of young boys, and under his inspiration and guidance many young boys dedicated themselves to the life of sacrifice and service. As an instance of his love for me, later when I was at college in Dacca and was staying in one of our college hostels, Jnan Maharaj came from the Math on a pilgrimage, as he used to call it, to visit the Rama-krishna Ashramas of East Bengal. When he visited Dacca he came straight to our hostel and asked me to accompany him during his pil-grimage. I regarded it as a blessing and accompanied him with great delight. Jnan Maharaj brought with him a young boy of my age and we two together now attended on him. In many parts of East Bengal boats were used for all classes of transport and communication. Jnan Maharaj hired a boat for the purpose of visiting the different places he had selected. He thus moved from place to place with his two attendants and completed his holy pilgrimage. He was simple like a child and could very quickly endear himself most intimately to young boys. Wherever he went he inspired all, old and young alike, with the life-giving teach-ings of Swamiji. His life's special mission was to spread Swamiji's mes-sage, to which he dedicated himself completely, and his dedication has borne abundant fruit. His inspiration brought into being during his own lifetime a number of ideal educational institutions which bear eloquent

testimony to his lifelong dedication to the spread of the message of
Swami Vivekananda.

In retrospect

Before I conclude I wish to share with you my later revelation that
behind all the scenes I have described, something happened that at the
time remained unseen and unknown. This unique event was that the Holy
Mother was present at the Math throughout the day of the celebration and
watched its various functions. Or it may be said in the words of the Holy
Mother herself ("He who is Sri Ramakrishna, he is I myself") that Sri
Ramakrishna himself attended the functions of the celebration of his own
birthday anniversary, as he had done at Dakshineswar in Sri Ramakrishna
Form during his lifetime. Even now when I meditate on this event I visualize that I spent the hours of that Sunday, March 1, 1914 at my own spiritual home with my own eternal God the Father and God the Mother in
One. I imagine and visualize that the Holy Mother, sitting on the veran-
dah of the then Sri Ramakrishna Temple, as she used to do on all such
occasions, was watching and listening to *Kali Kirtan* being sung under the
mango tree, when I spontaneously came there and watched and listened to
the same music. I feel how blessed I was to have been under her feet at the
Belur Math though at that time I was absolutely unconscious of this
extraordinary event of my life.

Swami Premananda

Sri Ramakrishna's birth anniversary celebrations at Rarikhal

Now I am going to tell you about the incident which became the
turning-point of my whole life. This happened in 1915. I was in the
final class of my high school education.

I heard that the birth anniversary of Sri Ramakrishna would be
observed at a village named Rarikhal, the home of the celebrated scientist Sir Jagadish Chandra Bose. That village was about four or five miles

from our village, which was named Sholaghar. Sholaghar was a very important village in that area, and it had a primary school, a middle school, a high English school, a charitable dispensary, and a big shopping centre which opened daily. People from adjoining villages for miles around used to come and do their shopping there and the boys alike used to come and read in the high English school of the village.

As soon as I heard that the birthday anniversary of Sri Ramakrishna would be celebrated in Rarikhal I decided to go and the day previous to the festivity I went there. I found that preparations had been made for the celebrations in a very big way. A temple was there. A big tent had been set up. Arrangements for preparing food for distribution during the celebrations had also been made.

Swami Premananda's arrival

I heard that Swami Premananda, a direct disciple of Sri Ramakrishna and the head of the Belur Math, was coming that very evening to attend the celebrations. I was deeply interested to see what was happening. As soon as I arrived I found that a meeting was going on and a gentleman was speaking on some particular aspect of the life of the Gopis and Sri Radha and their relationship with Sri Krishna as described in the *Bhagavatam*. He was describing in great detail episodes in the love affairs between Sri Krishna and the Gopis and Sri Radha. At that very moment Swami Premananda arrived at the meeting in a palanquin and was given a seat. The gentleman continued his speech, and Swami Premananda listened. Of medium stature, with a well-built body and very fair complexion, the Swami seemed to have descended from heaven to earth and at once became the cynosure of all eyes.

Warning against discussions of love affairs between
Sri Krishna and Sri Radha and Gopis

When the gentleman concluded, the Swami was requested to say a few words. For the first time I had the rarest privilege of my life—to see a child of Sri Ramakrishna. The whole audience was looking intently towards him. The words that fell from his lips were the first words that I heard from the lips of one of the dearest children of Sri Ramakrishna. He struck quite a different note altogether. He uttered a stern warning against such discussions of the love affairs between Sri Radha, the Gopis, and Sri Krishna. He said that these matters which happened in the lives of Sri Krishna and Sri Radha and the Gopis related to an extraordinary supersensuous state of spiritual development. Ordinary people, whose minds remained at a low level of spiritual growth, and whose minds were attached to consciousness of the body and the senses, would never be able to appreciate the spirit underlying these love affairs. Rather, listening to and pondering over these affairs would do great harm to them. In particular, householders, who led a worldly life, should guard against indulging in these discussions. Extreme purity of mind, complete restraint of the internal and external senses, and the uttermost detachment from the objects of the world were the prerequisites to the correct apprehension of the suprahuman divine relationship between Sri Radha and Sri Krishna. What ordinary people should try to do was to listen to those teachings of the scriptures which helped to purify their minds in order to proceed from a lower state to a higher state of spiritual consciousness. Lastly, he dwelt upon how we could develop a spirit of love for and devotion to God and a spirit of detachment and unworldliness through worship of God in man. The audience was overwhelmed by a surging wave of spirituality that swept through the whole area. I became completely dumb with wonder, and silently moved away from the crowd. I went back home.

Radhika Mohan Das

Incidentally, the name of the gentleman who was addressing the assembled people just at the time of the arrival of Swami Premananda was, as far as I remember, Radhika Mohan Das. He was editor of a Bengali social monthly *Samaj Bandhu*. He came from Calcutta especially to participate in the celebrations. Since the very day of his having seen Swami Premananda and having heard his comments on his speech, Radhika Mohan became deeply attached to him and would always try to live close to him. His spiritual outlook underwent a radical change and he tried to mould his religious ideas in the light of the inspiration he now received from his day-to-day association with Swami Premananda. He used to say that he was so unfortunate that even living, as he did, in Calcutta, so near to Belur Math, he never met with Swami Premananda before. He compared himself with the musk-deer which runs about here and there in its pursuit of the source of the smell of the musk without knowing that the source was within its own navel itself. From now on whenever he met Swami Premananda he bowed to him and tried to be in his holy company as long as possible. He expressed particular delight to tell me that I was uniquely fortunate to come to the feet of Swami Premananda at such an early age. He was a very humble and lovable person and was most appreciative and receptive. He became completely transformed by the magnetic touch of divine love of Swami Premananda.

Joy of celebrations

Swami Premananda's arrival had created a stir all around. People from different parts began to assemble at the village to share in the celebrations. Great enthusiasm prevailed. I went again the next day to take part in the celebrations. The scene I saw I shall never forget. That a spiritual person could exert such a tremendous influence over a vast crowd in the way the Swami did, I had never seen in my life, and I do not expect that I shall ever have an opportunity to see anything like it again. It was unique. The Swami moved from place to place in the grounds where the celebrations were going on. Here there was devotional music, and elsewhere *kirtans* were being sung. In one place huge quantities of khichuri and curry were stored in small country boats, used as improvised containers, and later distributed among the assembled people. Groups from different parts of the adjoining villages gathered in different places and each group continued to play its music in its own way.

Swami Premananda's dance in ecstasy

I was standing near one of these groups, when Swami Premananda suddenly appeared. The group at once became surcharged with an extraordinary wave of emotion. Then I found to my surprise that Swami Premananda entered the circle and began to dance and share with them the song that they were singing. The spirit of the place suddenly changed completely. The whole group became mad with the excitement of spiritual fervour. They danced and danced and danced, moving round in a circle, their songs repeating the names of the Lord. Practically it became a spiritual lunatic group, completely absorbed in a devotional mood. The scene continued for some time and then Swami Premananda became a little calm and silently moved to another place. The scene I saw that day I have never seen repeated anywhere in any way. It happened once and only once in my life. I saw with my own eyes what one can become in the name of God. Now, I only read in *The Gospel of Sri Ramakrishna* how Sri Ramakrishna became immersed in God consciousness while singing and dancing in the name of the Lord.

Swami Premananda becomes Pir of Muslims

During the presence of Swami Premananda in the village the whole area became vibrant with a spiritual wave. Men belonging to different religions—Hindus, Muslims, and all groups, began to gather round him every day. The Muslims used to call him their Pir—their own saint. They would go to him at any time and the Swami received them at all hours. They would go and visit him where he stayed and entertain him with folk songs sung to different tunes, in different ways, as was their custom. They became one with the Swami who was always full of love and sympathy for them. He inspired them with spiritual teachings such as they had never received at any time in their lives.

Faith and devotion generates tremendous strength

The most distinctive trait in Swami Premananda's personality was divine love. It was so very expressive in every movement of his life that whoever came in contact with him, at any hour of the day, could not but be attracted to him. He was a magnet. Once attracted by his magnetic love, no one could ever separate himself from him. Through his divine love, he drew everybody to himself and by his own example helped them develop their faith in and devotion to God. The faith and devotion he wanted to inculcate was not in the least passive, but vibrant, full of strength and vigour. It was most life-giving.

An example. Keshto Babu was a very sweet singer of devotional songs. He came from Calcutta and attended the celebrations at Rarikhal. He entertained Swami Premananda and the devotees by frequently singing in his sweet voice. One day Swami Premananda asked him to sing a most devotional song beginning with the words: "O Mother, come and let there be a spiritual fight between Mother and child. Let there be a test whether Mother is defeated or the son is defeated." Keshto Babu sang the song very nicely. When, however, he finished singing, the spiritual fervour which should have animated the song had not been aroused. Swami Premananda mildly said to Keshto Babu, "Well, Keshto, you have sung the song very nicely in your own way. Let me now sing a little of this song in my own way." The moment Swami Premananda sang the words, "O Mother, as your child, I am heir to all your spiritual wealth, and today, with your strength, which I have inherited from you, I shall defeat you in our fight," his face completely changed and became aflame with deep spiritual emotion. A heavenly scene and atmosphere was created. The tremendous spiritual fervour manifested in Swami Premananda at the moment of his singing pervaded the whole audience. It completely surcharged and elevated those who were fortunate enough to be present there on that occasion. He then spoke to the people and dilated upon the fact that true faith in God generated such tremendous strength in man that he could easily fight against all odds and win the battle of life.

First personal contact with Swami Premananda and his prediction

Now I shall not continue further what I saw happening from day to day with the presence of Swami Premananda in that village. Instead, I shall come straight to what happened to me. Arrangements for Swami Premananda's stay in the village had been made at the parental house of the scientist, Sir Jagadish Chandra Bose. It was a nice house, with a small building and a pond facing it. The front room of the building was provided for Swami Premananda and his two attendants, Swami Arupananda and Swami Dayananda, who had accompanied him from the Belur Math. As yet I had not had any personal contact with Swami Premananda. One day I went straight to this house in order to meet the Swami. I stood near the door of his room. Swami Premananda was there, seated on a cot. The Swami just looked at me and said, "Here (he) has come again! Well, come inside."

I went inside. He asked me to sit down. I sat on the floor at his feet. Immediately he asked, "Where have you come from?" I named the village, Sholaghar.

"Who are there in your family?"

I replied, "Father, mother, four brothers, and two sisters."

"What does your father do?"

I told him.

"Your brothers?"

I told him.

"You?"

"I am in high English school, reading in the final class."

Immediately he said, "Oh, then it is all right. You will live at the Math. But not now. You will come after you have passed the B.A. examination."

To live at the Math after my having passed the B.A. examination—a prediction made within one minute! Past, present, and future seen through! Since 1915 a whole life spent as he had predicted! My light and guide and polestar!

At the time the Swami made the prediction, Swami Arupananda and Swami Dayananda were both present. From that day until the last day of their lives I was very close to them and they showered unfailing affection upon me.

Days with Swami Premananda

The moment Swami Premananda made the prediction about me I felt that he had made me completely his own. He knew my past, my present, and my future, and guided me accordingly. I became one with the whole group and began to live and move and have my being with them as long as they remained in that village. I attended to the small needs of Swami Premananda. When he went to bathe, I accompanied him and washed his clothes. In the village one had to go a little distance for toilet purposes, and I carried the water jug and waited to go back with him. In short, wherever he went, I went too.

The Swami continued his spiritual ministration not only among the men of the village, but he would visit other places also. In those days women did not come out and attend public meetings, so special meetings were organized for them. I went with Swami Premananda to those meetings, along with another friend who was a good musician.

Swami Arupananda, Swami Dayananda, and I became so close that they asked me whether I was prepared to go with them to the Math. I could not give them a definite reply at the time. My mind wavered. Those who came to know what was happening to me had warned me not to do anything without much thought.

Scenes on Swami Premananda's departure

Soon the time came for Swami Premananda to leave. The day of his departure from the village is still vivid in my mind. That memory will never be erased. Men and women from the village and adjoining villages assembled in the Ashrama grounds from where the Swami would leave. A unique scene was created. I have never witnessed one like this in all my life.

The moment the Swami began to get into the palanquin, the whole crowd burst into tears! The women began to weep aloud, as they used to do in the villages when anyone in the family died. That happened on this occasion. The Swami was moved. He could not get into the palanquin. He stood and blessed them all with sweet words of love and consolation. Finally, he got into the palanquin and it started moving. We all followed on foot. As we moved on, people from the wayside villages came running. They wanted to have a look at the Swami and receive his blessings. The Swami spoke a few words and blessed them all. The palanquin again started, and gradually we all came to the bank of the river Padma. There the Swami stood, ready to board the steamer. We bowed to him before he went on board. The steamer moved along the river, and we watched and watched until it went out of sight.

Impact

This whole episode moved Swami Premananda so very deeply that he himself expressed his feelings to one of his brother disciples. He said that when he left the village of Rarikhal he was reminded of the scene which occurred when Sri Krishna left Vrindaban for Mathura, and how the Gopis felt at Sri Krishna's leaving them behind. The events of that day in 1915 became indelibly imprinted on my mind. Even today I see with my mind's eye the same scenes, and I see them all as vividly as on that day, so long ago.

After the whole episode ended I went back home, but that home no longer existed for me. I now felt the real impact on my mind. The old world had vanished. I could not think of anything but the Belur Math. It flashed into my mind as my real home. How to go there and when to go was the only question.

Hem Dada and preparations for going to Belur Math

I heard that a devotee and disciple of the Holy Mother was the headmaster of the high English school at Abdullapur, a village about fifteen miles from our village. I longed to meet him and know from him how I could fulfil my desire to live at the Belur Math, as Swami Premananda had suggested. Accordingly, I went to the headmaster and met him and talked with him. He was a bachelor and wonderful person. His name was Hem Chandra Datta and he was addressed as Hem Dada, meaning Brother Hem. He inspired many students who came in touch with him. He became very fond of me and promised that he would make all arrangements for me to visit the Belur Math. It was arranged that in the near future I would meet him at a place called Teota, near Manikganj, where his father lived and worked. From there we would go together to Calcutta and then to Madhupur, a place of retreat, where we would spend a few days. After that we would return to Calcutta and go to the Belur Math where he would leave me. Soon afterwards, school vacation time came and I took the opportunity to realize the plan as he had devised it. I left home, and went to the steamer station, about ten to twelve miles away. I took the steamer, and managed to go to the place where Hem Dada was staying with his father. We then left together for Calcutta and stopped there.

M., Master Mahasaya

Hem Dada knew M., Master Mahasaya, the author of *The Gospel of Sri Ramakrishna*. So when we reached Calcutta we went to meet him. This was the first time I met Master Mahasaya. What a personality! Broad-faced with a long beard, sweetness itself, calmness itself, so loving, I was deeply moved. This was a unique experience for me—to be at the feet of one who had sat at the feet of Sri Ramakrishna so often. The whole of humanity is indebted to M. for the spiritual treasures he has preserved. Hem Dada talked to Master Mahasaya, and I was a mere witness at that time. In my later life I had many occasions to sit at his feet and again listen to his words of nectar. I recall with deepest reverence and joy and wonder my last visit to him on the evening of June 3, 1932 when he offered me with his own hand a mango to eat in his presence. He was divine love itself. Alas, that was his last day on earth. He passed away early next morning.

Belur Math and return home

According to our plan, Hem Dada and I went to Madhupur, and after a brief stay there we went straight back to Calcutta, and from there to the Belur Math. Swami Premananda was there and we met him and bowed down before him. I felt at home and so happy to be there with the idea that my dream was going to be fulfilled. I told Swami Premananda that I wanted to stay at the Math. "No, no," he said, repeating what he had wanted me to do during my first meeting with him, "you must go back and pass the B.A. examination and then come and stay at the Math." I felt very sad but I had to go back home and complete my studies and take my B.A. degree. Now as I look back I find that his will was done. My time is over, but this story is just beginning. Thank you.

PART TWO

As I said in the first part of my story, I left home and visited the Belur Math in 1915 and wanted to live there; but Swami Premananda said, as he had done before during my first meeting with him, that I must get my B.A. degree and then join the Order. I therefore had to go back home and prepare for the matriculation examination to be held the next year, 1916.

Swami Brahmananda and Swami Premananda at Dacca

In the meantime, I heard that Swami Brahmananda and Swami Premananda, with a large group of swamis and brahmacharis, were visiting Kamakhya and then would visit Dacca and lay the foundations of the Ramakrishna Math and the Ramakrishna Mission there. I immediately began to think how to take advantage of this event to meet them. I heard that they would be coming in February. So, in order to have an opportunity to meet Swami Premananda again and to meet Swami Brahmananda and other swamis while they were in Dacca, I made arrangements with one of my classmates to go to Dacca before my examination, stay there, take the opportunity to be with the swamis, and then sit for the examination. The examination would begin on the first of March. Students from all schools in the district of Dacca would go there to sit for the examination. That was the plan in those days. Accordingly, I made arrangements with my family. My classmate and I went to Dacca and arranged to stay there in a boarding house.

The swamis came as scheduled. I immediately went to the place where they were staying, introduced myself, and became very intimate with those who were looking after Swami Brahmananda, Swami Premananda, and the group accompanying them. It was a very fine house where they were accommodated. It was named Agnes Villa. I do not exactly remember the number of swamis and brahmacharis in the party. It was quite a big party, including some devotees.

Agnes Villa becomes a place of everyday visit

I had gone to the city to prepare for the examination, but my principal interest now turned to thoughts of this group. I spent some time every morning, reading and preparing for the examination. In the evenings, I went straight to Agnes Villa where Swami Brahmananda and Swami Premananda and all the other swamis were staying. That house became a place of festivity. Swami Brahmananda and Swami Premananda regularly met the devotees there, and I took every opportunity to be with them.

Mantram *given by Swami Brahmananda*

One day, as I went and bowed to Swami Premananda, he asked me to go and bow to Swami Brahmananda. I went and bowed to him. We used to call him Maharaj. We never used his full monastic name when we mentioned him to any other person. When we refer to Swami Vivekananda we only use the word Swamiji. Everyone understands who are referred to when the mere words Swamiji and Maharaj are used. In the case of other swamis, it is our custom to add Maharaj to the end of their personal or sannyasin names. Swami Premananda was called Baburam Maharaj, Baburam being his personal name. As I bowed to Maharaj, he looked at me. I was only 17 years old. Maharaj said to me, "Do you want to do anything to develop your spiritual life?" I folded my hands and expressed my heart's desire to do so. Maharaj gave me some instructions about how to think of Sri Ramakrishna, and then he said very solemnly: "Well, I would like to tell you just a few words for your spiritual development. If you really seek God, if you really seek spiritual growth, try to observe three things with deepest devotion. Never deviate from these three things. Under all circumstances try to stick to these three things that I am going to tell you. These three are: *Sincerity, Simplicity,* and *Truth.*" He was speaking with me as usual in Bengali, but these three words he uttered in English. He gave very special importance to these three spiritual values, and insisted on my sticking to them under any circumstances whatsoever. He warned me against deviating from these three prerequisites to spiritual life. These three words were the *mantram* given to me by Swami Brahmananda. These three spiritual values I have tried to follow most scrupulously throughout my life. I have not told an untruth in my whole life.

After meeting Maharaj and Baburam Maharaj, I always dreamt of them, and thought of them, and yearned to be with them. My mind always remained in their company. In the morning I would do some studying for the examination, but almost every evening I spent with the Swamis.

Sensitive nature

The manager of the boarding house noticed that early in the evening I went out and came back late in the evening. So, as a well-wisher, he said to me one day, "Well, Chintaharan (my personal name), you came here to study and prepare yourself for good results in your forthcoming examination, but you are spending almost every evening outside." I have always been of a very sensitive nature, and I reacted very sharply to the slightest adverse opinion expressed about me in any way whatsoever. I still continue to be so, though to a much lesser degree. As was my habit in those days, I at once reacted to the manager's remark saying, "If you desire, I shall leave your place and go elsewhere." He immediately said, "Why do you think that way? I have heard that you are a very good student and are expected to do very well in your examination, but if you neglect your studies in the way you are doing just before the examination, your results will be adversely affected." I felt ashamed, and humbly responded, "Sir, I am grateful to you for your kind thought. But you will kindly excuse me, I shall not be able to persuade myself to act in a different way."

Laying foundations of Math and Mission

On February 13, Swami Brahmananda and Swami Premananda laid the foundations of the Ramakrishna Math and the Ramakrishna Mission on the new land donated by one of the big landlords of the city of Dacca, Jogesh Chandra Das, a great patron of religion and culture. I was present on the occasion and had the opportunity to see everything with my own eyes. It was a sight to see how two divine children of Sri Ramakrishna laid the foundations to carry on the message of their Lord for the peace and progress of humanity.

Egolessness of Swami Premananda

An incident comes to my mind, and while it may appear small, its spiritual implications are too deep, and too abstruse to reveal themselves to the uninitiated soul. Egolessness is the very precondition, the primary means, and the end and fulfilment of spiritual life. This rare state reached the uttermost perfection in the life of Swami Premananda and not only transformed his mental consciousness but also completely metamorphosed his physical body so that both body and mind reacted exactly in unison against the least touch of egoism in any form whatsoever. This trait of egolessness thus became part of a physico-mental indistinguishable blend, forming one unity in the life of the Swami. This spirit of egolessness therefore became so natural with him that even his body involuntarily shrank from doing anything which would appear to detract from that state. Swami Premananda's life was a most concrete example and illustration of egolessness and fulfilment of the highest state of spiritual enlightenment.

What happened was this. After the foundation-laying ceremony, arrangements were made for taking a photograph. Swami Brahmananda was seated amidst all those assembled. The seat of Swami Premananda was found vacant. He did not go there, and was found behind the group outside the range of the camera. Viswaranjan Maharaj, a tall, able-bodied, senior Swami and attendant of Swami Brahmananda, went near Swami Premananda. Standing behind Baburam Maharaj, he stretched out his arms, and with all reverence humbly said, "Maharaj, please come and take your seat for the photograph." He then led Baburam Maharaj to his seat. Baburam Maharaj looked like a puppet, completely unconcerned. A photograph was taken of the whole group.

The incident left such a deep impression on me that its lesson is still as fresh in my mind now as it was over seventy years ago. To repeat, egolessness, indeed, is the very precondition, the primary means, and the end and fulfilment of spiritual life. At the present time, such an incident is entirely inconceivable.

Impact on the youth of Bengal

Dacca was the capital of East Bengal, which produced many revolutionaries in the struggle for the independence of India. Without any exception, all these revolutionaries were inspired by the teaching of Swami Vivekananda. The movement for the freedom of India came to a high pitch at the time when Swami Brahmananda and Swami Premananda were visiting Dacca. A large number of young people, inspired by the ideals of sacrifice and service for the freedom of India, as preached by Swami Vivekananda, were at that time studying in different colleges. Many of them used to visit Swami Brahmananda and Swami Premananda. The Swamis received those students with great love and sympathy and guided them in directions that would benefit them personally in particular and the country in general. They were so deeply attracted to the divine personalities of these two Swamis that many of them either joined the Freedom Movement of India or embraced the life of renunciation and joined the Ramakrishna Order, for their own spiritual salvation and for the service of humanity. It may be of interest to you to know that some among those who joined the Order happened to take charge of some American centres.

Swami Premananda's self-revelation

I am reminded now of another incident that took place in connection with Swami Premananda. The students of the Dacca College organized a meeting in their hall to receive and hear the Swami. A most learned professor, named Aswini Kumar Mukherjee, was presiding over the meeting. Swami Madhavananda, who later became the president of the Ramakrishna Order, accompanied the party of Swami Brahmananda and Swami Premananda. Swami Premananda took Swami Madhavananda with him to the meeting. Swami Madhavananda gave a very nice speech. Later when Swami Premananda addressed the meeting, he became, as usual, completely absorbed. He began inspiring the students, telling them how to mould their lives with spiritual ideals and how to fulfil their ultimate mission of self-realization. The hall was surcharged with an extraordinary wave of spiritual fervour. The time allotted for the meeting was exceeded. At this time Swami Premananda, while speaking, was completely lost within himself. He was in another world altogether, oblivious of time and his surroundings. At that very moment the chairman looked at his watch and this attracted Swami Premananda's attention. The sudden break in his extraordinary emotional mood caused a mental shock to the Swami, and he exclaimed, "Sir, through the grace of Sri Ramakrishna, I have gone beyond the domain of time." This remark, though quite embarrassing to the chairman, was yet impregnated with a deep spiritual significance. Properly understood, it was rather a blessing in disguise, and, in this case, it really proved to be so. The chairman was a very fine person and was most appreciative and receptive. He had the proper insight and took the remark in its true spirit and in a very humble manner.

Vijay Krishna Goswami's mother-in-law

Vijay Krishna Goswami was a great devotee of Sri Ramakrishna. He had an ashrama in Dacca, at a place called Gendaria. His mother-in-law was staying at the ashrama at that time. She was a very old and spiritual-minded lady. Swami Brahmananda knew her well, and she was very fond of him. In fact, she loved him most dearly and looked upon him as her child. Swami Brahmananda and Swami Premananda went to visit her at Vijay Krishna Goswami's ashrama, and I accompanied them. Thus I had the blessed opportunity to be a witness to the mutual spiritual treatment and behaviour between Vijay Krishna Goswami's mother-in-law and Swami Brahmananda. The scene reminded all of us of Yasoda's relationship to her child Sri Krishna. It was, indeed, a scene to see.

Vijay Krishna Goswami's vision of Sri Ramakrishna

When Vijay Krishna Goswami was living at this ashrama, he one day had the vision of Sri Ramakrishna in his physical form. He said that he had even touched and felt his body. Sri Ramakrishna was at the time still living and staying at Dakshineswar.

Farewell lunch and departure

Swami Brahmananda, Swami Premananda, and their party left Dacca by the end of the third week of February and went to Narayanganj where they had to take the steamer on their return journey. Nibaran Choudhury, a disciple of Maharaj, invited all to have lunch at his house before seeing Maharaj and his party off at the steamer station. The lunch was elaborate and I still remember that it ended with a most delicious melon. Everything went according to plan, and we all assembled at the steamer station and saw the party off. It was February 24.

Passed matriculation examination

The days I spent in the company of Maharaj, Baburam Maharaj, and the party at Dacca will ever remain enshrined in my memory.

After the departure of the party, I awoke to my own situation. I realized where I stood in relation to my preparation for the matriculation examination to be held on March 1. I studied hard and finished my work as quickly as possible. I sat for the examination and passed it in the first division.

College education

Now began my college education. As ordered by Swami Premananda, I proceeded with my college studies. I took admission into Jagannath College in Dacca. At that time, some friends of mine were staying at Agnes Villa, the very house where Swami Brahmananda and Swami Premananda and their party had stayed. I joined my friends and began to live with them. The head of our group was later to become Swami Gnaneswarananda, the founder of the Chicago Vivekananda Vedanta Society.

Swami Mahadevananda

At this time, Swami Mahadevananda was in charge of the Ramakrishna Math at Dacca. Swami Mahadevananda was a disciple of the Holy Mother. His birthplace was Koalpara, a village very near to Jayrambati. There is an ashrama at Koalpara where the Holy Mother used to stay on her way from Jayrambati to Calcutta and back. At this ashrama the Holy Mother installed with her own hands a portrait of Sri Ramakrishna and a portrait of herself. From his very boyhood, Swami Mahadevananda came in very close contact with the Holy Mother and served her with the utmost love and devotion. Swami Mahadevananda now told me that the Holy Mother had gone to Calcutta and that he was going to visit her there. It was the month of December, 1916. As soon as I heard this, I told Swami Mahadevananda that I would like to go with him to visit the Holy Mother. He agreed.

Visit to Holy Mother and initiation

Accordingly, on December 23, 1916, we left Dacca and reached Calcutta early the following morning. We went straight to the Holy Mother's house at Baghbazar. At once we went to the Ganges, had our bath, returned to the Holy Mother's house, and were waiting to bow to her. At that time, the Holy Mother was worshipping Sri Ramakrishna in the shrine on the first floor. We were waiting on the ground floor. Swami Mahadevananda, who was quite at home there, went upstairs to see what the Holy Mother was doing. By then the Holy Mother had finished her worship, but was still seated in the shrine where she had been worshipping Sri Ramakrishna. Swami Mahadevananda made his obeisance to her and then came back downstairs and told me that the Holy Mother was still seated in the shrine after her worship. He asked me to go upstairs and make my obeisance to her. I went upstairs and entered the shrine and made my obeisance to her. The moment I bowed to her, she looked at me and said, "Well, will you have initiation?" I was overwhelmed. She immediately said to me, "Take your seat. Perform *acamana* (just sprinkle a little Ganges water into your mouth)." Then she said, "Which God or Goddess do you love most?" I immediately told the Holy Mother the name of my only God. She then gave me initiation. I had not taken any gift with me to offer at her feet, as is the custom at the time of initiation, for I did not know that my initiation would take place in this manner. The Holy Mother asked me to bring some fruits from those under her bed in the shrine room. Accordingly, I brought some and she asked me to offer them at her feet, which I did. Then I bowed to her, left the room, went downstairs, and told Swami Mahadevananda all that had happened.

One of my friends, Jay Chandra Chakravarty, a disciple of Swami Brahmananda, was present there. He was the eldest son of Sarat Chandra Chakravarty who was a disciple of Swami Vivekananda and author of *Svami-Shishya Samvad* (Conversations between the Swami and His Disciple). This was a wonderful book and was a source of great inspiration. It was read by all young people in those days. My friend's mother's house and our house were in the same village and very near to each other. We knew each other very well. He read at our village school for some time. After my initiation, my friend and I went out and bought a piece of cloth with a very narrow red border, the kind of cloth the Holy Mother used to wear. We also purchased some grapes. They were then offered to the Holy Mother. At noontime I had the Holy Mother's *prasad* at her house.

Prediction

Swami Mahadevananda told me that after I had had my initiation the Holy Mother said to him, "This boy will make his mother and his brothers weep," indicating thereby that I was meant for the life of renunciation. This prediction fulfilled the prophecy that had been made by Swami Premananda at the time of my very first meeting with him in 1915.

Christmas Eve at Belur Math

That evening, I went to the Belur Math and witnessed for the first time the celebration of Christmas Eve, which is observed by all the Ramakrishna Math and Ramakrishna Mission centres all over the world.

Conclusion

To conclude: The Holy Mother, in one of her letters to a devotee, wrote: "He who is Sri Ramakrishna, he is I myself." Sri Ramakrishna said to Yogin Ma, a woman devotee and close attendant of the Holy Mother: "Never have any doubt about her (Holy Mother). She and this (referring to himself) are one." Both Sri Ramakrishna and the Holy Mother declared that they were one. Coming to the Holy Mother's feet is coming to Sri Ramakrishna's feet. Thus it was that I came to the feet of Sri Ramakrishna.

Divine Rights of the Sangha opened with separate epigraph and dedication pages, as in Back to Vivekananda, *condensed under the title below.*

DIVINE RIGHTS
OF
THE SANGHA

BACK TO VIVEKANANDA
Part I
Revised 11 March 1992

SWAMI NITYA-SWARUP-ANANDA

BELUR MATH

BACK TO VIVEKANANDA

The Only Way of Salvation for the Sangha

THE WAY

All activities of the Math will be carried on
with the approval of all its members, and in
the absence of unanimity, with the consent of
the majority. (The Math I – Rule 14)

DEDICATED TO

THE UNITED SANGHA

With an Earnest Prayer
for its Coming

BACK TO VIVEKANANDA

DIVINE RIGHTS OF THE SANGHA
BACK TO VIVEKANANDA
Part I
Revised 11 March 1992

I
PREAMBLE

I.I   PROPHET OF THE DIVINITY OF MAN AND THE GLORY AND FREEDOM OF THE ATMAN

Prophet of the New Age, Swami Vivekananda, gave to humanity, on a spiritual level, a basic message which centered on the bedrock of the divinity of man and the glory and freedom of the Atman. To bring this noble truth to bear on every aspect of the material and intellectual levels of the lives of individuals and to elevate and leaven the mass of mankind at large, Swami Vivekananda incessantly preached the fundamental right of every human being to manifest his potential divinity, his real nature, the fulfilment, the *summum bonum*, of human life.

I.2   ESTABLISHMENT OF THE ORGANIZATION AND CREATION OF THE CONSTITUTION

To this end, Swami Vivekananda established the Organization of the Ramakrishna Math, with its headquarters finally at Belur.

Before passing away he enacted and gave to the Organization, with its fullest consent and acceptance, a firm and comprehensive constitution designed to help manifest every member's potential divinity in every aspect of his life—either on the material, or the intellectual or the spiritual level. The Organization's Constitution now goes by the name of "Rules and Regulations of the Ramakrishna Math, Belur: Framed by Swamiji in 1898."

1.3   THE CONSTITUTION EMBODIES THE SPIRIT
      OF SRI RAMAKRISHNA

Sri Ramakrishna before his passing transmitted his spiritual self into
Swami Vivekananda and charged him to continue to fulfil his mission
on earth. True to his Master's divine dispensation, Swami Vivekananda
moulded his Master's charge into the formation of the Ramakrishna
Sangha to fulfil his Master's mission by his lifelong work through the
Sangha and, before his passing, he in his own turn, breathed into the
Sangha the spirit of his Master, Sri Ramakrishna, "in whom is the universe, who is in the universe; in whom is the soul, who is in the soul,
who is the soul of man; knowing him—and therefore the universe—as
our self alone extinguishes all fear, brings an end to misery, and leads
to infinite freedom." This spirit of Sri Ramakrishna in the form of the
Word which was with Sri Ramakrishna and which was Sri Ramakrishna, was now embodied in the Constitution bequeathed by him to
the Sangha for its guidance and administration throughout its life. The
Constitution is thus the Word which was Sri Ramakrishna—the Veda
of the Sangha breathed by Swami Vivekananda, the Vyasa.

II

THE CONSTITUTION

RULES AND REGULATIONS OF THE RAMAKRISHNA MATH, BELUR
FRAMED BY SWAMIJI IN 1898

II.1   THE CONSTITUTION

Swami Vivekananda moved the Ramakrishna Math from Nilambar
Mukherjee's garden house to its own abode at Belur on 3 January 1899
with its own Constitution, being "Rules and Regulations of the Ramakrishna Math, Belur: Framed by Swamiji in 1898." The Constitution
was now bequeathed to the Sangha at the Belur Math. The members of
the Math included the following disciples of Sri Ramakrishna besides
the disciples of Swamiji:

1. Swami Vivekananda
2. Swami Brahmananda
3. Swami Premananda
4. Swami Shivananda
5. Swami Saradananda
6. Swami Akhandananda

7. Swami Trigunatitananda
8. Swami Ramakrishnananda
9. Swami Advaitananda
10. Swami Subodhananda
11. Swami Abhedananda
12. Swami Turiyananda

II.2 THE CONSTITUTION ACCEPTED AS THE VEDA
OF THE SANGHA

All members of the Math bowed to the Constitution as the Veda of the Sangha and accepted it with the fullest consent of each and every one of them.

II.3 THE CONSTITUTION SECURES DIVINE RIGHTS
TO EVERY MEMBER

The Constitution, through its divine declarations, secures to every member of the Organization his divine right to:

JUSTICE   in all forms of community life;

FREEDOM   of thought, expression, faith, and
            worship in community life;

EQUALITY   of status, opportunity, and
            privilege in every form of
            community life;

FRATERNITY assuring divine dignity of every
            member in community life based
            on the spiritual unity of the Order;

AND ENSURES
AND VIVIFIES every member with the belief that:

(1) "This Sangha is his (Sri Ramakrishna's) very body and in this Order he is ever present." (The Math II – Rule 13)

(2) "Every member of this Math should feel that in every act of his he may manifest the glory of the Lord and that wherever he may go or in whatever circumstances he may be, he is a

representative of Sri Ramakrishna and that it is through him that people will see the Lord." (The Math II – Rule 4)

(3) "Whatever the United Sangha commands, is the command of the Master; whoever worships the Sangha, worships the Master; and whoever disobeys the Sangha, disobeys the Master." (The Math II – Rule 14)

(4) "All activities of this Math will be carried on with the approval of all its members and in the absence of unanimity, with the consent of the majority." (The Math I – Rule 14)

(5) "Unity is the chief means of progress and the only method of gaining strength. Therefore, if anyone tries to disrupt this unity by thought, word or deed, the curse of the whole Sangha will fall on his head and he shall lose this world as well as the next." (The Math II – Rule 10)

III

THE BASIC CRITERION OF ADMINISTRATION
OF THE RAMAKRISHNA MATH ORGANIZATION

III.I THE SANGHA IS SRI RAMAKRISHNA'S VERY BODY

"The Sangha is his (Sri Ramakrishna's) very body and in this Order he is ever present." (The Math II – Rule 13)

This divine declaration by Swami Vivekananda in his Constitution (1898) is the bedrock of the divine origin of the Ramakrishna Math Organization. This divine statute of the Sangha declared by Swamiji made it absolutely incumbent on the Sangha to regard itself, in its totality, as Sri Ramakrishna's divine body, as well as to regard its individual members severally as the divine limbs of Sri Ramakrishna's divine body itself.

The recognition of this divine status of the Sangha is the indispensable condition by which to comprehend the living inspirational soulforce of the Order. Comprehension produces insight and insight produces sensitivity. The degree of sensitivity is therefore proportionate to the degree of comprehension. As is comprehension embodying insight, so is insight embodying sensitivity. In degree, therefore, comprehension, insight and sensitivity are mutually in exact proportion. In this particular case also the degree of spiritual sensitivity which Swami Vivekananda inspired into the Ramakrishna Sangha is in exact proportion to the spirit embodying his declaration that "This Sangha is his (Sri Ramakrishna's) very body and in this Order he is ever present."

Swami Vivekananda made comprehension, with corresponding insight and sensitivity, of this divine declaration the Basic Criterion of Administration of the Ramakrishna Sangha, and as such, the Touchstone of the correctness of judgement as regards the administration and the carrying on of any activity in any aspect of the life of the Ramakrishna Math and Mission. In accordance with this *sine qua non*, any activity of the Organization is to be deemed essentially worthy in spiritual content of the Ramakrishna Sangha only to the extent that it fulfils the spirit of Swamiji's declaration and is an activity which is, therefore, inherently divinizing in its momentum. On the contrary, any activity in any aspect of the life of the Ramakrishna Math Organization which is bereft of the spirit of Swamiji's declaration of the Sangha as the body of Sri Ramakrishna will automatically lose the right to be regarded as worthy of an activity of the Ramakrishna Order. Swamiji's own crystal-clear instruction to the Math in this regard is: "Only that kind of work which develops our spirituality is work. Whatever fosters materiality is no-work." (Letter from USA – 1895 to Sashi Maharaj).

Swami Vivekananda, in giving the Sangha its divine status of being Sri Ramakrishna's very body, created the Ramakrishna Order as the divine Temple of Worship embodying the Universal Divinity of mankind, and, ipso facto, *as an absolutely spiritual organization in its strictest sense, never to be conceived of otherwise.* As an absolutely spiritual body, its essential vitality and continuity depend upon its innermost spiritual purity of content and not in the least upon its varied external expressions. These external expressions in the form of Diksha (initiation into discipleship), Ramakrishna Temples, ritualistic worship of gods and goddesses, classes and lectures, hospitals and dispensaries, schools, colleges and orphanages, publication of books and journals, relief works and other such activities, instantly meet our eyes and capture our minds; but the real essential divinizing spiritual soul inhering in and pervading them remains absolutely underground, unseen and unperceived by those who are externally minded. As a matter of course, therefore, more often than not, it is not the grain, the substance, the spiritual soul, but rather the shell, the external expression, which naturally engenders a strong appeal as the driving force of the Organization.

As the spiritual soul-force of the Organization declines, the external shell gradually masquerades as the internal spiritual soul-force, attracting unqualified, externally-minded spiritual aspirants, and misleads them into an apparently attractive abyss of doom. It was for this very reason that the ancient spiritual teachers and the founders of our Order prescribed the severest conditions for the aspirants to prepare for the ultimate fourth stage of life of monastic renunciation, so that those who are not fully and completely purged of impurities of the least trace of lust for enjoyment in this life and in the life hereafter are declared unqualified for the monastic life of renunciation, lest they should drag down the highest spiritual ideals of life of renunciation of a monastic organization to the lust for temporal enjoyment and power. This lust for enjoyment and power fosters a mentality of "materiality" which is a condition of "no-work" in a monastic organization according to Swami Vivekananda, the divine creator of the Sangha.

Salvation for the Ramakrishna Sangha, therefore, lies precisely in Swami Vivekananda's declaration, that the Sangha is the divine body of Sri Ramakrishna himself. Through the continuous inspiration of this divine declaration, comprehended with corresponding spiritual insight and sensitivity, it becomes the dynamic process to preserve the divinizing soul-force of the Order as well as the Criterion by which all activities of the Order are to be judged as to their spiritual content of worthiness in the truest sense—whether they develop spirituality or materiality. The yardstick against which this is to be measured is Swamiji's declaration that "whatever develops spirituality is work and whatever fosters materiality is no-work." In this way, when inspired by this highest ideal of Swamiji, all activities of the Order become divinized and have the power of divinization within them—as envisioned by Swamiji for the Ramakrishna Sangha, and, *ipso facto,* for the whole world.

III.2 EVERY MEMBER OF THE SANGHA IS A REPRESENTATIVE OF SRI RAMAKRISHNA HIMSELF

"Every member of this Math should feel that in every act of his he may manifest the glory of the Lord and that wherever he may go or in whatever circumstances he may be, he is a representative of Sri Ramakrishna and that it is through him that people will see the Lord." (Math II – Rule 4)

In this divine declaration, Swami Vivekananda not only wanted every individual member of the Sangha to be regarded as a divine limb of Sri Ramakrishna's divine body, but he also wanted every individual member of the Sangha to regard himself as a divine limb of Sri Ramakrishna's divine body and, *ipso facto,* as a representative of Sri Ramakrishna himself.

As such, Swamiji charged every individual member of the Sangha to identify himself fully and completely with Sri Ramakrishna and to manifest and exemplify his identity with Sri Ramakrishna in every movement of his own thought, emotion, and action. It is to this end that he climaxed his charge to every member of the Sangha by laying down his final declaration in that regard which commands that "Every member of this Math should feel that in every act of his he may manifest the glory of the Lord and that wherever he may go or in whatever circumstances he may be, he is a representative of Sri Ramakrishna and it is through him that people will see the Lord."

III.3 THE COMMAND OF THE UNITED SANGHA IS THE COMMAND OF THE MASTER HIMSELF

"Whatever the United Sangha commands, is the command of the Master; whoever worships the Sangha, worships the Master; and whoever disobeys the Sangha, disobeys the Master." (The Math II – Rule 14)

Swami Vivekananda's declaration that the command of the United Sangha is the command of Sri Ramakrishna himself, added the unique divine consummate dimension to his absolutely democratic administrative dispensation for the carrying on of any activity in any aspect of the life of the United Sangha.

Swamiji's warning that "Whoever disobeys the Sangha, disobeys the Master" underscores his intent that the voice of the United Sangha would be heard as the divinizing democratic force throughout the life of the Sangha, as representing the voice of Sri Ramakrishna himself.

III.4 SWAMI VIVEKANANDA'S DIVINE DEMOCRATIC COMMANDMENT

"All activities of this Math will be carried on with the approval of all its members, and in the absence of unanimity, with the consent of the majority." (The Math I – Rule 14)

In this foremost declaration of Swami Vivekananda, in which he provided the foolproof unequivocal administrative dispensation in his divine Constitution (1898), he mandated the right to consent and approval of every member of the Sangha in the carrying on of all activities of the Order. The basis for this inbuilt divine democratic provision rests in Swamiji's own words that every member of the Sangha is a divine limb of Sri Ramakrishna's divine body. This spiritual basis is further strengthened by his still higher spiritual declaration that every member of the Sangha "should feel that in every act of his he may manifest the glory of the Lord and that wherever he may go or in whatever circumstances he may be, he is a representative of Sri Ramakrishna and that it is through him that people will see the Lord."

This crucial basic foolproof unequivocal divine democratic commandment has thus attained the supreme divine status as the administrative dispensation built into the Constitution framed by him in 1898 with the divine insight of keeping the soul of the Sangha ever vibrant and united and guiding all its activities in every aspect of its life in fulfilling his Master's mission.

III.5 SWAMI VIVEKANANDA'S STERNEST WARNING AGAINST DISRUPTION OF THE UNITY OF THE DIVINE SANGHA

"Unity is the chief means of progress and the only method of gaining strength. Therefore, if anyone tries to disrupt this unity by thought, word or deed, the curse of the whole Sangha will fall on his head and he shall lose this world as well as the next." (The Math II – Rule 10)

Swami Vivekananda's foregoing declaration constitutes a direct warning against those who would disrupt the unity of the Sangha by any attempt of thought, word or deed.

As Sri Ramakrishna is himself the body of the Sangha, the Sangha is inherently united. To be a member of the Sangha, divinized as the body of Sri Ramakrishna, is to be oneself divinized, to manifest this divinity within oneself, and from there to divinize the whole world in order to usher in the Universality of Divine Birth on earth. Thus, the mission of the divine Sangha is to fulfil the establishment of Divine Life on earth, as exemplified by the life of Sri Ramakrishna.

This inherent united-ness of the Sangha as the body of Sri Ramakrishna himself, based on the declarations of Swami Vivekananda in his Constitution (1898) extends, therefore, to its very purpose in manifesting the glory of the Lord. The crucial importance of unity in fulfilling this purpose relates to the unity of the voice of the Sangha as a divine united command and, *ipso facto*, the command of Sri Ramakrishna himself, as well as to the divine right of consent and approval of every member of the United Sangha. As representatives of Sri Ramakrishna himself, therefore, cognizance must necessarily be taken of the approval of every member of the Sangha in accordance with Swamiji's democratic administrative provision that "all activities of this Math will be carried on with the approval of all its members and in the absence of unanimity, with the consent of the majority."

Against this background of the necessity of unity of the divine Sangha for it to be the divine vehicle to fulfil Sri Ramakrishna's divine mission, Swamiji's sternest warning against those who would disrupt this unity by thought, word or deed, becomes both irresistible and self-evident. Thus it is that any attempt to disrupt or undermine the united-ness of the Sangha will destroy its very purpose and will cause "the curse of the whole Sangha" to be brought to bear on those who will "lose this world as well as the next."

III.6 THE DIVINE FORTIFICATION OF THE SANGHA: ITS BASIC INBUILT DEMOCRATIC ADMINISTRATIVE PROVISION

The transcendental prophetic vision of Swami Vivekananda, his sacred trust to the Sangha, was fortified by him in the declarations of his divine Constitution (1898), wherein he provided the mandate that every member of the Sangha, as a limb of the body of Sri Rama-krishna, is a representative of Sri Ramakrishna himself; and that *the consent and approval of every member of the Sangha in the carrying on of all the activities of the Math is the basic divine inbuilt foolproof unequivo-cal democratic administrative provision.*

It is now incumbent upon the Ramakrishna Sangha to examine with extreme care its responsibility in the fulfilment of its sacred trust by Swamiji in every particular and in every aspect of all its activities, administrative or otherwise. Specifically, it must be recognized that any undemocratic intent in the carrying on of any activity of the Order which deprives a single member of the Sangha of his divine right of consent and approval is absolutely contradictory to and inconsistent with the life and teaching of Swami Vivekananda, the Prophet of the New Age. And, in particular, any such undemocratic induction will be tantamount to depriving Sri Ramakrishna himself of his consent and approval in the administration of the Sangha which is his own body and in which he is ever present, and *ipso facto,* equivalent to denying and betraying Sri Ramakrishna as well as Swami Vivekananda.

IV
THE CONSUMMATION OF THE DIVINE MISSION OF THE SANGHA

IV.1 THE SANGHA REPRESENTS THE HARMONIZED CONSUMMATION OF DIVINE LIFE ON EARTH

The consummation of Swami Vivekananda's declaration that the Sangha is Sri Ramakrishna's very body is nothing less than that the Sangha will unite the whole of mankind in the impersonal universal divine body of Sri Ramakrishna, representing and explaining the very purpose of the harmonized consummation of the whole history of Divine Descent on earth. This divine harmonizing mission of the Sangha thus becomes the vehicle of completion and the fulfilment of Sri Ramakrishna's Divine Life on earth and the explanation of the whole history of Divine Descent on earth. Swami Vivekananda exquisitely elaborates this explanation when he says: "We believe that every human being is divine, is God. Every soul is a sun covered over with clouds of ignorance; the difference between soul and soul is due to the difference in density of these layers of clouds. We believe that this is the conscious or unconscious basis of all religions, and that this is the explanation of the whole history of human progress either in the material, intellectual or spiritual plane—the same spirit is manifesting through different planes. We believe that this is the essence of the Vedas" (Letter from Chicago, 3rd March 1894 to Kidi).

And he culminates his declaration of this harmony saying: "We want to lead mankind to the place where there is neither the Vedas, nor the Bible, nor the Koran. Yet this has to be done by harmonizing the Vedas, the Bible and the Koran. Mankind ought to be taught that religions are but the varied expressions of THE RELIGION which is ONE-NESS, so that each may choose the path that suits him best." (Letter from Almora, 10th July 1898 to Mohammad Sarfaraz Hussain of Nainital).

By representing the consummation of Harmonized Divine Descent on earth, Sri Ramakrishna's birth thus becomes the fulfilment of the explanation and purpose of the whole history of Divine Descent. Now, therefore, mankind will become consciously aware that their ultimate destiny is Divinity and that the fulfilment of their destiny lies in the manifestation of this potential divinity in every movement of their life. Every human being, therefore, has the fundamental inherent divine right to manifest in his own individual distinctive way his potential divinity, his own real nature. This divine right, in its very nature, is the ultimate basis and, *ipso facto*, the *raison d'etre* of all forms of human rights to freedom. All such forms of human rights to freedom, however, are merely a prelude to, but indispensable for, gradual development in different stages of collective life. But the democratic right to freedom is universally accepted to be the highest form of human rights as an instrument conducive to the highest development of any form of collective living in human society. This democratic right, however, as stated before, is still unconscious of its ultimate quest for its divine goal like that of the musk deer, but will eventually and inevitably lead man to realize his divine right to manifest in his own distinctive individual way his own real nature, his potential Divinity, his ultimate fulfilment, the *summum bonum* of human life on earth.

It is against this divine foundational background scenario that the inevitable ultimate quest of every human being is now being symbolically but unconsciously demonstrated by the quest for democratic movements currently being witnessed in all parts of the world. This quest for democratic right is therefore basic to mankind's unconscious ultimate quest for Divine Self-realization. When the quest for democratic freedom will become conscious of its ultimate goal and lead to the realization of Absolute Divine Freedom, the Divinity of Mankind as declared by Swami Vivekananda, Prophet of the New Age, will become his Universal message, as exemplified in Sri Ramakrishna's divine life. Swami Vivekananda's own words of his prophetic vision are: "India will wake up again and the great tidal wave that has arisen from this Centre will like a mighty deluge inundate the whole of mankind and carry them towards liberation. This is our faith and we have girded up our loins to achieve this very objective to the best of our capacity through the successive generations of disciples" (Math Rules (1898) – Plan of work for India – Rule II).

In order for the Sangha to consummate Swamiji's sacred trust to it in fulfilling the universal divine mission, the spiritual strength and purity of the Order must be perfectly aligned with the declarations bequeathed to it by Swami Vivekananda in his divine Constitution (1898). Thus, the members of the Sangha must feel themselves to be the holy limbs of Sri Ramakrishna and Sri Ramakrishna's representatives in their individual thoughts, emotions and actions; the glory of the Lord must be manifested within each member of the Sangha, through whom people will see the Lord; and the whole world must be enveloped by the Divine Sangha as the impersonal universal divine body of Sri Ramakrishna, the harmonized consummation and explanation of the whole history of Divine Descent on earth.

The Sangha thus brings to humanity the Divine Message of the New Age that the whole history of mankind's development either on the material plane, or on the intellectual plane, or on the spiritual plane represents the varied expressions of the One Universal divine spirit through the different planes of mankind's development and that this is the conscious or unconscious basis of all religions—the divinity of mankind and the need to manifest this divinity in every movement of its life.

IV.2 THE SPIRITUALIZATION OF THE HUMAN RACE IS THE SANGHA'S ULTIMATE SACRED TRUST AND INDIA'S MISSION

As mentioned before it is thus that the Sangha becomes Sri Ramakrishna himself, "in whom is the universe, who is in the universe, who is the universe; in whom is the soul, who is in the soul, who is the soul of man; knowing him—and therefore the universe—as our own self alone extinguishes all fear, brings an end to misery, and leads to infinite freedom. Wherever there has been expansion in love or progress in well-being, of individuals or numbers, it has been through the perception, realization and the practicalization of the eternal truth—the oneness of all beings." *The impersonal universal spirit of Sri Ramakrishna inhering in the Sangha, now in its turn, must pervade the whole world and make it One Harmonized divine humanity with its every single individual soul harmonized into the divine body of Sri Ramakrishna, as envisioned and predicted by Swami Vivekananda as being the divine mission of India's life in the spiritualization of the human race.*

In most trenchant language in "India's Message to the World," Swami Vivekananda declared: "Aye, a glorious destiny, my brethren, for as far back as the days of the Upanishads we have thrown the challenge to the World—'Not by wealth, not by progeny, but by renunciation alone immortality is reached.' Race after race has taken the challenge up, and tried their utmost to solve the world-riddle on the plane of desires. They have all failed in the past—the old ones have become extinct under the weight of wickedness and misery, which lust for power and gold brings in its train, and the new ones are tottering to their fall. The question has yet to be decided whether peace will survive or war; whether patience will survive or non-forbearance; whether goodness will survive or wickedness; whether muscle will survive or brain; whether worldliness will survive or spirituality. We have solved our problems ages ago, and held on to it through good and evil fortune, and mean to hold on to it till the end of time. Our solution is unworldliness—renunciation. This is the theme of India's lifework, the burden of her eternal songs, the backbone of her existence—the spiritualization of the human race. In this her life-course she has never deviated, whether the Tartar ruled or the Turk, whether the Mogul ruled or the English."

V

THE FULFILMENT

V.I SWAMI VIVEKANANDA FULFILLED SRI RAMAKRISHNA'S MISSION BY MOULDING IT INTO THE FORMATION OF THE RAMAKRISHNA SANGHA

With the future vision of the Sangha to envelop the whole world in the universal divine body of Sri Ramakrishna, the harmonized consummation and explanation of the whole history of Divine Descent on earth, Swami Vivekananda fulfilled his Master's mission by moulding it into the formation of the Ramakrishna Sangha. Swamiji thus established the significance and the *raison d'etre* of the prediction his Master himself had made immediately at the very first sight of his first photograph showing himself fully merged in Absolute Divine Consciousness. Sri Ramakrishna's own words of his own prediction were: "This photograph will be worshipped in every home." Strangely enough, as if in fulfilment of his own prediction, one day Sri Ramakrishna chanced to visit the small room below the Music Tower of Dakshineswar Temple where the Holy Mother used to live to serve the Master, and in which she had enshrined and worshipped in a niche of the room the selfsame photograph. The moment Sri Ramakrishna saw this photograph he immediately worshipped the Universal Divine Man-Gods represented in the photograph within the divine abode of the Divine Holy Mother of the Universe.

With the creation of the Ramakrishna Sangha, Swami Vivekananda explained and fulfilled the purpose of his Master's mission and prediction and declared unto humanity the significance of the Divinity of Mankind and the Universal Birth of Divine Life on earth, and at the same time established his own prediction that "The day of Sri Ramakrishna's divine descent heralded the dawn of the Satya-Yuga, the Age of Divine Enlightenment."

Reminiscences

INTRODUCTION

THE REMINISCENCES that form the heart of this second volume
were solicited at the onset of the commemorative activities in
Swami Nitya-swarup-ananda's honour, when the author wrote a public
circular on behalf of the "Friends of Swami Nitya-swarup-ananda"
requesting contributions to his commemorative volume. While reminiscences were being collected by the author in America during 1993,
those in India were being received by Mr. Raghunath Goswami and
other friends. Several years passed, however, before the contributions
were all in hand and could be selected and edited for the current publication. The author gratefully acknowledges the translation of the reminiscences from the Bengali by Mrs. Shubhra Chatterji (translations are
identified by an asterisk after the writer's name).

Although Swami Nitya-swarup-ananda often looked askance at reminiscences and seldom reminisced himself, it is hoped that he would
have gazed affectionately on these sincere acts of friendship. On the
other hand, it seems likely that he would have sympathized with the
hesitancy of some friends to put pen to paper, whose lives he no doubt
touched just as deeply.

The seventy-three reminiscences in this section span as many years—
from the early 1920s until 1992. They are arranged in chronological
groupings so that the reader can refer to them while going through the
biography in Volume 1. Each reminiscence is placed according to the
writer's first meeting with Swami Nitya-swarup-ananda, or later if incidents of particular interest in the narrative occurred in subsequent years.

A number of India's most distinguished scholars share these pages
with respected monastics, artists, professionals, entrepreneurs, and
others from various walks of life who knew Swami Nitya-swarup-

ananda and wanted to pay tribute to him. There is sufficient material within each chronological grouping to satisfy a variety of interests; the reader is free to pick and choose. But even the humblest reminiscences offer a wealth of personal incidents and perspectives, poignant and often amusing, that add to our perception of Swami Nitya-swarup-ananda and enrich his story.

As the compiler of these reminiscences, the author gratefully acknowledges the generosity of those willing to share experiences close to the heart. With a sense of regret, but out of necessity to minimize the redundancy inevitable with seventy-three contributions, many heartfelt opening and closing statements in appreciation of Swami Nitya-swarup-ananda had to be edited out, along with many of the discussions about his ideas, educational philosophy, and the work of the Institute of Culture, which are covered elsewhere in his own words.

The profiles of the contributors (often given with reluctance) provide a fascinating look at the diverse and often remarkable accomplishments of Swami Nitya-swarup-ananda's worldwide circle of friends.

1920s
(As family friend and young monk)

The earliest reminiscences are those of the Basu Thakur family, who knew the young Chintaharan Sarkar during his pre-monastic days in Dacca, now in Bangladesh.

For the purposes of this narrative, the family included Mr. Nalini Kumar Basu Thakur, his wife, Sailabala, and their three sons: Sukumar, Sunil, and Chinmoy. Both Sukumar and Sunil were tutored by the young Chintaharan, but the reminiscences focus on the eldest son, Sukumar, who did brilliantly in the Indian Civil Service before his premature death in a tragic accident.

This patriotic Bengali family includes in its history a number of prominent leaders and freedom fighters in India's struggle for independence, such as the late Samarendra Nath Basu Thakur (Sukumar's paternal uncle) and the late Chinmoy Basu Thakur (Sukumar's younger brother), whose reminiscences open this section. The third reminiscence is that of the late Sunilava Guha (Sukumar's maternal cousin), whose memories of Chintaharan Maharaj span more than seventy years. Three other members of the Basu Thakur family—the late Sujata Basu Thakur (Chinmoy's wife), Dr. Phulrenu Guha (related to Nalini Kumar Basu Thakur on her mother's side), and Miss Rooma Basu Thakur (Sukumar's niece)—have contributed reminiscences to the 1950s section, since they first met Swami Nitya-swarup-ananda at Russa Road. The author is grateful to Miss Rooma Basu Thakur for her initiative in collecting the reminiscences and for her clarification of the family tree.

The fourth and final reminiscence in the 1920s section was written by the late Rabindra Nath Sen, a distinguished public figure in Bengal (unrelated to the Basu Thakur family) who knew Swami Nitya-swarup-ananda in Dacca as a young monk.

SAMARENDRA NATH BASU THAKUR

I met Chintaharan Maharaj for the first time in Dacca at the house of my cousin, Mr. Nalini Kumar Basu Thakur, the father of Sukumar

Basu Thakur. Chintaharan Maharaj (then Chintaharan Sarkar) was Sukumar's guardian tutor, and I saw him in the same house very frequently. He used to discuss spiritual matters with Sukumar's mother, Mrs. Sailabala Basu, and under his guidance she took *diksha* [initiation] from Swami Saradananda Maharaj. Chintaharan Maharaj told me that he held Basanta Kumar Basu Thakur and Satyananda Basu Thakur [two other members of the family] in high esteem as great leaders in the public life of Bengal.

A particular phase of my student life at Faridpore College pleased Chintaharan Maharaj very much. The Principal, K. N. Mitra, was a staunch nationalist as well as a great devotee of Thakur Ramakrishna and Swami Vivekananda. A committee was formed under his initiative in the name of Thakur Ramakrishna with Mr. Mitra as President, Prakash Chandra Ghosh (an Advocate) as General Secretary, and Harendra Chandra Chakraborty and myself as Joint Secretaries. When the committee was given a small house with four rooms rent-free, it was utilized to start a little four-bed hospital for treating patients free of charge; with further small donations, the committee was able to purchase a plot of land, which put the new Ramakrishna Mission Seva Pratishthan on a permanent footing. It so happened that, in the course of two or three years, Prakash Chandra Ghosh and Harendra Chandra Chakraborty both joined the Ramakrishna Order at the Belur Math.

I met Chintaharan Maharaj again after several decades when he was staying at the Ramakrishna Mission Institute of Culture in Calcutta. He asked my whereabouts and was so very glad to learn that I had survived some nine years of imprisonment, detention, and solitary confinement for my activities in the freedom movement. As he requested, I used to go to the Institute very often to visit him.

The calm, sober, and serene character of Chintaharan Maharaj attracted me the most and his affectionate attention for me rather overwhelmed me, which even after his sad demise keeps me fresh and lively at my present age of about ninety-two years [written in 1994].

CHINMOY BASU THAKUR

It is my proud privilege to narrate something about Swami Nitya-swarup-ananda, who was a great philanthropist, a great scholar, and above all a true disciple of Sri Ramakrishna and Swami Vivekananda. Here I shall only say something about one who was a friend, philosopher, and guide to our family throughout his life.

We lived in Dacca in the locality named Wari. Perhaps it was in the early twenties when my father, the late Nalini Kumar Basu Thakur, engaged a tutor for my two elder brothers, Sukumar and Sunil. The tutor's name was Chintaharan Sarkar, and he lived in our house as one of our family. We looked upon him as our own elder brother, sharing our sorrows and joys. Whenever there was any problem my mother would seek his wise counsel, and Maharaj would gladly help her in all possible ways. My mother not only loved but respected him, and it was through his guidance and inspiration that she became a disciple of Swami Saradananda.

He took great care in teaching his pupils. Sukumar had always been a brilliant student, but under his tutor's able guidance he stood first in the I.Sc. Examination of the Dacca Board. He then proceeded to England, where he passed the difficult Indian Civil Service Examination. By that time Sri Chintaharan Sarkar had left our house and had become a brahmachari in the Ramakrishna Mission (henceforth, we called him Chintaharan Maharaj, or just Maharaj). Maharaj was very proud of Sukumar's success, and of the rare good qualities that Sukumar had developed. Sukumar's character had been moulded under his influence, and Chintaharan Maharaj had also imbued Sukumar with the idea that mundane benefits were not all there was to life—that there was a need to reach higher to the sublime realm of the spirit. Through his inspiration, my brothers Sukumar and Sunil both became disciples of Swami Shivananda (Mahapurush Maharaj).

After a period of short service, my brother Sukumar lost his life in a motorcar accident. Maharaj was greatly shocked—though he was a monk, his personal relationship with us was never severed. He never forgot the days when he had lived with us.

Throughout his life he remained the great well-wisher of our family. In spite of his intense involvement in various works, he corresponded with my mother or with us to inquire into our whereabouts. During the "Quit India" movement, a call given by Gandhiji, I was detained in various jails for my involvement as a Freedom Fighter for five years, from August 1942 to July 1947, and Maharaj was anxious about my safety and my health. Later, he always found time to come to my quarters and houses in different locales, and he never came empty-handed.

He was a man with an impressive personality. He always shunned publicity and was meticulous in his work. A staunch disciplinarian, he led a disciplined and exemplary life. Maharaj is no more with us, but his image will remain ever bright in our hearts.

SUNILAVA GUHA

I am an old man of seventy-four [written in 1994]. I cannot remember a time when I did not know Swami Nitya-swarup-ananda. We looked upon him primarily as a family friend—a friend of three generations—more than as a monk. He was known to us as Chintaharan Sarkar, and it was not until much later that we became familiar with the name that he acquired when he donned the garb of a sannyasin. For decades there was hardly any change in his physical appearance, and to us he seemed unchanged and unchangeable.

Under his watchful eye as tutor, my cousin Sukumar grew into an outstanding student and ultimately joined the Indian Civil Service. The tie that was forged between teacher and pupil remained after Chintaharan Maharaj had joined the Order and was living at the Belur Math, even though Sukumar was posted at Sangar in Madhya Pradesh. I distinctly remember the terrible day when the news came about our Sukumar's death in a motorcar accident. On hearing about it Chintaharan Maharaj rushed to our house and almost broke down.

After Sukumar's death, Chintaharan Maharaj continued to be a friend, philosopher, and guide to our family. Indeed, he was our source of unerring counsel. It was at his suggestion that my elder brother, my younger brother, and I all became students at the Ramakrishna Mission Vidyapith in Deoghar, sitting at the feet of the teacher-monks each one of whom might prove an acquisition to any institution in the world. When my elder brother Amitabha (nicknamed "Bob") also died under tragic circumstances in another family tragedy, Chintaharan was shocked beyond measure and almost wailed like a child. He lavishly showered praises on his "dear Bob," calling him a "jewel" and "one in a million." He gave us, particularly my wife, a thorough dressing down for having failed to fence in the roof from which my brother had fallen to his death.

Whenever I travelled widely throughout the length and breadth of India, Maharaj gave me letters of introduction so that I might have safe and comfortable accommodation at the guest houses of the Ramakrishna Mission. And when I was stricken with a deadly disease, again it was Chintaharan Maharaj, our never-failing friend, who made all the arrangements with Dr. Shelley Brown and was present at the Institute during the consultation. The way he spoke about our family on that occasion almost made me blush in spite of my dark skin—I recall that day with gratitude.

The last time I saw Swami Nitya-swarup-ananda he was in a coma, lying ill at the Seva Pratishthan. How strange it seemed that the man who would have been all smiles to see me could not even recognize me! I realized then that his days must be numbered. When he passed away some time later, we lost a cherished friend who had stood by us in weal and woe, while society had lost one of its most brilliant visionaries and organizers. The Ramakrishna Mission Institute of Culture bears eloquent testimony to his power to conceive an idea and to translate that idea into reality. Our Chintaharan Maharaj lives on in his achievements, as well as in our hearts. I often meet a gentleman, another ardent admirer of Swami Nitya-swarup-ananda, who expresses it eloquently when he says that amidst the galaxy of monks in this holy land, Maharaj's name shines like a pole star.

RABINDRA NATH SEN*

[Abridged for the current volume from the article by Rabindra Nath Sen, "The Passing Away of Swami Nityaswarupananda," *Robibasar,* April 8, 1993 (Calcutta: Bengal Books): 115–18.]

On October 22, 1992, Swami Nitya-swarup-ananda left us all to join the lotus feet of Sri Ramakrishna in his characteristically unassuming manner. When I heard the news I felt that the world had lost a great worker—one whose deeds are proclaimed by all, but who himself chose to remain silent about his achievements. I had the good fortune to come in contact with this great monk of the Ramakrishna Order from a very young age, and subsequently had the opportunity to work with him in close proximity for a number of years in my professional capacity.

It was the year 1924. I was in my first year at Scottish Church College and staying with my family in a rented house in Muktaram Babu Street in North Calcutta. A few monks of the Ramakrishna Mission started living in the house adjacent to ours and Chintaharan Maharaj was among them. Also living there were Bharat Maharaj, one of the most venerated and seniormost monks of the Order who acted as its custodian for several years, Swami Dayananda, who later founded the Ramakrishna Mission Seva Pratishthan, and Swami Madhavananda and Swami Vireswarananda, both of whom eventually became Presidents of the Order. What a luminous group of monks we had staying there! The other three monks (Bhupen Maharaj, Upen Maharaj, and Satyen Maharaj) were no less illustrious, and commanded deep reverence from all who came in touch with them. We all became quite attached to this family of monks and that attachment flowered into a deep bond, for which I consider myself blessed and uniquely privileged.

On the meeting place of five roads in the southern part of Calcutta stands one of the city's most magnificent buildings, the Ramakrishna Mission Institute of Culture. I was involved with the Institute right from its inception. This temple of culture, now resplendent in its glory, had a humble beginning. The Institute shifted from a small bylane off Wellington Square to Russa Road just at the time when the Calcutta Metropolitan Development Authority was entrusted with the task of developing the area around Gol Park. Swami Nitya-swarup-ananda took this opportunity and went about requisitioning land and resources for building up the grand institution he had envisioned, single-handedly and in his usual meticulous and well-organized manner.

I was with Price, Waterhouse, Peat and Company, a well-known auditing firm which also did the auditing work for the Institute. It was through this that I came to know the exact nature of his functioning on the professional plane. The great "Karma Yajna" [work on a grand scale] undertaken by him was executed with due dedication and painstaking perfection. His sublime thoughts and keen perception, coupled with his exquisitely refined taste, made the Institute possible. Nothing short of the very best would meet his standards. The best architectural firm, Ballardie Thompson, drew up the plan, and the best construction company, Messrs. Martin Burn Ltd. (who had also constructed the Belur Math temple), was entrusted with the job. There is an all-pervading atmosphere of serenity and purity in the Institute. Everything about it is grand and exquisite, starting from the shining brass plate at the entrance, to the stairs, the lecture halls, the meditation room and the library—it is all sublime and yet without any trace of ostentation. This has been possible because the building is but a projection of grander visions and ideals.

For the last few years of his life, he led an almost anonymous existence within the walls of the selfsame Institute he had built up with so much love, dedication, and perfection. An example of perfect self-effacement and nonattachment, it is truly a symbol of renunciation as cited in the teachings of the Bhagavad Gita.

Another facet of his personality which left a deep impression on me was his wonderful combination of tenderness and firmness. Isolated incidents crowd my memory of his high standards and his attention to details. Swami Nitya-swarup-ananda came to my new house in South Calcutta in 1955. "Try to maintain the standard you have set," he cautioned me. "Unfortunately, standards tend to degenerate—seldom do they go up." I am sorry to say that I have not been able to follow his advice. On another occasion I took him to see the "Old Age Home" which I founded in Joka. He was very pleased with what he saw. At the same time, he came out characteristically with his word of caution, "Rabi Babu, will you be able to maintain the standards set by you and be able to continue running the Home like this? We are so very undisciplined as a nation."

On our way back he said, "We were together when the Institute was brought up—come, let us go to America and set up an Institute of Culture over there." I begged to be excused under the plea that at the age of eighty-three I was too old to undertake such a venture.

Let us not forget the lofty ideals to which he dedicated his entire life. Let us fervently hope that the temple of culture which he founded will continue to serve as a reminder to humanity of the great need of true intercultural and interracial understanding.

1930S–40S
(Albert Hall and Wellington Square)

AMIYA KUMAR MAJUMDAR

It was in the year 1936 that I first came to know Swami Nitya-swarup-ananda (Chintaharan Maharaj). I was then an undergraduate student of Scottish Church College. The Birth Centenary of Sri Ramakrishna was being celebrated with great enthusiasm and excitement, and Swami Nitya-swarup-ananda was one of the members of the Working Committee formed by the Ramakrishna Mission. Though many of the veteran monks of the Mission were occupying senior positions, the young Swami Nitya-swarup-ananda had to shoulder great responsibilities.

We came to know each other well as the years passed by. There was a special reason for my attraction towards him. My guru, Swami Gnaneshananda (who was my uncle before his initiation), was a monk of the Ramakrishna Order, and as a brahmachari he had been very close to Swami Nitya-swarup-ananda at the Ramakrishna Mission in

Dacca. They were fellow perfectionists; neither could tolerate any lapse, negligence, or laxity. My uncle (then known as Brahmachari Abhed Chaitanya, or Abhed Maharaj) was also very methodical in his work, and both he and Swami Nitya-swarup-ananda were initiated by the Holy Mother.

Swami Nitya-swarup-ananda had a firm belief that behind all the diversity in societies and nations there was a wholeness of world culture. Every single culture, he felt, was just a manifestation of this more universal human culture, though social scientists, particularly anthropologists, had no faith in this kind of sweeping concept. Swami Nitya-swarup-ananda discussed these matters for days on end with such eminent scholars as Benoy Kumar Sarkar, Ramesh Chandra Majumdar, Kalidas Nag, Niharranjan Ray, and others. He became ever more convinced about the value of world culture, and it was just a matter of time before he linked up with UNESCO.

It was in the late fifties that Dr. N. Bammate came to the Institute on behalf of UNESCO to prepare a comprehensive report on it. He was the Head of the Section of Philosophy and Humanistic Studies in the Department of Cultural Activities. I remember receiving an urgent call from Chintaharan Maharaj to stay at the Institute for a couple of days. I dared not ask him the reason. The Institute was then located at 111 Russa Road. On arrival, I saw a foreigner engaged in writing something with all seriousness. Maharaj introduced me to the gentleman, Dr. N. Bammate. Then began the explanation of what the Swami meant by world culture and the details of the School of World Civilization. Dr. Bammate and I were taking notes as dictated by Maharaj. I still remember vividly all that happened on that day. I noticed on the Swami's face a glow of satisfaction, just as a glow suffuses a child's face at the unexpected recovery of his lost toys from some unknown corner. With great pains, Dr. Bammate wrote the draft along the lines indicated by Swami Nitya-swarup-ananda.

I helped him to the best of my ability. Dr. Bammate, however, had misgivings about the foreign scholars who would be required to stay in the Institute for a period of five to six years while engaged in research. "Even if they agreed," he argued, "would it be possible for us to offer them appropriate fellowships?" To remove his misgivings, I asked him if he was aware that Swami Nitya-swarup-ananda had started the Institute with a very meagre amount received from the Sri Ramakrishna Centenary Celebration Committee, and had eventually been able to build, at a cost of Rs. 75 lakhs, the magnificent edifice which now housed it at Gol Park. Maharaj never worried about finance; it was his conviction that a good work never remained incomplete for want of funds.

Swami Nitya-swarup-ananda had the unstinting support of many great men. Dr. Radhakrishnan wholeheartedly endorsed Swami Nitya-swarup-ananda's plan for the School of World Civilization, and went so far as to declare, "If anybody opposes it, then I shall be prepared to speak for it." Dr. Malcolm S. Adiseshiah, Deputy Director-General of UNESCO, told him, "Your plan will be complementary to the UNESCO project." While travelling throughout Europe, America, and the Middle East in 1962–63, Swami Nitya-swarup-ananda discussed the feasibility of his plan with various experts and gained widespread appreciation for it.

His thinking was way ahead of many illustrious contemporaries. When Arnold Toynbee said, "To be human is to be capable of transcending oneself" and "Anything that an individual does accomplish has meaning and value only in the larger context of society and history in which the individual plays his tiny part," he was probably echoing the thoughts of Swami Nitya-swarup-ananda. Dwight Eisenhower, the former President of the United States, had plans to build an international university, its purpose being "to attack the enemies of truth." Similarly, Chief Justice Earl Warren of the United States Supreme Court suggested the establishment of a School of Wisdom of the World to ensure the removal of anxiety, tension, and insecurity, and "to help create the foundation for a world culture." Evidently, Swami Nitya-swarup-ananda anticipated them all.

Many will remember that Sarat Chandra Chattopadhyay, the eminent Bengali writer, drafted the Welcome Address on behalf of his countrymen on the occasion of Rabindranath Tagore's sixtieth birthday. The opening sentence of the Address was "When we look at you we are overwhelmed with boundless admiration." The same applies to Swami Nitya-swarup-ananda. He had comprehensive knowledge in a variety of subjects. In fact, whenever I had the privilege of discussing any subject with him, I was amazed to see his range. His knowledge was really encyclopaedic. Whether it was psychiatry or constitutional law, philosophy of history or gastronomy, printing technology or ecology, theological proof or linguistic precision, he always felt at ease in discussing any subject.

In one striking example, his knowledge proved crucial to the safe construction of the Institute's building at Gol Park. It happened during a meeting with the architects and engineers (Ballardie, Thompson, and Matthews and the Martin Burn Company) to discuss the details of its construction. Swami Nitya-swarup-ananda intervened, pointing out that on the way to the first floor, a certain part of the wall would develop cracks: "I have struck at the place with a heavy object," he said, "and I heard an unusual sound." The next day that particular section of the wall was opened, and a four-by-six-inch piece of glass was inserted into the hole for observation. A few days later, it could be seen that the glass piece had cracked horizontally. Thus his conjecture proved to be true. In other such meetings, he used to discuss with the engineers how the library could be made soundproof, or what would be the appropriate matting for the floor, or how high the readers' counter would be—but before taking the final decision, he would consult with Mr. B. S. Kesavan, who at that time was the Librarian of the National Library.

While I was a student, I read Wordsworth's poem "To the Skylark," two lines of which are often quoted: "Type of the wise who soar but never roam / True to the kindred points of heaven and home." Swami Nitya-swarup-ananda truly reflected this ideal in his character. I have seen him reading newspapers, answering telephone calls, dictating letters, seriously engaged in metaphysical discussions such as "freedom versus determinism"—doing all this simultaneously. In the midst of all this, a devotee was explaining to him how the workers were destroying his industrial organization in the name of trade unionism. Maharaj at once switched to a new subject. He began to inquire into the nature of participation by workers in the field of management. "Why can't we apply the principles," he asked, "What prevents us from applying these principles?" He posed three questions and then went on to answer them like a veteran management expert!

Whatever work came into his hands, he would try to accomplish it flawlessly and elegantly. He was always meticulous about the absolute faultlessness of anything in print. I remember that he spent about four hours in the house of Dr. Shashi Bhusan Dasgupta, deciding whether a comma or a semicolon would be inserted after a clause in one of his articles ready for publication in the Institute's monthly *Bulletin*. He was also uncompromising when it came to maintaining the time schedule. On one occasion when the Institute was celebrating Human Rights Day, the meeting was to begin at 5:30 P.M. The chief speaker had arrived before the appointed time. But the President of the meeting, Sri Prasanta Bihari Mukharji, Chief Justice of the Calcutta High Court, had not yet appeared. At precisely 5:29 P.M. Maharaj invited Professor Nirmal Chandra Bhattacharyya, who was seated in the audience, to ascend the stage and preside. A little later, Justice Mukharji hurriedly entered the hall. Maharaj led him to a seat in the audience instead of offering him the Presidential chair.

One of the remarkable traits of his character may be mentioned here. When he became convinced of the validity of an idea after careful deliberations and severe tests, he would never deviate from it. On one occasion in an academic matter, Maharaj did not agree with the eminent historian Dr. Ramesh Chandra Majumdar, which resulted in the complete breakdown of communication between the two for more than a month. One day Maharaj said to me, "Ramesh Babu is an excellent scholar; he is also a close friend of the Institute. So I should go to

his house and settle the dispute amicably." And he did so without further delay. He never harboured in his mind any feeling of resentment
born out of a difference of opinion.

Everyone knows the line of a verse from Rabindranath Tagore: "I
have made you the pole star of my life." It would be no exaggeration to
say that Swami Nitya-swarup-ananda made Vivekananda "the pole
star" of his life. While discussing important matters, or finalizing the
menu for the invited guests who would dine with him, or giving
instructions over the phone, Swami Nitya-swarup-ananda was often
heard murmuring to himself, "Religion is oneness, religion is oneness,
religion is oneness." It was evident from his conduct and mode of
work that he did not arrive at this truth through a process of reasoning.
This truth—Religion is oneness—came back to him again and again
like the refrain of a song. This truth was the result of his intuitive
apprehension, a flash of revelation. He valued action more highly than
ratiocination. Therefore, Vivekananda's "Practical Vedanta" was, to
him, not just an article of faith but a matter of actual realization.

Many of the intellectuals of our country discussed in detail with
Swami Nitya-swarup-ananda the ideas contained in his *Education for
World Civilization*. At the conclusion of these discussions, some were left
with the impression that Swami Nitya-swarup-ananda was an "idle
visionary"; they thought that it would be almost impossible to realize the
ideal as he envisaged it. I often ventured the remark, "Yes, but he is a
pragmatic visionary." Yet I, too, had some misgivings. After prolonged
discussions with him, some but not all of my doubts were removed.

His conviction was that changes would occur in the minds of men in
the course of time. Human nature has a duality, on the one hand per-
ceiving truth in a fragmented manner which leads to anxiety, unhappiness, and mutual hatred; and on the other hand, sensing the cosmic
vision embedded in the human psyche. A continual warfare is being
waged between these two attitudes. He believed that the human mind
could be transformed by global education which viewed the world as a
whole. Unfortunately, the present system of education consists in the

mere collection of information. If there is no change in this system, then how shall we acquire a global education? The upshot of the whole thing comes to this: Is it through global education that our minds will be transformed, or must we change our attitudes in order to receive global education? If we affirm that changes of mind will occur through global education, and at the same time assert that global education presupposes a change in psychology, shall we not commit the fallacy of arguing in a circle? Maharaj certainly did not intend to say that one should learn how to swim on land and then plunge into the water. In fact one has to learn how to swim by taking the plunge into the water. The important thing is to take the plunge towards global education.

In this context we can remind ourselves of two observations of Sri Ramakrishna. He used to say that coins in circulation during the Mughal period would not be acceptable during the British period, and that four litres of milk cannot be contained in a one-litre bottle. The present system of education is based on fragmentation and analysis; one learns by dissecting. But in reality the universal existence is indivisible. Hence the necessity of changing the method so that the whole can be apprehended as the whole. In other words, the knife which slices bread cannot fell a banyan tree. Man is essentially a nondual integral consciousness. This self-luminous consciousness exists by transcending the body, mind, and senses. The individual consciousness and the universal consciousness are identical. Therefore, man whose essential nature is universal consciousness can easily go beyond the fragmentary nature of mental process. Swami Nitya-swarup-ananda has drawn the attention of all towards this fundamental truth.

There is yet another thing which one cannot afford to ignore. When Swami Nitya-swarup-ananda spoke of "education for human unity and world civilization," he had carefully considered the nature and quality of the method of teaching. The method of imparting global education could not be the same as one which aims at transmitting information to a group of passive listeners, an education lacking any relevance to life. He felt that education must be a vital experience shared by both the teacher and the student. In his own words, "The outcome of the educational programme will be a *living experience* enjoyed by teachers and students alike." This is an echo of the Upanishads: "O Brahman protect us both (teacher and student); teach us both equally well, see that both of us are equally capable and equally well versed."

Swami Nitya-swarup-ananda was undoubtedly far ahead of his time. He had far-reaching insight into the future of mankind; his feeling was deep and his thoughts were cogent and clear. An extraordinary man of action, Swami Nitya-swarup-ananda sought to make one conscious of one's real self, one's glorious heritage, and one's dignity. Whenever I had an opportunity to discuss his plans or new psychology with him, I was reminded of the words of Sri Aurobindo: "Man is to be judged not by what he is, but by what he is going to be in future." I have detected similarities of thought between Sri Aurobindo and Swami Nitya-swarup-ananda. I cannot resist the temptation of quoting a few more lines from Sri Aurobindo: "Truth cannot be attained by the mind's thought but only by identity and silent vision. Truth lives in the calm wordless light of the Eternal Spaces; she does not intervene in the noise and cackle of logical debate. Thought in the Mind can, at most, be Truth's brilliant and transparent garment, it is not even her body."

Swami Nitya-swarup-ananda has again and again spoken about the spiritual solidarity of mankind. His ideas were scientific; to him, human values were really spiritual values. What Dr. Fritjof Capra has said in his treatise *The Tao of Physics* echoes the perceptions of Swami Nitya-swarup-ananda:

Penetrating into ever deeper realms of matter, he (the physicist) has become aware of the essential unity of all things and events. More than that, he has also learnt that he himself and his consciousness are an integral part of this unity. Thus the mystic and the physicist arrive at the same conclusion; one starting from the inner realm, the other from the outer world. The harmony between their views confirms the ancient Indian wisdom, that Brahman, the ultimate reality without, is identical with Atman, the reality within.

Swami Nitya-swarup-ananda has departed with a feeling of regret. In a world which is extremely self-centred and which is torn asunder by the love of power and insane jealousy, few people have realized the significance of the School of World Civilization as conceived by Swami Nitya-swarup-ananda. My firm belief is that if we devote ourselves to the fulfilment of Swami Nitya-swarup-ananda's dream, only then will our tributes to his memory become meaningful.

ARUNA HALDAR

I came to know Swami Nitya-swarup-ananda from 1938 onwards when I was a student in Calcutta University. I was introduced to both Swami Nitya-swarup-ananda and Swami Madhavananda, then Secretary of the Ramakrishna Order, by Swami Abhayananda (widely known as Bharat Maharaj).

Bharat Maharaj sometimes used to stay with Swami Nitya-swarup-ananda when the Institute was situated at Wellington Square. Whenever I attended various festive occasions there, Swami Nitya-swarup-ananda would talk to me about various aspects of Swami Vivekananda's writings, most of which he seemed to have committed to memory. He appeared to be intellectually inclined towards scholarship and propagating Swamiji's ideas in uncompromising and not always popular ways, but as a young student of philosophy, I liked the way he spoke.

After a few years, while I was working as a teacher in the University of Patna, I came to know that the Ramakrishna Mission Institute of Culture had moved to Gol Park, as organized and supervised by Swami Nitya-swarup-ananda, who had ever been its presiding spirit. The why and wherefore of his leaving Gol Park were unknown to me for some time. But I met him again at Gol Park after he had returned as Secretary in 1970 when my husband, Mr. Gopal Chandra Haldar, was delivering the Vidyasagar Lectures in the Institute's Vivekananda Hall, organized in collaboration with Calcutta University. Swami Nitya-swarup-ananda was present at all the lectures and appeared to be pleased. After the end of the meetings, we met him in his room and received his blessings.

I saw him last in our Calcutta residence, where he very kindly came to visit me when I was stricken with a cardiac attack in 1981. I was touched by his unforgettable kindness and unselfish display of charity, then a retired monk working for the society at large. I bow down to his memory with grateful respect.

TRIGUNA SEN

What I am today is because of Swami Nitya-swarup-ananda—his teachings, his guidance, and above all his love!

Yes, his capacity for giving love indeed knew no bounds, such an abundance of pure, unselfish love. Yet who would guess from his somewhat stern exterior that he was capable of so much tenderness? He came down to Kankhal on more than one occasion just to see me, just to be with me. It is through such pure unselfish love that one gets an inkling of the real import of the Vedantic dictum, "Religion is Oneness." It is the bond of such love that dissolves all differences between soul and soul, man and man. The words of Swami Vivekananda come to mind:

> Listen friends, I will speak my heart to thee
> I have found in my life this Truth Supreme
> Buffeted by waves, in this whirl of life
> There is one ferry, that takes across the sea
> Formulae of worship, control of breath,
> Science, philosophy, system varied,
> Relinquishment, possessions and the like
> All those are but delusions of mind
> Love, love that's the only thing.

"You will have to create an atmosphere of love," Swami Nitya-swarup-ananda used to say to me often, and these words had been so ingrained in my mind that I held it my duty to consciously implement it in the new institution I was then striving to set up. Today when that love comes reflected back in the smiling faces of my students almost half a century later, I feel overwhelmed. Truly, it was a great lesson that I had learnt from him.

It was in the early forties that I first came in contact with Swami
Nitya-swarup-ananda. I was at that time totally committed to the task
of bringing up a new university in Jadavpur, which was quite an uphill
battle in those days. He came to me one evening and said, "Triguna
Babu, I, too, am working to create a new kind of educational institution. Let us walk together." The Institute of Culture had then just
shifted to Russa Road, which was not very far from my place of work.
We would meet in the evenings and walk together, quite literally. People used to mistake us for brothers: both of the same height, same
stoutish physique, and bald-headed—he a sannyasi with his clean-
shaven head and me with my one-hundred-percent genuine bald pate!

We would spend hours discussing the topic so dear to both of us:
education. I must admit that I benefited a great deal from these discussions. The scope of his vision went beyond ordinary conception. He
crystallized my ideas and gave me the strength to follow some of my
innate convictions to complete fruition.

"A man should not be one-sided, he should have literary, technical,
and cultural education—a full-fledged education," he would say. I,
too, held similar views, having come in contact with Sri Aurobindo and
his educational thoughts through his "National Institution" during my
formative years. Although the nucleus of Jadavpur University was an
engineering college, I saw to it that there was provision for all-round
education. Swami Nitya-swarup-ananda suggested that I visit the University of the Sorbonne in Paris to see how the Department of Comparative Literature functioned there. I did so, and subsequently this
subject was introduced at Jadavpur. The famous *littérateur* Buddhadeb
Bose was invited to take charge. It was a novel step, a bold step.

During this time, I became intimately involved with the functioning
of the Institute of Culture as a member of its Governing Body.

In 1966, I suddenly decided to leave Calcutta and go on a pilgrimage. Jadavpur University was by then firmly established and I felt it
was time for me to relinquish all responsibilities. My work was done. I
went to Hrishikesh, where I met Swami Saradeshananda for the first

time, which later on developed into a deeply enriching relationship. Swami Nitya-swarup-ananda was very happy when he heard of this. He wrote to me, "You are lucky to have been blessed by one like Swami Saradeshananda, the like of whom is rare today."

After my pilgrimage I returned to Calcutta. I had no place to stay. So I decided to go straight to the Institute of Culture. Swami Nitya-swarup-ananda was no longer there. Swami Ranganathananda was the Secretary. He welcomed me with these words: "Chintaharan Maharaj has kept a room reserved for you. He had told me that Triguna will come back one day!"

After some time I was suddenly summoned to Delhi and sworn in as Education Minister to the government of India. Dr. Radhakrishnan, the President, told me that he truly expected something worthwhile to happen in the field of education, an educational policy which would rank among the best in the world. I worked hard, but disillusionment came soon and I realized that everything was so enmeshed in politics that it was not possible to do anything worthwhile in real terms. I gave up my ministership and started staying in an ashrama in Dehradun.

During my tenure as Education Minister, Swami Nitya-swarup-ananda came to see me on more than one occasion. And when he heard of my resignation he immediately came down to Dehradun. The ashrama where I was staying and the Ramakrishna Mission Ashrama were housed in adjacent buildings. He called me up, "Triguna Babu, I have come here for you. Why have you wrapped yourself up in a bundle of emotions and sentiments? Come out with me. Let us both work together once again. There is so much work to be done."

Yes, indeed, he always had so much work to do. Ever enthusiastic, energetic, and so totally undeterred by external circumstances, he was in fact the only person in the entire Order who was capable of translating Swami Vivekananda's grand ideals into practice, and he worked for it unrelentingly till his very last breath.

SATCHIDANANDA DHAR*

I had the good fortune to come in contact with Swami Nitya-swarup-ananda about fifty years ago and to witness his *seva-yajna* [service on a grand scale]. I first met him in 1941, three years after the Ramakrishna Mission had inaugurated the Institute of Culture in Calcutta to embody Sri Ramakrishna's ideals. In 1943 I visited the Institute in its rented building at Wellington Square. There was a Students' Home where a few college and university students used to stay. I recall that one of them was Bipad Bhanjan Goswami (later Swami Swahananda), and there were several students from Srihatta in East Bengal. Two others, Phani Sanyal and Mani Sanyal, were the brothers who later became famous professors and economists. We used to go to the Institute at Wellington Square from the Ashrama at Pathureaghata, which was started the same year. We viewed Chintaharan Maharaj from a distance, seeing that he was always busy talking to very respectable people with a sheaf of papers in hand. Bipad Bhanjan Goswami and a few others shifted from the Institute to the Pathureaghata Ashrama in 1943, and Pathureaghata itself shifted to Narendrapur in 1956.

After the Institute moved from Wellington Square to Russa Road, my younger brother, Subodh, became one of the residents of the Students' Hostel while attending an engineering college. The Russa Road house had many small rooms and Chintaharan Maharaj used to stay in one of those rooms; foreign visitors were also accommodated. While there, he planned out the huge building at Gol Park and its international scheme of action. At that time, we could not even imagine the magnitude of his plan, and how far-sighted he was! To present Indian culture holistically to the world, to bring world culture to India, and to bring about an interaction of all cultures—this whole idea of Chintaharan Maharaj, and the way he implemented it, was truly wonderful. His thoughts were far-sighted, his vision was like that of a rishi, and his action had boundless courage, dependence on God, *rajas* without a trace of ego.

The palatial facility of the Institute of Culture at Gol Park today bears witness, on the one hand, to Chintaharan Maharaj's refined artistic sensibilities, and on the other, to the remarkable scheme of diverse activities which he originated in its programmes. It became recognized internationally as a meeting ground for different religions, cultures, and races. The memory of Chintaharan Maharaj is inextricably linked with this institution which stands for international understanding and the ideals of liberal humanism and world unity as envisioned by Rama-krishna-Vivekananda.

Yet Swami Nitya-swarup-ananda was greater than his deeds. He was devoted to Sri Ramakrishna from his boyhood, and initiated by the Holy Mother. It was his conviction that to see Holy Mother was to see Sri Ramakrishna. And he was blessed with the love and affection of many of the direct disciples of Sri Ramakrishna.

He always kept himself hidden and did all his work in the spirit of "nahang, nahang" ["not I, not I"]. Although shy of coming to the forefront of any public meeting, he would always be the centre of attention in informal gatherings—and undefeated in any argument. He used to entertain many distinctive personalities from all over the world with great respect, as an equal.

In his personal life, he was always at ease under any circumstances. He had the sannyasi attitude of being content with whatever he received. He was a connoisseur of good food but he was happy with even the simplest of meals. Outwardly very reserved, but among his close associates, very exuberant.

He had a special power of awakening one's dormant potential and helped others to exceed their innate capabilities. Many famous researchers and scholars became established through his encouragement, and also by his financial support. Even the slightest of virtue in others was emphasized and used to inspire them to uplift themselves. He himself would never desist from any project till it had been successfully executed.

Over the years, the Institute of Culture had to face numerous obstacles and hard times. Chintaharan Maharaj accepted all these stoically, as the Divine Will. He gave himself no rest even after he retired, still

lamenting that "I have not been able to complete the tasks I had set
forth." This lamentation referred to the Institute of Culture, out of
frustration that a proper arrangement had not been carried forth to put
his ideals into practice for the service of Thakur and Ma. He spent his
last few years at the Institute, the temple of his *sadhana*. He felt in himself as well as in others the *swarupa* [spirit] of Brahman. This was the
predominant mood in his last days, ever the Vedantist, but also the
playful child of the Holy Mother.

PARIMAL KAR

As I sit down to write my reminiscences of Chintaharan Maharaj,
memories of innumerable events crowd my mind, some very personal,
some trifling, and some concerning his dreams about the Institute of
Culture and other multifarious activities. I did not keep any diary so it
is difficult to place these disconnected events in a proper sequence. I am
also conscious that even my best efforts cannot bring out the entire
gamut of his many-faceted personality. I will write a few lines, however, only to pay my respect to his memory.

   During my long association with him from 1945 onwards, I had the
privilege of knowing him intimately as a member of the family, as it
were, joining him in various activities from prayers early in the morning to postdinner discussions at night. The topics were varied and very
wide in range. I distinctly remember how he brought his critical faculty to bear on everything we discussed. This was usual for him. Every
fortnight some of us used to hold an afternoon discussion on selected
readings from Swami Vivekananda. Chintaharan Maharaj invariably
attended those sessions, and he could always summarize the subject
under discussion by giving its quintessence. I personally found it very
rewarding. It was remarkable how he effortlessly touched the central
theme shorn of all trivialities. At that young age, it seemed to me that
he had a third eye.

   This capacity to hit the bull's eye was reflected in other activities
also. When the blueprint of the Institute building at Gol Park was

being processed, he often used to argue very competently with the architects about the changes he proposed. I found to my surprise that in most cases his suggestions were accepted. It would not be an exaggeration to say that the Institute building at Gol Park was entirely his creation. His penchant for details was largely responsible for the massive structure as it stands today. The building is not only functional and aesthetically designed, but it also embodies the vision of Chintaharan Maharaj—a vision carefully nurtured and affectionately nourished for over a decade.

When the Institute moved from Keshab Chandra Sen Street to a more spacious accommodation at Wellington Square in 1943, he was very happy because of the opportunity to expand its activities. There was a lecture hall of a moderate size, which was a great improvement over the room at Albert Hall, College Street. Then, after years in rented rooms, the Institute moved into its own building with eight large-sized apartments at 111 Russa Road. Swami Nitya-swarup-ananda told us that at last he would be able to execute his plan and fulfil his life's dream. But it wasn't long before he found the new premises too small for the Institute's expanding activities, and after only a few years at Russa Road he began looking for a more spacious accommodation. I accompanied him to various places seeking a suitable plot of land or a building to house the Institute. At long last he succeeded in getting the plot of land at Gol Park.

Under his instructions, the blueprints of the building were being prepared and altered, subsequently to be replaced and altered, subsequently to be replaced yet again! This continued for about two to three years. During this period, he kept the blueprints hanging on the walls of his bedroom. He used to look at them intently and note down the changes he contemplated. I remember on one occasion he held a discussion after dinner on some of the changes he proposed and continued the discussion till midnight. But, to my surprise (and, I must confess, to my annoyance), he woke me up at about 4:30 the next morning to say that the changes he had suggested about five hours earlier contrary to my views were not really necessary after all. The proposed building apparently occupied his mind so fully that he did not even have sound sleep.

Once construction was under way, the projected cost of the building based on his plans for it was taking quantum leaps every five to six months. Sometimes I used to ask him: "Maharaj, where is the money to fund such an ambitious project?" But he was not at all concerned about where the money would come from. It seemed to me that Maharaj was building a castle in the air. I never thought it would at all be possible for him to execute his ambitious project. But, belying our worst apprehensions, he succeeded in collecting more than Rs. 85 lakhs (quite a large sum in those days), and was able to give shape to his dream within an unbelievably short time.

Immediately after the end of the Second World War, Chintaharan Maharaj thought about bringing out an enlarged seven-volume edition of *The Cultural Heritage of India* in order to present before the world various facets of Indian culture in greater detail. He asked me to act as Secretary to the General Editor of the Second Edition. I joined sometime in 1947 and was therefore associated with the publication from the very beginning when the preliminaries of the revised scheme were discussed. There were very eminent scholars on the Board of Editors. Maharaj played a key role in the formulation of the scheme and the disposition of the topics. I still vividly remember his finesse in tackling delicate issues concerning scholars of diverse susceptibilities and opinions. After the scheme was finalized to his satisfaction and the prospective writers selected, Swami Nitya-swarup-ananda left the entire responsibility to the General Editor. He never interfered with his work. He did not even question me except to ask me casually how the work was progressing. This was another remarkable trait of his character. He knew precisely where to step in and at what point to withdraw. Like a true Vedantin, he gave everyone free scope to grow and develop in his own way.

Those who came in contact with him are familiar with the perfectionist traits of his character. He was never satisfied with anything, however satisfactory it might be in the estimation of others. His motto was "Even the best can be improved." He followed this ideal scrupulously all his life. He spared no pains to live up to this ideal.

The readers may get the impression from the above narration that he was stern, an austere and hard taskmaster. Yes, he was. But he was also a man endowed with very soft human qualities—very sympathetic, generous, and understanding, and with a keen sense of humour. So often he used to excite our laughter by his witty remarks.

I heard from some of the monks who were his contemporaries in the Ramakrishna Order that Chintaharan Maharaj was very strict as a brahmachari, uncompromising in the observance of the monastic duties enjoined upon him. One day in the course of conversation, I told Chintaharan Maharaj what I had heard about his early years in the Order. He laughed and said that he had sometimes stretched the proscriptive injunctions enjoined upon a brahmachari too far! He told me the following incident. During those days private buses used to ply in Calcutta, and some of these buses bore different female names, such as Alaka, Kadambari, etc. One day after leaving out a few buses bearing female names, he finally boarded a bus having no female association at Baghbazar. Again, during those days the number of female bus passengers was negligible. But when the bus on which he was travelling reached College Street and a female passenger stepped on board, he immediately got down. While narrating this incident, he explained to me that such extreme observance of injunctions was an outcome of the feebleness of a creative mind. Gradually, he succeeded in freeing himself from the shackles of meaningless taboos and emerged as a true Vedantin, both in thought and action. In the light of what he said on that occasion, I could imagine that his was a truly spiritual journey in order to make his inner life more perfect, more comprehensive, more universal, and, in fact, more truly human.

When I was working for *Cultural Heritage*, the Institute did not have a duplicating machine. So occasionally we had to go to the Belur Math and get the materials mimeographed there. On one occasion a monk and I worked almost throughout the night at the Belur Math in order to complete the job. The next day Chintaharan Maharaj took the monk to task for having failed to do the assigned job. It very much pained me because I thought that Maharaj was not being fair to the monk, and I expressed my disapproval rather strongly. He didn't know that we had worked through the night at the Belur Math, learning it for the first time from my statement. So he kept quiet. Then I started avoiding him and after four or five days he called me. "I hope you have calmed down," he said smilingly when I met with him, "I deeply appreciate your feelings." This was typical of Chintaharan Maharaj.

I have had the good fortune of enjoying his love and affection in abundance. I have also had the privilege of observing his activities very closely during the formative period of the Institute of Culture, of which I have narrated only a few incidents to bring out the traits of his character which left a deep impression upon me. If I am to give an epithet to describe Chintaharan Maharaj and all he stood for, I shall call him a "Visionary with a Spade." He had not only dreams in his eyes, but also the capacity to give a concrete shape to his dreams.

The construction of the new building at Gol Park began in July 1955. The formal opening of the new building took place on November 1, 1961. Chintaharan Maharaj retired from the Institute in 1962. He was, therefore, at the helm of the Institute's affairs hardly for six months after the grand inaugural events. It gives me pain to think that he could not apply his magic touch to the School of Humanistic and Intercultural Studies in its formative stage and give it a solid foundation. He had visualized the newly inaugurated School as one of the major activities of the Institute of Culture in the new building. That would have been the fulfilment of his life's dream. His was a global view marked not simply by tolerance but by acceptance of all world cultures.

This is my humble tribute of respect to the memory of Chintaharan Maharaj, who passionately dreamt of the Universal Brotherhood of Man, cutting across boundaries of religion, nationality, language, and race.

SANTWANA DASGUPTA

I met Swami Nitya-swarup-ananda in 1948. I had just joined the Lady Brabourne College as a Lecturer after receiving my M.A. degree in economics. The All-India Commerce Conference was being held at the time in the Calcutta University campus, and I was attending it as a delegate. On the evening after the open session towards the end of the conference, Dr. Benoy Kumar Sarkar (the eminent economist who was the Convenor) announced, "We will now proceed to Belur Math, the headquarters of the Ramakrishna Empire, which every modern man should visit." When we all arrived at the Belur Math, we, his students, were introduced as "Young Bengals," and Swami Nitya-swarup-ananda (who was standing in front of the then Math office, opposite the Temple) was introduced to us by Professor Sarkar in his inimitable manner as a "Generalissimo in the spiritual army of Sri Ramakrishna." Nityaswarupanandaji invited all of us to visit the Ramakrishna Mission Institute of Culture, of which he was the Founder-Secretary.

Shortly afterwards, I visited the Institute, situated at the time at the Russa Road campus. I was accompanied by Madame Lizelle Reymond (Mrs. Jean Herbert), who was a friend of Professor Benoy Kumar Sarkar and well known to Nityaswarupanandaji. We were very well received by him. I had been deeply impressed by the way Professor Sarkar had introduced him to us on the very first encounter—he was to me a "Generalissimo in the spiritual army of Sri Ramakrishna." Thereafter I attended the discourses, meetings, and seminars at the Institute regularly. These regular visits brought us (myself, my two sisters, and two other friends) close to Nityaswarupanandaji Maharaj. And we noticed how hard he worked to make the Institute an inter-cultural centre for preaching the universal ideas of Ramakrishna-Vivekananda. He was eager to see us develop as inheritors of these universal cultural values.

Soon we were enlisted as workers. We participated in the discussions during the lectures, served tea at the assembly of scholars, assisted the library staff to prepare the catalogue, etc. After I started joining the discussions, he appreciated my efforts and encouraged me to continue, thus helping me to mature as a speaker. Like my teacher, Professor Benoy Sarkar, he was also keen on seeing me develop as an independent thinker. There were always persons at the Institute, even among the eminent scholars, who expressed the opinion that my first duty as a woman was to get married and rear a family. But neither Professor Sarkar nor Nityaswarupanandaji ever regarded womanhood as a disability in leading the life of an intellectual. Actually, Nityaswarupanandaji particularly believed in absolute equality between men and women in all respects.

When my first book, *Vivekanander Samaj-Darshan* [The Social Philosophy of Swami Vivekananda], came out in Bengali in 1963, he heartily congratulated me with the words, "This is the book which we have needed for a long time." After that, he introduced me to the assembly of learned scholars at the Institute as "the author of a very good and much awaited book on Swami Vivekananda."

One day I remember he brought Swami Vijayanandaji, the head of the Argentina Centre of the Ramakrishna Mission, to our home for a copy of the book. When I presented the book to Swami Vijayanandaji, both were overjoyed. A few days later, when I met Vijayanandaji at the Belur Math, he also spoke highly of the book and asked me to publish an English version so that the whole world could better understand Swami Vivekananda.

When Nityaswarupanandaji left the Institute for the first time in 1962, I was struck by his detachment. After all, he had built the Institute with motherly care. But he was a true sannyasin and a true disciple of Holy Mother, believing in the dictum "nothing greater than renunciation." He came back as the Secretary of the Institute in 1970, but again left it in 1973, this time for good. His last days were passed at the Institute without any official post as a retired person.

In the interim, he became for several years the Head of the Udbodhan Office (Holy Mother's House). One day I went there for a visit to the shrine, as I often did at the time, and when I went to see him I got a good scolding. He admonished me, "Only those who care to do nothing for the mission for which Thakur, Ma, and Swamiji lived and laid down their lives come here to offer pranam to the shrine, take *prasad*, and go away. Tell me what *you* are doing to spread their ideals." He was very excited that day over the fact that the present generation was being uprooted from its cultural heritage and yet those who utter the names of Ramakrishna-Vivekananda don't feel bothered to do anything to remedy the situation.

During his last days, whenever I met him at the Institute, often during or after a function, he would always greet me as a "worthy student of Professor Benoy Kumar Sarkar, living up to the ideal of Ramakrishna-Vivekananda." I felt blessed at these meetings with him. When my next book, *Vivekananda, the Prophet of Human Emancipation*, came out in 1991, I went to present him with a copy. He was overwhelmed with joy and exclaimed, "What a caption, exactly the right epithet for depicting Vivekananda's role in human history! Oh, you have done a grand job."

That was my last meeting with him. I was very busy writing the new enlarged Bengali edition of the book and never went to see him again, even when this volume was published. I was thinking of going to him one day when I heard that he had passed away, giving me no more opportunity to have his vigorous encouragement, which I considered his blessings.

I remember him as a perfectionist in all matters, and it was not easy to please him. He showered his inspiring encouragement, gave us all sorts of help when needed, but he did not spare us if and when we failed to reach the standard, and then we would get a good scolding from him. Yes, he was an uncompromising perfectionist, but always true to the ideal of Ramakrishna-Vivekananda. I think Professor Benoy Kumar Sarkar described him rightly—he was truly a "Generalissimo in the spiritual army of Sri Ramakrishna."

SUMITRA CHAUDHURI

Swami Nitya-swarup-ananda was well known to my late father, Dr. R. C. Majumdar, for many decades. Maharaj always had a high opinion of his advice and consulted him on various matters regarding the Ramakrishna Mission Institute of Culture, especially when *The Cultural Heritage of India* was under preparation for publication and he became a regular visitor to our house.

In 1949, when the Institute was still at Wellington Square, I went there with my father to attend a lecture by a Russian cultural attaché entitled "Russia Under Stalin's Rule." She gave a vivid description of a prosperous Russia, full of happy and contented people. After the lecture some questions were asked by members of the audience, and my father ventured, "If anyone disagrees with government policy, what is the procedure to communicate it to the authorities?" "It is *preposterous*," the speaker replied indignantly, "to think that any citizen would want to disagree with the High Command!" Swami Nitya-swarup-ananda was angered by her rude response and apologized to my father after the meeting. But my father replied that he did not mind, because he had been given the answer (his suspicions had been verified).

Swami Nitya-swarup-ananda came to my father for advice when the High Court ordered the eviction of the recalcitrant tenants of 111 Russa Road after the house had been donated to the Ramakrishna Mission Institute of Culture. The Swami had been advised to eject the tenants with the police, but he felt that such a direct confrontation was unbecoming for a monk. My father, however, advised him to follow his advocate's advice, so Chintaharan Maharaj requested my older brother to accompany him, and to enter the house with the police in his stead.

On another occasion, he was very hesitant to accept a car offered to him by one of his admirers so that he would not have to use time-consuming public transport to visit the consultants located in different parts of Calcutta while the Gol Park building was being planned. But he was not convinced that it was befitting for a monk to use a car. He came to my father to seek his advice, and my father reassured him that using the car was not for his own comfort, but only in the interest of saving time.

These two incidents show how conscious Swami Nitya-swarup-ananda was of the sanctity of the saffron robe he had donned, and how he sought in every particular to maintain the high standard of that life.

1950S

(Russa Road)

BHABATOSH DATTA

I had been hearing about the Institute of Culture and Swami Nitya-swarup-ananda for many years, but I only came into contact with him in the early 1950s. We had a long talk, and I was deeply impressed by his sincerity of purpose, devotion to the cause of the Institute, and modesty about himself. It was admiration at first sight.

The Institute was then functioning in a set of rooms in Russa Road. The lecture hall wasn't large, but the listeners were all enthusiastic and interested in the subject of my talk, which, as far as I remember, was on some aspect of Indian economy. After that I went there many times, sometimes to give talks and sometimes to listen to talks given by others. Swami Nitya-swarup-ananda, whom we called Chintaharan Maharaj, came to my house frequently.

The grand building near Gol Park came up in the early sixties. I admit that I was at first critical of the lavish style and grandeur. I even told him jokingly, "If Sri Ramakrishna Paramahamsa comes back to life, will he recognize the grand palace as a temple of culture named after him?" Chintaharan Maharaj said quietly that we would realize later the value of the Institute, of the halls, hostels, library, etc. I did realize later that he was right. It is not necessary for me to go into any details about the work of the Institute. I was a participant in the activities of the Institute for a long time, and was for some time on the Governing Body.

Suddenly one day we heard that Chintaharan Maharaj was being transferred to another Mission Centre. He accepted the decision with perfect equanimity, but we all felt disturbed. At the farewell meeting, some of the speakers could not restrain their tears.

His connection with this Institute did not, however, cease. He used to come to all the major functions, including particularly the Foundation Day. Every time we met he asked me affectionately about my health and my work. I met him last some five years ago when he invited me to his room and told me about a book he was writing.

We had a long talk on various subjects, and I cherish the memory with great regard. I've met many persons in my long life, but I do not remember having met anyone with Swami Nitya-swarup-anandaji's selfless devotion to work, creative power, and ability to attract others, combined with a quiet acceptance of the entire discipline of the Mission he served.

DINESH CHANDRA BHATTACHARYA

Probably it was in May 1950 that I came to my Calcutta home during the summer vacation of the Haraganga College, Munshiganj (now in Bangladesh), where I had been serving as Professor of Sanskrit and Indian Philosophy since 1940. I had remained in Munshiganj after it had been partitioned into East Pakistan because it was a beautiful place situated by the rivers Dhaleswari and Meghna, and there was no communal disturbance at that time.

On one occasion when I was in Calcutta I visited the Ramakrishna Mission Institute of Culture situated at Russa Road near my house, and there I met Swami Nitya-swarup-ananda for the first time. He received me very cordially after learning my name and profession. I was a Professor of Vedanta in the study centre at the Bhubaneswar Ramakrishna Math, where I had the privilege to teach such scholar-monks as Swami Madhavananda and Swami Pavitrananda, among others. Swami Nitya-swarup-ananda asked me whether I could recommend any of my students to teach Vedanta and deliver weekly lectures on the scriptures at the Institute. A meagre allowance could be provided, as one gentleman had promised to donate a small sum for that purpose. I said that I could come myself if he so desired. He immediately replied that he had not expected such a thing, but would be very glad if I agreed. I was keen by then to leave Munshiganj as serious communal riots had erupted at Narayanganj just across the river. I returned to Munshiganj, resigned from my post, and flew back to Calcutta with my precious books to join the Institute of Culture as a Professor of Vedanta.

Swami Nitya-swarup-ananda was very respectful to me and appreciated my weekly lectures on the Upanishads. The pupils at the Institute were earnest—university students who had come to study the Vedanta texts included in their syllabi, and some senior persons. I felt a little embarrassed when he said that I was one of the few who could present a correct exposition of the Vedanta. I remember a very interesting incident when Swami Nitya-swarup-ananda was seated in his office at the Institute asking for an elucidation of some Sanskrit text and I was trying to explain according to my understanding. One gentleman, probably an admirer of the Swami, said to him, "Why don't you ask these questions of Pandit Dinesh Shastri who, I think, will be able to answer all your queries?" Swami Nitya-swarup-ananda smiled and replied, "This is Pandit Dinesh Shastri with whom I am speaking!" The gentleman was somewhat abashed.

Swami Nitya-swarup-ananda once handed me a copy of his published English translation of the *Ashtavakra Samhita* so that I might offer my comments. I did so and returned the book to him. In academic matters, he was so very modest, and once he came to my poor abode at Baghajatin Colony to discuss certain possible changes in the text.

I continued my evening classes at the Institute when it moved to Gol Park, though in a different capacity, sometimes as an honorary teacher, and sometimes as the Kumar Pramatha Lecturer, which was a salaried post. One day after the construction of the Institute had been completed, Swami Nitya-swarup-ananda took me round the rooms of the International Guest House, fitted with all kinds of modern amenities. "Will you blame me for having spent so lavishly on these luxurious rooms?" he asked me; "My reply to you will be that these rooms

must meet the requirements of foreign scholars." He explained further, "There are many foreign professors—English, German, and
American—who are willing to serve India without remuneration if we
can provide them with board and lodging. You are aware that this
Institute had a humble beginning at Keshab Sen Street and then at
Wellington Square. But I was always dreaming of an Institute like this
which would be a centre of world culture. Even some of my brother
disciples laughed, saying, 'Your dreams will never be realized'—but
today the dream has become actuality through the grace of the Holy
Mother. Pandit Mashai [a term of great respect], I tell you that if you
are to dream at all, always dream lofty dreams." His words are still
ringing in my ears.

Many years passed. Swami Nitya-swarup-ananda later visited America and other foreign countries where he had the opportunity to discuss
with experts his plans for establishing a one-world perspective through
religious and cultural education. Though he received support and
encouragement from both Western and Indian thinkers, I doubt
whether it was adequate to fulfil such a grand vision. A few years ago
when he was living a retired life in the Institute of Culture, I met him
again in his room. He was very glad to see me and spoke to me for
hours about culture and religion, bold ideas which were drawn from
authentic Indian culture as rooted in Vedanta, and also presented me
with a copy of his book *Education for Human Unity and World Civilization*, which articulated his vision and proved his undaunted determination to propagate it.

In 1990, when my Bengali book *Vivekanander Vedanta Chinta* was
published by Swami Lokeswarananda, I felt that it was my first duty to
present a copy to Swami Nitya-swarup-ananda, who had brought me
to the Institute in 1950. When I handed him the copy with words of
gratitude, he was simply overwhelmed and exclaimed, "Pandit Mashai,
you have remembered me so long, I am so glad!" and spoke of me
highly to a visiting engineer who happened to be present, with words
revealing the nobility of his love for Vedanta and Sanskrit culture.

Perhaps he overestimated my learning and ability by saying repeatedly that I was the only man who could do some real good to the world
by preaching Vedanta, if only I could go abroad. This loving reproach
was hurled at me even when I met him last in his hospital room on the
monks' ward of the Seva Pratishthan hospital, where I had also been
admitted for an operation. In spite of his illness and inability to say
much out of weakness, he exhorted me again and again to leave my
idle corner at home.

He is no more among us, but I shall remember him as a great constructive genius with a loving and amiable nature. His purpose in
introducing higher Sanskrit at the Institute was to provide a clearer
insight into the Vedanta and Indian culture, which was the foundation
of his grand dream of religious and cultural unity.

SWAMI ABJAJANANDA*

[The following selections are abridged from Swami Abjajananda's three-
part series of articles, "Swami Nityaswarupananda-Asphuta-Smritirek-
haye" (Swami Nitya-swarup-ananda: a sketch), published in *Dhru-
vatara:* Part 1 (no. 35, June–July 1995, pp. 13–31); Part 2 (no. 36,
September–October 1995, pp. 72–84); and Part 3 (no. 37, December–
January 1995–96, pp. 112–24). They were translated from the Bengali
and edited with Swami Abjajananda's final approval, for use in this reminiscence and in sections of the biography in Volume 1. Beautifully written and sensitively perceived, they present a monastic portrayal of
Swami Nitya-swarup-ananda over decades of observation.]

(From Part 1)

"Memoirs! I am very wary about your so-called memoirs. Most of the
time reminiscences become autobiographies of the writer—full of
cock-and-bull stories, or like a disjointed novel. I am very cautious
about memoirs." I had heard these words from Swami Nitya-swarup-
ananda himself when I was the editor of *Udbodhan* magazine and he
had come to stay in the Holy Mother's House for a few days. I was

discussing various things about the magazine with him, and this comment came up in the course of talking about reminiscences written by the elders.... He even cited an example of how a very venerated person had given two versions of the same event in two different articles!... He advised me to take a very firm stand about publishing memoirs.

Sitting down to write this article, and a memoir at that, of the same Swami, I still hear his words of caution ringing in my ears. Naturally I feel hesitant and apprehensive. The strokes of this portrait have therefore been made very tentatively, very cautiously and timidly. May I not fall a victim to exaggeration or untruth of any kind!

Swami Nitya-swarup-ananda was a person of great deeds, for which he was recognized in India as well as abroad. But in a reminiscence, one has to look for the essence that was flowing deep within his being, which, like the fabled underground river Phalgu, was the hidden source of all his outer actions. This deep inner current lent a glow and vitality to all his talents. And we cannot escape the great truth that it is our *kriti* [inner power] which gets transformed into our *kirti* [external actions]. The present essay will attempt to do just that, to draw attention to that aspect of Swami Nitya-swarup-ananda's personality which lay carefully hidden from the world. I embark on this bold enterprise because I have had the good fortune to see him from very close quarters....

Swami Nitya-swarup-ananda was an intensely humane person, a powerful individuality, a forceful personality. He was not easy of access. There was a clear line of demarcation which set him apart from the rest. Yet, as the more familiar "Chintaharan Maharaj," he had a different aspect—very simple, unassuming, lively, full of humour; one who could empathize with young and old with equal ease, and a dear friend to all. This aspect was no less unique and extraordinary, for he was everyone's well-wisher, close friend, and confidant. He was a brilliant conversationalist who was quick to appreciate the fine qualities of others. Yet, as a critic, he could be outspoken and forthright, which sometimes made him unpopular with those on the receiving end.

Strangely, as frightened as people were of his lashing criticism, he never failed to attract the deepest reverence and affection of all those who came in touch with him.

In his personal life, he was a highly erudite monk of the Rama-krishna Order, an Advaita Vedantist. His vision was on the cosmic plane, constantly focused on the serenely meditative form of Swamiji. In his heart was ever enshrined the glorious "*shakti-samudra-samutha-taranga*" [wave of Shakti] form of Sri Ramakrishna. But perhaps he was most widely known and recognized for being a specially favoured child of the Holy Mother, whose image was impressed on the very core of his being, who was the divine wellspring of all his action-medita-tion-knowledge. The last years of his life were full of Mother, and he departed from this world to rest on the lap of his Eternal Mother. Here we might recall that the Holy Mother had given initiation to this unknown young boy without his asking.... Right from his childhood he was not the least worldly-minded, and that is why Mahamaya who "sees through all the transient" had bestowed her Grace on him imme-diately upon seeing him.

His love for perfection was reflected in the way he approached or looked at everything in life, and in all his interactions with people, events, and objects; his quest for the Beauty in Perfection was evident in every single little thing he attended to. This was another remarkable trait of his character which made him unique, and his perceptions so different from the rest. This was one of the reasons for his greatness as a man. A few sketches will depict some of these characteristics of Chintaharan Maharaj's personality....

My acquaintance with Chintaharan Maharaj spanned a period of five decades, but I knew him personally only after 1951, and I became close to him later during the centenary celebrations of Swami Viveka-nanda in 1963. I was initially cognizant of him from a distance when the Institute of Culture was housed in a rented building in Wellington Square, before it shifted to its own premises in Russa Road. At Russa Road, his austerely simple and orderly way of life drew admiration

from us young monks of the Order. There was no dearth of space
within the Institute at Russa Road, but he always stayed in a small
room which he shared with a brother monk in the monks' quarters.
The room was sparsely furnished, just two simple cots covered with
spotless white sheets and with two pillows, very ordinary and yet so
very extraordinary and attractive in its orderliness and neatness. A
small table, a couple of chairs, and a small bookshelf were all that was
there for the Founder-Secretary of the Institute!

In spite of his reticence and gravity, there was something magnetic
about his personality which drew me to him. I took the opportunity to
meet him whenever I visited my friend, Sudin Maharaj, who was staying at the Institute. Sudin Maharaj was always full of praises for him as
he had a great deal of respect for Chintaharan Maharaj's austere
ways—such as his self-discipline, his extremely controlled and regulated lifestyle, and his strictness regarding the practice of spiritual disciplines, japa, and meditation. All these accounts sowed in my heart a
deep reverence for this unique personality. We also took pains to see
him whenever he was at the Belur Math. There he used to spend most
of his time with Bharat Maharaj, meetings which clearly indicated the
extent of their closeness.

In 1963, the colleges attached to Saradapitha [a large educational
complex run by the Ramakrishna Mission, directly adjacent to the
Belur Math headquarters] were in a festive mood with the preparations
for Swami Vivekananda's Birth Centenary celebrations. The centenary special issue of *Sandipan* published by "Shikshanmandir," the
postgraduate teachers training college, had attracted a lot of attention,
as had *Swamijir Padaprantey,* the book I had written about Swami
Vivekananda's disciples. These two publications had caught the particular notice of Chintaharan Maharaj. One day Swami Vimuktananda,
the Founder and Head of the Belur Saradapitha, and an intimate friend
of Swami Nitya-swarup-ananda, called me and said, "Go and see
Chintaharan Maharaj, he wants to talk to you." I felt quite intimidated
at this sudden request, but Swami Vimuktananda reassured me, "Chin-

taharan Maharaj has really liked your book, *Swamijir Padaprantey*. He also wanted to know the main person behind this special issue of *Sandipan*, and I disclosed your name. The writing, editing, printing, paper, layout, cover—everything has been to his satisfaction. My dear, to get something appreciated by his discerning eyes and to win his spontaneous praise is no mean achievement. It must be the result of some past good deed. You are indeed very lucky. You will go and make your pranam to him personally." He was at the Math and as soon as I went and made my pranam, he congratulated me with very touching words and asked me detailed questions about *Sandipan*. His profuse blessings on that day became a point of inspiration for me in later years. This occasion also revealed to me for the first time the depth of his keen aesthetic sensibilities and artistic sense. Several future incidents furnished further proof of this.

The pure white marble relief statue of Swami Vivekananda at the Belur Math, the whiteness of which brings out the radiance of Swamiji's meditative form, had once fallen prey to aesthetic distortion. It so happened that the backdrop of the statue was painted dark blue by some "knowledgeable" soul. The distortion was noticed by all and it created a few minor ripples, faint murmurs of disapproval by a discerning few, and even praise by some. One day Chintaharan Maharaj went to make his pranam at Swamiji's temple. He stopped short at the entrance. His eyes were ablaze. His body trembled with emotions he could scarcely suppress. He quickly made his pranam and straightaway went to President Swami Vireswarananda's room and burst out, "I grant you have lost your eyesight. But we who can see—what is this we are made to see? What is happening in this Math, in Swamiji's temple? The pure white image of Swamiji which has been worshipped in this form all these years has been tainted. The blue paint has ruined the natural beauty of the image. It is intolerable!" This outburst of his deep anguish and anger subsequently effected the restoration of the image. We owe the restoration to Swami Nitya-swarup-ananda's spiritual and aesthetic sensitivity.

I keep remembering his exquisitely refined taste, without a trace of ostentation. It was inborn. His aesthetic taste was wonderfully projected in the exquisite architectural structure of the Institute of Culture at Gol Park, which was constructed under his direction and guidance. But significantly, he kept his own living area away from the palatial building. He stayed in a small mezzanine room on top of the garage, furnished in his characteristic manner with just a cot covered with a clean white sheet. There was a small room adjacent to this one which was used as the meditation room. It had a small wooden altar on which were placed the three photographs he worshipped. There were a small flower vase and a tiny incense stand, that was all. Yet that meditation room had such a serene and sombre atmosphere, resonant with a spirit which is hard to describe. The stark simplicity, austerity, and orderliness of the living room and the meditation room were a reflection of his inner nature, his exquisitely refined aesthetic sensibilities, elegant and simple, without a trace of display or excess. Even today, the picture of that meditation room keeps coming back to my mind, the room that was a witness to his years of silent *sadhana*.

How many of us are really aware of the source of all the energies of this great worker? I was once lucky enough to witness this very carefully hidden facet of his personality. I had come to Calcutta from Shillong to undergo investigation and treatment for some serious ailment. I had expressed my extreme reluctance to be admitted to Seva Pratishthan, or any other hospital, in a letter to Bharat Maharaj. I had also written to Chintaharan Maharaj expressing my views. It was then that I became aware of the gentle and affectionate side of his nature— a mother's heart which lay hidden behind the stern exterior. He sought Bharat Maharaj's permission and made arrangements for me to stay at the Institute under his guardianship while all the required tests and treatment were being performed. The specialist doctors from Seva Pratishthan used to come twice a day to examine me at the Institute and sometimes I was also sent there by car for checkups.

I was totally bedridden. My room was adjacent to his room. It was practically like staying in the same room as there was no door in between, making it thoroughly accessible. I would watch him absorbed in meditation in the late hours of night and early hours of dawn. In spite of his extremely busy schedule he made time to come and sit near me several times during the day and find out in detail about my treatment and medication. He reminded me of the Himalayas, full of rocks and hard stones nurturing cool streams and refreshing green wealth in its bosom, and offering asylum to those in need. During my illness, I came to know Swami Nitya-swarup-ananda as a worthy child of the Holy Mother. His steadfastness regarding spiritual practices, meditation, and study, and his great love for all of this was a source of inspiration, an example, and a great learning experience for us. Here by saying "us" I mean those of us who have had the good fortune to come in close touch with him....

Pictures like these abound and need to be culled and brought together to complete the portrait of a figure which is hidden from the eyes of the world, to try to know his total personality. His saintly character is of greater glory than the more manifested aspects of his personality, or shall we say that it is this inner glow which gave resplendence to his outer qualities, the source of so much attention from everyone?

I saw him quite closely during his three-week tour of Assam and Meghalaya, at which time he spent considerable time in Shillong, where I was posted. Before leaving for Shillong I had gone to seek the blessings of Bharat Maharaj. While giving his loving blessings, he had said, "I have never been to that part of the country. Somehow things did not work out. I have been nurturing a wrong idea in my mind that the State of Assam is full of jungles with hardly anything to see over there. Perhaps Thakur now wants me to shed this illusion which is why he is sending you over there. You go and settle down first and then make all arrangements for my visit. I am now feeling a great pull in my heart for that region. I have not talked about this to anyone else but you so far. I will be waiting for your call." I felt so elated and inspired that I had no words to express my great joy. When he saw that I was willing to shoulder this responsibility, he put another onerous responsibility on my shoulders and said, "If I go I will not go alone. Swami Dayananda and Chintaharan will accompany me. And if Lokeswarananda wants to join us too, it will be even better. You will have to invite them separately and take full charge of their board and lodging, travel, etc. Will you be able to do it? It will be your test in a way."

All arrangements were made accordingly with Thakur's guiding hand to help me. Bharat Maharaj and his companions expressed their pleasure with all the arrangements and showered their blessings. Their visit created quite a stir in Assam and Meghalaya, and all the Mission Centres there were inundated with festivities and celebrations during their stay. In those three weeks of tour and travel we saw various facets of Chintaharan Maharaj's character, a few of which will be presented here.

In the hilly region of Shillong darkness descends fast. Our dinner used to be over by half past nine in the evening and all the monks and brahmacharins residing in the Ashrama used to assemble in Bharat Maharaj's room. Swami Dayananda was present, as were the other elderly monks. Chintaharan Maharaj was of course always there. One day we were trying without success to draw Bharat Maharaj out to discuss the olden times at the Math, but he deftly managed to steer the conversation away from any such talk. Seeing our disappointed and defeated faces, Chintaharan Maharaj very subtly brought in the topic of how Swami Premananda used to keep a sharp eye on the observance of daily routine at the Math and how novel was his way of instructing and disciplining the sadhus and brahmacharis. This worked like magic. As soon as he heard Baburam Maharaj's name, words started pouring from his lips as he became immersed in the memory of the saintly soul. There was hushed silence and Chintaharan Maharaj too was listening enthralled. Swami Dayananda, Swami Lokeswarananda, Pashupati Maharaj, and all the other elderly monks too were lost in rapture, for these new unheard-of facts about Swami Premananda transported them to the distant past. It was well past two o'clock in the morning and Bharat Maharaj started shivering in cold. We covered him up with thick blankets and put the room heater on. With great reluctance we broke up for the night. The bitter cold was affecting everybody. We all stood up and, one by one, started taking our leave, making our pranam to Bharat Maharaj. But Chintaharan Maharaj continued in the same posture, his face with a blissful expression, eyes closed, but one could see teardrops glistening in the corners even in that dim light. Bharat Maharaj went to bed and after quite some time asked, "What time is it now?" When he heard the answer, he was surprised and exclaimed, "Chintaharan, will you not go to sleep tonight? Go and sleep, the night is almost gone." Chintaharan Maharaj then slowly left the room.

The memory of that wonderful night at Shillong is still ingrained in our minds: A musical instrument is lying in an assembly, but only the person who knows how to play it will be able to bring it to life and create a resonance of melody. It needs his master fingers to bring out the sound of music; without his touch, its potential to give so much joy will remain unexplored. Bharat Maharaj was extremely reticent, yet he had a treasure trove of precious memories hidden inside—because his life was a virtual museum containing many priceless treasures, unmatched to this day. He would never have opened up that treasure chest of his own even if one had spent a thousand hours with him. Chintaharan Maharaj was very close to him and one of his very own. Therefore he knew how to unlock these innermost chambers. The memory of Swami Premananda was the key to get access to those innermost chambers of his heart. He knew how to break his reserve and make those outpourings possible. We had noticed even in that dim light that Bharat Maharaj's eyes were wet, his face was all aglow, and his voice charged with emotion. This was a rare treat, and we owe it all to Chintaharan Maharaj. The manner in which he himself was also immersed in the memory of that beloved soul—that memory too is unforgettable.

Similarly a few incidents during the Assam travels revealed this side of his nature, the strong undercurrent of his devotional life, while outwardly he remained a staunch Advaita Vedantist. This Advaita was for him no dry intellectual exercise, devoid of the softer and sweeter strains of devotion. His Advaitism was not a doctrine but a matter of realization whose expression was soft, gentle, dipped in the nectar of devotion. This sweetness radiated itself in his meditation, and his bhakti-tempered *jnana* found perfect expression in his work. This is why the whole of his spiritual life was steeped in Swamiji's teachings and thoughts.

When he went to visit the famous shrine of Shaktipitha Kamakhya, he observed all the rituals meticulously and with great devotion, as shown by the temple priests. He climbed down the dark and slippery staircases leading to the shrine, sat on the wet floor, and recited all the mantras; after finishing the *puja* he came up the stairs without taking anyone's help, slightly overcome with emotions. . . .

[In the concluding section of Part 1 and at the beginning of Part 2, Swami Abjajananda gives several more episodes from their travels in Assam before continuing his narration about the close relationship between Swami Nitya-swarup-ananda and Bharat Maharaj.]

(From Part 2)

There was a deep bonding between Bharat Maharaj and Chintaharan Maharaj. It can be compared to the deep love and attachment between two brothers, an element of respect and regard for the older from the younger in an ideal family. It was never very overt, but it was not difficult for the intimate to notice this. Even in his very old age when Chintaharan Maharaj stayed at the Belur Math, we observed that every morning he made his pranam at all the temples and the place of samadhi of all of Sri Ramakrishna's disciples at a fixed hour, no matter what the season was. Then, after making these morning rounds, he used to go up to the second-floor room where Bharat Maharaj was staying. Their meeting was a part of his daily routine and he never veered from it even when he was ill. This consistency was something quite extraordinary, and even in Bharat Maharaj's last days, when he was totally infirm and unable to talk or even sit up, even then Chintaharan Maharaj made no exception to his daily visits; he used to go and sit there quietly, just look at him silently and then come away. And yet Chintaharan Maharaj was a person who hardly ever stepped out of his room to visit others. His routine visit to Bharat Maharaj was an exception, and he sometimes met him in the evenings as well.

We used to notice that the topic often discussed between the two was the "Rules and Regulations of the Math" as formulated by Swami Vivekananda in 1898, and their implementation—or, at times, the problems in applying some of those rules in the changed context of the present, and the ways to overcome such difficulties. Sometimes the discussion would come to such a point that a casual visitor would think that an argument was going on. Bharat Maharaj loved intelligent criticism, and he therefore used to provoke the sharp logical mind of Chintaharan Maharaj by some statement guaranteed to initiate a heated discussion. If Swami Dayananda also happened to be present, the discussion would become so utterly absorbing that only someone who witnessed it personally would be able to understand how uplifting such a conversation could be. Dayananda Swami was also extremely fond of Chintaharan Maharaj, the two were extremely close. Swami Dayananda, Bharat Maharaj, and other senior monks used to affectionately call him "Chintu"—we have heard it thus too. . . .

[Here Swami Abjajananda goes into detail about Swami Nitya-swarup-ananda's well-regulated and austere life, quoting Swami Vimuktananda about his steadfastness as a brahmachari, and how his character had been moulded by the saintly Shukul Maharaj (Swami Atmananda). This section has been widely quoted in Chapter 2 of the biography in Volume 1, and only the concluding paragraph is given below.]

The two main traits of Shukul Maharaj's character—a yogic detachment and a dynamism of heroic proportions—were very much evident in Chintaharan Maharaj too. A very small incident will help to elucidate this statement. The annual Foundation Day was being celebrated at the Institute of Culture. This important function is attended by many learned and famous people. Swami Nitya-swarup-ananda, who was then staying at the Belur Math, was duly invited to attend the celebrations. He had gone there (by public transport) and was present in the packed auditorium seated among the general public, as one among many, watching all that was going on with great interest and attention, and after the function concluded he went away unnoticed and unrecognized by those around him. He had not waited for, nor had any expectation for, any kind of special treatment. And here we might recall that he had been associated with this very institution as its life-force, shaping its very destiny right from its inception, for more than three decades.

(From Part 3)

Swami Nitya-swarup-ananda was not a public speaker in the conventional sense, although he was a brilliant communicator. He was no orator, which is why we have never seen him on a stage, yet his facility with words was extraordinary. People were simply enthralled by his conversation. Ironically, his strict adherence to truth made him so forthright that people found it difficult to accept his ideas in spite of being charmed by his words. This outspokenness was taught to him by Swami Atmananda. Shukul Maharaj used to say, "Doing Thakur's work means propagating his ideals, not appeasing people. Encouragement of falsehood and injustice is the same as being untruthful and unjust. Not to fight against falsehood is a sign of weakness."

His Advaitic thinking had raised his consciousness to such heights that he could not conceive of the entire human society and civilization as anything but One. We find the culmination of his thoughts in his monograph *Education for World Civilization*, in which he also gave his plans for its practical implementation. It was his cherished dream that the Institute of Culture would become the primary centre for the study of world cultures, the seat of research, and the practice of humanism. He worked to realize this ideal till his very end. He explained that man is essentially one. The diversity we find in different cultures, religious sects, and rituals is but a difference of expression. Man is trying to express this single truth through all his activities, and all his expressions are but different facets of this one universal idea. He wrote,

"Neither the body nor the mind, nor the senses constitute man's real nature. The real nature of man is the spirit beyond them. It is existence itself. It is therefore universal and not limited. It is infinite, not many. Humanity is essentially one, Existence is one, Civilization is one."

This Advaitic consciousness permeated his being and found spontaneous expression in his everyday life. I will mention a small anecdote which comes to my mind in this connection. I was then posted in Shillong and had gone to Delhi for some official work. Swami Lokeswarananda had come from Calcutta. Chintaharan Maharaj was in Delhi, probably for some work connected with the Institute. One evening he came and said, "Let us go and visit a place." Swami Lokeswarananda also joined us. We went to a newly constructed palatial building. The interior decoration work was still in progress. This was to be a guest house for international celebrities, and the idea was that the décor would be artistically done in traditional Indian style. The art forms of different regions, both ancient and modern, would be represented. It was but natural that a connoisseur of art like Chintaharan Maharaj would particularly feel interested to visit such a place. We went around looking at every nook and corner, very much appreciative of what we saw. Chintaharan Maharaj was particularly pleased to find that the folk and rural art of India were given prominence.

We were climbing down a flight of stairs, absorbed in talk. Chintaharan Maharaj was explaining to us about the evolution of art: *Satya-Shiva-Sunder* (Truth-Goodness-Beauty) is God; all beautiful things are manifestations of the Divine and that is why we are attracted to beauty; this world is full of beautiful things—the Eternal Beauty which is immanent in Nature, etc. In the meantime, four or five gentlemen were climbing up the stairs. One could not make out from their dress or speech which province they were from. They spoke a mixture of Hindi and English. Anyway, we must have struck them as pretty odd for they kept looking at us askance. They were saying among themselves, "Who are these ochre-robed people, of what religion?" We were quite amused. Suddenly one of them came up to us and asked the question directly. Chintaharan Maharaj immediately replied:

We are human beings
We belong to humanity
Ours is human religion.

I do not know whether this reply satisfied their curiosity, but they went away sheepishly. I for one was struck with admiration at this prompt reply. He had made these lofty ideas so much a part of himself that they seemed to be flowing in his veins—so much so that even in jest they found such simple and spontaneous expression.

Chintaharan Maharaj used to remind us often of Swamiji's saying that our ideal should be to build up our character by synthesizing knowledge, meditation, devotion, and action. Never before in the whole history of humanity has there been a perfect synthesis of all these four yogas, as in the person of Sri Ramakrishna. We observed Chintaharan Maharaj's own efforts to realize this ideal in his life, work, and *sadhana*. His daily life was a living example of the harmonized expression of the four yogas. But above all lay his spirit of surrender, like a child, to the Mother. Holy Mother was the theme in all his joy and sorrow, in life and death.... He was quite unique in his expression of emotion, love, affection, affliction, and devotion, and crowning it all was his "mother-centredness."

Seldom did the world get to see this aspect of Chintaharan Maharaj, his loving heart, his love for meditation, and his adherence to devotional practices. Only towards the end when he was freed from the claims of the workaday world did these hidden aspects get more revealed. Many saw and marvelled at him at the Math during Kali Puja celebrations, seated in one unbroken posture from 9:00 in the evening till 4:00 the next morning. This can only be the result of years of spiritual practice. Those who have seen him at Udbodhan or at Jayrambati must have noticed how transformed he would be, calm and serene, so very childlike in front of the Holy Mother's image.

In spite of serious illness he always had the three photographs of Thakur, Ma, and Swamiji by his bedside. He also always had the pictures of all the direct disciples of Sri Ramakrishna in his room, all in one frame. I remember one day in particular. He was then in great pain and very seriously ill, staying at the Institute of Culture. It was 12:00 noon. I had gone to see him. On entering his room I found it vacant. I assumed that he must have gone to have his bath. I waited for him all by myself. After some time he came out. He saw me and yet seemed to take no notice of me. He did not utter a word and straightaway went to the corner of the room where the pictures of Thakur, Ma, and Swamiji were kept. He sat in front of them and was lost in silent prayer for quite some time. After that he went in front of the pictures of the direct disciples and spent some time in silent prayer. All this while I felt that he was so absorbed in his act of devotion that he was totally oblivious of the presence of anyone else in that room. After he had finished he looked at me and smiled and said, "Sit down, sit down. How long have you been waiting for me?" I have been attracted again and again by the manner in which his mind was always in communion with the divine, every moment of his life.

I had gone to see him a few days before his passing away. He was then at the hospital; his speech was not very clear and he showed great reluctance to speak. Yet the memory of that last meeting is still etched very vividly in my mind, and it will remain so till I breathe my last. He held me close to his bosom and softly spoke a few words which I cannot publish here because they are very confidential. That was his last blessing—as he mentioned to me explicitly. He placed his hands on my head when I took leave, and then again held me close to him for a while. He said, "This is my last conversation with you. I was waiting to say all this to you. I have told you my last words. Spend your days in joy with Thakur. We will not meet any more."

A brother monk wrote to me on October 22, 1992: "Swami Nitya-swarup-ananda left his body at 12:30 P.M. today. We got the news at 4:00 P.M. He was at Gol Park. He had lost all appetite towards the end. I believe, a few days before the end he had looked at Holy Mother's picture and complained, 'Can't you see? I am suffering so much,' with tears streaming down his face. But today he was quite well. He had even spoken on the telephone at 12:20 P.M. The end came suddenly, even before the doctor could arrive."

He spent his last days at the Institute. He breathed his last in that temple of culture he had helped to shape, the seat of long years of his *sadhana.* . . .

If these sketches of Swami Nitya-swarup-ananda are found wanting in any way, the fault lies entirely with the artist whose tentative strokes could not do them justice. If they have been able to depict him properly in some places, it is because the inhibitions of the writer have been swept away by the sheer force and greatness of his subject matter, and the emboldened strokes assumed a vitality of their own.

Swami Nitya-swarup-ananda—his understanding was so wide and comprehensive, his wisdom so deep, his knowledge so vast—he was truly an extraordinary personality. His idealism touched sublime heights. We can only glory at the range and depth of his being. Standing on the footsteps of a great mountain, aspiring to scale the summit, we become aware of how difficult it is to reach those heights. But surely we can draw our inspiration by thinking of him, and herein lies the relevance of this entire exercise.

PREM KIRPAL

The enclosed jottings were inspired by Swami Nitya-swarup-ananda, a rare human being and a truly great soul whose memory I cherish. I believe in the attainment of a Global Brotherhood which Swami Nitya-swarup-ananda expressed in his Scheme of World Civilization, and which I tried to promote at the national and international levels.

> *Salutations!*
> To Nitya Swarup Ananda
> Who came to my home
> Like fresh breeze of morning
> With Surya from the East
> I offer Love and Salutations
> On this First April Morning!

To that Great Global Citizen
Of Education for World Civilization
Exalted by the Noble Shelley Brown
And inspiring my Life and Memories
I offer Mind, Heart and Soul
To make me one and whole!

With growing awareness of the Cosmos
And new Consciousness unfolding
I invoke the Swami's Dream
Of a New World Order
Of Learning and Revering
All Cultures and Civilizations
For Mind's Luminosity
And Human Solidarity
In Quests of Education
And practice of Compassion
To live, love and Serve
And Take Care of each other!

The Space Within the Heart
Somewhere in space there must be people
Who are born in love and grow in its fullness
Blending truth, beauty and goodness
In the effortless practice of love and kindness,
Devoid of pride, fear and pettiness,
Untouched by lusts of greed and power:
Defying decay, pain and suffering
By expressing the self in joy of acceptance.

Somewhere in time there must be people:
Who can transcend the human condition,
Casting away its frailties and confusion,
Mastering the self with near perfection—
Yet retaining utter humility—
Nurtured by the power of compassion.

Burning with the zest of life.
Poised in still centre of action.

Inside my heart there are such people:
Glimpsed here and there in far flung space.
Emerging from the flux of time,
Created in sweet fancy's flame.
They are the best of my treasures,
Strong sources of my life's sustenance,
Companions of my dreary hours—
Dear radiant friends who can never fade:

I bless these souls and bless myself,
And ask of the gods that be
To grant such shrines of love and beauty
To the lonely hearts wherever they be!

SUJATA BASU THAKUR*

I became acquainted with Swami Nitya-swarup-ananda Maharaj in March 1953, after my marriage to Mr. Chinmoy Basu Thakur, the third son of the late Nalini Kumar Basu Thakur. We had unbroken contact with Chintaharan Maharaj from that time, so I got to know him somewhat over the years, though his spirit was so vast that it isn't possible to describe him in a few words.

He had a special fondness for me. In the beginning I used to treat him with excessive reverence and approach him very timidly, his personality commanded such respect. But, gradually, I came to realize the deep affection he had for me and for all the members of my family. Maharaj used to give my mother-in-law various books on religion, and once referred to her as "a flame of purity." She herself held him in the highest regard, and told us, "In one sense Chintaharan is my guru. He has showed me the way to peace and spirituality. It was at his insistence that I took initiation from Swami Saradananda."

From the core of his heart, Maharaj wished for the spread of higher education among women and for their development. He was very pleased when he found out that I was the Principal of a High School for Girls, and blessed me earnestly. He sometimes used to give me his books and published lectures to read.

Whenever he had the opportunity, he came to visit us in our house, or even in the various temporary quarters which we occupied in the course of my husband's postings. I observed that he liked things to be spick and span, and for all work to be done with perfection. He used to say that cleanliness is next to godliness. So whenever he was coming to our house, I took great care to have everything in perfect order. I could sense his pleasure. I remember once I had some problem with the school authorities. The matter was even taken to court. I told Maharaj about it and sought his advice. He asked for all the papers related to that problem, and then he arranged them meticulously, taking a long time. He never wanted anything to be done in a rush.

There was not a hint of intellectual pride. He was averse to any display. He used to always keep himself occupied with different kinds of work, but he seldom discussed these things. The ideals of his life were discipline and a strong sense of duty, and he ever upheld them in his words and deeds.

I have observed another aspect of his personality. He greatly appreciated good food of all kinds—Indian, Western, simple and home-cooked. He was very fond of feeding others. I had gone to see him one afternoon at the Udbodhan office just after my marriage, and he asked us to have lunch with him. With what gentle care and affection he supervised our meal! I will never forget that. In turn, whenever he liked some dish in our house, he used to ask us about its preparation in detail.

I went to see him at the Institute of Culture a few months before his passing away. He distributed the fruits and sweets we had brought to all who were present in the room. My husband was narrating many amusing anecdotes from his childhood days. Chintaharan Maharaj also spoke to us about these earlier times and when the subject turned to my husband's elder brother, who he had tutored in earlier days, he said, "You know, I am proud of Sukumar."

PHULRENU GUHA*

I heard about Chintaharan from my childhood since he was the private tutor of Sukumar, the eldest son of my mother's cousin, Nalini Kumar Basu Thakur. I was told that he was a very good teacher, very affectionate, and that Sukumar's mother, Mrs. Sailabala Basu, was fond of discussing spiritual matters with him.

We first met Chintaharan Maharaj when the Institute was at Russa Road. He invited prominent personalities to hold discussions there, which included one of Mrs. Sailabala Basu's brothers, Nripen Chandra Guha, whenever he was visiting from Dacca. All three of Mrs. Sailabala Basu's brothers used to stay at her father's house in Calcutta, which was on Janak Road adjacent to the Institute, and Chintaharan Maharaj would go over there and have animated discussions with them.

It was at Russa Road that Chintaharan Maharaj planned the Institute of Culture at Gol Park. He always used to talk about the Institute and his plans for it, and we felt as though he even dreamt about it. I remember one occasion when he invited a few people to dinner after the building had been constructed at Gol Park but some of the furniture was still lacking—he borrowed a few chairs and the sofa set from our house. Our house was situated in Gol Park and he used to come over quite often.

Chintaharan Maharaj shared the sufferings of his acquaintances. He could instil fearlessness and inspire them to work. It was rare to find such an open-minded person, so well read and with such a range of knowledge. He would discuss not only religion, but all manner of things happening worldwide. He had an especially deep feeling for India and loved to dwell on how our country could be developed.

He was very fond of my husband, Dr. Biresh Chandra Guha. Maharaj often used to tell me, "I have rarely met a person like him." Only a few words, but it gave me courage to go forward in my life.

Chintaharan Maharaj was a lively person, an extraordinary worker. Everything had to be done properly and in a disciplined manner. The teachings of Vivekananda, of the Ramakrishna Mission, touched every moment of his life till the very last. After taking sannyas, Chintaharan Sarkar's name became Swami Nitya-swarup-ananda, but for us he was ever our Chintaharan Maharaj.

ROOMA BASU THAKUR*

While still a college student in search of a job, I knocked on the door of 111 Russa Road on August 8, 1958. The first part of the interview was a handwriting test. I was thinking, "That's it! No other questions, and then I'll get the job." Just then, a very pleasant looking, serene sannyasin came and stood in front of me. "How long have you been practising your handwriting?" he asked me. I could barely answer—my limbs froze, my throat was parched! But he not only offered me the job, he also opened up the door to the world of Ramakrishna-Sarada-Vivekananda; I entered that door, and was blessed.

Chintaharan Maharaj was a philosopher, a *jnani,* a lover of learning, a skilled architect, a great artist, a worshipper of *karma,* and an efficient organizer. Even half a century ago, when India was still not very advanced in the knowledge of science, even back then all the projects and plans of Maharaj had a scientific outlook.

The Gol Park building which houses the library at the Ramakrishna Mission Institute of Culture was constructed as a synthesis of Eastern and Western art forms, and its perfect architecture, visited by so many, is an expression of Chintaharan Maharaj's aesthetic taste. His thoughts, his plans, and their implementation were expressed, as it were, in every pore. It took indomitable willpower to implement a project of this dimension in the India of those days.

His projects were so big, yet his unique sensibility was applied to even the smallest details. This huge building in Gol Park has no *choukath* [raised doorsills dividing rooms, found in most of the older houses]. Maharaj said that this building should be constructed in such a manner that no one should face any obstacles, and that even a blind person should be fully mobile and secure. Nowadays we find a number of blind, handicapped people moving freely around the Institute, who are the beneficiaries of his progressive ideas.

After receiving a large donation of books from Dr. Barid Baran Mukherjee as a starting point, he built up a huge cultural library. Chintaharan Maharaj gave Mrs. Anupama Roy and Mrs. Amita Brahma the responsibility of organizing the books at Russa Road. I saw them climb up huge stairs with handkerchiefs tied on their noses, dusting the books and arranging them neatly on wooden shelves. Chintaharan Maharaj used to watch them at work. He was always inquiring what they needed. Sometimes they used to ask me to assist them. A huge *yajna* was under way and everybody was happy. Those scenes are still fresh in my memory.

Chintaharan Maharaj used to make arrangements for our food. He was very fond of Anupama Roy and Amita Brahma, and used to call Anupama Roy by a pet name, "Anu." Anupama Roy served the Institute till her last breath, and Chintaharan Maharaj was deeply affected by her untimely death in 1986, which also made me feel very sad.

The library was his life! I personally consider Maharaj to be a great librarian. In those days most people did not have a clear conception of a library, and I saw Maharaj putting great emphasis on Professor S. R. Ranganathan's theory of "the Five Laws of Librarianship." He used to discuss with us time and again how these laws should be put into practice at Gol Park. On other occasions, he would pick up a few passages from a book on library science and question us to see whether we could understand their meaning ("What is your concept of a library?" etc.).

The Children's Library at the Institute is one of the best in India and stands as an example of his fine sensibility and practicality. Because he understood the child's mind so well, he made this Children's Library open access. He wanted children to have the freedom to choose their own books, to be able to browse. His direction to me was to be keenly observant so as to guide the children whenever necessary. His understanding of child psychology extended to every detail. He had colour-coordinated tables, chairs, and shelves made to child size. A blackboard was hung on the wall where children could draw pictures to express themselves. Even the ceiling fluorescent light covers had beautiful pictures painted on them. Throughout the planning, he was a scientist as well as an artist in his outlook. He even had the wiring concealed, most unusual at that time, and to keep the library free of white ants (which eat books), he contacted pest-control experts right from the start of construction. Needless to say, he used to supervise personally every little detail.

All these features created wonder in the eyes of most visitors. Chintaharan Maharaj's plan for the Children's Library was so farsighted that librarians from all over India requested the blueprints, even down to the measurements of the tables and chairs. The Librarian of the National Library, Mr. B. S. Kesavan, who had consulted on the Institute's General Library, himself became interested in the Institute's model of the Children's Library.

When the library was being shifted from Russa Road to Gol Park, Maharaj said that the books should be transported from the shelves at Russa Road to the shelves at Gol Park following their call numbers, without getting them mixed up in any way. I remember how the books were packed under his supervision, serially, according to their call numbers, with a kind of relay system between the two sites, and stacked straight onto the shelves in the new location. This entire experience was not only educative but also gave me great pleasure. I am amazed even now how this complex task was accomplished smoothly under his guidance. I remember every working moment of those days as a joy.

While he was building up the library bit by bit from a mere sapling to a huge tree, he took it upon himself to train the library workers. He instructed us that each task was to be perfectly executed, and in order to do that, he told us, one needs to have *nishtha* [thoroughness], perseverance, and meditation. He used to say that no work was too small for perfection. Everything was Thakur's work. "Treat your work as service," he always emphasized, "not as salaried employment." His sharp eye never failed to detect any imperfection. He used to tell us that a

paper has to be folded in such a way that the corners do not stick out.
When papers are to be punched before filing, see that they are all even.
No book should be askew on the shelf. And he used to come and see
whether all these details were being observed. So we used to become
really apprehensive when we heard his voice coming in our direction.
He used to tell us that one has to prepare oneself to cope with all situations. To Maharaj, *karma* was *dharma*. He himself used to be immersed
in work day and night. While at Russa Road, I observed that he always
kept one eye on the construction at Gol Park. He had a unique capacity
to spread his observation and direction over both localities.

We saw his organizing abilities during the inauguration of the new
building and the East-West Conference. The scale of operation was
unprecedented. Dr. Sarvepalli Radhakrishnan was the President of the
Institute when Prime Minister Jawaharlal Nehru inaugurated the building. The ceremony took place on the beautiful and spacious lawn. The
entire lawn and all the verandas were packed with people, and yet everything was so disciplined and beautiful. The opportunity to be a witness of
such a big event is a matter of great pride and joy to me today.

We saw him give shape to the ideas of Ramakrishna-Vivekananda
in a special way through the Students' Day Home. He understood that
knowledge cannot be attained with an empty stomach, so he wanted a
place where students from poor and lower-middle classes could come
and have a good meal at a negligible sum (two annas). Thus, they were
able to strengthen themselves both physically and mentally, and
Maharaj kept a very keen eye on their progress. This was one example
of his *seva-dharma*, just as the Children's Library was also free and
open to rich and poor alike.

Swami Vivekananda declared that a race could not be awakened
unless the women were elevated. We have seen a reflection of this ideal
in Swami Nitya-swarup-ananda also. He felt that women were equal
and he wanted them to develop equally. He used to say that women
should stand on their own feet and should not be dependent on anyone.
Even in those distant days, he had opened up the doors for the libera-

tion of women. Today's society could use his liberal outlook! When he gave a job to a woman like myself, it meant breaking the barriers of orthodoxy and paving new roads for our development. His affection and encouragement led me to attain some academic qualifications later on. My graduation and my specialization in Library Science was done at his behest—and he never ceased inquiring about my progress in studies. "You have to be properly qualified," he used to tell me.

After joining the staff at Russa Road, I met with an accident and I couldn't come to work for some time. In those days, we were given a small monthly allowance rather than a regular salary. A few of my seniors, Mrs. Anupama Roy and Mrs. Amita Brahma (Roy), as well as myself, felt that I probably would not get the entire allowance. But two days before the payday, Maharaj called me and asked, "What, don't you need money?" I replied, softly, "Yes, I do." He then asked me to write an application for it, and he even told me what to write. He was so sensitive!

Another distinctive aspect of this Karma Yogi's life was that he had a word of hope or consolation for anyone with problems in life. I remember a small incident. My mother was admitted to Seva Pratishthan hospital. For certain reasons, I had to stay in her room and attend to her; the situation was such that I could not leave her unattended for a single moment. My brothers were out of town, so my father used to bring me my food. Maharaj was very upset when he came to know that my father had to go in the afternoon heat every day. He scolded me and asked me why I hadn't let him know about my problems. He took up the matter with the hospital authorities and made arrangements for my food. From then on, hospital food was served to me along with my mother, free of cost.

My life has been influenced in many ways by this great soul. My heart is filled with joy even today when I think that I have had the experience of working under the personal care of such a great artist, a tireless worker, superstition-free and a man so far ahead of his times in scientific outlook that he became a torch-bearer for the modern generation. I once more offer him my pranam.

NANDITA BHATTACHARYA*

By the grace of Sri Ramakrishna-Sarada, we had contact with Chinta-haran Maharaj for nearly forty years. He was an ocean of love, and that ocean was boundless. It gives me immense joy to retrieve these few memories.

I have experienced the Lord's Grace from the dawn of my conscious-ness, and I grew up listening to the strains of devotional hymns and chanting in my parental home. I was married at the age of fifteen, and since my husband was inspired by the same ideals of Sri Ramakrishna and Swami Vivekananda, we tried to conduct our domestic life accord-ingly and were frequent visitors to the Belur Math. This dear companion which the Lord had chosen for me was a true friend, simple, unaffected, and godlike, before he passed away and left me after fifty years.

We first knew Chintaharan Maharaj when the Institute was at Russa Road. It was our good fortune, because a very intimate kind of rela-tionship grew up with all who were acquainted with him. Nothing remained hidden from his powerful insight, everything was revealed. His mind was absolutely pure, a perfect example of a devoted sadhu. He was fond of my husband, whose name was Ram and who had made many sacrifices to fulfil his father's wishes at a young age. Perhaps this devotion and sense of duty of my husband had touched Maharaj.

Gradually, we became close to him. His name, Chintaharan ("one who takes away all anxiety"), was truly meaningful—he really could remove our anxieties and replace them with love and compassion. A symbol of power and determination, he was an apt successor of Swami Vivekananda. We felt it a blessing to know this great monk, and con-sidered him as a father figure; his behaviour towards us was also just like that of an affectionate parent.

People were entranced with his lively conversation, even on every-day topics. With any new acquaintance, he would immediately inquire about all the details of a person's life. If someone had a problem, he would be concerned and try to solve it. We knew of his work and were aware of his fame, but we were more satisfied with that aspect of him as a loving well-wisher.

Maharaj came from East Bengal and had the vivacity of that locale. One day he rang me up and said in his East Bengal dialect, "I feel like eating *sak* [a leafy green vegetable]. Tell me how many varieties of *sak* you know about." I listed the names, so he could note them down meticulously. Thus, in every little thing he had perfect *nishtha*, from choosing the menu, to shopping in the market, to cooking and serving—nothing escaped his attention. He didn't allow any deviation or mistake and he didn't accept slipshod work. Whenever he was invited to have a meal, he would inquire in detail about every step of the process, making the hostess feel that her service was purposeful. His praise would be spontaneous. Even if he saw the slightest good in anyone, he would praise them to the sky and encourage them to forge ahead. He used to say that if everyone in the world would follow one simple rule, there would be no discord, and no dearth of peace and happiness. That simple rule was to say, "What can I do for you?"

When the construction of the Institute at Gol Park was in progress, Maharaj was extremely busy, but in spite of that he called us, showed us around, and personally explained everything. Whenever he could find time, he would come to our house. Many devotees would collect on these occasions to listen to him. Sometimes he would spend hours immersed in spiritual discussions. He loved to listen to these three songs from the *Kathamrita*, sung by myself and my daughter-in-law: "Aye Ma Sadhan Samaré" [Mother, come to this battlefield of Sadhana], "Nath Tumi Sarbaswa Amar" [Lord, you are my all in all], and "O Raj-Rajeswar Dekha Dao" [King of kings, O king of kings, come and show yourself].

My M.A. examinations commenced three days after my daughter's marriage. He encouraged me and asked about my exams, and then sent me a huge bouquet of flowers with his blessings the day my results came out. On another occasion, he somehow came to know about my husband's birthday. He arrived that evening with a huge cake, lighted the candles, and sang "Happy Birthday." How easily he could mix with us and come down to our level, even though he was so great and powerful and we were so small compared to him.

In 1977, we were celebrating the Silver Jubilee of our organization, "Sri Ramakrishna Sarada Samsad." The twelve-day-long celebrations were conducted under his direction and supervision. Many monks participated from different centres of the Ramakrishna Math and Mission. The President, Swami Vireswarananda, and Bharat Maharaj were coming to our house, so Chintaharan Maharaj gave us detailed instructions about welcoming and hosting them properly. I had no words to express my gratitude.

Chintaharan Maharaj breathed his last in the Institute which he had built up from his dreams. After his passing away, when he was brought to Mother's House at Udbodhan on his last journey, I went there to pay him my final respects. I had an intense desire to offer him a garland made of his favourite jasmine flowers. I was surprised to find a flower seller sitting on the road selling only jasmine flower garlands (uncommon in October). I felt that Thakur was fulfilling my wish, and that by His Grace I was able to board the hearse with the help of a monk, in spite of my failing health, and to place the garland as my final offering.

SUHRID MAJUMDAR*

While writing about Swami Nitya-swarup-ananda, I feel hesitant—how much of his great personality can I put into words? I came into contact with him in 1955 during the construction of the Ramakrishna Mission Institute of Culture at Gol Park. I was attached to the building department of the Martin Burn firm, involved with the construction on behalf of my organization. Swami Nitya-swarup-ananda was the Secretary of the Institute, which was then at Russa Road. He had long cherished a dream for a bigger facility, in order to expand and to establish contact with the wider world. He wanted to make this possible through the new building which was being constructed at Gol Park. A huge amount of money was needed to fulfil this task, which was collected under his initiative in spite of many hurdles.

People often repeat, "Everything is God's will." Swami Nitya-swarup-ananda never subscribed to this facile view. He did not believe that the Institute of Culture would be completed without any effort, purely by God's will. I was struck by his determination and integrity during this period, he was so very hardworking. He used to come twice daily to supervise the progress of the construction, and everything had to be perfect. When he detected a defect in the construction of the Vive-kananda Hall, he had it rectified at a huge expenditure, but without the slightest hesitation. He had to appoint people for executing different kinds of jobs during the construction, and his selection was always appropriate. While the construction work was in progress, he frequently arranged feasts for us, he was so fond of giving others a treat.

He had wanted to go abroad after the construction was completed and his wishes were fulfilled. Before his travels he had woolen trousers and coats tailored, and sought various opinions in a lighthearted manner. But after his return from the West, immediately he was exactly as before. One could gauge his profound knowledge in all his conversations.

His faith in me was expressed in many ways. Some years ago, while he was at the Belur Math, he asked me to see him about some work. Once again, about two years ago [in 1992] when he was staying at the Institute, he called me and wanted to give me the responsibility regarding the expansion of the Gol Park building which was then under way (he was dissatisfied with the construction of the third and fourth floor of the Scholars' Residence, being done in a manner which altered the correct architectural perspective of the Institute as a whole). He breathed his last in the Institute which he had built. His great life will forever remain bright in our memory.

1960s
(Early Gol Park)

GOVINDA GOPAL MUKHERJEE

There are six bold truths about Swami Nitya-swarup-ananda that come immediately to mind and that I offer here in his memory.

1. The catholicity of Swami Nitya-swarup-ananda expressed a unique understanding of Sri Ramakrishna and Swami Vivekananda, in keeping with the true Indian tradition.

What I most admired in Swami Nitya-swarup-ananda was his catholicity. He had a huge vision, and at the root of his vision was Swamiji and Sri Ramakrishna. That is why I felt he had a true understanding of the meaning of Sri Ramakrishna's advent, and how Swami Vivekananda had wanted to give it form. Swami Nitya-swarup-ananda's perception was absolutely unique in the Order—although not unique in the historical sense in that it converged to the original Indian psyche, to the deepest cultural wellsprings of India's national ideal.

His universalism was apparent to me from the very beginning, even on a personal level. I didn't belong to the ranks of the Ramakrishna Order, but he consulted me on so many scriptural details, inquiring about whether something he had written was precisely correct in terms of the scriptures, and repeatedly asking me the question, "Is it in conformity with your shastras?" He really understood the exacting discipline of scholarship, and he was faithful to the scriptures in every detail.

He was very fond of a quotation from Swamiji. It was the translation of an old Sanskrit verse whose refrain was "from that which everything comes, to that One Self of All is our obeisance":

> yasmin sarvam
> yatah sarvam
> yah sarvah
> sarvatas ca yah
> yas ca sarvamayo nityam
> tasmai sarvatmane namah

He used to recite this again and again, for that was his view, that everything is He. And he also favoured another quotation from the *Isha Upanishad*, "Isha vasyam idam sarvam" [All this must be completely encompassed by the Isha, or the Lord]. Everything is that One Principle. So that was the viewpoint of one man, Swami Nitya-swarup-ananda, which is why my admiration for him knew no bounds. I never found anyone else like that—so vast.

In his time, he never allowed any picture of Sri Ramakrishna or Swami Vivekananda at the Institute. He had placed an altar with only a single lamp on top in the Universal Meditation Hall as a symbol of the universal light, the divine spirit that is common to all. "All the world, all the world, should come and converge at this Centre," he used to tell me, "that was my original idea of how to make this Institute a universal gathering place where all could freely exchange their views." So broad, so wonderful was his vision! It was only after he left the Institute that the pictures and the shrine were put into place and a more sectarian conception began to dilute his original idea.

His idea was pure Vedanta, and he was a real Vedantist. He translated and did a precise commentary on that difficult text, the *Ashtavakra Samhita*. It is not a text meant for everybody, but he brought out the very cream, the very essence, of Advaita Vedanta. His exacting and lucid translation was praised by such a respected scholar as Dr. Satkari Mookerjee, who wrote the Introduction to the book, and who was also my teacher. The *Ashtavakra Samhita* is such an austere writing that few people are familiar with it. So one day I said to Swami Nitya-swarupananda that perhaps I should start giving classes on the *Ashtavakra Samhita* based on his translation. He was delighted: "Oh, are you thinking of that?" he replied with enthusiasm. But unfortunately I could not fulfil my desire.

Nobody really has any proper conception about the *universal* principles of Vedantic thought. And to bring this out and disseminate it was the one aim in Swami Nitya-swarup-ananda's life. And this came to him through the study of the *Complete Works of Swami Vivekananda* and through the *Kathamrita* [Gospel of Sri Ramakrishna]—these were his inspiration, the basis of his grasp of the universal principles. It was Swami Vivekananda who said that Vedanta should be the universal religion of the world. So Swami Nitya-swarup-ananda took the cue from him and tried to give it proper shape, devoting his entire life to this.

His vision was such that it was not confined to the establishment. One day we were discussing how many people really reach the highest realization, attain to this stature, when he suddenly said, "Possibly that man from the South, he possibly had something like that." He was referring to Ramana Maharshi. So that also touched me so much, that a monk of the Ramakrishna Order could speak so highly of Ramana Maharshi—he could sense it. I truly cherish all these memories of Swami Nitya-swarup-ananda's catholicism.

2. In contrast, the Indian spirit of universality is being lost today in the Ramakrishna Mission and in other religious groups which are becoming too rigidly sectarian.

Sri Ramakrishna's life was the very embodiment of catholicism. Whenever he heard that someone was great in spirit he would seek them out of his own accord and make friends with them, such as Vidyasagar, a pioneer in the education field, and Keshab Chandra Sen, the Brahmo leader. That was the habit of Sri Ramakrishna himself, but I find that liberalism lacking in the present-day Ramakrishna Mission; an exclusivist mentality has crept in that says Ramakrishna is the *only* way. This is also completely foreign to the Indian tradition.

In my own makeup, I was brought up in the Indian tradition of universal acceptance. There is the famous utterance of Sri Ramakrishna based on his own realizations, "Yato mat tato path" [The paths are many, the ultimate goal is one]. Swami Vivekananda conveyed the same idea in his famous Chicago address when he quoted a verse from Puspadanta's famous *Siva Mahimna Stotra*, which uses the imagery of all rivers flowing towards the one ocean. That is true universality. And as Nitya-swarup-anandaji used to quote Swami Vivekananda, "I shall be happy when each one of you will have his *own* way"—when each individual will be following his own unique path to spiritual realization. It was never Sri Ramakrishna's or Swami Vivekananda's view that "through Ramakrishna alone you can reach the goal, Sri Ramakrishna is the *only* way."

Other faiths are making the same error in these days of narrow sectarianism. Sri Aurobindo, for example, was also broad in his own utterances when he said that "all life is Yoga." But if I go to his Ashrama in Pondicherry today, they will say, "Sri Aurobindo is the *only* Yoga." Or again, Anandamayi was herself a great lady, an exemplar of the spiritual life, but her disciples today assert that "Anandamayi alone is that highest thing, she is the Divine herself." It is quite all right to worship anyone as your guru, in the sense that the guru is an emblem of Brahman, of the Lord Himself, and there must be absolute adherence in terms of one's faith, one's Chosen Ideal. But when you make it propaganda and try to thrust it upon others—that is foreign to the Indian spiritual tradition. And that is why Swami Nitya-swarup-ananda's opposition to sectarian ideas and his fidelity to the true Indian spirit of universalism struck me as so unique and so admirable.

3. Swami Nitya-swarup-ananda had a unique ability to intuit the inherent qualities in a person, and to put them to proper use.

Another of Swami Nitya-swarup-ananda's distinctive characteristics was his ability to intuit the inherent qualities of a man, to sense that, "yes, this task can be accomplished through him." He always perceived the best to be drawn out of others, to realize their full potential. In every instance, he would get the right man in the right place, doing the right things, and then doing them correctly.

And he was such a perfectionist that everything had to be done "A-One" or he would immediately complain, "No, no, this is not a good quality thing, you have to do it in *this* way." Yet he was also aware of the burden of his exacting standards. When I was working with him, he would repeatedly apologize, "I am taking too much of your time.

You must be getting disgusted." "Why?" I would hastily reply, "I am getting such a good training under you in how to make it come out right." He was just as exacting with himself. He would ask, "Is this the right word in this context? This other would be better, what do you think?" The very next day he would again come with a new change in the word and I would sometimes get exasperated and say to myself, "What is this old man doing with me?" But then I would find that precisely the correct word was ultimately found after all these changes, and that this was the only way to hit the mark. At every step he would fine-tune it further, until the word and the interpretation were strictly in accordance with the scriptures. He used to quote Swami Vivekananda that we must always have the support of the shastras.

What I have become today as a lecturer is because of Swami Nitya-swarup-ananda. The story of how I got involved lecturing at the Institute of Culture is an example of how he could draw things out of people and foster their potential. It happened in 1959 when I had just joined the Sanskrit College, Calcutta, and was teaching there. I was living in Keyatala, very close to the Institute's new building under construction at Gol Park. Early one morning when I was taking my breakfast, I found a sannyasin at my door: Swami Nitya-swarup-ananda himself had come to my residence to request me to undertake some classes at the Institute. "But I have never lectured in public on anything," I protested. "No, no, you will be able to do it!" he was insisting. Possibly he had received an earlier impression of me from some discussion groups with friends, but in any case he was so confident that it overcame my initial hesitation.

Then he himself told me the background of his request. The Institute was just then in transition moving from Russa Road to Gol Park. Swami Omkarananda, the monk who was giving the *Bhagavat* classes at Russa Road, was a great scholar, but with some old-fashioned ideas. At Russa Road his students used to take off their shoes outside and then sit on the floor cross-legged while listening to the scriptures, in the old-fashioned way. The new Vivekananda Hall at Gol Park was not to his liking. One day he went to Swami Nitya-swarup-ananda and said, "You have made such a wonderful hall, but the people will enter it with their shoes on and will sit down on chairs to hear the *Bhagavat*. Ah, I can't *bear* it! I can't give classes there." So Nitya-swarup-anandaji had come to ask me to fill this void. "It is a wonderful new hall and Omkarananda has refused," he told me. "The hall must be utilized for this purpose, and you will be lecturing only once a week."

So that is how he just pulled me in and put me there as a lecturer from 1960 onwards. You can't imagine the spirited atmosphere with him at the Institute in those days. His presence was unique, everyone used to say that, so animated and encouraging. He just used to stand at the entrance with folded hands when the multitude of listeners used to leave after being saturated with the divine ambrosia of the scriptures for a full one hour. He never projected himself as a teacher or a lecturer. He felt that his only duty was to provide the rich repast, that he had no other role but to welcome all to this grand feast. When he left the Institute, I felt quite miserable and wanted to leave. It was only because of Nitya-swarup-anandaji that I had come to the Institute. But I remained to continue the tradition he had begun there, and I ended up giving regular scripture lectures at the Institute for more than thirty years.

4. Two of Swami Nitya-swarup-ananda's lessons: Work is worship when done in the right spirit, and one must go beyond all limiting ideas.

It was Swami Nitya-swarup-ananda who taught me the lesson that work is worship when done in the right spirit. He opened my eyes to its actual purpose, that work is a mentality, *a state of being*. I always remember how he remonstrated when he found everybody just praising the perfectly spick-and-span and tidy atmosphere in a Mission hospital without regard for its sterility of spirit: "What is all this, is this the spirit *Shiva-Jnane-Jiva seva*—is this the worship of everyone as Shiva Himself?" I learned from him that when a doctor comes with his stethoscope, instruments, and medicines to treat a patient, whatever he brings, these are the objects through which he is actually worshipping the Lord. That must be the spirit in a hospital run by the Ramakrishna Mission, he insisted. "If you enter the temple, you carry some flowers and incense in order to worship," he explained. "In the same way, the doctor should enter the premises of the hospital carrying their instruments in order to worship. Do the doctors here go in with that spirit?"

The same holds true for lecturing, or for any other activity. There is the story he told me one day of a direct disciple of Sri Ramakrishna who lectured to an empty hall, save for one listener, his attendant, Swami Nitya-swarup-ananda. When he asked him afterwards why he had gone to the trouble of speaking for a full hour with nobody to hear, the saintly monk had replied, "I have come to worship Thakur through my discourses, I have not come to lecture to the people." In the same way, Swami Nitya-swarup-ananda inspired in me a new vision of lecturing. I began to examine myself, "What is it that I am doing; am I doing it in that spirit?" Whether or not people are coming to hear, the attitude must always be simply, "I am worshipping."

So many things he taught me, and often with such wonderful humour. He was fond of feeding and entertaining people. One day I was at the Institute with my wife, and he suggested, "You come and have your dinner or lunch with us." So I had to tell him that I was a strict vegetarian. "Oh," he said, "in that case what can I offer you to take?" Then he said, "but I can't entertain you in such a way!" Turning to my wife, he enjoined her, "Come, let us *break* all his restrictions." Next he charged me, "You shouldn't have these vegetarian, nonvegetarian, limitations, or anything of that sort, because you have attained the height of scholarship in the scriptures." "But my ideas are not restrictive," I replied, "because in my house everyone takes fish and meat. I eat with them at the same table, so it is just my personal habit to take this vegetarian diet. I have no prejudice about these things. If you ask me to take fish I could do so, but possibly the smell of it would make me vomit because I am not used to it." He pounced on this answer: "No, no, the idea of a good smell or bad smell, that should also not be with you, you must be beyond all that—the smell of fish, that reaction should not be there." Finally I could only reply, "I have not attained to that height!" So in that very humorous way he was always trying to instil the knowledge in me that one must go beyond all these limitations, beyond all divisions, beyond this small vision of things, transcending all dualities.

On another occasion my wife and I were going to Benares. We were worried about getting the tickets and the proper reservations. "Don't worry," Chintaharan Maharaj said to my wife (who used to sing), "You just perform one or two pieces of your wonderful music, and allow him to go on lecturing. All these arrangements will be done by his many devotees. There will be no problem getting bookings or a place to stay, everyone will be volunteering for the honour." "But only one thing," he said as he embellished the scene to my wife, "many ladies will be coming and will fall down at his feet—at that time you must shut your eyes." How much we always enjoyed his sense of fun!

I must mention here that I used to admire him even as a student. As students, we used to go to the Institute at Keshab Sen Street in the late 1930s, shortly after it had been founded. He was much admired as a revered inspiring teacher even then, surrounded by eminent philosophers and scholars, even Dr. Radhakrishnan himself, who was then working at Calcutta University. Of course, as a young student I never knew him intimately in any way. But we realized, young as we were, that something new and wonderful had been started in that small space—such a small beginning from which he eventually built up a great institution.

5. Swami Nitya-swarup-ananda's vision of Sanskrit education was to rekindle the national spirit, a much-needed concept today.

There have been some grand visions of education in India with the object of instilling the true national spirit. With this aim, the National Council of Education was started in 1905, at the time of the nationalist movement. Sri Aurobindo was the first Principal of that national college, from which the present Jadavpur University has come into being.

Similarly with that end in view, Rabindranath Tagore founded his Visva-Bharati in Santiniketan, and his motto came from the Veda itself: "Yatra visvam bhavati eka nidam" [Where all the world becomes one nest]. Gandhi also in his own way tried to experiment with this type of purposeful education, which he named *Nayi Talim* [New Training]. But all these experiments ultimately failed, because what you find now at these places are just ordinary universities where learning is a commodity and people are getting their degrees for the sole purpose of making their way in the world. The original purpose of inculcating the true spirit of Indian culture has been lost.

The same question must be put to the schools run by the Ramakrishna Mission, such as Narendrapur and Purulia. Do they have any stamp of their own? What are the products coming out? Yes, they pray morning and evening and the discipline is very nice, and they achieve some remarkable results so that children will become very successful in life, in that way. But what Swami Vivekananda called *man-making education*, what of that in these schools? Is that achieved? I have received no answer when I have asked this question.

I found that Nitya-swarup-anandaji was the one man who tried without fail to instil the national spirit, to implement it through the educational programmes he developed at the Institute of Culture in his day. That was his dream. Whatever he did and wherever he went—and he sought out UNESCO and so many other sources in this effort—he was bent on imparting the national ideal through his unique scheme of education based on Swami Vivekananda's vision and conception. Even in his own Order few could appreciate his vision or come to his aid in that way. Now the Order is getting the benefit of the magnificent building he created to house the Institute, which they are using in their own way. But he himself had a much bigger vision of the place which still remains unfulfilled in most ways. He had the dream that from this pulpit at the Institute of Culture he had founded would go forth the call to the entire world: "Hark, hear ye all," *Srinvantu visve*, the message of universal unity.

Swami Nitya-swarup-ananda always turned to the shastras for support, and it was his vision that the Upanishads and other scriptures along with Swamiji's works must be studied to rekindle Indian national culture. That is why he included Sanskrit education at the Institute of Culture from the beginning, and finally developed the classes into a School of Sanskritic Studies. He enlisted me to help form the syllabus, divided into various groups, and from there into so many classes for each aspect of study, to give it proper shape. His conception of it was very broad but very intense. There was so much that he wanted to achieve in the School, built on solid foundations but soaring to such a high level.

It was not meant to be ordinary Sanskrit studies in the sense of just taking classes and doing translations from the Sanskrit language, but rather Sanskrit studies with the aim of instilling the multifaceted Indian culture in the minds of students. As they advanced, they were to take up the philosophies, literature, and sciences. It was a tremendous venture in those days with a definite aim. Rekindling national culture is still the most important task before us even after fifty years of Independence, but unfortunately the Institute's current program of Sanskrit studies lacks any such aim or capacity. Few teachers these days are properly equipped to enlighten students about Indian culture through Sanskrit studies in the way that Nitya-swarup-anandaji envisioned.

It was again with this purpose of rekindling national culture that he started publishing the volumes of *The Cultural Heritage of India*, and his idea was that each of these volumes would later be elaborated and multiplied into more numerous volumes. It was a unique project, unparalleled, which he could not complete.

6. The legacy of Swami Nitya-swarup-ananda's work was to fulfil Swami Vivekananda's vision.

Swami Nitya-swarup-ananda always kept with him and was always quoting from a little book written by Swami Vivekananda for the Ramakrishna Order. One day he handed it to me and pointed out this quotation:

The ideal of this world is that state when "the whole world will be full of Brahman" again, when there will be no need of the Sudra, the Vaisya or the Kshatriya powers; when a child will come to the world endowed with Yogic powers from the very birth; when spiritual force will have full sway over material force; when disease and grief will no more be able to affect the human body and mind; when the sense organs will not be able to run counter to the mind; when the application of brute force will be completely effaced from human memory like a dream of the past and when love will be the sole motive force in all actions in this world; then only the whole of mankind will be endowed with Brahmana qualities and become Brahmana. It is then only that caste distinctions will disappear and the Satya-Yuga visualized by the ancient Rishis, will come into being. That kind of division of caste alone which gradually leads along that path will have to be adopted. Only that kind of division into castes will be cordially accepted which is the best means to the elimination of caste distinctions. [From "Plan of Work for India," *Rules and Regulations of the Ramakrishna Math, Belur: Framed by Swamiji in 1898*]

After reading out this portion from Swamiji's book, Nitya-swarup-ananda asked me: "Is not this the vision and dream of Swamiji that has been developed by Sri Aurobindo in his *Life Divine*?" I had to concur, and it was a revelation to me. Only then did I realize why during his imprisonment in Alipore jail the spirit of Swami Vivekananda is reported to have visited Sri Aurobindo day after day, possibly to fulfil his unfinished task.

The quotation epitomizes the ideal for human fulfilment: "When a child will come to the world endowed with Yogic powers from the very birth"—only then will he require no training; and "when spiritual force will have full sway over material force"—only then will mankind find its true fulfilment in Oneness. Such was Swamiji's huge vision, and it was this huge vision which inspired Swami Nitya-swarup-ananda to move forward in his lifelong struggle to find the ways to educate mankind for world civilization and human unity. Few could understand either Swami Vivekananda's vision or Swami Nitya-swarup-ananda's attempt to translate that vision into reality, he was so far ahead of his time. That was his vision of "Thy Kingdom on earth" which he had inherited from Swami Vivekananda and wanted to usher in.

In his final years, he lamented to me, "I couldn't fulfil everything," and for that reason, in that respect, he died a brokenhearted man. But his legacy of universalism is there for others to pick up—to retrieve the true Indian spirit from which Swami Vivekananda drew his fire, and to go forward in the Ramakrishna Mission with the universal message of its Master, Sri Ramakrishna, unshackled from sectarianism and the motivations of narrower minds.

KESHAB CHANDRA SARKAR

I was thirty-five years old when I was interviewed by Swami Nitya-swarup-ananda for a position at the Institute of Culture at Gol Park. I remember the date exactly, December 30, 1960, and the location. We were just next to the staircase of the new International Scholars' Residence, Maharaj on the first step and myself standing on the lawn. After questioning me about my background, he asked me, "How much do you want?" It had been recommended to me by those who sent me that I should try to obtain 150 rupees per month, so I requested that amount with folded hands. "And if we don't pay you that now?" he replied. I quickly suggested 100 rupees a month, and again the same reply. "We will pay 70 rupees now," he said, "and after seeing your work for one month we will increase it." I agreed, and after the trial period Maharaj raised my salary to 100 rupees.

I was engaged as a telephone operator–cum–receptionist for the reception desk at the main entrance, which I shared with an elderly brahmachari. At the time I knew nothing about operating a telephone switchboard, but Swami Nitya-swarup-ananda trusted that I could understand the principle and learn it. He had the knack of choosing the right person for the right job. After that he would give the worker plenty of space to perform the task but would also keep an eye on whether that work was being done correctly.

Every afternoon at 4:00 he used to come and stand by the reception desk to see how I talked to people, because my job was also to attract people, to make them interested about Institute affairs. One day someone asked me a question which Nani Brahmachari was going to answer, but Maharaj said, "Let Keshab speak," and in such ways he would quietly observe. He didn't give suggestions, and I had the impression that he was satisfied with how I was talking. I was fluent in English and Hindi as well as Bengali, which gave an added advantage.

But six months later I was sacked. I had been asked to write down all the calls I made at the switchboard. One Saturday Swami Nitya-swarup-ananda came and asked me to show him the register. "I asked you to record all the calls," he said, rather unexpectedly a bit harsh, to which I replied, "It is not possible. My first job is to make the call as soon as possible—these two things cannot be done together." "Well," he said, "if you think it is too much for you, you need not sit here." "Well then I will not sit here!" I retorted. I was very adamant. When I arrived for work the next day I was directed to the accountant, who paid me off. A terrible moment, and I left.

For the next three months, now that I was an accomplished telephone operator, I tried to find another job. I learned that Maharaj used to ask Mr. Samiran Sarkar, "What is Keshab doing now?" I called Samiran one day and he asked me if I would like to return. Next, I received a letter from him to come and see Chintaharan Maharaj immediately ("Treat this letter as a telegram and see Maharaj as soon as possible"). It was the time of Durga Puja, and I went to see him in the late afternoon. Maharaj talked to me for one and a half hours. "You are exactly the fit person for the Institute," he said, "but you have so many defects. Well, if you think that nobody will criticize you when you work, then leave. But if you want to work here, if you like, you may join from today." I told him, "Maharaj, if I do anything wrong, you kick me out." He immediately took me to the corner office where they were making preparations for the inauguration of the building and for the East-West Cultural Conference, and he said to all present, "Ah, Keshab, he worked with us for some time, and he has come back. You give him some job, some position." I was reinstated at the Institute on October 16, 1961, a day I can never forget—I so valued Chintaharan Maharaj's long talk with me and his affection. After that I remained in the employ of the Institute right up to the time of my retirement in October 1997.

I had been an actor on the stage, and I used to enjoy acting out certain incidents before an impromptu audience. Chintaharan Maharaj used to relish this, and in his last years at Gol Park he would prompt me at the breakfast table, "Oh, Keshab, you tell them, how did I sack you, and how did I reinstall you, tell the story!" I would mimic all the parts, including his own, and by then it was so delightfully hilarious to myself as well as others.

Preparing for Maharaj's Return in 1970

Troubles between the administration at the Institute and the employees began soon after Swami Nitya-swarup-ananda left as Secretary in 1962. They were being ill treated and I had sympathy with them, and later when I joined the employees' union I felt that the union activities were being misrepresented to the Belur Math authorities by their informants.

The relationship had become so bitter that the employees were very much in favour of Swami Nitya-swarup-ananda's return as Secretary in 1970, and this included the union members. By that time I was working in the administration of the Language Department, and I was one of the staff considered as fit to represent the employees in talking to Swami Nitya-swarup-ananda about his return.

Mr. Hiren Das and I met with Swami Nitya-swarup-ananda at the Mission's Seva Pratishthan hospital in the Secretary's office (who absented himself for this occasion). We gave him our support and told him that we wanted him to return, reassuring him that old grievances with management would be forgotten—a "clean slate." On our part, we were reassured as to his magnanimity of mind.

In those days, the union people used to take assistance from political parties, and our union was affiliated with the Forward Block [a non-

Congress party, now part of the Left Front Government led by the Communists]. They had considerable force, quite strong, and there were posters and writings all over the walls of the Institute and even hanging from the trees. I was given the responsibility of ensuring that all these had been cleared, as Swami Nitya-swarup-ananda had made that a condition of his return. I received a call from the Seva Pratishthan, where he was then staying as a guest—Maharaj was on the line, saying, "You see, it is reported to me that still you did not clear all those writings by the unions on different parts of the building. So I tell you, either you clean all these things, or I will not enter at all." I straightaway went to our union secretary, Mr. Nani Das, also a worker at the Institute, and told him what Maharaj had just said. "What shall we do?" I asked him. "I am going away from here," Mr. Nani Das replied, "do whatever you like." So Mr. Nani Das took shelter in a tea shop near the lake, and in the meantime I got some people to remove all the union writings and posters. Then I telephoned Swami Nitya-swarup-ananda: "Yes, Maharaj, you please come. Everything has been removed."

He was welcomed back warmly, I remember, and was surrounded by many employees as well as the union leaders as he was being garlanded near the entrance to the Library. We had decided that we would stand by him while a lower-level employee, the humblest worker, placed the garland. And then as we were all standing round, Swami Nitya-swarup-ananda said to us, "Ami seva karte asechhi" [I have come to serve the people, not to exploit]. This set a new tone at the Institute, a new hope which we felt very deeply.

He wanted to settle all the disputes amicably. The first step was to reinstate Mr. Nani Das, who had been suspended prior to his return. Chintaharan Maharaj held his first meeting in the Reception Room on the ground floor of the Auditorium Section, and at that meeting a resolution was passed to drop the charges against Mr. Nani Das and to sanction his back pay. I heard that Dr. Prem Kirpal, a government official from New Delhi (Education Secretary), was present at the meeting along with the members of the Managing Committee. Mr. Samiran

Sarkar played a vital role in this matter, the constant skipper in a way, since he understood what was needed to be done to get things back on course. We were all very happy after this meeting, including Nani Das, because his arrears were all paid. He gave some of us a big party.

Chintaharan Maharaj also seemed very happy, perhaps because he was relieved that the heart of the people at the Institute had been won. He was keen to know our reaction. Nani Das and I had gone to the house of the Institute's treasurer, Mr. J. C. De, and when we returned Samiran said to me, "Maharaj waited for you for such a long time, he wanted to talk to you."

After a few days, Samiran said to Nani Das, "You do something as a token of gratitude to Maharaj, please go to him." So out of the money he had received, Nani Das bought a fine dhoti for Maharaj, and as we entered the lawn from the back side we saw him trying to present it to him. "No, no, I cannot take it," Maharaj was saying, and he adamantly refused. Nani Das pleaded for some time, and finally Maharaj said, "All right, I accept it, you give it to your father in my name, that I have given it to him." I could see that Maharaj was moved, emotional, but what happened next was astonishing. Maharaj was telling Nani Das, "I will go to your house and meet your father." I was dumbfounded that the Secretary of the Institute of Culture would commit to visit the humble dwelling of an ordinary worker!

One day Nani Das appeared at my house: "Keshab Babu, Maharaj is coming to my house, I don't know what to do, I don't dare to go with him alone," he said anxiously, "you please help, you come with us." So we three—Maharaj, Nani Das, and myself—went in a small black Austin car to Nani Das's house in Garfa Road where they were living in a refugee colony. I can assure you that no other Maharaj of his status, age, and position would ever have condescended to visit such a house in that way. The father of Nani Das was getting ready, for he had only one dhoti and he was tying it with extra care. I think that Maharaj had agreed to come to further heal the wounds between the management and the workers at the Institute, festering so long in such a bitter relationship. We could never have imagined such an emotional gesture on Maharaj's part.

That day we also visited a nearby plot of land as a possible site to construct a house for the monastics working at the Institute of Culture. Maharaj was always on the lookout for this because he did not think that monastic people should stay inside the Institute after it had closed for the day. Nani Das took us to the plot, but when we actually set foot on it Maharaj looked around in displeasure and said, "Characterless land! It is characterless." No entreaties by the owner for him to purchase the land were of any use after that.

Working Under Maharaj Again

I had been managing the School of Languages along with Mr. Tarakeswar Giri, but when Chintaharan Maharaj returned, I told him that I didn't feel capable of running the Language Department independently. He was also thinking of hiring a more highly qualified director (later, he changed his mind, but I still didn't feel that I could accept). A Principal's post was created, and for his use an old table was to be polished, a table that I knew as I had been using it myself. The polish men came and polished it nicely for the newly appointed Principal, and when it was ready they asked Chintaharan Maharaj to come and see it. He asked them to turn it upside down, and found that the underside was caked with dirt. As soon as he saw this he shouted at them, "Clean it and come back!" No one else would have examined the work done at the Institute with such care. This was very important to him, to get things done properly and to have everything very clean.

Maharaj used to ask me to show visitors around the Institute and explain about it to them in English. I had free access to his office and could escort any visitors there who wanted to meet and talk with him. He would immediately lay aside everything he was doing. He had this idea that if the Scheme of Work and the goals of the Institute were properly explained, the ideals would be appreciated and the Institute would grow to fulfil its objectives.

Maharaj used to consult many persons of consequence about the Scheme of Work. On one such occasion, the former District Magistrate of Dacca, Mr. D. L. Majumdar, came to stay at the Institute and Maharaj wanted to seek his comments. "Keshab, go get such-and-such a paper," he told me. And I well remember his displeasure when I couldn't find it right away. "Where have you been?" he admonished me, "He has left!" I had been a bit late since I never knew exactly what he might ask for. But Chintaharan Maharaj expected everything to be kept perfectly in place and ready to retrieve at all times. Later Mr. Majumdar came back and was given the paper for his opinion.

Soliciting expert opinions was one aspect of his untiring willingness to learn. One time Mrs. Etah Ghosh (wife of Mr. Kanti Ghosh, the well-known translator of Persian poetry) had come all the way from Santiniketan. Maharaj happened to be out when she arrived, and her room had yet to be booked (in those days no one could be accommodated without his permission). "Maharaj has asked me to come," she said, "Where is he?" "You please wait," I replied, "I will try to contact him." I knew Maharaj had gone to visit Dr. Nihar Kumar Munshi, an eye specialist, whom I also knew, so I called his residence and was told that Maharaj was still there. "What is he doing?" I asked. "He is looking at my bathroom," the doctor replied. You see, the architect of that building had gone to Dr. Munshi's house to closely examine the materials, arrangement, and other features of the interior, and Maharaj had therefore gone there himself, to observe and to learn. His willingness to learn was a lesson from Maharaj that I also took to heart.

Maharaj's Confrontation with a Legacy of Discontent

I got a glimpse one day of what I felt was the predicament at the Institute that Maharaj had stepped into after his long absence. I had been there for a long time, and in the meantime I had seen a change in guards, a change in policies and procedures, activities, mode of approach, and maybe some change in outlook too. Chintaharan Maharaj had come back into a volatile situation, full of uncertainty and vested interests. It was natural that he would look for support from those workers he felt he could trust. He suddenly called me from my house. "Were you sleeping?" he asked me (in Bengali); then he added, "I don't know to whom I have come. You should be available." He wanted to get on with his plan for the Institute, with his Scheme of Work about which he was passionate, and for this he had tremendous energy. He wanted to do something for the welfare of the country, for the people as a whole, and he had his own ideas and ideologies and wanted to adhere to those steadfastly. Now he was contending with employees who had worldly needs and who, as a rule, wanted more money (something that he was not in a position to give immediately).

This may have been secondary to his main thrust, and perhaps he had an incomplete idea about the harsh realities of the workers, yet he was exceptionally considerate and liberal and went out of his way. He attempted to increase the government grant to the Institute. There was a gentleman from Kashmir who had taken the name of Swami Vivekananda as his own, a Mr. Narendranath Datta who was doing voluntary work at the Institute following his retirement from the central government. He was very much trusted by Chintaharan Maharaj. Mr. Datta prepared a voluminous report to approach the government for increasing the grant, which included provision for new scales of pay. Samiran Sarkar commented at the time, "If even half the amount we ask for is granted, we shall be in a better position financially." Unfortunately, it didn't come through, the increase was not sanctioned, so the pay increases also could not be given.

Since the union people were expecting some fat ready money from the management which they did not receive, and perhaps also because Swami Nitya-swarup-ananda was adamant about pursuing his progressive ideas for the Institute even in the face of any discontent, the worker unrest which had been rampant before his arrival began brewing again. He circulated new Rules of Participation to create allegiance to the ideals of Sri Ramakrishna and Swami Vivekananda as the motivation for all work, just as for the monastics, but some of the conditions were not appreciated, especially since this had been written in

English, which could be reinterpreted and misinterpreted for the lower class of workers. The perception was there among some that their rights were being usurped rather than reinforced. Maharaj called in Mrs. Purabi Mukherjee, a Member of Parliament, to pacify things, and she was also put on the new "Staff Welfare Committee" (an amendment to the Rules of Participation of which the workers approved).

The union secretary, Nani Das, and Swami Nitya-swarup-ananda still had a good relationship. In fact, Nani Das took advantage of Maharaj's kindheartedness and asked him for money to tide him over, a kind of charity, since he was a poor man. But Nani Das was underhanded. He was telling the union workers that he was against Swami Nitya-swarup-ananda because he represented management. That tactic was his weapon and the way he held onto his power. He never made public that he took money from Maharaj. But in mid-1973 it all came out when a loyal senior staff member told the union about it. Nani Das was revealed, and when he saw that his position was jeopardized, he fought back to save himself by starting serious agitation at the Institute. He began work stoppages, demanding for himself a promotion for which he was unqualified, stirring the workers to demand dearness allowance, etc. That was when Swami Nitya-swarup-ananda was *gheraoed* in his office. It came to total defiance of all authority. Nani Das used to go around saying, "I am the Secretary, Nitya-swarup-ananda is not the Secretary, everybody will be guided by me." Work at the Institute came to a standstill, and that was intolerable to Swami Nitya-swarup-ananda. The workers were not keeping to the ideals of being participants, conditions were not being met. Nani Das was sacked with the other troublemakers shortly after Swami Nitya-swarup-ananda left the Institute at the end of 1973. Maharaj's cause was for the Institute, for the good of many, for the *Indian* way of doing things from the perspective of higher ideals.

After he left I think he was continuously writing, working on those two books. In 1975 I saw him coming out of the Institute's Library. I had written him a long letter a few days back to his Belur Math address when I had completed my fiftieth year (I was born in 1925). As he was coming out he said, "Yes, Keshab, I have received your letter," and he patted my back.

Maharaj's Blessings

I married very late in life, at age forty-five. I couldn't afford to marry earlier since my pay was only 210 rupees per month and there were five in the family to support. After I got quarters at the Institute in 1969, I began thinking of marriage, and when a proposal came for an arranged marriage in 1971, I agreed. I broached it with Maharaj while I was walking with him across the lawn: "Maharaj," I said a little hesitantly, "I forgot to tell you one thing." "Have you married?" he replied. "No, Maharaj, I am going to be." Then he asked me all the details, when, where, etc. He had in his hand a box of sandesh, and he opened it and said, "Take." I took one, but when he said, "Take one more," I demurred. "You take!" he insisted affectionately, from such a depth of sentiment. I can never forget it. After our marriage in Madhya Pradesh, my wife and I went together to make pranam to him. My wife had an M.A. in Hindi. "Go to the Library," he told us, "and in my name ask Mr. Bimalendu Majumdar (the Librarian) to take your wife on staff." It wasn't possible because my old mother was staying with me at the Institute staff quarters and needed looking after. But I was touched by Maharaj's suggestion and his concern for us.

I always sought his blessing for the major events in my life. After I completed twenty years of married life, I went again to make pranam in his room. He asked me, "Is there anything special?" and I told him, "Yes Maharaj, on the day I left for marriage I made pranam, and today I have completed twenty years so I felt I should come." Nothing was complete without his blessing.

That was in 1991, nearing the end. The last time I saw him was when he asked me to show around an American visitor. He gave detailed instructions, that I was first to take her out of the gate and from there to the main entrance, etc., and to explain to her in detail all about the Institute—ever the perfectionist.

Later, I attended his Memorial Lecture at the Birla Sabhaghar. I was seated near the back, among so many paying homage to the great monk who had touched our lives over many decades, and to whom we felt so close.

1962–63
(First visit to the United States)

BETTY ROBINSON

The first time I met Swami Nitya-swarup-ananda was during his trip to the United States in 1962, at the Ramakrishna-Vivekananda Center in New York, where he was staying with Swami Nikhilananda. I had heard that he had translated the *Ashtavakra Samhita*, the ultimate non-dualistic treatise, and I made a serious attempt to read it. Of course it was extremely difficult to understand, but years later, after the Swami himself presented me with a copy, I finally developed some kind of insight into its profundity. It was poetically beautiful and deeply moving.

One very amusing incident occurred during his stay at the Ramakrishna-Vivekananda Center. The assistant swami at that time gave lectures by reading from his notes, and although the visiting senior swamis seldom attended the evening classes by the assistant, Swami Nitya-swarup-ananda decided to do so. He sat by himself in the balcony with the rest of us downstairs. During the course of the lecture, we heard some gentle snores, but gradually this faint snoring became louder and louder to the point where the entire chapel eventually seemed to be reverberating with the snores. All were smiling discreetly, but the amazing thing was that this incident was remembered with the greatest happiness rather than any embarrassment because everything the Swami did had that childlike joy.

The summer of 1962, Swami Nitya-swarup-ananda went to Thousand Island Park, where the Ramakrishna-Vivekananda Center has its summer retreat. Swami Nikhilananda and Swami Aseshananda were both there to greet him. These three disciples of Holy Mother seemed just like boys together, full of fun, and full of sweet mischief. I remember one event where all three of them were quoting with booming voices from a high-powered Sanskrit scripture, going on and on from memory for more than half an hour, while the assistant swami (who was also present) fell far behind, much to his chagrin.

Often after dinner, at night in the Vivekananda Cottage, there would be an informal class. On one occasion, Swami Nitya-swarupananda was present and some of us asked him to give his reminiscences of Holy Mother. We begged and begged but he did not reply, just keeping silent. I had the feeling that his reverence for her was so great that he could not speak. Later at the Vedanta Society in New York during his 1987 trip, he gave a lecture, "How I Came to the Feet of Sri Ramakrishna," in which he told us his reminiscences of the Holy Mother. It was such a joy to hear this from him after all those years.

I recall an incident that was particularly helpful to me while Swami was at the Vedanta Society in New York. Right after his lecture, he went upstairs to answer any questions from the students. Swami Tathagatananda, his host, was encouraging us to go up and ask the Swami spiritual questions. I asked him a vague, general question, in response to which he replied, "Tell me, how many desires have you had since the last time I saw you in India?" This reply was like a shock treatment! It made me aware of how many-branched were my desires, and spurred me on to new disciplines. He put his finger on the problem instantaneously!

I saw Swami in India in the 1970s when I was staying at the Ramakrishna Mission Institute of Culture doing research on my doctorate. I felt his protective influence throughout my stay. He seemed aware of every detail. Later, I was astonished that he could remember even the smallest things.

Earlier, I had the opportunity to see the beautiful Christmas card which he had sent to Mrs. Max Beckmann, with whom I was staying in the late 1970s and early 1980s. He had known Mrs. Beckmann in America and also later in India, and they had great respect and affection for each other. In this particular card he had written that although she was

American, and he was in India, they were both Indians, the implication being that they were part of the same family. He went on to write that India was not just a geographical place but a set of values. He elaborated so beautifully what these values were, reflecting his deep love both culturally and spiritually for India. Because he, himself, loved India so much, he was able to include others as part of it. We always appreciated his broadness, and we never felt "different" in nationality from him, nor did his brethren here. His broad acceptance and his internationality remain deeply impressed on my mind.

Swami Nitya-swarup-ananda always spoke of the philosophy of Advaita, echoing Swami Vivekananda's belief that it would become the future religion of mankind. His entire personality reflected this expansive dimension of thought, bringing to mind the universality described by Shankaracharya: "The concept of the unity of Consciousness revolutionizes the relationship between the individual and the world," and, from the *Hymn to Annapurna,* "Parvati is my mother, Shiva is my father, Shiva's devotees are my friends, and all the three worlds are my native lands." Truly a world citizen, Swami Nitya-swarup-ananda was an exemplar wherever he went of the spirit of universal religion and the understanding of a universal heart.

WILLIAM CONRAD

When I first saw Swami Nitya-swarup-ananda in 1962, shortly after he arrived in New York, I caught a glimpse of him riding in the back seat of a devotee's Cadillac. My initial impression was that of a powerful man of great authority, someone who could overcome all obstacles; perhaps it was the expression of command on his face and the tilt of his head, capped by a stylish beret, which bespoke a firm self-control. Yes, this definitely was someone who could have founded a large and important cultural institution!

I saw Swami again six months later, following his tour of the United States with friends as a guest of the U.S. State Department. He was in the back of the same car, but on this occasion his face seemed relaxed to me; a calm almost childlike smile played on his lips. He still had his penetrating glance, but he was quick to laugh and a new aspect of this swami was revealed to me. Yes, his demeanor gave me the impression that here indeed was a man of the spirit.

Some twenty-five years later, Swami returned to America as the guest of the same two friends who had toured with him on his previous visit. We were all concerned about his health, given his age. There were several occasions when he was ill, which gave many of us at the Vedanta Society the opportunity to do personal service. I recall specifically the time I brought a flower arrangement to his room consisting of only two or three flowers in a small vase. Instead of being annoyed at such an offering, he said delightedly, "Oh, it is Japanese arrangement!" His graciousness made me feel very close to him.

It was a great privilege for me to participate in the initial taping of Swami's reminiscences, which eventually he gave in the form of a lecture at the Vedanta Society (and which were subsequently published as "How I Came to the Feet of Sri Ramakrishna"). He was not inclined to reminisce, and so this took considerable prompting. Once he started, however, he was like a locomotive going full speed! In the midst of this mighty flow of words, I would feel impelled to say, "But, Swami, is that relevant to the point?" or "But, Swami, can you give a concrete illustration?" I did this so often that he affectionately came to call me "Mr. But," a well-deserved nickname, I must admit.

One of my hopes was to hear his reminiscences of his initiation by Holy Mother. Naturally, this was a sensitive topic for him. He would acknowledge in a general sense the historical importance of initiation by Holy Mother, but he preferred not to speak of it in a personal sense. As a substitute, he told how Swami Brahmananda had instructed him while he was still a student. When pressed, he recounted that Maharaj had summarized spiritual life as *Ishwara vastu ar shahb avastu* (God alone is real, all else is unreal). He emphasized that Maharaj had not said "the world is unreal" but had added the watch words "sincerity, simplicity, truth," which were spoken in English. Swami said that these words

were almost as important to him as his initiation. He said that afterward
he could never deviate from truth. Then he smiled and asked, essentially, "Are you satisfied now?" I could "but" him no "buts."

These words he put into practice in his life. Surely his demand for
accuracy, his scrupulous attention to detail, and his vigorous devotion
to truth were like the protracted reverberation of a great gong struck
by a master hand.

In the spirit of Swami Nitya-swarup-ananda, I cannot keep from
adding a charming story he told on himself. Whenever he did anything
he paid attention to the smallest detail of the work. He said that when
the Institute of Culture was being built, he oversaw the design and
construction, and reconstruction, of every part. One day he overheard
a discussion at the Institute with the architect about some details of the
work in progress. Swami asked them, "What are you whispering
about?" They replied, "We won't tell you, because if we do you'll ask
for changes!" This was the impish sense of fun with which he could
deflate any pomposity, even at his own expense.

MOTHER SERAPHIMA

I remember when we first met Swami Nitya-swarup-ananda. It was in
1962 when he was in the United States as a guest of the United States
government, and he was busy all day long seeing important people.
Swami Pavitrananda, the Head of the Vedanta Society on West 71st
Street and one of his hosts in New York City, loved and respected him
enormously. He told us that what we didn't see of this charming and
energetic monk was the sadhu who rose at 3:00 A.M. for hours of meditation and japa before his busy day began.

JOHN SCHLENCK

I first met Swami Nitya-swarup-ananda in 1962. He stayed for several
days at our center, the Vedanta Society of New York, shortly after he
arrived in the United States. I remember him sitting next to Swami
Pavitrananda in our Vivekananda Room. Close devotees of our center

were invited to two question-and-answer sessions. He was very careful in answering questions. If he had the least doubt, he would first repeat the question as he had understood it, then ask, "Is this your question?" About Holy Mother he said that he had only met her a few times. When he was asked about Swami Brahmananda, he deferred to Swami Pavitrananda, who was a disciple of Swami Brahmananda. But about Swami Premananda he spoke at some length. He replied, "He was like a magnet. His love drew people like a magnet. He made no distinction between Hindus, Muslims, Christians or anybody else. Muslims regarded him as their own prophet." Swami Nitya-swarup-ananda felt that compartmentalizing life into spiritual and temporal was artificial, seeing life as *either* one or the other. He emphasized that we should try to see life as spiritual in everything we do.

On my first trip to India in 1971, I visited Swami Nitya-swarup-ananda at the Institute of Culture in Calcutta. I was interested to see the institution which embodied his life's work. I was newly on pilgrimage, staying at various ashramas and seeking a devotional atmosphere, so I was less receptive then to what seemed to me to be the relatively academic atmosphere at the Institute, though I could appreciate his achievement intellectually. I was struck by the large, free-form desk in his office. Sitting behind it as I faced him, he was a figure commanding respect. After asking me with genuine personal concern about the close members of our Vedanta Society, he posed two challenges. "Can you send us people with organization skill?" he asked first. "All these large centers you see here in India were built up on the initiative of individual men. There is no overall plan." His second challenge was: "You American devotees from all your centers should get together once or twice a year to discuss ways and means of expanding Vedanta work in the West." This was a revolutionary idea. We Western devotees had always deferred to the swamis in charge of our Vedanta centers in such matters. What could I reply? I said something to the effect that I was more interested in meditation and developing my spiritual life than in organizational matters. I don't remember exactly what he said, but the gist of it was that there was no conflict between the two.

On my third visit to India in 1982, I met the Swami at the Rama-krishna Mission in New Delhi. He was staying in the room at the end of the corridor on the ground floor of the monks' quarters. As I recall, he asked me what I thought of his book (an earlier version of *Education for Human Unity and World Civilization*). To be honest, I had always found his writing to be overly general, lacking specific concrete plans. My reply was similar to what I had said eleven years before: I was more interested in developing spiritual life. He rejoined rather impatiently, "You are still saying the same thing! Who is against meditation?"

On his second visit to the United States in 1987–88, Swami Nitya-swarup-ananda stayed much of the time with a close friend of mine in upstate New York. There, and also at our Vedanta Society in New York City, where the Swami was our guest for some time, I had a chance to get to know him more intimately. At the home of my friend, I stayed for several days on two occasions. On the first of these visits, the Swami asked me to read his book carefully and give him my honest reaction. He assured me that he wanted open, critical dialogue. This in itself was impressive, coming from a man of his standing. I found that although he argued his points vigorously, he never resented or dis-couraged honest disagreement.

He again took up the question of American responsibility for Vedanta work in America. He said, "These are *your* centers. They don't belong to the swamis. It is *your* responsibility to spread Vedanta in America." Like other swamis of the Ramakrishna Order, perhaps even more so, he emphasized principle before personality. His devo-tion to Ramakrishna and the Holy Mother was profound, but it was difficult to persuade him to speak about them. For him, Vedanta was universal and transpersonal. His great passion was to make the Vedan-tic vision relevant to all areas of human life. He would often quote Vivekananda, especially Swamiji's first letter to Nivedita: "My ideal . . .

is: to preach unto mankind their divinity and how to make it manifest in every movement of life." Then Swami Nitya-swarup-ananda would repeat, "how to make it manifest in every movement of life!"

After years of thought, I have concluded that he was right. I now see that there is no conflict between developing one's own spiritual life and thinking of ways to make Vedanta available to more people in the West. We Vedantists do have a responsibility for the growth of the movement in our own country. Those committed to Ramakrishna-Vivekananda idealism should work together and make long-range plans. And, above all, the Vedantic vision must be made relevant to all areas of human life. As Swami Nitya-swarup-ananda said, we should not compartmentalize, everything must be spiritualized.

ERIK JOHNS

When Swami Nitya-swarup-ananda first visited New York in 1962, my friend Jack Kelly and I were partners in a seasonal business. This proved most fortunate for us as it provided the opportunity to spend long stretches of time with the Swami, during which we were privileged to chauffeur him to many places in the eastern and midwestern parts of our country.

Those were halcyon days. How many facets of his knowledge and interest we found—how deep his appreciations and penetrating his criticisms! We were particularly intrigued by the Swami's broad application of Vivekananda's message, especially as expressed in the Ramakrishna Mission Institute of Culture. This great institution which has received worldwide recognition rounded out the Mission's works already developed along the philanthropic lines of schools, hospitals, and emergency relief. The Institute was clearly a step in the plan that Vivekananda had set forth. For Jack and me, all this was of great moment in 1962 as we saw the Swami meeting and sharing his ideas with prominent persons, from U Thant, then Secretary-General of the United Nations, to Supreme Court Justice Earl Warren.

The global outlook of humankind "as a whole" so imbued the
Swami that we could feel the fire of Vivekananda radiating through him
to us, and we were caught up in that fire. When the Swami returned to
India, he wrote to us as follows, dated April 23, 1963:

> Dear Erik and Jack:
>
> How to express how I miss you? I am always feeling a void on
> account of your absence. My life in the USA had been so inextricably
> linked up with you ever since I landed there. So often I referred to
> you to others as my umbrella. The bond of relationship was so
> marked that it could not escape others' notice. Swami Nikhilananda
> asked me what would happen to you after I left. Truly, I cannot
> express in words the depth of feeling I bear towards you. I shall ever
> remain indebted to you for all you have done for me. May you both
> prosper in life and find fulfilment and bliss and peace is my highest
> prayer to God....

In 1964, I was able to make a three-month pilgrimage to India. I was
deeply touched to find the Swami at the airport to greet me upon my
arrival. He took consummate pains to work out my travel plans in
India, always sensitive to my needs and interests. He guided me
through the Orissan temples, the Bengali museums and monuments,
and of course the places of pilgrimage connected with the *lila* [divine
life and play] of Sri Ramakrishna. At every turn he smoothed the way
for me, making the blessings I felt seem as natural as air. And though
many letters were written after I returned to the States, I was prepared
for the fact that the Swami's intense interaction with those in immediate contact would preclude him from being a regular correspondent.
Still, on March 20, 1965, he wrote the following:

> I must apologize for my long continued silence in spite of your many
> letters which are always lying before me. I do not need to tell you, par-
> ticularly, that this is due to my very bad habit of not writing letters and
> is in no way an indication of indifference. You have written me so many
> letters and I take this as "a tribute to your patience" with me which was
> the expression you applied to me in connection with sending the brass

pots [a reference to the packaging and shipping of altar items for the Vedanta Society of New York]....

You are very familiar with my way of thinking and I must say that you are one of the very few devotees I have met in America who are able to appreciate the universal application of the teachings of Sri Ramakrishna and Swami Vivekananda. You do understand how their teachings, if presented from the universal standpoint, can render most effective service to all sections of humanity. I firmly believe that this is the most vital need of the world today and that this has the potentiality of revolutionizing every aspect of thought in every stratum of society in every country of the world and lead all people to the consummation variously sought.

Since I sent you a copy of the scheme of the School of World Civilization I have developed it further and it has now assumed much better form. It has greater clarity and concrete suggestions for the studies. I am now showing it to various important people and inviting their comments, criticisms and suggestions. After some time I am thinking of having it printed so that I may send it out into the world....

I need not tell you or Jack how deeply dear to my heart both of you are. I shall never be able to forget what both of you have been to me. Please remember that you both always live in my memory. An intimate American friend while in India referred to us three as an inseparable group. I feel proud of this....

Aside from being humbled by his personal affection for us, we were glad to hear he was continuing to put into tangible written form the visionary plan Vivekananda had disclosed as a future project for the Mission. As we struggled to cope with the reality of a world locked in a Cold War threatening annihilation, we found hope in the Swami's optimism and fervor as through the years he planned for a school that would train scholars and thinkers in the context of global consciousness. Then in 1977 our teacher, Swami Pavitrananda, Head of the Vedanta Society of New York, died. The letter the Swami sent was our most valued consolation:

The news of the passing of my most respected and beloved brother Swami Pavitrananda has given me a rude shock. It has been most unexpected to me. The vacuum created in my mind by the Swami's passing will never be filled in. I bow to him today with my warmest love and devotion. May his soul find supreme fulfilment in absolute existence, absolute knowledge, and absolute bliss!

Swami Pavitrananda was a rare personality imbued with extraordinary ethical and spiritual virtues. You are all very fortunate indeed to have enjoyed spiritual relationship with him for so many years and served him so well. You are really blessed....

For some time we had offered to bring the Swami back to the United States for a second visit. He was now staying at the Belur Math, and though continuing to refine his ideas and publications, he was relatively free from the responsibilities of an official post. Still, his own health had received some setbacks, so Jack and I managed to extend a commercial trip to Japan and China and include a short stay in Calcutta. Dated December 19, 1978, Swami's letter welcomed us:

...I am now at the Mission's hospital in Calcutta undergoing treatment for some ailment including acute cough. I hope to be well within a week....

You know very well that I am fully possessed of one idea of Swamiji and that I have ever dedicated my thought, emotion, and acting to this and this alone. And this has been the solace of my life....

I wonder whether each of you has received a copy of *Human Unity and Education for World Civilization*.... This I did about a year ago when it was published. I enclose a copy of the latest folder which was published recently. I am now yearning to discuss the whole scheme with you both.

I am extremely happy to receive your letter of 2 December which has come to me just now. It was really so nice and generous of you to have thought of extending your trip for Japan to India. I shall join you the day you reach India and be with you till you leave. Kindly let me know your programme. I feel you will first land at Calcutta. If so, kindly let me know immediately so that I can make arrangements accordingly. You may include me in your holiday tour programme. Why have you made your India tour programme so short? Can you not extend it?

Our visit, lengthened at his suggestion, found the Swami in good health and able to "move" with us, as he would say. Our own feelings about the trip were echoed by Swami's in his letter dated February 22, 1979:

> It was indeed so kind and affectionate of you and Jack to remember me before you embarked on your way to China and to make it possible to visit India. I need hardly say that since my return from America in 1963 I have not been able to enjoy the amiable company of Jack and yourself in the way I did this time for full three weeks at a stretch from the time of your arrival till almost the hour of your departure. It was indeed a great opportunity you both gave me to enjoy ourselves in the fullest measure and in the friendliest and frankest possible manner. I shall never forget these days. I have been particularly happy because I am alive to the fact that my life and work have come to an end.... Please remember me to Swami Tathagatananda.... I fondly cherish the memory of the devotees of your Centre. Please give all of them my love and best wishes....

We continued to hope that Swami's health would stabilize and the trip to the U.S. would be possible. In the meantime, I was encouraged to attend the open convention that was held at the Belur Math at the end of 1980. No small part of this encouragement was the chance to see Swami again. But when we met, I realized that, aside from minor health problems, he was beginning to feel isolated. He began to look upon the day-to-day workings of the Math as warning signs for the future. He felt the frustration of sensing the purity of the early days under the guidance of the direct disciples slipping away as the Mission, beset by modern problems and constraints, resorted to what he perceived as commercialism and compromise. His letter of May 10, 1981, underscored his dissatisfactions:

I have your loving letter of 18 April which I expected much earlier. You created a void in me when you left India. I felt so happy as long as you were in this country but felt so sad in your absence. I was particularly unhappy as I could not make you feel absolutely at home with me here and could not entertain you in the least to my heart's desire. In fact I could not do anything whatsoever as I wished to.

You must have noticed that I feel completely out of tune with the present state of affairs.... Spirituality is rapidly becoming a commercial commodity.... To him [Swamiji] everything in the world could be given up for truth but truth could not be given up for anything whatsoever. He compared truth with a corrosive substance, which inevitably, though gently and slowly, makes its way even through granite. But alas! compromise now looms large for us for quick (or no?) results....

It seemed more important than ever that Swami be given a chance to benefit from a change of scene. We renewed our invitations. Soon, however, as his health improved, he started to work again on the clarification of his ideas and he brought out several publications as noted in his letter of October 31, 1984:

> ...In 1982–1983 I spent most of my time in Delhi and Kankhal. I worked on the revision of *Human Unity and Education for World Civilization* and made the second edition ready with many additions and alterations. This has been done at the instance of the Government of India (Education Ministry) which has decided to publish it as Government's own publication and thus ensure its wider circulation. Besides, I made two other brochures ready for publication. One is called *India's Message to Herself and to the World* and the other is called *The World Civilization Centre* (revised and enlarged second edition)....
>
> Now that I am all right I have decided to go to Delhi and complete my unfinished work. I shall submit to the Government the manuscript of *Education for Human Unity and World Civilization* (as it has been now renamed) and arrange for the distribution of the brochures. All this I shall complete before the end of December....

And in the same letter he gave us hope with the following news:

> As I mentioned before, I shall be absolutely free after December.
> When is the best time to visit... and for how long should I be there?

Our joy was mitigated by a letter in March 1985 advising us of the death of Swami Vireswarananda and also fluctuations in Swami Nitya-swarup-ananda's own health:

> Swami Vireswarananda, President of our Order passed away on 13 March at 3:17 pm. He was 93. His body was kept in a spacious room till 14 March. As the news spread through the different media and news broadcasts over radio and television the same night and published in newspapers the next morning, streams of thousands of disciples, devotees, and friends started pouring in at the Belur Math from the evening of 13 March. His body was cremated on the 14th at 1 pm behind Swami Vivekananda's Temple at the spot set apart for the cremation of the Presidents of the Order. It is estimated that between 75,000 and 100,000 persons came to pay their last homage to the Swami. The President of India, the Prime Minister of India and the Chief Minister of West Bengal offered their respects to the memory of the President of the Order by sending special floral wreaths. Special puja and bhandara will be held at the Belur Math on the 13th day, 25 March. About 40,000 devotees are expected to participate in the function and have prasad....
>
> In my last letter I informed you that after treatment in Calcutta I came back to the Math on 29 September, 1984 and was feeling quite well. But unfortunately I again fell ill and was under treatment in Calcutta from 15 November to 28 February. I came back to the Math on 1 March. I am keeping well but I am still very weak.

Despite weakness the Swami managed a trip to Delhi in April to complete work on his book and still planned a trip to the States. The letter was dated May 6, 1985:

> Your Easter Sunday April letter (redirected from Belur Math) over-whelmed me. I am caught in my own trap. My health permitting (I am still very weak), I shall make the trip. I am accordingly dropping

my plans for spending the summer at the Lucknow Ashrama's Retreat near the Naini Tal hills.

I am trying to complete my work at Delhi and return to Belur Math by the middle of May. I hope to make travel arrangements and get ready for departure by the first week of June....

...I showed your letter of 7 April to Swami Hiranmayananda who was at Delhi at the time. He is the present general secretary of the Math and Mission. He told me that there would be no objection if the doctors approved of my proposed journey. On 11 May, I came to the Math and on 13 May, I came here at the Institute to make preparations for the journey....

I then saw my doctors—a cardiologist (regarded as topmost in Calcutta) and a general physician (of the Mission's Seva Pratishthan). I have been under their regular treatment for a long time. They examined me. Though recently I badly suffered from bronchial cough and asthma, I do not have any trouble now except weakness. The two doctors consulted together and gave in writing their opinion "that Maharaj (myself) should not undertake the strenuous journey considering his state of health." I immediately sent to you a telegram (15 May) which read: "Doctors' opinion against my undertaking proposed journey. My plans dropped. Do not send ticket."

He went on in the letter to tell how he had tried to convince the doctors that he would be well taken care of in America but to no avail, and added, "My long-cherished dream is dashed." Our plan to receive the Swami in America also seemed doomed. But we took heart from the postscriptum (in longhand) from which we deduced that bodily weakness had not daunted the Swami's spirit: "P.S. Please excuse me for sending this letter typed in a most ugly manner. You may guess under what circumstances I am now living. I do not think have sent any letter like this in my whole life."

Then a year later in June 1986 a letter came to Jack—

...Have faith in yourself with the firm belief that the blessings of Swamiji attend you for ever and ever. This faith will work as an eternal source from which will flow continuous power expressing itself in innumerable forms of service....

—and ended with:

I have written a long letter to Erik which will give you all my news and *big surprise*. I am keeping much better health now.

The surprise was of course that the doctors had finally approved of his making the journey. However, another obstacle surfaced in the letter of October 7, 1986:

...On the 10th of last month three sample copies of the completed book [*Education for Human Unity and World Civilization*] were given to me. I was deeply shocked when I went through it. There were many errors. I could never have imagined that the book would come out in the form it did. As I was possessed by a ghost which compelled me under any circumstances to see it through in some presentable form, I have suffered hell all these days, and my plans to visit you and Erik have been completely frustrated....

The next step for me will be to have the book printed by a very good publisher in a fitting manner and thus complete my humble mission in life. The rest may take care of itself. The experience of human nature I have had during this period has done me much good and bids fair to do me more good in future.

Now after all this, when I shall be able to leave Delhi I do not know as yet. I shall try to keep you informed of what happens and what I shall be able to do....

All of us who know of Swami Nitya-swarup-ananda's fastidious attention to the details of perfection will understand his pain and unhappiness in connection with the production of his book. But he managed to stay with the project during that winter, completing it to his satisfaction, and by May 19, 1987, he was able to send the following short letter:

In response to my letter to the General Secretary of the Math, the Trustees at their meeting yesterday approved my visit to the USA.

I am now having my passport renewed and visa granted. As soon as I get them I start and meet you.

I shall keep you informed about the day-to-day progress of my arrangements.

Prayers were answered. There were no further complications and Swami Nitya-swarup-ananda arrived in New York in June of 1987. With no serious problems of health, he spent fourteen months traveling in the United States, visiting most of the Vedanta centers, accepting speaking engagements to present his ideas and making contacts with many notable thinkers and professionals who could admire his global vision; they received his book with respect and reverence.

For Jack and me, besides being the long-awaited fulfillment of a fervent desire, it was a renewal of spiritual enthusiasm and outlook, as it was for other friends, old and new, whose lives he touched.

Then, not a year after Swami returned to India, Jack died suddenly. There was immeasurable solace for me in Swami's words dated August 13, 1989, 10 P.M.:

I was waiting and waiting, and waiting for details of the saddest news you gave me through the telephone messenger.... In the meantime I remained in constant suspense, thinking and thinking, and thinking of Jack. I cannot think of any other person who looked upon me as dearly as his own as Jack did. But my criminal habit (as Swami Pavitrananda described it) of not responding to his letters now pains me very deeply. But it is too late for me to make good my misdeed which I myself will never be able to forgive. It is very difficult for me to restrain my tears when I think and feel that Jack is no more. While writing this letter, tears are rolling down my cheeks and my throat is choked. Oh Jack, shall I not see you again? Why have you left me behind? I feel so guilty to you. I beg you with folded hands to forgive me. I have proved myself so ungrateful to you. Nobody in the world has done for me what you have done and in the way you have done. I felt that you kept me under your arms as long as I was there. But that America has now vanished for me. To me Jack was America and America was Jack....

My heartfelt prayers to Sri Ramakrishna and Holy Mother that they may draw their loving child Jack to their feet for eternal rest and bliss.

I do not find words to console you in your bereavement. I wish I were with you at this time to be of any service whatsoever. May Sri Ramakrishna and Holy Mother give you all strength to get over all difficulties.

A "P.S." at the end of his letter began, "My physical condition is very bad" and went on to list various problems. And so, the next year, 1990, I made a pilgrimage to India, mostly to meet again with Swami Nitya-swarup-ananda.

His movements were now curtailed and his strength failing, but it did not keep him from providing many comforts during my stay. We were able to make a pilgrimage to Cossipore Garden together, spending some precious moments in Thakur's room.

When the time came for me to go, he insisted on taking me to the airport. He must have felt as he kept waving as much as I did, that we would not meet again in this life. And yet his mind was then, as it remained to his death, as sharp and clear and loving as when we had first met so many years ago.

JOAN FOX

I first met Swami Nitya-swarup-ananda when he came to the Vedanta Society in Portland, Oregon, in 1963. I still recall three statements from that visit which affected me profoundly. When the Swami was asked, "What is the greatest hindrance to spiritual life," he immediately replied, "Self-deception, self-deception is the greatest obstacle in spiritual life." The second lesson was his explanation that India's contribution to the world is the science of the soul. The third statement instilled confidence: "Don't worry or concern yourself with things you don't understand; work with the understanding you already possess and the rest will come."

During Swami Nitya-swarup-ananda's 1987 visit to America, he again came to the Vedanta Society of Portland, perhaps expressly to

see Swami Aseshananda, but we were all blessed with his holy company for three glorious weeks. He and Swami Aseshananda came to
the foyer every midday after the worship, and every evening after *arati*
to listen to the reading of *The Gospel of Sri Ramakrishna* and to answer
the questions of devotees. Seeing these two disciples of Holy Mother
together, and being in their company day after day, was a bright and
unforgettable experience.

Swami Nitya-swarup-ananda marvelled amusedly, on certain occasions, at the apparent disregard for time at the Portland Society. A
clock was diligently and strategically placed for all to see during the
readings, but even so the evening question-and-answer sessions went
on for a very long time before the residents of the Temple sat for their
evening meal. Since it was a fairly large clock, it could hardly go unnoticed. Finally, one evening Swami Nitya-swarup-ananda laughingly
said, pointing to the clock: "What is that for?"

Holy Mother's birthday was observed during Swami Nitya-swarup-
ananda's visit, with Swami Aseshananda performing the *puja* and *homa*
[sacred fire] ceremonies. Many devotees were present that day, and
after the worship everyone sat to take *prasad*. Swami Nitya-swarup-
ananda was seated at the head of one of the tables set up for that purpose. Certain of the devotees had the responsibility of serving the
prasad, the writer included, so we were all very busy. Suddenly, Swami
Aseshananda called my name, and when I turned to him he said, "Sit
there now," pointing to the chair just to the right of Swami Nitya-
swarup-ananda. It was then I realized that a silent wish of mine had
just been fulfilled, the opportunity to talk quietly with Swami Nitya-
swarup-ananda, however briefly, to receive his explanation of some
incidents relating to the Holy Mother. Writing this, I am once again
captivated by those precious moments. He graciously answered my
questions, elaborating and expanding until, I believe, he was satisfied
that I understood. At length, and by way of summary, he said: "That
was her life, these things happened, it is a fact, that's all. Read everything there is of Holy Mother. To understand Sri Ramakrishna, read

everything there is of Swami Vivekananda, read about Sri Ramakrishna. Then you will never have to ask another question." He also
said to me on that occasion, so helpful, "Depend on no one—ever."

It was characteristic that almost every time someone asked him a
question he would initially respond by saying, "Why do you ask that
question?" Then it was incumbent upon that person to explain to the
Swami why he or she was asking that particular question. The result of
this approach will be obvious to the reader. I remember Swami Aseshananda saying: "A good question is one that comes from the heart."

Later, after everyone had partaken of *prasad* and everything had
been put away, I came down the hall and there in the library sat Swami
Nitya-swarup-ananda talking with a few devotees. As I joined the
group I realized he was talking about the practical implementation of
Vedanta. "If you are truly living Vedanta," he was emphasizing, "you
will not even have to say anything about it. Those with whom you
come in contact will see it, sensing that there is something worthwhile
happening in your life and will be silently influenced by that. Just live
the life." He talked a long time on this theme, and listening to him one
felt the mind being propelled beyond its current capacity in order to
absorb what he had to say. One was infused with a renewed sense of
purpose, direction, and commitment, wishing with all the heart for the
strength and dedicated love to help fulfil his dream for us ("us" meaning not only the relatively small group before him but, in his vision, all
the inhabitants of a spiritually united world).

The evening before his departure from Portland, he appeared to me
to be in a very exalted state. He seemed much more indrawn and was
listening intently to the reading of *The Gospel of Sri Ramakrishna*,
leaning slightly forward in his chair, eyes closed, repeating softly every
now and then, over and over, "Always remember, you have a Mother.
Always remember, you have a Mother."

SWAMI YOGESHANANDA

I had a number of encounters with Swami Nitya-swarup-ananda over a period of many years, all of them brief, but none forgettable.

The first time was in the Church of Universal Philosophy and Religion in Sacramento, California (later the Vedanta Society of Sacramento), when he was making his first visit to the West, and the Sacramento center was under construction. Swami Ashokananda and he had been friends at Mayavati, and the former used to tell us that up there in the mountains it was he who had insisted that Swami Nitya-swarup-ananda translate the *Ashtavakra Samhita* into English. He had pleaded no intellectual talents of this kind, but Swami Ashokananda would not let him go.

A part of the "package" of Swami Nitya-swarup-ananda's visit to see his old friend, Swami Ashokananda, was to survey the new work going on in Sacramento. We of the monastery were not far along in the construction of the Temple, and Sunday services were still held in the foyer, a small anteroom of what would become the future chapel. It was here that Swami Nitya-swarup-ananda was asked to give his discourse. Anticipation was keen because it was well known that he usually did not give lectures, hardly ever. How had he been persuaded to speak to the Sacramento congregation? Was it Swami Ashokananda, that same arm-twister of old? Perhaps not. I suspect that Swami Shraddhananda, the resident Minister, had soothed him with words such as "very few will be present, you have come such a long way, please give them something," and so forth.

So he began. Impressive in size, and very dignified in speech and bearing, he spoke eloquently for a brief time. Then, lo and behold, he turned toward the photographs of Sri Ramakrishna and others which were set into the temporary shrine, and utterly broke down. With big tears rolling down his cheeks, he could barely carry on: "When I look at these pictures, sitting here so many miles away from India and think what that means … ," his voice almost trailed off into sobs, and soon he gave up and sat down.

Another aspect of Swami's personality was revealed during this visit in his intimate talks with monastery members and devotees, in which he emphasized the impersonal, and cautioned against the idolizing, self-indulgent emotionalism of bhakti-groupies.

During my stay in India, from 1965 to 1968, I caught many glimpses of him. He would come to Narendrapur often, and was always in the company of its Head, Swami Lokeswarananda, with whom he seemed very friendly. They could be seen together at all sorts of functions, such as athletic events, musical concerts, public meetings, and festivals. Swami Nitya-swarup-ananda never spoke publicly or made himself prominent, but rather seemed to be giving moral support to his younger friend. I believe that on some occasions he stayed overnight in the Guest House. When he moved to the New Delhi Ashrama, I visited him there also. In his large room at the end of the hall he would talk to me about the Western work, and he would also ask me questions. This was the Swami's wonderful quality, that he did not make you feel like an ear on the wall, something to be talked *at;* he was genuinely interested in where you were coming from, both geographically and ideologically.

He spoke mostly of what he felt was the mistake being made by the Heads of Western centers: the ingrownness, the too-limited vision, the lack of universality of appeal in the lectures, and the tendency to form little mutual-admiration societies. Yet he did all this in a bubbling, piquantly humorous way. At that time, I had to care about my proprieties since I was an aspirant for the taking of sannyasa vows, and I was also heavily under the influence of some of the swamis he was talking about, so I may not then have altogether appreciated the drift of his thought.

While stationed at the Vedanta Centre in London, I made a trip back to India in 1970. When I visited the Advaita Ashrama in Calcutta, I found Swami Nitya-swarup-ananda among those who were staying there, perhaps as a temporary guest. He recognized me, recalling our Narendrapur talks. He had heard about the new mansion in Holland Park that had recently been given to the London Centre, and he was curious to hear all about it. His fascination with detail astonished me. I was expected to give him a room-by-room tour in words. He sat cross-legged on his bedstead and I in a chair close by (he wouldn't have me on the floor), and he asked question after question. What is on the ground floor? Who all are living there now? Gradually I suspected that he was using this rather prosaic checklist to induce sleepiness. And sure enough, in a little while the eyelids became heavy. It would have made *me* sleepy at that hour of the day, typically India's siesta time. Suddenly Swami said, "Now finish quickly, because very soon I shall be off in the other world." He lay flat and was not long in falling asleep, but that did not let me go, for just before he had advised, "Go on telling me about it." All who knew him will surely recognize this playfulness with which he charmed us.

Our next meeting took place in England, at the London Centre, and although I cannot date it, it must have been on his way to, or from, India. I accompanied him in a car on a trip out into the countryside to see "typical English villages." His interest extended to small details and he was obviously enjoying himself. He wanted to know the history of things. What I remember most vividly, and it is an indelible picture in my mind, is the time he went into one of the many shops we saw and asked the attendant for something. Regretfully, she could not produce it (I forget now what it was), but what lingers in my mind is the way in which he spoke to her—so affectionate, so intimate in manner and with jollity, as if they had been dealing with each other for years. I do not think I have ever seen another swami display such ease and tenderness with a total stranger. Evidently he had taken very much to heart Holy Mother's injunction to "make everyone your own."

He was not at all well even at that time. At our final encounter in 1987 during the Vedanta Convention at the Vivekananda Monastery in Ganges, Michigan, it was evident that he could not last many years longer. Yet the stamina and vitality of the man was proven by his going on into his nineties, and this despite his large bulk. Rarely, we know, do such builds attain these years. Although he had always voiced strong opinions about the work of the Order, and especially about what he felt was ineptness in dealing with Westerners, this time he was on his high horse. He continued to sound one note through all the speeches and discussion of the Convention: Go back to Swamiji. He made it clear that he felt Swami Vivekananda's mission had been lost in provincialism, Hindu chauvinism, and devotional smugness, and he railed against this. By this time I had sufficient experience of my own to feel *en rapport*, and I silently championed his courage. And I must say, whatever the radicalism of his pronouncements, they were usually delivered in a gentlemanly, dignified, almost affectionately pleading manner.

The last conversation I had with him in the Ganges Monastery is one I remember well. He scoffed at the term "comparative religion." "I do not understand all this about dialogue among 'religions,'" he said, "there is only one religion throughout the world." I did not understand just what he meant, and had no time to ask. Probably he was alluding to the idea of Swami Vivekananda which he so often quoted: "Mankind ought to be taught that religions are but the varied expressions of THE RELIGION which is ONENESS, so that each may choose the path that suits him best."

Numerous were the dicta which Swami Nitya-swarup-ananda gave out, precious gems for our day and our future. Thank you for giving me this opportunity to honor his memory.

1964–69
(Back in India)

SANKARI PRASAD BASU*

I do not remember exactly when I first met Chintaharan Maharaj, but it was during my early college days, sometime after 1944. It began as a casual acquaintance. I used to go with Badalda (Mrigendranath Mukherji) to meet him when he was Secretary of the Institute of Culture at Wellington Square, and later on at Russa Road. Badalda, I should explain, was in a real sense a sannyasin, though formally he did not wear gerua cloth, and he was one of the main founders of the Howrah Vivekananda Institution and Ramakrishna Vivekananda Ashrama. He was a gifted singer, endowed with an exceptionally melodic voice, adored for his devotional songs, and was invariably asked to sing the opening and closing songs of all the big meetings held at the Math. He was a disciple of Mahapurush Maharaj, who had experienced samadhi while listening to him sing. Badalda was handsome and graceful, with a sweet smile, and his benign personality was characterized by modest behaviour. All the monks of the Order, young and old alike, treated him with love and respect, and his requests were seldom turned down. Chintaharan Maharaj also treated him graciously. It should be remembered that Chintaharan Maharaj was a great worker and very particular about the value of time, yet he always spared time for Badalda and never let him go without offering him food.

Chintaharan Maharaj had a strong physique, rather stout, and a voice that was deep, resonant, and sweet. His statements were always clear-cut and forthright, without unnecessary emotionality. His personality had a hypnotic quality. Such a man could not but attract me, but as a youth of sixteen coming from a lower-middle-class family, I was no less attracted by the sumptuous breakfast spread, comprising buttered toast, eggs, fruits, sweets, etc. Over the years I noticed that Chintaharan Maharaj never neglected the matter of eating. Even when he was in his nineties, one would see him at the monks' dining hall of the Institute at Gol Park with his napkin tied round his neck, still able to appreciate a multicourse meal, comparable to a multiorchestrated concert. He was a connoisseur of food in the truest sense of the term, giving each and every item of food its due value. He never rushed his meals, and because he had a sophisticated taste he would point out the good and bad points without hesitation. His culinary exploits during his younger days in the company of his brother monks have now become a legend. His feats at that time seemed heroic, as if he was a warrior stocking up energy before marching into battle. Yes, he was a great fighter, fighting his life's battle, the life which he dedicated to the cause of Swami Vivekananda.

Getting back to the point, the reason I used to go to Chintaharan Maharaj with Badalda was to make arrangements for speakers and chairpersons for the various functions which were to be held at the School or the Ashrama. He readily used to help us out. I found that he was acquainted with most of the cream of Calcutta, and no one ever turned down his request. As a result of this we were able to get many famous people to come to our Ashrama situated in a remote part of Howrah town.

I may be wrong, but I feel that Chintaharan Maharaj became well known to the public when the Institute's fame was spreading at Russa Road, and when *The Cultural Heritage of India* he was publishing was gaining wide acceptance as a major work. The Institute at Russa Road became one of the nerve centres of cultural life in Calcutta. Dr. Tripurari Chakravarti's discourses on the *Mahabharata* drew a big crowd, and Swami Nitya-swarup-ananda even managed to get someone as austere and erudite as Swami Omkarananda to give regular classes on the Upanishads. A list of all the people who delivered lectures at the Institute in those days would have included the names of the most famous personalities and scholars from all over the world. And as for the illustrious team of editors and writers for *The Cultural Heritage of India*—one wonders how it was possible to gather all these precious gems together; we have been told that it was Chintaharan Maharaj who accomplished this difficult task.

Chintaharan Maharaj was no doubt an Indian monk, but a monk of a different type. His India was ever for expansion ("Expansion is life and contraction is death," had said the great Vivekananda); thus, in some of his tastes and methods he favoured Western ways. For example, he kept a sharp eye on discipline and was extremely particular about keeping time. I remember Dr. Shashi Bhusan Dasgupta's remarks to me in this regard. I had gone to see the ailing Dr. Dasgupta at the Department of Tropical Diseases at the College of Medicine. It was late afternoon. Outside the light was fading. He was seated on a chair at the spacious veranda—so scholarly, humble, calm, cool, collected, self-disciplined—he belonged to the ancient tradition of teachers of India. Unaware of the fatal cancer which was consuming his body, he was busy making plans for the future. And thus came up the topic of the lecture series he was to deliver at the Institute. He spoke about Chintaharan Maharaj for quite some time with great reverence and respect. I remember two of his comments. He said, "I have not seen such punctuality in this country like that of the Institute. The car would pick me up and drop me back at the exact stipulated hour. The meetings would commence and end exactly at the scheduled time— here would never be any deviation. Swami Nitya-swarup-ananda's clock would never err." He further said, "I feel Chintaharan Maharaj is acquainted with each and every brick of that huge building at Gol Park. Perhaps his flesh and blood is mingled with the mortar that binds the bricks together."

The Institute of Culture at Gol Park is the abode of Swami Nitya-swarup-ananda's *sadhana* and *siddhi* [fruit of *sadhana*]. He had a dream and because he was a great worker he could realize his dream. Although Ramakrishna and Vivekananda were born in Bengal, he felt they belonged to the whole world, and the whole world had to become united with their ideal. The Mission has set up many centres from which the services of health, education, and spirituality flow to rich and poor alike. But the Ramakrishna Mission had more to accomplish, because Swami Vivekananda had the vision that there should be a meeting of East and West, places where the accumulated wisdom of mankind could be transmitted. Swami Nitya-swarup-ananda was inspired with this idea and he thought of a centre in which a world-body would be created, carrying through its veins and nerves the entirety of mankind's cultural heritage. Swami Nitya-swarup-ananda was the man to give it shape. And he stepped in. The Ramakrishna Mission Institute of Culture was created. There was a storm of criticism that Nitya-swarup-ananda had "built a palace," had "made a hotel," but he remained firm in his conviction that what seemed like a huge palace today would in the future seem tiny, because the wings of Ramakrishna Paramahamsa were ever spreading and the number of people seeking their shelter would never cease to expand.

Because this is a memoir there is bound to be some personal allusion. Here I will acknowledge with great reverence that I am deeply indebted to Swami Nitya-swarup-ananda for my research work on Swami Vivekananda. Furthermore, he practically took me by the hand and introduced me to the intellectual society of Calcutta as a speaker on Swami Vivekananda. It happened as follows:

I was present at a meeting at Howrah Ramakrishna Vivekananda Ashrama in April or May of 1969 as a volunteer. At dusk, a small black Austin car entered and Swami Nitya-swarup-ananda got down, looking for me. He had gone to my house, and not finding me there, had come to the Ashrama. He began talking to me without even sitting down, saying, "I have heard that you are doing some research work on Swamiji. How far have you progressed?" I said, "A bit—a huge book called *Vivekananda in Indian Newspapers* is being published. It has been jointly edited by Mr. Sunil Bihari Ghosh and myself." He asked me, "Have you got any new information about Swamiji?" I said, "Plenty." Then, "Are you thinking of writing something based on all these materials?" "Yes." "That's good. You come and deliver a series of lectures at the Institute on all this." I was very surprised. Not that I was unused to lecturing, it's my profession, but lecturing at the Institute! Good heavens! Now, thirty-seven years later, it is impossible to explain what it meant in those days to lecture at the Institute. Scholars from all over the world came there to lecture, the newspapers regularly published reports of these lectures (then the newspapers had a different character), and the Calcutta intellectuals used to keep a sharp eye on the content of those talks. Giving a lecture at the Institute was like being knighted into intellectual royalty. I said, "Give me some time, let me get prepared, let me finish writing the first draft of the book." Maharaj said, "All right, you give a lecture after six months, and see how it goes, and then start your lecture series." After this, he immediately left the place without talking to anyone else. He was a busy man.

I took some time to recover and stood there thinking, "A few years back I used to go to him with Badalda to arrange for speakers, and today he has come to ask me to speak"—the famous Swami Nitya-swarup-ananda, the Founder-Secretary of the Ramakrishna Mission Institute of Culture, he had come looking for me just because he had come to know that such-and-such person has found out hitherto unknown information about Swami Vivekananda. I realized the extent of his devotion for Swamiji and the intensity of his desire to see Swamiji in a new perspective. Here it was not important who the speaker was; it was the novelty of the content which was his concern.

I had given my first lecture on November 27, 1969. On May 18, 1970, there was a function at the Institute on the occasion of the publication of *Vivekananda in Indian Newspapers*, with Dr. Satyendranath Sen, the Vice-Chancellor of Calcutta University, presiding. (The book took seven long years to come out of the press, for various reasons. But for the sustained efforts of its publisher, the late Janaki Nath Basu, it could not have seen the light of day.) Soon after that, my weekly lectures started and continued for one and a half years. I was accompanied by Mr. Bimal Kumar Ghosh, my close associate in Swamiji's research work (who is presently the Secretary of the Howrah Rama-krishna Vivekananda Ashrama).

Maharaj was frequently present at my lectures. One day he sent for me. He handed me a packet of letters and said, "Read at least one of them." I did, and found that a particular professor had raised a serious objection about one part of my lecture, accusing me of misrepresenting a Brahmo group and its leaders. The other letters were in the same vein. Maharaj asked me, "Have you got anything to say on this?" I replied, "I can do one thing—instead of going into confrontation, I can stop my lectures. Or, I can publicly refute these allegations." Maharaj said, "There is no question of stopping the lectures. You adopt the second course of action." And that's what I did.

While the lectures were going on, Maharaj again called me one day and said, "Is it possible for you to do further research work on Swamiji?" I said, "It is." Then he asked, "What are the factors which make it impossible for you to carry on?" I answered simply, "Money."

Maharaj knit his brows, looking thoughtful. "So much money is being spent on so many things," he said, "and you mean to say you won't get money to do your research? How have you been carrying on so far?" "Mainly by spending from my own pocket," I told him, "but this is no longer possible, all the more so because now I would need to tour all over India; Swamiji created a wave in South India and it would be necessary to collect all that information, and I would also have to complete the work that I have started in West India." "Also," I added, "it is not possible for me to accomplish it alone, I would need assistance." Maharaj listened to me quietly and said, "Suppose we get you the money. Will you go?" I said, "Yes, but in six months, I am not free before that." He said, "Let us see. I have a feeling you *will have* to go."

Two or three months elapsed following that conversation. I was continuing my talks at the Institute and was seeing Maharaj regularly, but he didn't bring the subject up again. I was becoming impatient and restless, being so keen to collect more information on Swamiji, and also because my departure plans could only be accommodated within a limited time frame and needed some advance preparation. Bharat Maharaj had also come to know about this and kept asking me, "When are you leaving?" to which I had to reply repeatedly, "I don't know."

Then one Monday evening after my lecture Maharaj sent for me. He told me, "Come to the Institute at 8:00 A.M. on such-and-such a day and have breakfast with me." He didn't mention the reason. I agreed to come. I went to see him, had a good breakfast. Then Maharaj asked someone to bring a book. I saw that it was none other than the volume I had co-edited, *Vivekananda in Indian Newspapers*. He picked up the book and said, "Come, let us go." I was still totally in the dark. The car entered a narrow road and stopped in front of a house. I had been to this house in Bipin Pal Road once or twice before. It was the house of Dr. Ramesh Chandra Majumdar. We went upstairs and took our seats in the drawing room. Shortly thereafter, Dr. Majumdar entered the room and Maharaj introduced me and said, "I was talking about this person." Then he handed over the book and said, "This is the book."

Dr. Majumdar looked at the book carefully, turning the pages, and said, "Good! Well done! I had also wanted to do something like this, but somehow couldn't do it." Then he started talking about the influence of Swamiji on the freedom fighters. While writing the history of the freedom movement, he had seen two huge files on the Ramakrishna Mission marked "Strictly Confidential" in the Delhi archives. He wondered whether they were still there.

Then, with enthusiasm, Dr. Majumdar started talking about a discovery he had made: "I have gathered a piece of information on Swamiji from a New York newspaper which has not been published anywhere as yet—I have published it in my book. I will show you the book." He brought the book from inside and showed me the relevant passage. I was already aware of this and of his claim on this. I told him, "This passage had been published long back in the *Indian Mirror*." Dr. Majumdar asked with surprise, "Is that so?" I said, "Yes sir. Just see this passage in our book." Dr. Majumdar carefully compared the bit published in our book from the *Indian Mirror* and his own book, and said, "Yes, now I see." Then he said to Maharaj, "All right, we will talk about it later on." The expression on Maharaj's face revealed that he was feeling both relieved and happy.

On the way back, Chintaharan Maharaj discussed the episode with me briefly. It seems that when Maharaj had put up the proposal of bearing my travel expense to the Governing Body of the Institute, Dr. Majumdar had objected. His view had been that there was no point in spending money on an unknown researcher of uncertain capability ("Who is he? What are his credentials? No, no, I cannot say 'yes' to this proposal"). Since Dr. Majumdar was very influential, particularly in the field of research, it was almost impossible to override his opinion. So the proposal had been turned down. Maharaj was deeply hurt. His affection for me and faith in me, and his dreams of new research on Swami Vivekananda—in view of all these factors, Dr. Majumdar's rejection had been a jolt. That is why he had taken me straight to Dr. Majumdar.

After this meeting, he asked me to come to the Institute one evening. As usual, he didn't give any reason. He called me into his office. When I entered I realized that the meeting of the Governing Body was taking place. Many eminent people were present, including Dr. Majumdar. As far as I can remember, Dr. Suniti Kumar Chatterji and Swami Lokeswarananda were also there. As soon as I appeared Dr. Majumdar said, "I was just talking about him," and then he began to lavish praise on my research work related to the book. What he said next made me realize to what extent the historian is committed to truth. He confessed, "I became afflicted with pride after discovering a newspaper report on Swamiji in New York, completely unaware that these people had already unearthed not only this report but a host of other new information. That is why I had raised an objection to bearing their travel expenses." When Dr. Majumdar finished speaking, Maharaj had a bright expression on his face as he turned to me and said, "Now you may go."

The Institute bore most of my expenses as I started my research travels on October 3, 1971. It took me seven months to complete the tour from the southernmost tip of India to Baroda in West India. The university authorities had granted me study leave, and the Vice-Chancellor, Dr. Satyendranath Sen, had been most helpful in this respect. My companions at different stages were Bimal Kumar Ghosh, Lakshmi Kanta Boral (who had borne his own expenses), and Biswanath Basu. And my wife, Maya Basu, was in our group for most of the journey, helping our research. The huge amount of information which I had collected was used in my seven-volume Bengali book, *Vivekananda O Samakaleen Bharatvarsha*. (The material accumulated during this time is being published by the Ramakrishna Mission Institute of Culture in several volumes, of which the first, *Swami Vivekananda in Contemporary Indian News*, Volume 1, came out recently in 1997. At the behest of the present Secretary, Swami Lokeswarananda, the Institute agreed to undertake this project.) But here I will admit without any hesitation that if Swami Nitya-swarup-ananda had not taken the initiative, those research travels would not have taken place and my subsequent books and articles on Swamiji would not have been so enriched with facts.

I kept visiting Swami Nitya-swarup-ananda on a regular basis. He was always anxious for further research on Swamiji, and encouraged me to do more of it. Towards the end, I found him at times depressed and at times agitated about the moral decline of West Bengal and India, and the lack of public outcry over an all-round state of degradation. He used to cry out in agony, "What has happened to Swamiji's Bharatvarsha [India]—why aren't you doing anything about it?" He was, of course, aware of individual limitations, but this was his way of expressing his internal anguish. And at times he would be possessed by a big dream. Then it would no longer be Swamiji's Bharatvarsha, but Swamiji's *world*. Swami Nitya-swarup-ananda would then become a global citizen of the new world order of which Swamiji was the centrepiece. This world had not yet been born, it was yet to be, but it had to be accomplished, he knew, for Swamiji's advent could never remain unfulfilled. With the progress of science, he used to say, men were being brought closer physically, but mentally were many miles apart; they were becoming more and more dehumanized, the slaves of machines. The only way to reestablish human contact would be to inundate the world with Swamiji's consciousness, and in that united world, Vivekananda would be the sun shedding life and light to all. He used to literally catch hold of us and say these things to us. We used to feel restless and sad, for we thought that Maharaj was in a dream state, unable to see that the world had fragmented, had become so devoid of joy and moral judgement that it had rejected its Prophet, Vivekananda. Maharaj was like Coleridge's "Ancient Mariner," not condemned but blessed with the trust that he had to utter to anyone whom he could capture, till the last breath of his life, the message of great deliverance that was Vivekananda.

Swami Nitya-swarup-ananda wanted everything on a big scale. What he accomplished was great; the Ramakrishna Mission Institute of Culture stands for that as an example. But his vision was even greater. It was truly cosmic, for Vivekananda had given him that cosmic consciousness. And he left us with a huge cosmic vision for the future.

NAMITA GUPTA*

I first met Chintaharan Maharaj in late 1963 at the Belur Math during Swami Vivekananda's Birth Centenary celebrations. An incident at the time moved me deeply, and one particular comment is still motivating me to go forward. I had gone to see Swami Abhayananda (Bharat Maharaj). I found Swami Nitya-swarup-ananda (Chintaharan Maharaj to us) seated at the round table in Bharat Maharaj's room. In the midst of their discussion, Bharat Maharaj suddenly asked, "Can anyone remain silent for twenty-four hours?" I said, "I think if I make up my mind, I can remain silent for twenty-four hours. There is no reason not to." Bharat Maharaj insisted, "No, it is not possible." I do not know what came over me, but I took it up as a challenge and said, "Maharaj, why don't you test me and see whether I can do it?" Chintaharan Maharaj was listening to this conversation with a smile and was minutely observing the manner in which I was talking to Bharat Maharaj. When I later went to him, he used to refer to that incident to other devotees and praise me, saying, "How boldly she challenged Bharat Maharaj that day. She even asked Bharat Maharaj to test her." What he liked was my approach. His comment was "She is a burning flame."

I will now try to present the lessons I learned from Chintaharan Maharaj. He always used to say that everything should be done perfectly, because one can realize God only through perfection: "Perfection is the realization of God." He often gave the example of the cobbler who had spoken words of high philosophy but had kept his food on the dirty floor. When Maharaj had asked him, "Why have you kept your food on the dirty floor, you will fall ill?" the cobbler had replied with a smile, "From dust we are born, and to dust we shall return, so what does it matter?" Maharaj had been shocked at this unacceptable discrepancy of spouting highflown thoughts while neglecting basic hygiene.

One particular incident filled me with great faith. When my husband passed away, Maharaj came to our house. My mind was in an unsettled state. Maharaj did not utter any word of consolation. He had brought a garland which had been offered to Thakur and he placed it on my husband's body. I felt at that moment that my husband was freed.

He gave me valuable advice regarding the relationship of married couples which I often repeat to people even now. He said that there should be love between husband and wife but wrongdoing from one's spouse should never be tolerated. All my sorrow and suffering was washed away by Chintaharan Maharaj's unbounded affection. Throughout our life, his pure company cast the shadow out of many black days.

I was fond of cooking and he sometimes asked me to prepare different kinds of dishes for him. I cooked for him on many occasions. He was fond of food and was very lavish in his praise. That was our Chintaharan Maharaj. I really am not capable of writing about his greatness. People who have comprehended his intellectual powers or spiritual thoughts are in a better position to explain all these things to the reader. I can only express my crores and crores of pranam.

EULA BRUCE

Our first meeting was at the Belur Math in India in the winter of 1964. Swami Nitya-swarup-ananda had breakfast with us every day during the two weeks we stayed at the Belur guest house, and he made sure that we were served food which agreed with our digestion. He took us on many trips into the Calcutta area, sometimes accompanied by Swami Abhayananda (Bharat Maharaj)—what a wonderful time! I recall being impressed early on when Swami Nitya-swarup-ananda said that truthfulness was one of the most important factors of the divine estate, and that he had never knowingly told an untruth in his life. He once mentioned to us that his parents had in no way tried to prevent him from becoming a monk, and that even as a child he had longed to do this.

My husband and I took a two-week trip by train in India with Swami Nitya-swarup-ananda, during which he was always serene and in good humor. Even when I developed a mild case of pneumonia, we could not think of canceling the journey and losing his company. There was one

harrowing but amusing incident during this trip. At a railroad station
north of Calcutta, the Swami went out onto the crowded platform. I
could see him washing his face at a public watering place. Then he stood
with his back to the train viewing the countryside, lost in his own world.
The train began to move, so quietly it seemed by inches. Then it began
picking up speed, but to my alarm, the Swami, standing on the platform,
seemed to hear nothing. I tried to open a window, but it was sealed for
eternity! I looked at my sleeping husband, ailing and apparently lost to
the here and now. I was mentally wringing my hands, wondering how
we could ever get together with the Swami again. The train was now
moving at a fair speed when, all of a sudden, Swami Nitya-swarup-
ananda burst into our carriage at a moderate pace with his head held
high. He muttered, "That never happened to me before," but seemed
quietly amused. I was nonplussed—"How did you do it?" I asked. He
replied calmly and with a chuckle: "I just picked up my skirts and ran
faster than possible. I barely caught the last car!"

We also accompanied Swami Nitya-swarup-ananda when he visited
the farm of a great devotee, "Mohan" I think was his name, about ten
miles north of Calcutta. The devotee was much attached to Swami Nitya-
swarup-ananda and treated us all with loving consideration. His farm was
a model of productive efficiency; with a modest number of acres, he had
created a paradise of grapes, citrus, other fruits and vegetables—modern
in every way. When the Swami was relaxing on the patio, I noticed that
flies were becoming a nuisance to him. A wide feather duster lay on the
pillow, so I used it as a fan, waving it back and forth over his head. He
smiled faintly and looked at me with a glance of such sweetness and
impersonal affection that I was not the same, transformed by that
moment briefly from the merely human state.

When our Indian visas were running out, we went by the New
Delhi Ashrama to say goodbye. I said breezily, "We came to say goodbye, dear Swami." He looked stunned. "*Goodbye?*" he asked, his voice
breaking. Suddenly I felt the implications of that word, *goodbye*. His
face didn't change as he looked at us for the last time, but his eyes were

moist with tears. As we walked away, I was seized by a hurricane of grief. My husband took my hand. He said to me in a muffled voice, "I love him, too."

Many years later, during his last visit to the United States in 1987, Swami Nitya-swarup-ananda came to see us twice when he was visiting the West Coast. We had been keeping in regular touch with him by letters, so were aware that he had been planning another trip to the United States, but it was still unexpected when the first call came that Swami Krishnananda would be bringing him to visit us on his way down to San Diego. My husband had been paralyzed by a stroke and was unable to speak. The Swami embraced him affectionately and whispered a few words to him, which I didn't hear. The atmosphere of unconscious rapport immediately erased the years of separation, and we were once again in the joyful ease of his company, laughing at the same things, yet with an impact on the psyche which only in retrospect revealed the power of his presence on our lives.

PADMA MUKHERJEE

Chintaharan Maharaj! What can I say about Swami Nitya-swarup-ananda? Memories arise like misty clouds. Can words capture the infinite? But such joy has to be shared.

About thirty-odd years ago, when I was a teenager, one evening at our parental home at Shyampukur, I was playing the grand piano. Outside on the porch, my parents were quietly savouring the cool twilight hours. Suddenly a big car came to a halt and the clear resonant voice of Swami Sambuddhananda called out to my father, "Are you there, Ram? I have brought holy water from the Kumbha." Father rushed forward and was told, "Go to the car, Ram. I have brought someone to meet you. Take him upstairs." All this while I was observing what was going on with the casual curiosity of a child.

The doors of our home were always open to monks and devotees. An atmosphere of bliss pervaded the walls. The one goal of our parents was to live out life as one with Sri Ramakrishna in fullness and beatitude. As children, my brothers and I breathed in this atmosphere as our blessed birthright. An organization (Sri Ramakrishna Sarada Samsad) had been established in our home, and weekly sessions of hymns and readings from the scriptures were held. Seekers found contentment.

That particular evening, father escorted Chintaharan Maharaj out of the car. This was my first meeting with him. He was fair, of heavy build, and straight in bearing. I touched his feet. He sat down with my parents, asking me to continue with my piano practices. I complied.

Throughout my teenage years I had many chances to meet him. Once, my cousin and myself went to see him after school at Udbodhan, where he was then the President. His room was to the right of the main flight of stairs leading up to Sarada-Ma's shrine. He was reclining on his bed facing the door, reading and carefully marking a bottlegreen-covered fat volume with the name written in golden letters: *Sri Sri Ramakrishna Kathamrita*. Sitting on the floor with the restlessness of a girl, I was fascinated by the book and kept jumping up to get a better glimpse of it. Instead of five separate volumes, as was familiar in our house, here for the first time was the entire manuscript in a single book. Perhaps in those days he had plans of publishing the *Kathamrita* in one complete volume, annexed and indexed. He pointed out the side of the leaves wherein the numbers of the volumes had been carefully demarcated. "Do you like it?" he asked me. And when I nodded enthusiastically, he instantly, spontaneously offered it to me. I was dumbfounded. What renunciation! There was not the slightest hesitation in giving up his personal copy, something on which he was working, just because a child wanted it. The child little understood the gravity and depth of what she wanted. But some unseen force held me back from accepting something for which I was not ready.

Chintaharan Maharaj often graced our home from dawn to dusk. Devotees flocked to meet him. There were many "question-and-answer sessions," and we drank in as much nectar as we could. Maharaj analysed the three photographs of Thakur in samadhi. He said that *Bhagwan* [the Lord] had been photographed. All the three shots of Thakur were when he was in the transcendental stage of samadhi. His body had become one with Pure Consciousness, a rare phenomenon of Advaita where no difference exists between subject and object, where all is One.

The question was once raised why Thakur would give two different answers to the same query at different places. "It's a riddle," I ventured. Immediately, Maharaj pounced on the word "riddle" and kept repeating the word "riddle, riddle" as if to squeeze out of it the very essence of the question.

Some time ago I had gone to him at the Belur Math with a question. I wanted to know who in the *Mahabharata* had said that since this body would have to go in any case, it is better to do good work with it. Immediately Chintaharan Maharaj began to thumb through books with intense sincerity—there and then the answer had to be found! Just then Swami Gambhiranandaji chanced to stroll past and he too got involved in the matter. In the growing dusk I felt small in the presence of these two revered figures, while the Ganga lapped at the nearby steps of the ghat.

The river of my life flowed on. On the fourth day after my marriage, my mother sat for her M.A. examinations. Chintaharan Maharaj always encouraged her and made detailed inquiries about her progress. Mother was also gifted with rare musical talent and often used to sing, offering her voice and her compositions to Thakur and the devotees. As a wedding present he blessed us with two volumes of *The Gospel of Sri Ramakrishna,* and wanted me to have a book rack lined with immortal works. Later our daughter, Gargi, was born. I can still see Maharaj rocking the cradle and telling me, "Like Madalasa, keep repeating, *Tattvamasi niranjana* [Thou art the Stainless One]."

My husband was drawn into the magic circle of Maharaj's affection. Concerned inquiries were made about his business, and valuable advice given. But once Maharaj noticed that the water supply to our house was inadequate. Immediately my husband was sternly pulled up for neglecting the duties of a householder.

In the course of time our daughter bloomed into a young woman and married. Maharaj gave her a photograph of Sarada-Ma. It was not just a framed image, but was carefully thought out, and the wedding gift also included a personal note of blessing. Humble beyond words, Maharaj kept asking if the note had been correctly worded. He took great interest in the details of the wedding arrangement, even the size of the sweets! It was as if Thakur was always with me, sharing my worries and responsibilities. He never failed to ask newly married couples who went to him for his blessings, "Tell me, my dears, what will you ask each other: what will you expect from your partner? Always say, 'What can I do for *you*?' If all, from all walks of life, from all parts of the globe, asked this question, peace would ever prevail."

Swami Nitya-swarup-ananda was a perfectionist *par excellence*. To him the preparation and serving of food was an art. Uncompromising and strict, he often reduced me to tears. When instructing me how to peel apples he told me how to hold the fruit, use the knife, and shape the pieces—and he was relentless until I mastered the process. Attending on him at mealtimes, we had to serve the rice *boiling* hot from a small container with teaspoons of vegetables each time. He could discuss at length the various preparations of fish, such as smoked hilsa fish, and at Nimpith, I remember, he conversed expertly for nearly two hours about pisciculture with a professional in the fish trade. One day he had us prepare more than twenty varieties of *sak* [leafy green vegetable]. On another occasion, when he heard over the phone that our menu was to be just *shukto* [bitter vegetable curry] and mutton curry, he was audibly annoyed, insisting that a dal and a vegetable dish should also be included for a balanced meal.

Once when a group of us were returning from Jayrambati, Maharaj had asked us to halt en route at the home of Sri Satya Brata Mukherjee at Arambagh. Meanwhile, he had contacted our host and asked him to serve us *alu dum* [potato curry]. As per his detailed instructions, Satya Brata Babu and his family had to sit and sort out equal-sized potatoes! Another time, at the Belur Math, he was served slices of toast. Looking at the crispness of the two pieces, he divined that the person who had made them would easily scale spiritual heights. No detail ever escaped his notice.

I wander down memory lane. On my father's birthday, Maharaj would come with a cake, then light the candles and clap his hands in time with the birthday melody. Ever blissful, he rejoiced at every-thing—undiluted *ananda*. He chided us when we took my mother on a tour of South India with a travel agent. Considering my mother's age and health, he felt that she should not have been subjected to the rigours of a guided tour.

To his own comforts, however, Maharaj was totally indifferent. On the way to Mayavati, we made an overnight halt at Naini Tal. Due to a careless arrangement, Chintaharan Maharaj was allotted a room adja-cent to a dirty toilet. He suffered the whole night in a sitting posture without a frown or a grumble. At Mayavati, amidst idyllic surround-ings, we meditated, sang bhajans [hymns], and had the rare privilege of cooking and serving the monks.

When Maharaj was ill at Seva Pratishthan, he kept insisting that I should do something for Thakur. The idea of a weekly discussion ses-sion began to take vague shape in my mind. Maharaj gave it concrete form and suggested the name, "Mangalik." Broad and catholic, he stressed that there should be no orthodoxy about having only Sri Rama-krishna as a topic.

Maharaj was so close to me like a parent that I cannot draw back and gauge his qualities—his largeness, his scholarship, his vision, and his spiritualism that knew no bounds of time and space. To me, he was only Chintaharan Maharaj. Once at the hospital where I had gone to visit him, I was feeling a bit low and complained that there was no one to share my thoughts. Surprisingly, he too confided that he was alone and isolated with his dreams and visions. For two long hours he talked about sublime philosophy, the macrocosm and microcosm, oblivious to the lengthening shadows and peeping hospital attendants. Tears poured down my cheeks. Too small and humble to understand and take in his vastness, all I could realize was that here I was in the presence of something above and beyond my comprehension. All I could do was cry and wring my heart.

Chintaharan Maharaj was suffering greatly when I visited him for the last time. Even at that hour, he did not refer to his ailment but gesticulated with great difficulty, asking me how I was keeping. He left for Ramakrishnalok [the heavenly abode of Sri Ramakrishna] when I was away at Varanasi, so I was spared the pain of his passing. Maharaj was close to all who came in contact with him and made each person feel that he or she was his special favourite. Individually he made each devotee his own.

MARGARET GARLAND

My brief encounters with Swami Nitya-swarup-ananda stand out in my memory. He was such a warm, intelligent, and accessible human being. Though I first met him in India in 1957, and again during his trip to the United States in 1962, I especially remember a conversation in 1968 at the Belur Math guest house when the Swami joined us one afternoon. It was about "the common people." A visitor from South America, herself well-to-do, was saying that social reform wouldn't accomplish very much because of the mentality of the poor: "They all want cars and other material things," she complained. Swami's reply was: "Yes, of course they want those things, it is only natural in our world."

He seemed to me to be very much a person of his time, as well as a person who was very holy and lived in an Eternal Time.

1970S
(Gol Park rescue and afterwards)

SWAMI NITYANANDA*

My acquaintance with Swami Nitya-swarup-ananda was of long duration, from the time the Institute was at Wellington Square up until the time it finally moved to its present site at Gol Park. The Institute of Culture stands as Chintaharan Maharaj's immemorial achievement, a reflection of his spiritual sensibility and global outlook, though its full measure cannot be known by those of us who lack his intuitive power or spiritual realization. It exceeds our ordinary capacity, and we can only guess at it by observing how such a sannyasin lived his life, and by the fruits of his *sadhana*.

Swami Nitya-swarup-ananda's devotion to work and his staying power in the midst of obstacles are like ornaments in his life. Moreover, he had the encouragement and support of the General Secretary, Swami Madhavananda, without which this huge institution could not have materialized. Swami Abhayananda was also his friend and guide, although Chintaharan Maharaj was much younger. Whenever there was any good food prepared at the Institute, Swami Nitya-swarup-ananda used to ring us up, and we would discover Bharat Maharaj in his company, sitting informally at the dining table with just an undershirt. Bharat Maharaj's physique was better built than many a youth.

I was with the Ramakrishna Order for many years, and I was close to many senior monks of the Mission. I have neither the power nor the right to judge whether Swami Nitya-swarup-ananda was the best among these karma yogi sadhus, all of whom, according to the precepts of the Order, are the instruments of the Divine Will. But Sri Ramakrishna's Grace certainly flowed through Swami Nitya-swarup-ananda's consciousness in manifold streams for the good of many.

I can recall a number of things that were of a very personal nature, not all of which were beautiful or enjoyable (because Swami Nitya-swarup-ananda was extremely strict and serious in matters of work), but which were so beneficial that I will dwell on several instances in this reminiscence. He used to laugh and joke and mix very intimately, like a peer, whenever we went out with him, but in the field of work he could not forgive the slightest error in the sphere of *karma* since *karma* is a *sadhana*. He used to rebuke people sternly, but using language that never transgressed the ideals of a sannyasin.

I accompanied him to Bangladesh during the 1971 relief operations. We came to Jessore by car, where the government of Bangladesh had made arrangements for our stay in the evening. That night, I was present there as a humble *sevak* amid so many eminent people. A sumptuous meal was served and a variety of preparations of the famous hilsa fish of Bangladesh was brought to the table. The display of these specialities must have taken Chintaharan Maharaj back to his Dacca childhood, he so relished them. Seeing him so full of appreciation and eating with such gusto gave us more enjoyment that evening than the food itself. Swami Nitya-swarup-ananda went on to Dacca while I left for Barishal, where I was in charge of the relief operations.

After coming out of the Order, I received a long letter from him. This is part of the two-part letter, written from the Belur Math:

8 November 1977
Dear Krishnakamal,

Please accept my sincere wishes, affection, etc. for Bijoya. I have in front of me two letters from you. One is dated 28/2/77, addressed from the Ramakrishna Vivekananda Mission Ashrama, Barrackpore, and the second is dated 23/10/77, addressed from the Vivekananda Math, Barrackpore.

I was at Lucknow when the great furore at Rahara was happening. I was deeply shocked with the entire affair. I could not find a way of expressing my sympathy to you at that time and even now I have no words. All I can say is that we all have taken shelter at His Lotus Feet and He is our all in all. Truly, there is no one else whom we can call our own in this world. Wherever we might be, in whatever condition, we have to make Him our only support if we are to find fulfilment in life. No one can ever achieve the goal, whoever he is, by evading this. On the other hand, there is no need to have any fear from any source if you are following the path of dharma.

28 January 1978
I had started replying to your two above mentioned letters on 8 November, but had left it incomplete. I could not complete the letter and I could not send it to you. All this while, your two letters and my incomplete letter have been with me. Today I am replying to many old letters—I am completing my letter to you and giving my reply.

I have great love for you and am impressed with your dynamism. Whatever might have happened from the Sangha, many sadhus, devotees, and the general public are sympathetic towards you. This will be a great resource and support for you in future. Many people are prepared to help you out, seeing your life purified by service and your different types of service-oriented activities. What more can you expect? That people have this kind of feeling towards you will help you in your future service commitment.

Under these circumstances if you can regulate your future life with temperance, then your success is guaranteed. But if your working life sheds its selfless spirit of seva and gets influenced by unsadhu-like qualities of name, fame, recognition, pride, rivalry, jealousy, competitiveness, then whatever success you will attain at the initial stage will slowly erode and everything will be destroyed eventually. It is possible for you to do various kinds of good work, but only the highest order of the spiritually decreed [*adhikarik purush*] can establish a Sangha, so your work now will remain confined to a personal level. But if you are able to pursue the spirit of your work with purity, then only gradually the spirit will become the life-force of your future work and pave the way for the foundation of a Sangha. Hence, if you can work with a vision of the future, then only will your life become successful and fulfilled, and your entire effort directed at the welfare of the people will yield good fruit and get transformed to a Sangha in future. Try to embed this thought deeply in your heart, and do not undertake anything which will lead to further confrontation with the Math and Mission. In fact, your work should be regulated in such a manner that these boundaries will dissolve slowly and slowly get obliterated. This will be beneficial for both sides....

I don't know when I will be able to meet you again, so there will not be any occasion to exchange our views. Such is life. Now even the religious Orders are being penetrated by materialistic values. Alas, samsara [the world]! Alas, life!

I am going to Delhi in the first week of February and I will stay there for some time for some work. I can never forget Satyapriya

Babu, I am deeply attached to him. Give him my heartfelt affection and wishes.

Please accept my sincere best wishes and affection. I hope you are all right. May Sri Sri Thakur bless you. This is my earnest prayer at His Feet. Yours—

Your eternal well-wisher,

Nityaswarupananda

He used to keep track of my person till the very last. At times I used to go and make my pranam to him. His words would always be full of hope, encouragement, joy, and contentment. He used to quote the Gita and remind me—Arise, Awake, if you are killed you see the heavens, if you win you will win the Earth. Thakur is everywhere, within and without. We are all near Thakur. We are doing Thakur's work. Surrender everything to Him, all that is good, all that is bad. Never be discouraged, never be afraid, it is not your work, not your plan or your thought. You are His instrument. Whatever He is making you do, do accordingly. Wherever He keeps you, stay there. That is your real place. If you keep holding on to Him in each and every situation, then only you are saved, or else there is danger.

If you are afflicted by ego, he told me, it is dangerous. If you start thinking that I have done this or will do this, then darkness will descend on you. One has to go through a lot of suffering and pain. Thakur used to give the example of the kitten, and say that you do your work while remembering this. Innumerable sadhus and devotees think of your well-being. What greater boon can you get in this world than love. Your institution has won the acclaim of governmental and private sectors, you are taking care of the food, shelter, and education of the poor, this is an indicator of the blessings of Sri Sri Thakur and Holy Mother. Whether you are inside the Sangha or outside it, the real thing is to make Him the centre of your existence and hold on to Him.

I am remembering these words of Maharaj very much these days. Once I had gone to a village in Burdwan called Bhatar. The roof was thatched with straw. He had the desire of eating fresh fried fish caught straight from the pond in front, with coarse rice pounded in a mortar with a pestle. All arrangements were made. We had our food sitting on the mud floor of the humble cottage and talked of spiritual things. He was talking about the life of Holy Mother in the village of Jayrambati. He had this power of elevating the simple acts of daily life towards higher truths. This is the virtue of companionship of sadhus.

One whose life has been blessed by touching the feet of the Holy Mother has been able to see light amidst darkness, hope amidst despair. After joining the Order, he had to stay at home for some time. He had to leave the Institute of Culture for various reasons after having established it and brought it to its present state, but he had no complaint, no attachment. He left this body there in that same place and now he is enjoying eternal bliss in his own eternal being (*nitya-swarup*). I have placed his picture at the feet of Sri Sri Ramakrishna within my innermost self and am seeking his grace, and I am also feeling his blessing.

ABHAYA DAS GUPTA*

It is difficult to discuss anything about Swami Nitya-swarup-ananda, he was so different from the ordinary run of people. I will attempt to bring out a few of his unique qualities through little anecdotes. It was my good fortune to have his affection, and the way he manifested that affection was also unique, to be comprehended only through deep reflection. In this, and in everything he did, Chintaharan Maharaj was exceptional. The incidents given below bear witness to this.

This took place some years back. I was working at the Library in the morning when an attendant came in and placed a book on my table. It had come from the Secretary Maharaj of the Institute. I opened the book and found these words written (in Bengali): *Jekhane jemon sekhane temon* [whatever is done in a particular place, must be done according to custom—a quotation from the Holy Mother], and these words were underlined boldly with red ink. The meaning was clear to my mind: whatever work has to be done, must be done properly. There can be no exception to this rule: *any* work done improperly remains unfulfilled.

Later I came to understand Swami Nitya-swarup-ananda's point more fully. When arranging your room, each piece of furniture has to be placed where it enhances the beauty of the room and nowhere else. You cannot give the excuse that this entails extra work or time. Whatever is required, arrangements have to be made accordingly. We find a beautiful example of this from the Holy Mother, who said, "One day there was no *panchphoron* [spice mixture] at home. Didi [Lakshmididi's mother] said, 'Let us do it without it, it does not matter.' Thakur overheard this conversation and said, 'What is this? If you don't have *panchphoron*, why don't you go and get one paise of it? Whatever has to be given cannot be left out like this. I have come all the way from Dakshineswar to take curries seasoned with the scent of *phoron*, leaving aside precious fish preparations and bowls of payesh, and you want to leave *that* out?' Didi was embarrassed and asked someone to get it." If something has to be done perfectly, flawlessly, then it has to be done *jekhane jemon sekhane temon*. Without this ideal in mind, then no work, big or small, can be fruitful. Chintaharan Maharaj had realized this ideal in his life and he tried to motivate us to follow it. One has to totally surrender one's mind and heart and soul to the work—no arguments, no evasion, no rationalization. This is how he taught us.

The memory of another day is still bright. Chintaharan Maharaj had come to the Library quietly, and was looking around. Suddenly I was startled by the sound of his deep voice. He was holding the chair of one of my colleagues and saying, "Get up, get up, get up." This friend stood up apprehensively. Maharaj then straightened the chair, which had been crooked. "If you sit like this and stick labels," he said, "then your posture will also be crooked and the labels also will be crooked. If you sit straight, then your posture will be straight and your work also will be straight."

Then, after going round the Library, he called the Librarian, Anupama Roy, and said, "Your modern decoration is quite good." We were not able to comprehend what he wanted to say or what he was hinting at. Where did we make a mistake? Finally we noticed that there were cobwebs in the room, hence this sarcasm. We shared a joke amongst ourselves at that time, that if anyone should ever hang himself, and we informed Chintaharan Maharaj that "So-and-so has hanged himself," Maharaj would go there and say, "Good for nothing, he could not even tie the knot straight!" We used to enjoy this a great deal.

One day there was a phone call for Anupama Roy asking who on the Library staff had good handwriting. By some stroke of chance, my name was submitted, and I was in serious trouble. My colleagues all managed to escape in spite of the fact that their handwriting was commendable. So I alone set off with much trepidation to undergo the ordeal. I went upstairs, and then came the real danger. I had to make a fair copy of an article which was to be published in *Udbodhan*. Chintaharan Maharaj gave me detailed instructions on how to write it: each letter had to be of the same size, and the spacing of each letter as well as every word had to be perfectly even. I would have to measure the spacing with a ruler. Following all his instructions, I took great care in copying the article, but my efforts were in vain. He wasn't satisfied and sent it back. This time, instead of writing it in spare moments during work hours, I stayed up at night to do it without distraction. I again sent it to him, and again it came back. By now I was getting desperate. I felt I would never be able to complete this work. Finally, I sent him a third attempt, and this time it was not returned. But there was no phone call or message from him. I was feeling anxious—was it all right this time? In the evening I went up to him along with Anupama Roy, at her request, to make pranam to him before going to some function. As soon as he saw me, he said sarcastically, "Have you come here to listen to your praise?" We were both stunned. Was this any way to praise someone! Anupama Roy tried to protest mildly on my behalf, saying, "Abhaya did not want to come. It was I who asked her to come." But Maharaj was not ready to listen to this. He told Anupama Roy, "You don't understand anything. She was greedy for praise, and that is why she came." I heaved a sigh of relief listening to these bitter words, for he had finally approved my handwriting! I was overjoyed. In any work, in anything, Maharaj never accepted the slightest gap or imperfection.

Perfection was his goal. And we have seen that in all his actions and circumstances.

One day I invited him to have lunch in my house, but he did not agree. He asked me to cook food for him and send it over. Accordingly, I prepared some food and sent it to him. As I was returning to my room in the evening after finishing work, I noticed him on the lawn. As soon as he saw me he said, "Hasn't your mother taught you how to grind mustard?" From his words I could make out that he had liked the food and was happy with it, but since the mustard was not fine enough, he was pointing out the imperfection. He was constantly trying to remind us that even the smallest things have to be done perfectly.

Only once have I seen pure unalloyed happiness on his face. It was in the winter of 1979, when I had gone to see him at the Belur Math with my book, *Sri Sri Sarada Devi: Atmakatha* [Sri Sri Sarada Devi on Herself]. I was anxious for him to read it, but I was full of fear. Heaven knows how many mistakes he would detect! Perhaps he would chide me for presumption in anthologizing her sayings. I was thinking of all these things, but since it was a book on the Holy Mother, I had an intense desire to show it to him and I finally summoned up enough courage to hand it over. As soon as he saw the book his face lit up with an expression of spontaneous joy, and his eyes radiated beneficence. I had never before seen such a beautiful and joyous expression on his face. Of course he later on pointed out a few minor corrections to me, and added, "The second edition has to be exquisitely perfect in every detail." He even spoke of translating this book into English. He praised the book highly to several foreigners in my presence. But I somehow felt uncomfortable; something was out of tune somewhere. This kind of expression from Chintaharan Maharaj was somewhat odd. I began reasoning, "After all, he is a child of the Holy Mother, so if her life is published using her own words in a book, naturally he would feel happy. That was the joy he was expressing so spontaneously, and was only to be expected."

I have expressed my respects to Maharaj through these little anecdotes. I will conclude with excerpts of a letter written by him to me on 13 November 1980:

I was pleased to know that you all have come back from a visit to Mayavati.... Have you done anything about your book on Holy Mother? I think all the published copies have been exhausted. Now try to bring it out with perfection in every detail.

Whenever we talk of you, I remember your father. What a man! One never finds such a person in this world. And along with memories of your father, I am reminded of Sri Sri Baburam Maharaj. I had met your father for the first time in 1915 in Rarikhal along with Sri Sri Baburam Maharaj. It was at that time (I was a student of Class X) that Sri Sri Baburam Maharaj in his infinite grace dedicated me to the Math. But he had placed a condition that I could join the Order only after completing my B.A. graduation. His wishes have been fulfilled. Sri Sri Baburam Maharaj is the polestar of our life. The relationship of your father with him has tied us together forever with deep bonding love. The memories of your father enrapture my mind.

I hope you are all right.

Your well-wisher,
Nityaswarupananda

SHYAMA PRASAD MANDAL

I lost my godlike father in 1967, a physician who was devoted to the Ramakrishna Mission and spent his life for his patients, and in 1973 I found my fatherlike god in Swami Nitya-swarup-ananda, who guided me till his last breath in October 1992.

In December 1973, Chintaharan Maharaj was admitted to Safdurjung Hospital for an operation on his right upper limb, and I assisted Dr. B. Shankaran, an eminent orthopaedist, during the surgery. While the Swami was recuperating at the Ramakrishna Mission Ashram in Delhi, I had my first opportunity to be in close contact with him. I was staying nearby with my family, and he would religiously go for long evening walks and frequently visited my house. As we got to know him and his deep love and affection for us, we were drawn to him like a magnet.

As Chintaharan Maharaj spent time in Delhi for his treatment and for composing his books, he became like a family member to us. When I went to the United Kingdom in 1974 with my wife, Anindita (who was on a World Health Organization scholarship), and our two young sons (Pratip and Adhip, ages four years and six months, respectively), he wrote us touching and inspiring letters full of encouragement. Our stay in England was not very easy with small children, but his moral support helped us to hold on. After my wife and children returned to India in 1976 while I stayed back to complete my advanced degree in orthopaedics from Liverpool University, he was a great support and shelter to my family, who were alone in India.

During my stay in Liverpool, Swamiji unfailingly corresponded with me, guiding me in every step. I can narrate an interesting incident of this period. I was due to appear in the final examination, a very tough one to clear. Unfortunately, I fell ill and was incapacitated. In despair I realized that I would not be able to appear. One night I dreamt that Chintaharan Maharaj was standing beside me. He bolstered my courage to take the test and even assured me of success. It was no illusion! The next morning, I was allowed to take the examination from my sickbed and I performed so well that I passed with flying colours.

Soon after this, in 1977, I had to leave England suddenly to appear for an interview in Delhi which would enable me to get a consultant's job in India. Only my immediate family knew, and I had no time to inform Swami Nitya-swarup-ananda. I arrived at the Delhi airport early in the morning, underwent a successful interview of the Union Public Selection Commission, and went to my home in Delhi. Later that evening we heard familiar footsteps at our doorstep. On opening the door we were overwhelmingly surprised to find Maharaj! He had come from Calcutta to bless and congratulate us.

I was working as an Assistant Professor at the Lok Nayak Jai Prakash Narain Hospital in Delhi, but in 1982 I decided to leave the security of a government job and start my own private practice. It was a difficult decision spurred on by a crisis in my professional life. The future looked very uncertain, but Swamiji encouraged me to go ahead, undeterred, with my plan. I was able to join the Sri Ganga Ram Hospital soon after resigning. This was one of the best private hospitals in Delhi and proved to be a milestone in my career. Swamiji, like a father, had always been there beside me.

He continued to keep a constant vigil as my career unfolded, and even designed my prescription pad when he visited my clinic. He also guided my personal life. In spite of being a monk he had a profound knowledge of domestic affairs. In private practice I became very busy and preoccupied. My wife wrote to him, unhappy about my irregular timings and busy schedule. To this he replied (in Bengali):

> I am very pleased to get all the news of Shyamu (my pet name). That he goes out at 8:00 in the morning and returns at 9:00 at night is no great news for me. The day I hear that he is spending his whole night at the nursing home or is asked to visit patients one hundred miles away from Delhi—only then I'll be really happy. In my eyes and aspiration this is only the sunrise of Dr. Mandal. The day has yet to break. So there is no reason for you to get flustered. Now his only duty is to do his work carefully, cautiously and perfectly and build up a foundation for the future. The rest will take care of itself. I pray for his fulfilment.

This reminded me of Swami Vivekananda's preaching of "Work unto Death!" But his constructive comments were always the needful remedy.

He visited my parental home in Burdwan district of West Bengal as well as my wife's parental home in Calcutta. He met all our relatives, and his love of freshly cooked fish from the village pond is still fondly remembered, as are his praises to the cook after a hearty meal. He was with us in all walks of life, in all the ups and downs, until the very end of his days.

In October 1992 he fell very ill and my wife visited him at the Gol Park Institute. He inquired about me (in Bengali): "Will he come to meet me after I have become a dead log?" Hearing this, I rushed to Calcutta and I talked to his physician, Dr. Arabinda Basu. Swamiji used to always consult me regarding his health, often on the telephone from Calcutta. Within two days of my return to Delhi, he passed away. It seemed as if he was waiting to meet and bless me before he left.

In 1994, I suffered from acute pancreatitis, a potentially fatal disease. While lying in the intensive care bed, struggling between life and death, I often went into a trance. This is when, I distinctly remember, I conversed with him standing beside my hospital bed. He was, as always, giving me hope.

Swamiji always told me never to be astonished by anything that happens around us in this world; whatever happens, he said, try to search for the good in it. "Never consider yourself inferior to anybody," he insisted, "you have the potential and God will help you to achieve."

In the last few years of his life he was unhappy with the functioning of the Ramakrishna Mission and wrote the book *Back to Vivekananda*. During this time he also expressed his concern about the future of the Ramakrishna Mission Institute of Culture at Gol Park, Calcutta, which was his creation. He was never narrow or parochial in his following of Sri Ramakrishna, Swami Vivekananda, and Sree Ma, and could never tolerate any straying from principles. He felt that the Institute had deviated from its objective of being a seat of learning for universal brotherhood.

This is a very brief sketch of this saintly person. But I cannot express in words what it was like having him by my side. He touched my life with eternal hope, and I still feel his presence as a guiding star.

JAYANTA BHATTACHARYA*

Sri Ramakrishna realized the Oneness of all existence and his universal consciousness has enlightened the world. Swami Vivekananda was the Prophet of these ideas, and Swami Nitya-swarup-ananda was one of those rare souls in whom this Vedantic spirit was continuously resonating. I met this extraordinary sannyasin in August 1974 and have since felt his grace in my life. My reminiscence will reflect these personal benefits. It is beyond my powers to portray his character, his work, and his intellect, but the great Ramakrishna Mission Institute of Culture stands as a reflection of the universal principles of Sri Ramakrishna.

My great-grandfather was a friend of Narendranath Datta [Swami Vivekananda]. The connection between them was a gentleman by the name of Dasarathi Sanyal, who was Narendranath's classmate and a direct disciple of Sri Ramakrishna. Perhaps due to this fortunate legacy, our family has always been close to the Ramakrishna Order and our house was visited by monks from my very childhood. It was Swami Abhayananda [Bharat Maharaj] who made the arrangements for us to take initiation with Swami Vireswarananda. Here I would like to admit that my wife, who has chosen the path of bhakti, is more devout than myself, for I have a tendency to rationalize. As a result, she was quite uninhibited and free with Bharat Maharaj, who had a solemn and slightly aloof personality, and Bharat Maharaj also had a fatherly affection for her. We both depended on Bharat Maharaj and shared all our joys and sorrows with him.

Before meeting Chintaharan Maharaj, we had heard a lot about him from our friend Paromita, daughter of Dr. Kalidas Nag. Dr. Nag and Swami Nitya-swarup-ananda had been very close. I had also heard about him from Mr. Ajit Basu, the owner of Arora Films [one of the most famous film companies in Calcutta], who had met Swami Nitya-swarup-ananda in America and had enjoyed long conversations with him. Ajit Basu had known Sri Aurobindo and the Mother [of Sri Aurobindo's Ashrama] and many other famous personalities, but whenever he spoke of Swami Nitya-swarup-ananda, it was with unusual enthusiasm.

One evening at the Belur Math at dusk, when the water of the Ganges was calm and meditative, we had finished making our pranam to Bharat Maharaj, and as we left his room we saw Chintaharan Maharaj for the first time sitting on a bench just outside. We also made our pranam to this elderly, pleasant-looking, large-eyed sannyasin. He asked us our names and about my work. "I am a filmmaker," I replied, and I mentioned several of the titles of my films. In quality, these pictures had ranked well in Indian cinema. Maharaj was very enthusiastic and welcomed us to come and see him whenever we visited the Belur Math. I was amazed at the breadth of his knowledge about films! He told us that film as an art form had unlimited potential—to do either a lot of good for society or a lot of harm. In his admonition I found an echo of Andre Malraux's words, "A bad movie can be just as destructive in society as a hydrogen bomb."

My wife told him, "Pictures are all right, Maharaj, but 'there is no food at home.' He has been cheated all his life." "We have two sons," she added, "and we have to think about their studies. We have a roof above our heads, which is the saving grace." Maharaj replied, "This will not do, Thakur always said that you have to realize your dues. Why don't you see to it?" This was how he first drew us close to him on the first meeting, and this deepened as the years went on till the very end.

I told Maharaj about a film which I had made with my cousin, Raghunath Goswami, during the year of Swamiji's Centenary, a documentary called *Bhavdhara* [Flow of Ideals]. It was based on the teachings of Ramakrishna-Vivekananda. The film had earned a good name, but I could not recover the costs. Maharaj said, "I think I have seen the film and I liked it." Here it would be relevant to mention that in the interim Maharaj had become very close to my cousin Raghunath and his family.

Maharaj had a fatherly affection for my wife, who had mentioned our problems with such candour. Subsequently whenever she had a problem she used to rush to him. Once we sent our two sons to seek his blessings, and he told them, "Consider your mother as Jagaddhatri ["sustainer of the world," an epithet of the Divine Mother], and convey my respects to her." With Maharaj's blessings we prevailed over many obstacles and hard times, and our sons grew up and became well established. After Maharaj went abroad for some time, we kept in touch with him and wrote to him about our problems. He always provided encouragement.

He used to speak on such a high level. Listening to his words I could understand that he was the very embodiment of Swami Vivekananda's ideals. He spoke about the synthesis of the dynamism and scientific culture of the West with the spiritual culture of India, and of how the West was yearning for some internal deepening in the midst of its material prosperity. Concerning aesthetic endeavours he would say: "Not art for art's sake, but art for the sake of the Higher Self."

When my younger son received a fellowship from the Dutch government for advanced studies, I took him to meet Maharaj. He blessed my son and told him that he should acquire knowledge to serve the people of India. When he returned after completing his studies, I again took him to Maharaj, who asked him in detail of what he had learned, what he had seen, and what could be useful. My son replied that he had learned the need for discipline and dedication to work. Maharaj told him to implement those principles in this country. When my son expressed frustration about the work ethos in India, Maharaj thought for some time and said, "Keep trying, don't get discouraged." Then when Maharaj heard that he had refused a lucrative job offer abroad in order to fulfil his fellowship commitment to serve India, as well as for the sake of his parents, Maharaj placed his hand on my son's head and said, "Blessing, my blessing."

I will end my reminiscence with two anecdotes. The first occurred when Maharaj was very ill at Seva Pratishthan. We went to see him with a tin of Complan [a food supplement], but they told us that he was unable to eat anything at all ("You have brought this in vain, he is unconscious"). Nevertheless, we left it for him. The next day I recounted our experience of the previous evening to my cousin Raghunath (who used to see Maharaj daily). Raghunath told us with amazement, "But Maharaj regained consciousness last night and he wanted Complan, so it was served to him!"

The second incident occurred when we came to South Calcutta from our home in Howrah to do some shopping before a trip to Varanasi. We hadn't seen Maharaj for some time but had an urge to visit him and seek his blessings, as we had heard that he was ill at Gol Park. But we were informed at the Institute's reception desk that he was very ill and that visitors were not allowed. My wife pleaded that we would just make our pranam from his door and leave. With great reluctance they sought his permission, and the reception people were incredulous when Maharaj asked us to go up to his room. We found him seated with straps around his chair to support him. Our eyes filled with tears to see him like this. He asked me about my work and my children. I informed him that I was making a documentary film for Raghunath on the Ramakrishna Mission Lokshiksa Parishad [the social welfare wing of Narendrapur, Ramakrishna Mission]. He asked me whether I was being paid for the work. I will never forget the smile of contentment I saw in his face when I replied in the affirmative. I also mentioned that my younger son was about to get married, and that I would like to bring the prospective bride to him. He said, "You have already approved, therefore I give my blessings." Then he gave us some significant personal instructions. We realized after we left that he had been talking with us for almost half an hour.

The next evening when I came home from work, I found my wife weeping. She told me that Maharaj had passed away, she had seen it in the television news. I was stunned. I was thinking of the previous evening and all that he had said to us. Did he know that he was leaving? His guidance seemed to be his final grace, and he remains in our thoughts as an ever-burning flame.

RAMANANDA BANDYOPADHYAY*

I first saw Swami Nitya-swarup-ananda about forty years back, and continued to see him through the various phases of my life. The memory of our long association remains crystal clear and radiant until today. Thoughts fill my mind as I reflect on it, but here I will cull only a few which strike me as revealing his true stature. Although I cannot assess the depth of his life as a sannyasin, I can perhaps touch upon his spiritual greatness through the special path of his aesthetic genius.

His aesthetic sensibility is ever enshrined in my mind, for through it I had a glimpse of God as Pure and Shining Beauty. This revelation came by observing the way he lived his life, the way he left his mark wherever he went. So many places still bear the bounty of his rarefied aesthetic, for in whichever Mission centre he stayed he would work to make it more elegant and refined by adding his touches. It was not just a matter of giving passive instructions, for he would become instantly immersed in the task himself, and whoever used to work with him quickly realized that lame excuses or loose explanations would never do.

The Ramakrishna Mission Institute of Culture in Calcutta, an example of exquisite Indian architecture, bears testimony to his total involvement and dedication. Few are aware of how much thought, how many endless rounds of discussion, had to take place to give this distinctive shape to his dreams. Not many of us know about the meticulous plans which were formulated and reformulated to finally make it happen, or of the scores of artists, architects, and thinkers who contributed (even Frank Lloyd Wright, the world-famous architect, discussed some concrete suggestions with Swami Nitya-swarup-ananda at one point in its planning). At each step of its creation, Chintaharan Maharaj's rare and subtle artistic sensibility was working to see that perfection was attained.

Every corner of this building was the product of his deep reflection and expressive of some profound thought. In the foyer where guests are entertained, he designed framed wall spaces that he wanted to fill with great works of art from all over the world. He had also given much thought to the blue-tiled wall in the corner of the expansive green lawn of the courtyard, where he wanted to inscribe some symbol which would express the mantra *jato mat, tato path,* a symbol to give a visual expression to this great saying of Sri Ramakrishna. After holding numerous talks with artists, scholars, and sculptors he finally designed the symbol himself, and it was absolutely *unique*—so very modern, yet very simple and eternal, just like Sri Ramakrishna's life itself.

This was the symbol he designed:

He worked very hard to give this symbol its perfect expression. Because we were linked with the world of art, we also had to work hard and struggle to give it the perfect expression. Then one day the task was accomplished and after that he wanted to have the symbol inscribed in the blue-tiled wall in a golden colour. He wanted to mount it there because it would then provide an ideal setting for people of various religions to come and discuss the Universal Religion as preached by Sri Ramakrishna.

He never wanted Thakur-Ma-Swamiji to be represented blatantly, because they were so subtle in essence. Through this institution he had envisioned, he wanted all to enter deep into a very special kind of spiritual experience. His purity of vision was reflected in the way he had the Universal Meditation Hall done up: a simple room with just a soft light and no particular pictures or images so that people of all creeds would come and meditate. He drew his inspiration from the age-old spiritual traditions of India.

Anything too ostentatious was painful to him. I remember on the Foundation Day of the Institute he would express his views about the decoration on the stage in Vivekananda Hall. He had very strong reservations about the picture of Swamiji up there all done up with lights. Though different people may have different tastes, we have to consider his views in the light of his artistic sensibility, even though he didn't favour imposing one's own views on others. Another time he asked me, "How do you walk across the round park adjacent to the Institute?" I was rather surprised at this odd question, and yet I knew that he must have some good reason behind it. I told him, "Why, the way everyone does it!" Then he confided to me, "When I walk across it, I do so with my head down." Now I was really astonished and asked, "Why, Maharaj?" "Because of that doll-like statue of Vivekananda which has been installed there," he replied, "it gives me so much pain to see it." Such was his refined taste and sensibility.

I have a special preference for repeatedly referring to his artistic sensibility because he demonstrated that art was a *sadhana* and a path to perfection, in keeping with Swami Vivekananda's vision of art. Many are unaware of Swamiji's thoughts on art and aesthetics, but he clearly indicated that art is a path to spiritual life. Indeed, any creative work—whether it be music, literature, or the visual arts—is a spiritual endeavour.

I am an artist, a painter, and it was from that perspective that he always focused our talks on Swamiji's idea of art. Art, he explained, was not restricted to a piece of painting or sculpture, but was something which should permeate our entire being. He would invariably ask me about the pictures I was painting and what were the thoughts occupying my mind. He fastened on the essential relationship of art to life, how it could be manifested in one's daily activities, and how behind such manifestation there should be a consciousness of eternal truth, for art should be inspired by that sublime emotion.

I can give examples of his casual utterances about art which I found profoundly significant. I joined the Institute in 1975 to set up the Art Museum, and I frequently consulted Chintaharan Maharaj on various topics. He had a very modern approach and his discussions on all the contemporary trends just filled me with wonder. One day he said, "Why do you call them 'objects of art'?" I was surprised and asked him what was wrong with it. He replied, "No, no, it is not *wrong*, but instead of this, if you call them objects of aesthetics, then the expression is complete. That day I realized that "objects of art" had a greater dimension. His subtle point was that art is not mere objects but an expression of Eternal Beauty, a vital force through which to develop one's spiritual perception. This was the deeper meaning of art and its aesthetic enrichment of life, without which its understanding was incomplete.

Through our frequent dialogues about art I had the good fortune to witness a beautiful and artistic mind and a dedicated soul. Even now his words keep ringing in my ears and I do not feel that he is gone. I keep as a talisman a stern letter he once wrote rebuking me about some work improperly done, but in which he felt so bad for doing so that he concluded the letter with these loving words: "Forever your well-wisher, Swami Nityaswarupananda." I consider it a major gift, a great benediction in my life, this silent flow of affection beneath a stern exterior.

Small instances reveal some of his other exceptional qualities, such as his talent for design (for there was never an excess in his layout for the Institute's excellent publications, such as *The Cultural Heritage of India* and the monthly *Bulletin*); his meticulous attention to detail, as when he used to ponder which would be the perfect page and place to inscribe a book he was presenting; his uncluttered neatness, for one could instantly learn in his company that cleanliness is next to godliness; and the catholicity and breadth of his understanding, for he believed that truth was not confined to one's creed alone.

But through each and every thread of his life, thought, and work there was one central theme: his vision was illumined by the teachings of Ramakrishna-Vivekananda. He believed that their ideals, their teachings, were the means to our deliverance. In the last years of his life during his stay at the Institute he used to feel dejected by the structural changes being added to the building because they were not in tune with his idea of architecture as sculpture (from which nothing can be added or subtracted). His thinking followed a particular path and deviation used to hurt him deeply. Yet he always had an unusual degree of faith and conviction in his mind that the teachings of Ramakrishna and Vivekananda would bring about a New Age from the rooms of that very Institute.

Whatever his distress, his final years were permeated with a wondrous vision, and I could get a faint glimpse of that *Satya-Sundar* [Truth-Beauty] which used to fill his mind. Through Chintaharan Maharaj, a blessed disciple of the Holy Mother, I feel that I have had the privilege to witness the perfect expression of the life of a sannyasin, a monk of such impeccable integrity that he was an exemplar among his own. No one can question that integrity should be inherent to the life of a sannyasin, so why make special mention of it? Here I would like to add that the kind of purity and integrity he emanated was rare even among sannyasins.

I always knew that I was in the presence of a great sannyasin, but this sannyasin was also a great aesthete. As an artist myself it was my rare good fortune to come into contact with Chintaharan Maharaj's sublime sense of the aesthetic. He was the vital link which deepened my understanding of Swami Vivekananda's vision of art and of its importance in my own life and work. Each moment I spent with him was elevating and still influences what I do every day.

SATYAPRIYA CHAKRAVORTY*

I remember Chintaharan Maharaj as a monk who was always full of joy, full of fun, and full of good humour. It was only in the late 1960s that I got to know him personally, although I had heard much about him and his work at the Institute, and had seen him from a distance.

I was closely associated with the Ramakrishna Mission Centre at Rahara, and it was with Swami Nityananda, then its Secretary, that I made a trip to a place called Bhatar in the district of Burdwan at the invitation of one Mr. Murari Hazra who had a big garden house there. This trip was memorable to me in more ways than one, for it was the first time I got the chance to be close to Chintaharan Maharaj and to serve him personally. This was not easy because he was fiercely self-reliant and would not readily accept *seva* from anyone. But I persisted in doing little things for him, like putting his slippers forward for him to step into comfortably, or handing him the towel, or pouring water to help him wash his hands (there were no taps). Doing these little things for him gave me immense pleasure. But what he felt about it was not known to me. Following our trip to Bhatar, I only got an inkling when I received a letter from him by post written on July 21–22, 1976, in his inimitable style. It was a mock heroic poem written in Sanskrit:

Embodiment of complete service,
Adorned with many attractive qualities,
Bringer of great satisfaction and joy,
Of pleasant speech,
By your service have enthralled your friend Chintaharan,

You are an accomplished sadhaka,
In destroying the qualities of self-dependence,

And giving birth to many poisonous fruits
With the sweet nectarine flow of your service,
Which has the power of totally incapacitating,

    To dear Mr. Satyapriya Chakravorty
    You have brought with you
       a loving heart
    Which is why you are giving
       the gift of pure service.

              Your companion of Bhatar,
              who was enthralled by your service.

To make sure that I received this letter, he made two copies with his own hand and posted them separately. Just imagine my reaction when I got two copies of this hilarious letter in quick succession!

One or two very fond memories of the trip to Bhatar come to my mind. There was a large pond attached to the house where we were put up. Fishing was organized with great fanfare in the early hours of the dawn as Maharaj personally supervised the entire operation. Then when the net was hauled in he would give instructions: "Keep this one, and this and this, now free the remaining fishes." Then he entered into the kitchen and gave instructions on preparing tasty dishes. I remember that those fish dishes were very simple, without many spices, but they were very delicate. How we all admired his culinary skills!

Subsequently I accompanied him on another trip. This time it was to a place called Julu near Lucknow. Salil Maharaj, Secretary of the Lucknow Ashrama, organized this trip. It was a very beautiful garden house surrounded by orchards. Maharaj appreciated the calm beauty of the place very much and would say to me, "Satyapriya, how nice it would be to live a life of retreat in such serene surroundings." I would nod my head and also sigh a bit with the knowledge that such a thing was never to happen in my life with all my commitments. Somehow, when I think of the place today, I am reminded of Tennyson's famous poem "The Lotus Eaters."

In the mid-1970s, when he was leading a life of semi-retirement at the

Belur Math, I used to go and see him whenever I got some time off from my work. He was based at the Belur Math even though he sometimes travelled to New Delhi and other places. I have called it "semi" retirement because he was always busy with some work, mostly writing.

It was only after my own retirement from government service in the 1980s that I found some more time to visit him. He was then spending his last years at the Institute of Culture. Even then I found him busy writing a book. I never probed, but sometimes he would make me read out some passage. Once during such a reading session I got excited with the material and started reading very loudly. "Satyapriya," he said with a smile, "if these people get to hear this, they will not like you very much." It was only through such stray remarks that I got the idea that his stay at the Institute was not very pleasant.

He seemed to be carrying a great burden in his heart. Outwardly he was still full of laughter and would joke and make fun, yet one could sense that he was in great pain. Probably the sight of all-round degradation which had pervaded his beloved Order, and the careless manner in which things were being done—the lack of *nishtha* in everything—filled him with despair. He who was such a perfectionist in every detail, one who could spend months worrying over the appropriateness of a comma or a full stop in his writing, was bound to feel the lack of spirit of worship which should have been there in all the work.

He had undertaken this great burden, to caution his brother monks about their deviation, and to urge them to come back to Vivekananda. He fought for this cause until the very end, single-handedly, and he left this world with his head held high.

SREELA DEVI NAKACHI

"Not 'Chintaharan' Maharaj [one who alleviates worries], but 'Chintakaran' Maharaj [one who causes worries]," would giggle the Swami in a half-serious tone to one and many who came into his orbit.

He was of a fair complexion, with a broad build, but rather short of stature—a roly-poly cuddly swami when he sank into a chair, with sparks of fiery reprimand and sweetness alternating as he dealt with his visitors, friends, and devotees. A brilliant mind at work, he gave the impression that so much remained to be done in so little time at hand.

He possessed a vast social and liberal outlook, even to the extent of introducing his friends to each other with much pleasure and taking them to each other's homes. He spread friendship and affection in all directions through his wide circle of acquaintances. He took joy and interest in whomever he came across, keen to know about their life and soon to charm them with his warm concern. Small wonder we were all captivated!

It was sometime in 1977 that I first met the Swami. Rather interested to hear that I was wedded to a Japanese, he expressed a desire to try out Japanese cuisine. This provided a welcome opportunity to prepare Japanese culinary delicacies for him. Since my early days I had travelled extensively, and while I had enjoyed the language and arts of each culture, it was always the science and art of each culture's cuisine that had fascinated me the most. I felt that I came to know people most easily over the table and through the kitchen hearth.

Thereafter, it was with great joy that I looked forward on many occasions to the privilege of preparing some of the Swami's favourite requests, dishes such as caviar, mushrooms, cheese, and butter asparagus recipes. He knew how much I liked to present him with such dishes. To please me, the Swami like a child would make me happy, exclaiming: "All right now, put all this God talk aside for awhile, and tell me what you have brought for me. What have you prepared for me?"

But the sphere of the godly was ever present in his company. With his tremendous dimension, he was at one and the same time an idealistic visionary and a pragmatic down-to-earth realist. And with his wizardly vision, he moved easily from the personal to the global. His life recalls to me the utterances of the great and successful, that if one wants to do anything great and good, one will have to face mighty obstacles and even be disliked. For whatever is done is best done in a big and bold way. Reality is harsh, just as the truth is harsh when there is no compromise. The martial spirit and strength to triumph is not in one and all alike; but through those who possess it, the inscrutable cosmic power of Mahamaya enacts Her play in Her own inscrutable way.

A chosen receptacle and a true soldier of the great Swami Vivekananda, Sri Ramakrishna Paramahamsa Dev, and Sreema Saradamani Devi, Swami Nitya-swarup-ananda was fighting a crusade to bring back to light their highest ideals and principles before his physical departure, and to demolish the disintegrating forces which sway even a wise man in this realm of *maya*.

PRABHAT KUMAR BANERJEE*

Some twenty years ago, in about 1977, I had gone to the Belur Math. After making my pranam to Bharat Maharaj, I sat down on the bench outside his office, which was on the ground floor of Swami Vivekananda's old house near the Ganges, with the ancient mango tree on the courtyard side. In those days Bharat Maharaj used to greet visitors in this office.

I noticed a sannyasin sitting cross-legged in the chair on the opposite side of the veranda. Ochre-robed, he was stocky, short in height, fair-complexioned, and large-eyed. His head was held high and his person radiated peace and solemnity. His eyes seemed to be stretched to the far horizon, absorbed in thoughts in eternity. I was reminded of *Mahadeva* [Shiva]. I was fascinated and full of reverence, and kept thinking to myself, who can he be? I have been coming to this Math so often, why didn't I meet this enlightened sannyasin before? Just then, Montu Babu, Bharat Maharaj's attendant and companion, came and stood by me. I asked him the name of this monk. He seemed surprised and said, "Don't you know? He is Chintaharan Maharaj, Swami Nitya-swarup-ananda!" I was eager to go and make my pranam but somehow I could not disturb with my touch that quiet meditative figure in whom seemed to be streaming the powerful Falgu [a mythological underground river that signifies a hidden spiritual current].

Later on I heard that Chintaharan Maharaj spent most of his time for reasons of health outside of Calcutta. But I got acquainted with him at the Belur Math through a friend, Phani Bhusan Sanyal. Phani Bhusan

Babu was the son of Anukul Sanyal, a classmate of Swami Madhavananda and a disciple of Holy Mother, a favourite of Bharat Maharaj
and greatly liked by all the senior monks of the Order. He took me to
Chintaharan Maharaj's room. Maharaj was very happy to see Phani
Babu and asked him, "Oh, Phani, how are you?" They both talked for
some time and then Phani-da introduced me to Maharaj with praise
which embarrassed me. Chintaharan Maharaj was happy to know that I
had been close to Swami Shraddhananda from an early age and told me
that it was fortunate to be close to a sadhu such as Swami Shraddhananda (Bimal Maharaj). I told him that Bimal Maharaj had been my
father's student. Bimal Maharaj was then the Head of the Vedanta Society of Sacramento, California. "Sacramento is a beautiful place, and the
Ashrama has a wonderful atmosphere," Chintaharan Maharaj said to
me, "why don't you go there? Bimal is there, you will have no problems, you will enjoy it." I smiled but didn't reply.

After that I sought his pure company whenever I visited the Belur
Math. On one occasion I was describing my experience of meeting
Swami Virajananda at the Belur Math when he was the President of the
Order and Swami Shraddhananda was his Secretary. Swami Virajananda was staying on the first floor of Swamiji's house. I was then a
young student. Swami Shraddhananda took me to the President, and I
was awed. I was describing this experience to Chintaharan Maharaj
when he reacted sharply by saying, "You went to see him only *one* day.
Just *one* day! Do you know how fortunate it is to meet a great *tapaswi*
[one who does *tapasya*, or spiritual discipline]? And you went to see him
just *one* day?" I was filled with remorse. I then observed that Chintaharan Maharaj was lost in thought. Maybe he was remembering that
great *sadhaka*. He was looking out of the open window absolutely
quiet.

One day I entered Chintaharan Maharaj's room and found him reading a huge book with great concentration. I made my pranam. He just
gestured and asked me to sit while he continued reading. Suddenly I saw
Swami Gambhirananda standing at the door. He told Chintaharan

Maharaj that he remembered that so-and-so was in charge of something at Mayavati at a particular time. I cannot remember the details of that conversation, but I still recall that Chintaharan Maharaj was happy on hearing this and had nodded to show his consent. After Gambhiranandaji left, Chintaharan Maharaj started talking to me. A few of our friends had started gathering on Sundays at Phani Bhusan Sanyal's house to discuss the teachings of Thakur-Ma-Swamiji, the teachings of the direct disciples, and other spiritual matters. Phani-da was the moving spirit of the whole exercise. Chintaharan Maharaj was very happy and said, "Bah, ayee to chai [Good, this is what is needed]. What is the use of repeating the name of Sri Ramakrishna, you have to establish him in your heart. You will have to try to understand his teachings. You will have to think about him—only then you will advance. It is good to have these things discussed in small groups as you are doing. Good, good!"

I remember one evening. It was not yet dark. After coming down from Thakur's Temple, I met Chintaharan Maharaj. We started walking, and while walking he kept talking about Swamiji. I asked him to explain to me certain portions of the book which he had written in English, specially where he talks about the uniqueness of each country or race. He explained briefly. He also explained to me beautifully that India's uniqueness was religion. As he was talking I was very keen to ask him about the Ramakrishna Mission Institute of Culture which he had founded. I was aware of his great contribution towards building up this institution, but the topic had never come up. Even on that day, my desire to hear him speak about it was not fulfilled.

I used to notice that whenever he spoke about Swamiji, his face would become radiant with devotion and reverence, which cannot be described in words. He repeatedly spoke of Swamiji's life, and of his teachings to rejuvenate humanity in the spirit of Vedanta. One day while discussing Swamiji's letters, he drew attention to the diverse ideas therein and asked me, "Can you do something?" I looked at him quite puzzled. He added, "Many different ideas are spread throughout his letters. Can you classify them and group them categorically?" I told

him that I would try to fulfil this task with his blessings. He encouraged
me and told me, "After completing the task, send the manuscript to me.
I will go through it carefully and give you my opinion."

I took almost a year to finish it, written in two exercise books (I still
remember the date, May 10, 1980). I handed over the manuscript to him
with apprehension. I told him, "Maharaj, I have tried to do this work
according to your directions. I don't know whether I have been successful." I went to see him a month later. He praised me profusely and said,
"This is true *sadhana*. You have done good work. I had wanted to do this
personally, but could not for various reasons. Anyway, you have done it
quite well. Continue with this kind of *sadhana*." Later on another senior
monk went through the manuscript and advised me to write a comprehensive preface and get it published. The preface has been written but
the book has somehow not yet been published. But my satisfaction is that
I have obeyed the orders of that great *tapaswi*. After that I had lost touch
with him for some time. Probably he had gone out of Calcutta. Suddenly
after many days I saw him at Udbodhan, Mother's House. He was sitting
with quite a number of devotees in a room on the first floor. I made my
pranam and came away. This was the last meeting.

What an extraordinary life! Seeker of knowledge, Karma Yogi,
Founder of the great Ramakrishna Mission Institute of Culture, how
he withdrew from all that to lead a reclusive spiritual life towards the
end. The Gita has described such souls as One who surrenders everything, and how significant it was that he breathed his very last in that
very Institute which he had created.

I have been able to cull a few gems from my *jhuli* [knapsack]. Other
precious gems may lie hidden there, but I have lost them in the mean-
dering path of my life. At this advanced age it is not possible for me to
remember the exact time and date of our meetings, or even to remember his exact words, but I have tried to express the essence of his teachings with care in this reminiscence.

NANDITA DATTA*

Swami Nitya-swarup-ananda was, in his eternal essence (*nitya-swarup*), a sannyasin full of bliss (*ananda*). Wherever there was Bharat Maharaj, there you always found Chintaharan Maharaj. It is difficult for me to express any memories of the Belur Math which exclude Bharat Maharaj, so in this writing I refer to him quite frequently. I was a regular visitor to the Math with my father and aunts. My mother had died when I was very young, so I was brought up by my grandmother and paternal aunts. I still feel very deeply the affection I received from Bharat Maharaj and Chintaharan Maharaj, along with the holy company of other monks.

The Belur Math was like my beloved paternal home (as the monks would later tell my sons while asking them to take *prasad*). Those days are still fresh in my mind more than thirty-eight years later. In that propitious environment my sisters and I were initiated by Swami Shankarananda, and I was also in close contact with Surya Maharaj (Swami Nirvanananda), Jiten Maharaj (Swami Vishuddhananda), Swami Madhavananda, Prafulla Maharaj, Swami Gangesananda, and Swami Ranganathananda. Specially when I was a student at Indraprastha College, I used to make arrangements for Swami Ranganathananda to lecture in our college and various other places.

We used to stay in New Delhi but would go to the Belur Math during all our visits to Calcutta. My father's cousin was Swami Pavitrananda, the Head of the Vedanta Society in New York. My father, a disciple of Swami Vijnanananda, used to visit this Vedanta Society on his regular travels as a high-ranking official in the Ministry of External Affairs. Whenever Swami Pavitrananda came to Delhi, we would visit the Delhi Ashrama so frequently that it became like a second home.

Bharat Maharaj used to come to Delhi quite often, always letting us know about his arrival. When I used to talk with him about various details of my life, he would listen attentively and guide me. This was the relationship I had with him till his last days. Once Chintaharan Maharaj accompanied him to Delhi, and they both came to a dinner at our house. It was very cold that night. The *gerua* robes of these two monks brightened our drawing room. This was the first time I saw Chintaharan Maharaj. His manner was most pleasing, and his large expressive eyes lent a compelling appearance to his face. We were told that he was the Founder of the Ramakrishna Mission Institute of Culture, which had earned international recognition as a propagator of Sri Ramakrishna's ideals. They finished their dinner. Somehow Chintaharan Maharaj spilled some gravy on his punjabi [jacket], staining it with turmeric. I summoned courage and said, "Maharaj, give me the punjabi, I'll wash it." He gave it to me and I quickly washed and pressed it, and he was pleased.

I kept in touch with him through letters, which, though brief, managed to solve all my problems. Then we shifted to Calcutta after my marriage and I used to go to the Belur Math every Sunday and to the Institute on weekdays. Chintaharan Maharaj always encouraged my husband (a physician) in his work.

One day in 1978 he called me on the telephone: "Krishna (my pet name), a few disciples of Swami Pavitrananda have come to Calcutta. They want to meet the relatives of Swami Pavitrananda (who had just passed away). You invite them to dinner, and also introduce them to the other relatives of Pavitrananda Maharaj. It will make them happy." I implored Maharaj, "You also please come with them." He readily agreed, and even told me the menu.

Mr. Erik Johns from New York was one of the three visitors. He showed the coat he was wearing. "Do you know who it belongs to?" he asked, then added, "Swami Pavitrananda." I was very touched by their respect for the monks of the Order.

Another of the visitors was a disciple of Swami Pavitrananda, a Jewish-German actress who had undergone severe torture at concentration camps during the Second World War and was afflicted with Parkinson's disease. Her limbs were trembling but her mind was in a very serene state because she had taken refuge in Sri Ramakrishna.

Time passed. One evening I got a note from Erik Johns written in

English: "Krishna, I want to see you, will you be at home in the evening?"
I sent back a reply by messenger. Later on I came to know that Mr. Erik
Johns himself had come to deliver the letter. I rang up Chintaharan
Maharaj and told him that Mr. Erik Johns had come personally, but I
didn't realize it and didn't ask him to come up, and I was feeling very
bad about it. Maharaj started teasing me and said, "Don't feel bad about
it. Perhaps he had enjoyed the dinner and the conversation last time, so
he probably wants to repeat the experience. He will go to your house
with another friend. Give them a nice treat." I asked him, "Maharaj,
aren't you coming with them?" He said, "No, I am not keeping too well.
I have a fixed schedule for my meals, so I will not go." But I prepared
something light for him and took it to him, and he was so happy! He
always used to praise and encourage whatever I cooked. At the same
time he was severe in his reprimand for any deviation.

It was a very tragic event in my life when my youngest brother, who
had gone to America for higher studies, was killed in a car accident. I was
beside myself with grief. Chintaharan Maharaj told me not to be so overwhelmed with sorrow and he further said, "He has given life, and He has
taken it away. This world is impermanent. You cannot avoid fate."

We used to go to him quite often. Many people visited him and discussions were held on various topics. I noticed that he used to encourage all types of activities. I had just started publishing a quarterly magazine named *Divya-Jyotir Pathé*. When I sent him the first issue he
called me that evening, giving me his blessings and saying that he had
liked the magazine and considered it good work. Maharaj used to read
each and every issue with great care.

Whenever I visited him at the Institute, we used to go to the
receptionist first and ask his permission to go up. In spite of his failing health, he always welcomed us and would listen to us with a smiling face. I have great regret in my life that I was out of India when he
passed away. I got the news when I returned that another bright star
of the Ramakrishna Movement was gone.

GAUTAM CHATTERJI

The first time I saw Swami Nitya-swarup-ananda, I was a schoolboy in Class VIII. I used to see him walking around the Rabindra Sarovar Lake near the Ramakrishna Mission Institute of Culture at Gol Park with his dhoti tucked at the back. He walked for several miles, circling the lake boldly like a lion, and I used to follow him from a distance. No one dared to talk to him or come near him—even illustrious personalities living around the lake stayed clear of his path. So at that time, I didn't get to know him.

Then I met him at the Delhi Ashrama when I was there in 1978. He was seated with the Secretary, and he handed me his HMT [Hindustan Machine Tools] watch, because I was associated with HMT and he wanted to have it fixed. I had that done and he asked how much it cost. He wanted to give me the money but I refused to take it. There followed an animated discussion about how watches are manufactured, to what precision in twenty-four hours HMT can control deviation, whether HMT is the best as per the world standard, and so forth. I never forget that first lively discussion with this awesome personality that I had seen from afar in Gol Park. Afterwards he confessed to me that he had never realized he struck such an awesome figure.

I saw him again with my wife when we were visiting the Belur Math in 1984; he was sitting side by side with Bharat Maharaj on two chairs in front of Bharat Maharaj's room. There were benches set at right angles to their chairs on three sides. Devotees were coming and making their obeisance to them, and I pointed out to my wife, "There you see the two giants sitting side by side!" We also made our pranam to them, and stood by their side.

Swami Nitya-swarup-ananda asked us to sit down on the bench to the right, and started asking our names, whereabouts, what we do—and then suddenly, out of context, he started lamenting that within one hundred years of Swamiji, the movement had lost its force, its intensity. I replied by saying, "But Maharaj, we should not despair so much because one hundred years after Christ went, hardly anyone knew about Christianity in the world." "As a historical record," I continued my remarks, "there is only one letter from one of the Roman guards who was present at the crucifixion by the side of Christ, who had written to his home in the village: 'Today they have crucified a young man called "Joshua" who the Jews call their king.'" When I had finished Maharaj simply said, "But today man has set foot on the moon." Immediately I wanted to reply, but then in a flash the purport of his reply came to me: yes, he was absolutely right! He asked me, "Have you followed what I have said?" I replied, "Yes, it is an era of communication."

He paused briefly, looked at us, and quickly got up. He asked us to follow him. He started walking very fast, and we followed him through the Math making a detour to his room. He made us sit down in his room, and asked many questions we didn't understand at the time, but which we later realized were probing our lifestyle and mindset. Then he brought out two of his publications and presented them to us, and after going through them briefly, I said, "This is not practical." He said, "Why is it not practical?" I said, "The success for this type of work can be achieved only if Brahmajnanis [illumined souls] are at the helm of affairs." To that he replied sardonically, "So till you become a Brahmajnani, you won't make any attempt to do this work?" I think he wanted to make us realize that every one of us has to make an effort in our own way. The meeting ended inconclusively, and I was not fully convinced at that time. As was his custom, he came out of the room and stood on the veranda, watching us till we were out of his sight—that was always the case every time we went to see him at the Belur Math.

He made us realize that every work will have to be done properly and to perfection. He gave me the great privilege of attending to his daily chores, such as arranging his clothes in the almirah [closet]. After he used to come back from his evening walk of making pranam to all the temples in the evening, he would return perspiring and panting for breath with his walking stick in hand. I used to wait downstairs till he appeared on the horizon, then I went running to take the stick from his hand. He would then rest his right hand on my shoulder, and, one by one, we would ascend the staircase. The door of the room used to remain closed, so I had to rush, open the door, put on the light, and keep the stick by the left side of the almirah, while he would go straight for his cot and sit down there. I would open the fan, go to him, and take off his punjabi in a certain way which we were trained to do. The exact sequence had to be followed: next came the watch, then the socks. After that, the socks had to be put in the air on the veranda following which I rushed back to the toilet to wash my hands (not from the basin, because the hands had touched the socks, but from the bucket), dry the hands, and only then give him a glass of water. In all this, he would not utter a word, at the most he would gesture with his finger, and you had to understand the gist of it. He would be sitting with the banyan [sleeveless vest] and dhoti and recovering his breath. For three or four years, I went through this drill frequently in both the Math and the Institute of Culture, wherever he happened to be.

Then this incident came when I was with him and was going through the routine of removing his clothes, and had to put his watch in a box. When the lid closed, it made a snapping sound. He reacted sharply as if it had hurt him and reprimanded me, "Why did you have to do like that? There is a proper way of doing everything." Then he narrated a similar incident he had had with Shukul Maharaj, Swamiji's disciple, in the old Dacca Math; he had made the same mistake and Shukul Maharaj had become similarly upset and had showed him how the lid of a box will have to be closed by first pressing the knob at the bottom with the left thumb, then bringing the top lid down gently until it sits easily on the bottom surface, and then only the knob is released to lock it without any noise!

Another example: whenever I went to him by driving, he would ask, "From where have you come, and which route did you take?" It had to be the shortest possible route or he would be quite irritated. He mentioned that this had also been taught to him by Shukul Maharaj.

Next was his exact way of arranging a suitcase. That was a story by itself. I personally packed his suitcase for the United States trip in 1987, as I had done on several previous occasions. He would sit on his cot and I would be on the floor in front of him with that empty suitcase with the lid open. The layers of dhotis and punjabis and vests, sweaters and mufflers had to be packed in a logical sequence, with alternating longitudinal and transverse layers at exact right angles, so that not a square millimetre of space was left vacant. In this packing exercise, I have competed successfully with brahmacharis, and Maharaj always called me back. All these were preparations of the mind.

In the Institute of Culture generally I used to meet him before my day's work, and later in the evening after finishing it. I would stay with him till his dinner time at least, which was usually very light. He sometimes persuaded me to share his food. His casual remarks at such times have become deeply imprinted on my mind. On one occasion, he made his pranam to the photos of Thakur, the Holy Mother, and Swamiji which used to be by his bedside, and then to the combined photograph of Thakur, Ma, and Swamiji along with all the direct disciples. Then he just uttered, "These are the only photos to whom I make my pranam, none others." This impressed me. On another occasion when he was hospitalized at Seva Pratishthan, I remained in attendance up to 10 o'clock at night throughout his stay. One morning, around 9:30, he suddenly smiled to himself and said, "Why do you have to explicitly make your pranam [to him] so many times? Do it in your mind. There you won't have any restriction—there is no impediment or restriction." At that time, I had read about *manas-puja* [mental offering] and was under the impression that this can be performed only by advanced souls and not by beginners like myself. But later I came to understand the meaning of it by his grace, and even though he has left the body, I continue to feel his grace guiding my daily life.

ANADI DAS

My reminiscences of Swami Nitya-swarup-ananda are very personal. It may be worthwhile to write these experiences in order to bring out some aspects of this many-sided holy person. He was a classmate and lifelong friend of my late father, Mr. Bidhu Ranjan Das (a disciple of Swami Brahmananda). They used to study together for their B.A. degrees in Jagannath College of Dacca, and shared a room in the college dormitory. He told my father that if he dozed off while studying late at night, my father should pull his hair to wake him up!

He used to visit our family regularly during the last four decades and often shared our joys and sorrows like a family member. In 1978 when we visited India he gave my family some money from his own pocket to buy some special fish for us, and instructed us how to cook it. He told us several times that my wife and I were very fortunate to have served the very special holy man, the late Swami Vividishanandaji of Seattle.

I met Swami Nitya-swarup-ananda for the last time in December 1991 in the Institute. He said he liked my booklet "Vedanta and Relativity" very much and to send him more copies. When we saluted him goodbye, he blessed us with a peaceful smile. I was not sure if we would see him again. Although we know that Swami Nitya-swarup-ananda is resting in the lap of the Holy Mother Herself, still we shall miss him very much in this physical plane of existence.

1980s

(New friends)

RAGHUNATH GOSWAMI

I have had the good fortune of receiving a number of letters from Swami Nitya-swarup-ananda. Most of these letters are connected to memorable situations in my life. Therefore, rather than just talk about the contents of some of these letters, I will also try to describe the circumstances involved.

One of my cousins introduced me to Swami Nitya-swarup-ananda in early 1980, in the days before the International Convention of the Ramakrishna Mission. At that time the Belur Math was the Swami's usual abode. He lived in a room at the monks' quarters that were at the back of the main temple near the Ganga.

When I first met him in 1980, the walls of his room were really very bare except for a framed picture which was a composite of Sri Ramakrishna, the Holy Mother, Swamiji, and all the monastic disciples of Sri Ramakrishna. The individual photos in this composite were small, almost in postage-stamp size. "My gods and goddesses," he used to say when referring to the personalities featured in that picture.

He had two very spartan cots in his room, one which he used for sleeping and the other for visitors to sit on. The only other furniture in the room was a writing desk, one chair for the visitors (which he also used for his desk work), one very ordinary kind of easy chair near the window for Maharaj himself, and one innocuously placed meat safe [food cabinet]. Maharaj used to store very precious chocolates and bakery products, mostly brought by his foreign friends and admirers, in that meat safe. Maharaj was very fond of offering these tempting items to his visitors almost indiscriminately, but with the greatest affection.

I must mention something about certain developments which took place in Maharaj's room in course of time. A gentleman admirer of Maharaj, who was the owner of a carpentry shop, offered his services to construct storage cabinets in the very small anteroom which was nothing but part of Maharaj's bathroom. This gentleman gave him the idea that the bathroom could be partitioned with the storage units built up on one side of the wall. As a result of this project the entire room became completely crammed with partitions, which made Maharaj extremely disappointed and angry. After its completion Maharaj suggested innumerable revisions and corrections but the gentleman, despite his deep reverence and love for him, couldn't possibly conform to his precise standards. Finding no other option, the gentleman disappeared from the scene almost forever.

One day when I had been to the Belur Math and visited him, he told me to go to the anteroom and inspect the condition there. When I came back, he asked very candidly, "Could you possibly do something about it?" Just to minimize Maharaj's tension, I said, "What's wrong with this, Maharaj?" He told me with a grim face, "Being a designer, you are not supposed to ask me this question. Can't you find out the problems yourself?" Then he said, "There are six storage cabinets in various sizes fixed onto the wall projecting out, but they are not in a straight line. None of the shutters and doors of these function." I brought him one of our finest carpenters and also a supervisor to examine the extent of the problem in depth. Then we listed the things to be done in the anteroom, and enunciated all the items of work to Maharaj. Maharaj gave me a patient hearing, but at the end he said, "Don't you think it's much easier for you to pull the whole thing down?"

After a protracted discussion regarding design principles, aesthetics, functionalism, materials, process—everything—we came to some solution. We decided to pull down three-quarters of it, leaving only one cabinet which Maharaj somehow agreed to suffer. He used to put his soiled clothes and towels for the laundry in this cabinet.

Then to compensate this loss I suggested to Maharaj that he should have a small recessed cabinet projected from the wall in his room, to be used as his desk containing all his stationery and other writing needs, but with everything hidden when not in use in a storage area behind the hinged lid. He immediately was thrilled with the idea of throwing away the existing desk and using this in its place. The whole exercise proved to be a trying one on my part and I can well remember without exaggeration that I had to make innumerable trips to the Belur Math with my carpenters and experts in hardware, experts in polishing, etc., by turn. When it was finished, he remarked, "This polish on the *inside* of the desk doesn't look quite right, could you possibly change it?"

Somehow, by the grace of Maharaj, I eventually completed this difficult task of making him happy. After a week or so, he asked me to make an identical piece of furniture as a mirror image for the opposite wall. This proposed cabinet he wanted to use as his dining table, which complicated matters. I think I had learned certain lessons from the first project and made the second cabinet with fewer hassles. He was quite happy with these two cabinets and used to show them to his visitors with a lot of satisfaction.

Swami's room was on the first floor of the monks' quarters, and there was an adjoining veranda. His room was visible at a distance even from the entrance of the Belur Math campus. The very sight of his room with the doors open used to make us extremely happy. I can clearly remember an incident when the Swami was away in Delhi for a month or so. One day I came to the Belur Math with my wife, Bhabani. As usual, we stopped at the entrance of the campus and looked towards Maharaj's room, which was obviously locked up. We stopped there for some time for no apparent reason, and I discovered Bhabani was staring at Maharaj's room with her eyes filled with tears. In a subsequent letter, I hesitantly mentioned this small incident to Maharaj. I received his reply soon, dated 25 March 1982. He said, "You have mentioned that you saw Bhabani's tear-filled eyes on noticing a certain locked room in the Math. This remark is an instance of your extreme concern for Bhabani, but I have a feeling that you have not only been a witness to Bhabani's tear-filled eyes but of thousands of instances of actual shedding of these tears." He added seriously, "In fact, to keep Bhabani in unalloyed happiness should be your avowed objective, and hence you should maintain a solicitous watch for the slightest trace in Bhabani's expression of internal distress."

I still remember his first letter to me. I used to work at different sites at the Belur Math campus quite late in the evening to catch up with the time schedule of various exhibitions and presentations I was preparing for the Ramakrishna Mission Convention in 1980. I used to work alone or at times with some of my colleagues. During the day and most of the time in the evenings, Swami used to come regularly and silently watch our activities and work. Within a very few days I felt some kind of an urge of talking to Swami. I started conversing with him mostly in a fragmented manner in the beginning. The major portion of our conversation used to be concerning the Ramakrishna-Vivekananda movement and various important topics related to it. This conversation appeared to me as a very rare opportunity for me to illuminate my mind. I soon realized the depth of Swami's perception and clarity of thought. Somehow he made the whole atmosphere so congenial that it emboldened me to ask many more questions. His replies were very simple and direct as well as comprehensive. But Swami's communication was more than just passing on some dry information—it was information and beyond.

Our conversation in the midst of the serenity of the Belur Math was an unforgettable experience on my part. When the work was completed at the Math, I felt like writing him a letter. I wanted to communicate my deep feeling in this letter that he actually acted as a bridge between past and present, between darkness and light. I received his reply within a week. It was incredibly humble on his part. "No, no, you are wrong in saying so," he wrote to me, "actually it is you who are the bridge between the past and the present with your work." By the way, I am in the design profession. This simple comment gave me an entirely new perception and feeling about my work. Instead of making me self-conscious, it made me aware of the gravity and the almost overwhelming responsibility of my profession in the area of communication design.

I stayed in Dum Dum [in northern Calcutta] for a long period before I migrated to South Calcutta in 1987. Our abode was two-storied and pretty spacious. We kept the upstairs fairly empty, with a separate room meant for the swamis to rest when they came to visit. One day Maharaj visited us and after the meal he asked me to read out a few passages from *The ThreeFold Cord*, the monograph on the objectives of the Ramakrishna Mission Institute of Culture. He then explained something about his concept of universal education. Just after this I decided to play back Ravi Shankar's recorded piece which has music interwoven from East and West. Then I told the Swami that this is an example of universality through music. He listened to it with great interest, as I tried to annotate the music here and there while it was playing. I could see that he was quite absorbed in the music and with his kind of insight, trying to relate it to the theme of universality. "Maharaj, just listen to this—this is the oboe, this is the harp, etc.," I was remarking to him when he replied, "Yes, this is important, but don't get lost in the details. Rather concentrate on the spirit of the music." This was a great relevant caution for me. Maharaj himself attended to every detail, but he knew how to restrain his mind from being overwhelmed by such things.

Maharaj had excellent taste in food as part of an overall highly refined aesthetic appreciation. We had the privilege of working out menus for him on many occasions. I usually had to prepare at least three options to take to Maharaj at the Belur Math for his choosing. As an example: "Menu 1: Meat Soup with Wheat, Bakharkhani with Peanut, Sheek Kabab, Dal-Keemat, Paneer-Korma, Kashmiri Meat Preparation (with Almond), Salted Raita with Bundia, Papaya Salad with Salt and Black Pepper, Tarbooz Sorbet (with Ice)" *or* "Menu 2: Mulligatawny Soup, Meat-Puri, Urid Maah Dal, Paneer Korma, Meat Masala, Raita, Papaya Salad with Salt and Black Pepper." It was a great joy to cook for Maharaj; he was a genuine appreciator of the very best in all things because of his great sensitivity.

It was perhaps in July 1981 we invited Swami to our house in Dum Dum for lunch. I decided to prepare kabab (mincemeat treated with various spices, cake-shaped, fried over a slow fire). I have a strange habit of labelling all the vessels, bowls, jars, and bottles containing ingredients and spices with the quantity to be used marked on them, and also arrange them sequentially before I start cooking. I also label the back of serving plates, vessels, and bowls to be used. Frankly speaking, I never wanted Swami to see this ridiculous method which is so very personal. So I decided to set up a small kitchen in a tiny room (almost like a hideout) up on the first floor. We planned to make Swami comfortable in my study on the ground floor. Bhabani and others would keep him busy in conversation so that he wouldn't come up and see my strange culinary arrangement. While I was busy with my cooking, concentrating on the frying pan, I could sense someone's presence at the door. I looked up and discovered the Swami standing at the door watching me from a distance. He didn't speak a word, but came inside and to my utter nervousness started examining all those pots and pans with the labels. I could see that he was interested in the written words of the labels. I tried to be a little smart and told Maharaj, "This habit of mine is perhaps ridiculous and amateurish."

He simply kept quiet in a very grave mood. Strangely enough, we didn't discuss anything about this particular topic. We came out to the open terrace and started talking about completely different things. I was very thankful to him for not making any comment on what he had seen inside the kitchen. That would have been embarrassing for me. We came downstairs, had our meal, and then went to my study on the ground floor. Sitting in a chair he looked through the window and almost like a soliloquy, he said, "There is no such thing as 'end'; ends are nothing but the cumulative effect of means." After a pause, he continued, "What I have seen at your kitchen upstairs is something very important in life. One should pay utmost attention to perfect his means to reach a desirable end. Means are equally important as ends." He mentioned this incident in a letter, dated 14 July 1981, reminding me of how much means are inseparably connected to ends.

I received a letter from the Swami, dated 28 October 1981, informing me about his plan to travel to various places. He wanted to leave for Varanasi on 7 November and from there to Delhi via Kanpur and Lucknow. He was uncertain about his return. In the same letter he expressed his wish to see us before leaving the Belur Math. We requested him to give us the privilege to have lunch with him at our place. On the appointed day, the Swami arrived at our house completely drenched in sweat, and almost panting. Before we could ask any questions, he told us that he had come by bus all the way from Belur to Dum Dum, changing three times in between. I said in a complaining tone, "Maharaj, why didn't you ask me to send our transport?" Immediately I could realize the foolishness on my part to ask such a question to the Swami. I should have sent the transport on my own. I said so to him and apologized. The octogenarian Swami said, "It is none of your fault. I wanted to experience how people commute every day by such a crowded bus. I think I should *always* travel by bus."

Another incident regarding transport was related to me by a monk of the Swami's Order who actually witnessed it. The day after Swami Nitya-swarup-ananda retired from the Ramakrishna Mission Institute

of Culture, the monk was on a tram and saw Maharaj walking on College Street burdened by a huge suitcase which he was taking for repair.
The younger monk immediately got off the tram and asked him, "What
is the matter? Why are you carrying this heavy suitcase? Where is your
transport?" The monk knew that Maharaj had been personally presented with a Chevrolet car by a devotee during his tenure prior to his
leaving. Maharaj replied, however, "You must be knowing that I have
retired from the Institute of Culture and therefore I will not be using
the car anymore for my work." He had decided on his own that this
would be inappropriate.

When the Swami was in Delhi in 1982, he came to know about my
assignment in London on the occasion of the Festival of India. He
expressed his happiness about this in his letter to me dated 25 March 1982.
This was a four-page letter full of instructions and advice regarding very
mundane things, such as the admonition that I shouldn't be extravagant
in my spending and that I should save as much as I could from what I was
supposed to earn from the assignment. He was concerned and worried
about this particular aspect of my professional life. For some reason he
was always obsessed with the apprehension of my so-called overspend-
ing. In my earlier letter to him, I had written that since my fund didn't
permit me to take Bhabani along, she was to be left behind. But at the last
moment, Bhabani managed to get some money for her travel, so we
decided to go together. In his letter of reply, the Swami was curious to
know how Bhabani managed to get this fund. He was under the impression that perhaps she had sold some of her ornaments for this purpose.
Maharaj felt that if that had been the case, she should not have done that.
He was showing his concern for her and for the entire family in this letter. He gave very important advice in this letter. He wrote that you
should try to make yourself free from all your financial liabilities (loan,
flat, car, etc.) as soon as possible. He said, "You should know that unless
you have complete financial independence, it is not possible to have
peace in life as a householder."

His next letter, written four days later from Delhi, dated 29 March

1982, showed his genuine sense of humility which was an inseparable part of his personality. In the beginning paragraph of this letter
he apologized for writing the previous letter of 25 March, which he
considered to be full of uncalled-for advice and sermons. He asked
me to apologize to Bhabani as well on his behalf for this fault. It was
a startling experience for an innocuous man like me to witness such
humility—that a monk of his stature could show so much of modesty! The fact of the matter was that the letter of 25 March had been
far from immodest or uncalled for to my way of thinking, but rather,
as usual, illuminating and exceedingly helpful. In fact, that became a
guideline in our future life.

The larger part of the letter of 29 March was concerned with the
reprinting of his World Civilization Centre brochure. As most of
Swami's friends and admirers who had the privilege of becoming a little
intimate to him know, Swami was all the time preoccupied with the
dream of setting up this World Civilization Centre. This idea came up
after his tenure in the Ramakrishna Mission Institute of Culture, but
his vision remained unfulfilled and was always dynamic and expanding. With regard to the all-important reprinting of the World Civilization Centre brochure, Swami mentioned in the letter, "This particular
brochure is nothing but the outcome of Swamiji's vision and my life's
blood [*pranaswarup*]."

This letter was full of various details about the brochure. For
instance, he mentioned how many times he had revised the copy and
still the process of revision seemed to be continuously going on. He
very naïvely mentioned a truth about his obsessive editorial process
about which the printer had rightly commented, "There is no such
thing as final copy from Swami until it is completely out from the press
in the form of a bound volume." Swami expressed his unhappiness for
not being able to show me all these revisions and improvements!

The letter also showed his immense concern about having the right
kind of cover design with the right kind of imprint of title as well as the
symbol. He knew that at that time I was about to leave for London so he

wanted me to send him some design suggestion for the cover from London, if possible. At the same time he had enclosed two draft designs in pencil for the cover. One of them was definitely sketched by Swami himself. In his design he used the symbol which he had conceived: a pure circle with eight evenly spaced radii from the circumference to the centre. It was amazing how he tried to communicate his requirements for the symbol, with great detail and precision (should it be large, shifted, the exact placement, etc.). In the same letter he mentioned that the design inspiration was from the brochure of the United Nations University. He was always inspired by anything to do with a global context.

Swami's letter dated 30 April 1982 I received in London c/o Mr. Fred Lightfoot, Deputy Director, Commonwealth Institute. In the concluding paragraph of that letter he advised me to understand the qualities responsible for the ability of the British people to expand the world over. But he also mentioned that I should remind myself what Rabindranath Tagore had written in his last treatise, *The Crisis in Civilization:* "Today we witness the perils which attend on the insolence of might: one day shall be borne out the full truth of what the sages have proclaimed: 'By unrighteousness man prospers, gains what appears desirable, conquers enemies, but perishes at the root.'"

One time my wife and I went to Delhi to negotiate a professional assignment there. We stayed at a hotel at Connaught Circus due to unavailability of a better accommodation, and they had put us in a room at the terrace on the third floor. Swami was in Delhi at that time. I tried to get in touch with him at the Ramakrishna Mission Ashrama but he had gone out, so I left a message for him with the Ashrama operator giving my address and telephone number. I was waiting in our room for an important business phone call to come. It was a very hot blazing northern Indian noon. I came out of the room for some reason and certainly discovered the surprise of my life, seeing Swami coming towards me through the terrace. He was literally gasping for breath having climbed the stairs in that heat to see us. Incidentally, there was a lift till the second floor, but the climb to the third floor was still very rigorous even for us, what to speak of an octogenarian! He stopped before me and straightaway questioned me in a very candid and firm tone, "What is the purpose of your coming to Delhi?" I appealed to him to come into the room so that he could take rest and talk to us with ease. Finding Bhabani in the room, he candidly said to her in the same tone that he thought the purpose of our Delhi visit was perhaps because we had decided to sell our apartment in South Calcutta to get some money for tiding over our financial problem and were coming to seek his permission. In fact, Maharaj had instructed Bhabani many times not to sell the apartment for any reason. He was absolutely opposed to this idea of our selling out our future shelter (at that time we had rented the apartment and were actually staying in Dum Dum). Both of us tried to pacify the Swami and assured him that the purpose of our visit was something else. We didn't have any such idea to sell out our apartment against his will. But this visit from the Swami was a concrete example of a real selfless love, the first such experience in our lifetime, which words can only partially convey.

While Swami Nitya-swarup-ananda was in Delhi in 1986, I wrote to him about our feeling of loneliness in his absence. He wrote back from Delhi that rather *he* felt lonely "at your absence." He was unhappy because he felt there was a dearth of sympathetic people in that ambience. In the same letter he wrote about his plan to visit Naini Tal, Ranikhet, Almora, Kaushani, and finally Mayavati, hopefully by 28 May 1986. He expressed his desire to stay at Mayavati for a longer period "if my doctor permits." In the next paragraph he was absolutely full of praise about Mayavati, writing, "To me, Mayavati is a dream realized." Maharaj also said in the letter that Swami Vivekananda intended to fulfil the plan of a World Civilization Centre at the same site, which is why he established the Advaita Ashrama. He added further that, according to Swami Vivekananda's own writing, the words "in whom is the universe, etc." were to be the main motto of Swamiji's World Civilization Centre.

Maharaj went on to say that Swami Vivekananda had wanted to

establish a centre for the harmony of religions near Boston, the seat of many learned and intellectual people, the year after the Parliament of Religions. Swami Nitya-swarup-ananda wrote next: "For your information, when I was in Boston in 1962 I could sense that this was perhaps the right site for a centre like that. The environs included a number of universities such as Harvard, M.I.T., etc., and renowned public libraries, museums, art galleries, etc. My own desire was to establish a similar centre there. There was a beautiful plot adjacent to our Vedanta Society. The location was very central—it still remains vacant. This was quite feasible, to construct a 15–20 storey skyscraper and establish a small little centre for harmony of religions. But our Vedanta ideology is something different."

Then he added to this, "This plan of Swami Vivekananda remained unknown to people for quite some time. The description of this plan was published in the contemporary newspaper and Marie Louise Burke has quoted this in her book, *New Discoveries*. I am amazed to discover the similarity between this and my plan of action of WCC. The plan of WCC was the expression of Swamiji's original idea and that is the reason why I have an unflinching faith in it. But alas, it brings tears to my eyes while I write or talk about this—but even shedding tears does not bring me any peace. We are almost on the verge of abandoning the inner truth of Swami Vivekananda's thoughts and teachings. That such a disaster would take place so soon is incredible. I think this is a great tragedy."

However, Maharaj was a true believer in the indestructible nature of any great idea. He concluded his letter, "If I could ever have you by my side at Mayavati, I would be very happy. I would take you around that wonderful landscape of forests stretching for five or six miles... on a jeep. It would make you happy to see how this scheme could have come into fruition; it would beckon the world with the clarion call: 'Listen, you children of bliss—I am the way. Follow me, I shall save you to the uttermost.' We have completely disregarded this teaching of Swamiji."

His last major letter to me, dated 27 September 1987, was written from Moss Hill Farms, the home of one Erik Johns, one of his two hosts in the United States. He wrote, "I am spending my time here in great joy. The days just slip by, visiting various exhibitions, fairs, intellectual landmarks and other places of interest." He continued, "What has given me most joy is this anonymous stay at Moss Hill Farms. There is no match for this place. I have given details of my stay in my letter to Bharat Maharaj, which I enclose." It is of course needless to say that the copy of the enclosed letter was a long one and full of meticulously written minutest details of his travel and experience.

When I met him after his return from the United States there was a trace of sadness in his mind, seeing Indians holding very key positions in the United States but not having the slightest will to go beyond their private interests. He was equally disappointed to see that, in comparison to 1962, there had been a diminishing in the teaching of Vedanta in America. In spite of all those indelible marks of sadness on his mind, he continued with unvanquished zeal to focus on Swamiji's vision of human unity throughout his final years.

PRAKASH LOHIA

Maharaj saw everyone's strength, and to be in his company was to gain in strength, confidence, and self-insight. These are a few examples of how his company enriched my own life.

I first met him in 1980 while he was staying in the Belur Math. He wanted a bookshelf made for his room. After taking the measurement of the wall and making a sketch of the bookshelf, I commented, "With this design it will be symmetrical." An interesting discussion ensued on the notion of symmetry. He told me about an American architect who had written to this effect, then showed me his correspondence with this architect, for whom a postage stamp was later issued. In the course of this discussion, he said, "Harmonious design does not mean that it should be symmetrical." Later he used to illustrate this at the Institute of Culture by pointing out how its various buildings, while differing in

size, fit into a harmonious whole. The idea that everything need not be
symmetrical to be harmonious had a striking effect on my whole perspective; it carried into my personal life and made me more tolerant in
dealing with diverse people in our business organization as well as in
our joint family.

Whenever I was in Calcutta, I would go to see Maharaj almost daily
about 6:00 A.M., just after my morning jog. Thus I had the good fortune
of spending exclusive morning hours with him when no one else was
there. He used to dwell upon two favourite visions, one about universal
cooperation on the international level and the other, which appealed to
him personally very much, about the cooperative community life on a
rural farm. He would close his eyes as he visualized the whole thing and
begin to talk about a self-contained unit with agriculture, fish farming,
poultry, etc., one aspect feeding the other in a synergistic interaction.
The existence of the farm was just a starting point, and then he would
get into an expansive mood, slowly describing at great length how the
participants would be living there. He would give the example of how
everyone would hasten to help if a storm suddenly demolished one
house—some would come with bamboo, others with ropes, supplying
all the necessary ingredients to reconstruct it—all rushing to that person's aid. He once said, "To me, I sometimes feel that this is more
absorbing than the international work." This vision of cooperative living on the farm stuck with me, and had its implication in the management of my business. There is hardly a day when I don't remember his
words on one occasion or another. So many things he said to me were
relevant. Even when he remarked, jokingly, "Mr. Lohia, do you ever
say to the one you love most, 'What can I do for you?'"

His no-nonsense approach was sometimes very amusing. In the late
1980s, Maharaj spent a few days at Udbodhan while Ranjit Maharaj was
there. Holy Mother's birthday was being celebrated, so that day he was
sitting well-dressed on a cot in a room on the first floor opposite the
shrine, and naturally many people were coming to pay him their respects.
One lady was telling her children, "Do pranam to him, he is Mother's

son." I was sitting near Maharaj and in his characteristic way he mur-
mured ironically, "And all the rest are father's son?" *Everyone* is Mother's
son was the gist of his remark, so witty, for he didn't like this kind of
homage. On another occasion, in 1981 or so, I picked him up at the Institute of Culture to take him to my home. I have one cousin who is mentally
retarded, so while I was introducing Maharaj to everyone, I mentioned to
him about her, "She is my cousin and she is mentally retarded." He immediately replied in a very low voice, "It is a difference of degree only!"

He was a perfectionist even under the worst circumstances. When he
was very ill at Seva Pratishthan in the summer of 1992, I used to see him
every morning before going to my office. One day, I was there in the
room while he was being served his breakfast. He was too weak to sit in
a chair, so he had to eat lying on the cot on his stomach, just lifting his
head and resting it on his hands as he ate with a spoon. The whole
process involved first putting a towel on the cot, and then the plate on
which the tiffin box was placed, from which he would eat. Suddenly,
while I was sitting by the side, he called the hospital attendant over to
his bed. "What is happening?" the attendant asked. Maharaj pointed out
that the towel was crooked since the two sides were not parallel to the
cot. All of us were a witness to his perfectionism; sometimes it may
have appeared to us as fussiness, but it truly revealed how far the Ideal
had permeated into his grain. Everything had to be done just so. He had
been taught in this way by Shukul Maharaj [Swami Atmananda]. Shukul
Maharaj had even showed him how to arrange a mosquito net, and how
to make the bed without a single wrinkle. Even the smallest things mat-
tered. You might have seen Maharaj's table drawer, how the pen, the
pencils, and all else were arranged very neatly. Or how the Philips transistor radio that he had from the early 1960s was always kept inside the
original paperboard box, with the corners taped so it wouldn't come
apart. And he would take it out in the same way, put it back after use the
same way, always kept just as it should be kept.

When Chintaharan Maharaj was ill at the Seva Pratishthan in 1992,
President Maharaj was also a patient there. I was visiting on the day when

Bhuteshanandaji Maharaj was being discharged to go back to the Belur Math. About 11:00 A.M. Bhuteshanandaji was brought into Maharaj's room in a wheelchair, accompanied by several other monks; he had come to meet Maharaj before leaving. I was also there inside the room. Maharaj could not sit up at that time, he was lying on the bed, so Swami Bhuteshanandaji came to his bedside. Maharaj took Bhuteshanandaji's hand and held it for several minutes on his own head. Then he wished Bhuteshanandaji well, "Let Thakur give you good health so that a lot of work can be done." Afterwards, when they had left the room and I was sitting near Maharaj, he told me, "He is the Sangha Guru." This struck me so forcefully, for I knew on an individual level that he had opposed some actions of Bhuteshanandaji, but when it came to a question of principle, he saw Bhuteshanandaji as the Sangha Guru [the Head of the Sangha], maybe junior in age, but still he took his hand on his head for the blessing. His reverence for the Order changed my total thinking.

There were other examples. Out of our limited ways of thinking, we used to press him when he was ill at Seva Pratishthan to move to a better hospital. "Maharaj," we would say, "we would like to take you to Bellevue or to Woodlands." Yet his *oneness* with the Order was so complete that he could never think of any separation, even from their hospital. We could see incomprehension in his eyes at the very mention of it. Yes, he would criticize, he would do anything for the improvement of the organization, but he was forever inseparable from it, just as the roots are joined to the tree. No question! His last books may have been controversial, but I have heard from some of the more enlightened monks of the Order that they are relevant.

He was ahead of his time. Chintaharan Maharaj was a favourite of Swami Madhavananda, and one monk told me that Madhavanandaji had once said about him, "Nobody can understand him now," that he should have been born either in Swamiji's time or much later. Gopesh Maharaj [Swami Sarvadeshananda] also seemed to indicate that Swami Nitya-swarup-ananda could be appreciated in future. My wife, Neera, and I once accompanied Chintaharan Maharaj to Vrindaban, and while we were in his room, Gopesh Maharaj called me aside and said to me in a low but very distinct tone, "*Please see to it that the thoughts of Chintaharan Maharaj are preserved.*" Yes, let us see to it that the thoughts of Chintaharan Maharaj are preserved.

AMRITA SALM

While attending the Ramakrishna Math and Mission Convention in 1980, I heard about Swami Nitya-swarup-ananda. On Holy Mother's birthday while the delegates were away from the Math, Erik Johns, closely known to the Swami, took me to his room and introduced me. I entered the room. The Swami was sitting cross-legged on his bed talking to others. As soon as I met him I somehow felt very connected to him. We began to discuss the many direct disciples of Sri Ramakrishna whom he had known intimately, though he would not give much information on the Holy Mother.

It was already time for lunch, Erik and I were late, and he said to me, "Where will you take your lunch?" A dining room for foreign delegates had been set up downstairs, yet very quickly I responded, "If you give me lunch, I'll eat with you." As soon as the words came out of my mouth I realized that it was inappropriate to eat in the Swami's room in the monastery. He seemed very amused, and immediately gave us a delicious feast. That day he had numerous plates filled with special *prasad* offered to the Holy Mother. Both Erik and I were completely satisfied not just with the food but with his wonderful company.

Throughout the next few days I would go meet him in his room. Actually the next day when I entered his room he said, "Why are you so late? I have ordered special fish prepared for you." So I sat with him and ate lunch for a second day. He said, "You want to know how to make this preparation, don't you?" Of course I did, and he proceeded to name all the ingredients ("You will know what to do with them"). This fish dish became one of my favorite recipes.

During the course of the Convention, one of the swamis working in

America gave a lecture about Vedanta in the West. The next day, his photograph and the headlines appeared stating "America Is Not Ready for Vedanta." Swami Nitya-swarup-ananda handed me the newspaper and before I could utter one word he went into one of his intellectual rages. He said, among other things, "This swami thinks America is not ready for Vedanta and Swami Vivekananda felt it was!" It was, to say the least, a very stimulating monologue. All of us realized his conviction and love for Vedanta and for Swamiji. Actually, he was saddened by the proceedings of the Convention and was hoping somebody would finally say something relevant.

When Swami Nitya-swarup-ananda learned that I had written my dissertation on organization change, he was fascinated and oftentimes he was pumping me for information which he hoped one day could be used by the Order. He even suggested that I present my findings to the Trustees. He also encouraged me to study the Vedanta Societies in America in relationship to the theoretical findings of my dissertation.

Erik Johns had a wonderful relationship with Swami Nitya-swarup-ananda. One day, while Erik was going through the Swami's accumulated correspondence he found a letter written by a young woman from America who wanted to do some research and was requesting the Swami's assistance. The letter, unfortunately, had been written several years earlier and had remained unanswered. Erik was playfully remonstrating with the Swami for not answering his letters, especially those where his knowledge and advice would be beneficial. At that time, I realized the utility of trying to develop a correspondence with the Swami. In fact, many years later, I wrote him a Vijaya letter and said, "This is an exercise in detachment and karma yoga since I know you will not answer this letter." Strangely enough, several months later, I received a Christmas card telling me that I was not to practice too much detachment—he wrote me that I was to continue to write him!

In one of my letters to him, I asked him to please bless me with desirelessness. Although he did not respond to the letter, the next time I met him in India he continually introduced me to swamis and he would remark on these occasions, "She wants desirelessness." The first time he said this I felt embarrassed, but after that I was deeply moved to experience what I felt was an endorsement of this request.

Four years later, I returned to India for an extended stay of five months. I had the privilege and good fortune of his holy company on many different occasions. He was anxious to introduce me to people of like minds who appreciated Vivekananda and were trying in their own humble way to put these ideas into practice. One of the more memorable times was his visit to Jayrambati during Jagaddhatri Puja. Several days before this occasion, Indira Gandhi was assassinated. The country was in turmoil, and moving anywhere was difficult. Despite these obstacles, Swami Nitya-swarup-ananda insisted on his presence since he had promised me he was coming. Everyone was surprised to see him arrive because hundreds of guests were unable to attend. He did not often go to Jayrambati and all of the swamis there were over-joyed to have him in their company.

He made special arrangements for me to receive a personal tour of Jayrambati with Rammoy Maharaj, another direct disciple of Holy Mother. He also accompanied us and, along with the other swami, described many instances in Holy Mother's life. He insisted that I make diagrams of both of Holy Mother's cottages, even though I had a cam-era and was taking photographs. It was during this visit that I expressed my lack of appreciation for Holy Mother's statue in Her temple. He then, in his usual manner, looked at it from the highest Vedantic per-spective and began to quote Swami Vivekananda to the effect that one can see the moon from various angles.

It was also during this trip that, while returning to Calcutta, we went to the home of one of his devotees in Arambagh. It was interest-ing to see him with this devoted family as they prepared a tremendous feast in his honor which he thoroughly enjoyed in the traditional Indian way.

One day, the Swami requested a young man to meet me. As it turned out, I had known this person many years earlier. He began to tell me how much Swami Nitya-swarup-ananda loved him and guided him, and how he was able to discuss all of his problems with him. The young man continued to describe in detail how patiently the Swami listened to him, and then went on to enumerate some of the problems he had confided to him. This made me realize that the Swami, in fact, did not discuss on the face of it, the highest Vedantic truths where more mundane concerns were foremost.

Several times during this visit to India, I found the Swami in a mood that once again showed another side to his multifaceted personality. When he spoke of the direct disciples and his earliest contacts with them, he would become an altogether different person. He became deeply inspired and I saw him on the verge of tears when he spoke about their love, their conviction, and how he, himself, had been affected by their lives.

In 1987 Swami Nitya-swarup-ananda came to America for the second time for a prolonged stay. When I learned that he had arrived, I was anxious to meet him again. We discussed the possibility of my going to the East Coast for that purpose, but eventually he decided to include the West Coast in his travel itinerary. Erik Johns and I met him in San Francisco for the purpose of accompanying him by car to Los Angeles. I thought to myself, "How strange for a man of his age to enjoy the prospect of being in a car for twelve hours." It was decided by the Swami that we would take the longest possible route! We drove along the scenic route by the side of the Pacific Ocean. The Swami thoroughly enjoyed the beauty and became very childlike that day.

During this ride, we passed a very small town called Harmony. As soon as he saw the town's name, and the rolling hills, he began an extended discourse on the need for a community of scholars to join together and develop some of the ideas he had written about in his book *Education for Human Unity and World Civilization*. He strongly believed that America is the place where such a center of learning can flourish. Several times during his visit in Los Angeles he referred to this idyllic spot and its many possibilities.

It seemed the Swami was inexhaustible in his thinking and talking, with endless enthusiastic observations and reflections throughout this trip down the Pacific coast. His vitality was that of a twenty year old! Erik, some thirty years younger than the Swami, was in the meantime taking numerous catnaps in the back seat. Not until we were within an hour of the Vedanta Society—in other words, we had already been travelling for eleven hours—did Swami make his profound comment, "What time is it?" When I told him, he said, "Only now am I aware of my body."

While the Swami was staying at the Hollywood center, he did not want to limit his conversation to speaking only with devotees. He requested me to arrange for some talks at various universities and to meet with some well-placed professors and intellectuals. He was also interested in speaking with Indians who were living in America. On one such occasion, at the home of a professor, he spoke for over one hour to a group of Indian professionals living there. Challenging their lifestyle and their thinking patterns, he demanded that they reflect upon the purpose of their stay in the West. He encouraged them to remember their Indian heritage and how important it is that they share these ideas with their Western colleagues. I was spellbound by his emphatic demands and concern for their lives.

He was a brilliant conversationalist, though he avoided giving formal lectures. While in Hollywood, however, he was compelled to do so. Those of us who participated in the process of editing and re-editing (and re-editing again) will never forget the experience of his need for absolute clarity of ideas. Even the young monk who attended to him and received his unstinting affection and love reached the point of exhaustion as the Swami tried to perfect the public address system at the Hollywood Temple before the lecture. Needless to say, it all went beautifully.

One evening, Swami Nitya-swarup-ananda agreed to come with Swami Swahananda and some devotees to dinner at my house. For me, the most enjoyable part of the entire evening was his joy of entering the kitchen and watching me cook, counting all of the different dishes that were being prepared. On another evening in Santa Barbara he went to the home of two European physicians who were longtime devotees. He appreciated the way in which they entertained him and the variety of elegant items prepared. He requested them to write out the menu and he was continually showing this to others. The next time I met him in India, he was still talking about that wonderful meal in Santa Barbara.

Many evenings he sat in the Green House living room of the Hollywood center, meeting devotees and speaking with great conviction, candor, and humor. One evening, as he spoke about the need to bring Vedanta into the educational system and how it could be accomplished, he inspired many of those present to consider seriously the possibility of opening a residential school, not unlike those in India, where Vedanta and the message of Oneness and the Unity of Existence would become an integral part of the curriculum. The effect of that evening continues to inspire some of the devotees and monastic members who still contemplate the possibility of such an endeavor.

D. K. BUBBAR

The following meetings and discussions with Swami Nitya-swarup-ananda Maharaj are my obeisances, not reminiscences, for between the lines are deep instructions.

On 17 April 1978, Swami Nitya-swarup-anandaji Maharaj held in his hand a copy of my lecture, delivered in Bombay, wherein *Yoga Karmasu Koushalam* was defined by me. He had felt joyous at the definition and asked for the initial meeting. Thereafter, we were in constant touch.

In 1981, I invited Maharaj to Bombay. He graced my home ("Sea Shell") for almost thirty days. He wanted to see architectural buildings around Bombay. Whenever projects took me to Calcutta, he would call up the Grand Hotel in the morning, ask us to say "How wonderful am I" three times. Then, breakfast meeting at 6:30 at the Belur Math. After visiting the temples, I would come for breakfast, and he would fan me, and ask me to eat this or that. He would examine my dress, would ask me to turn around, observing the fall of sleeves, shoulders, cloth, etc.

He would enquire, "Did you design this dress?" "Yes," I would reply. He wanted perfection in every department. Then he would shower praises. He would always address me as "Mr. Bubbar." He was impeccable in habits and piccadilly accurate in his manners.

I mostly taped his utterances (in Bengali), which were later transcribed. There were many topics, but I have chosen three—Interpersonal, Spiritual, and Professional—so that, in the midst of crisis, these utterances of Maharaj will not only guide and uplift the spirits, but ASSUREDLY will make the practitioner a strong and evolved person.

INTER-PERSONAL

(1981: Bombay—Sea Shell)

My mind was disturbed. I was getting all kinds of negative thoughts, due to family, professional, and legal hassles. I was contemplating separation. On meeting Maharaj, he asked me how things were. Maharaj exploded when I told him:

M: Don't listen to whatever your mind says at different times!

DKB: Should I ignore the mind?

M: Not only ignore, but *stop* the mind. Stop—stop at once.

DKB: Then whom should I listen to?

M: You live in the mind, not in anybody, or WITH anybody. Fictitious mind. Where are these people who are troubling you? In Bombay? In Delhi? No, they are in your mind. Check your mind and order, "NOT with me." Ask yourself, "Why does my mind dictate to me like this?" The mind says, "That lady or this person is responsible for everything, she is making hell for me. If she was all right, then I could do wonderful things." Similarly, she is saying, "Due to this man, everything is bad." So the OTHER MAN is the troublemaker. So as soon as this thought comes, order your mind to stop it. Tell your mind, "If you can help me, give me peace. But you are creating discord and nuisance. You are my worst enemy. Try to be my friend." Always preserve the Self. One's own Self is the friend and foe. Listen to your Self.

DKB: I wish to be correct, right and good.

M: That is very good. Wonderful! (Maharaj felt relieved.)

DKB: But the problems have to be resolved?

M: In this world, there is nothing to be resolved. Don't you read
       newspapers? It is not only you who are having problems. This
       life is a problem. If you cannot adjust, then you cannot live. You
       are saying, "I cannot adjust." So, you are saying, "I am unfit."
       Go to America or Sweden, see what is happening. They are ruin-
       ing their lives—no family, no wife, no son. They are masters in
       this art of ruining. Today President Kennedy dies, the next day
       his wife goes and marries another person. In America they are
       doing big experiments in this line—forest life. They are going in
       for freedom, freedom, freedom. Is this freedom? Not at all. Con-
       trol your mind, mature your mind.

On another occasion, regarding problems with staff, clients, and
friends, he enlightened us thus:

M: Discord with any other person is an essential part of life. It can-
       not be avoided. Everywhere, one has to learn to adjust and to
       find solutions, not by running away, or creating separation or
       division. Just as the division of Hastinapura never brought any
       solution or peace, but led to war and destruction. The war over
       the inside is necessary to gain victory over ourselves. As Swami
       Vivekananda said, in this world you are going to be crushed by
       all outside forces, and life is that which rises above every obsta-
       cle. The secret of sea-bath teaches us this technique. Rise above
       every wave. If you don't, then you will die. This world is not a
       happy place. It is a miserable place, a place of constant struggle.
       But by use of appropriate intelligence, it can be made worth
       living. Therefore, don't imagine problems. Take steps on real
       problems. This can be done, if you don't harbour fear. While
       handling problems, don't leave any stone unturned. Don't
       ignore any condition. If ignored, then that condition will cause
       a further chain of problems.

SPIRITUAL

(1982: Belur Math)

Breakfast was served, and Maharaj was fanning me. Was he my mother, father, or a friend? Was he a man or a saint? HE WAS ALL IN ONE! That unalloyed love flowed bountifully.

M: How is everything?

DKB: Miraculously, my brother has returned part of my money.

M: Miracles never happen. Nothing comes from heaven. Nothing happens without a cause. Don't believe in miracles. It is cause and effect. (These utterances amazed me.)

(1985: Belur Math)

DKB: My mind is agitated with Thakur.

M: That shows you have a mind, not a stone or a wood. They do not get agitated. It is the normal function of the mind. But bad agitation about Thakur should be checked. Man always wants to depend upon something. So Guru is there. Still better is to depend upon your own Self. Practice the Mantra given by Guru, then the Self guides. Your relation with your Guru is NOT mechanical. It is spiritual. Follow his guidance. Love is a chastening and corrective force, but you must find it before you can give it. The more we lean on other people, the more we fall. None is indispensable—wife, child, father, mother, friend. Tell yourself always, "I am strong and shall face each challenge boldly and strongly. If I cannot, let me be effaced from the face of this earth."

(1981: Bombay—Sea Shell)

Our daughter, Devaki, told Maharaj, "Sri Ramakrishna is not Bhagavan. So I don't feel like worshipping him."

M: It does not matter to Sri Ramakrishna what you think of Him. There are millions who have not even heard His name. But what matters to you is important. So you must decide for yourself, and follow.

(1988: Belur Math)

Similarly, my foster mother, an American lady, who had influenced my formative years, came to Bombay and told me that all my problems were because I did not worship the God, Jesus Christ. She said this man, Sri Ramakrishna, was not a God, but a man. I argued against this, but she remained adamant. I referred this matter to Maharaj. Without hesitation, he said:

M: Do what is good for you. If you like to worship Jesus, it is all right. Important is your ease, comfort, and success. (I felt proud that a monk of the Ramakrishna Order had the breadth of vision to advise thus. How would any senior monk, of any faith, advise?)

PROFESSIONAL

(1987: New Delhi Mission)

I narrated an incident that took place with a multinational client. The new CEO invited me to his office, and said they were contemplating to build a headquarters complex in Delhi, if the government permitted. They might even hold a competition. I thanked the CEO, but regretted participation in any speculative project. I suggested they should give the project to us, for they knew our services. Besides, competitions had never produced any building of beauty anywhere. At this, the CEO had lost his cool. I referred the matter to Maharaj.

M: He lost his cool because that is part of his nature. It comes from an egoistic background. Forget his behaviour. Concentrate on getting the job.

DKB: If he is egoistic, and loses his cool, then how will we work together and produce something excellent? His work-method is ordinary.

M: First tell me why you are against competition. What is said, is usually done.

DKB: Any competition that a client wishes to call must adhere to the rules of the Council of Architecture, or it is illegal. Secondly, no competition in the world has produced a building which has stood the test of time. Only mediocre and third-rate buildings have resulted. Do you call for a competition if your loved one requires brain or heart surgery, or if you wish to find an advocate to fight your case in court? You don't. Then why here? It is a hypocritical and political attempt.

M: You are right. My charm for you is because of your guts, your thoughts, sense of honour, discipline, how you think and live. Make sure it stays that way. I am happy to hear this.

DKB: But that must bring me lots of big projects.

M: Then you must go along with people, or you will have to live alone.

DKB: I am already living alone.

M: For big jobs, you must go with people.

DKB: But most people want only the ordinary. Their methodology cannot get the extraordinary. They have barriers.

M: You cannot break their barriers. So?

DKB: I will suffer.

M: It is very easy to suffer. But it requires wisdom to avoid suffering. You must avoid suffering at all costs. The whole game is how skilfully we avoid suffering.

DKB: How do you do that?

M: By finding out, for yourself, how to deal with people—clients, contractors, staff, family, or anybody. People work the way they work. You have no control over that. Today one thing, tomorrow another. All over the world, it is like that.

DKB: As it is, I end up doing three times more work than normal. I feel tired.

M: Yes, you will feel tired, and this is your responsibility. They are all other people and cannot go by your directions. ALL THOSE WHO WANT TO DO GOOD, AND IN A PERFECT WAY, SUCH IS THEIR LIFE. Therefore, I respect your courage. But what are you going to do now—give up or fight? Whenever you meet a person, differences will be there. This is my point number one, in any dealing, with any person. So you must know how to deal effectively, with strength and vision.

DKB: How does one get that strength and vision?

M: By practice and patience. By understanding things, and the way they work. You will meet usual persons and unusual persons. Usual persons are afraid of unusual ways and unusual persons, like you, so their behaviour is difficult, through insecurity. But the world is standing on the shoulders of unusual people. Therefore, unusual people are enlightened people. They change their ways to get the best from situations.

DKB: Thakur neither listens, nor does anything!

M: Yes, then you have a gap. A gap between you and Thakur. What you are saying is, He is not responding to you. But Thakur says, "All my children say, 'Do like this, do like that,' and I say, 'You do like this and do like that.' THIS GAP IS NOT BRIDGED. The only alternative for Me is to pray to you, to give Me liberation, my child, because I cannot reform your thinking. But you are part of My being; how can I separate Myself from you? The only difficulty is, you don't feel that way. You don't live that way. You make Me responsible for what happens to you. But you go your own way, and charge Me for what is happening to you. Look upon Me as your own. You will remain untouched."

(28 March 1992)

I woke up with a start at 3:30 A.M. I told my wife, Chandrika, that I had dreamt that Maharaj was no more. We could not sleep. We waited until 6:00 in the morning to phone the Institute of Culture. Maharaj came on the line. He stated that his health was in VERY BAD SHAPE. But he was full of zest and cheer, and his smiles and love came through his intoxicating giggles. This was my last talk with him. The balance is history. OM TAT SAT.

SOMEN MITRA*

I first met Chintaharan Maharaj sometime in 1982 at the Belur Math. He had a distinctive personality with a sharp penetrating mind and subtle sense of humour, yet he seemed immersed in the knowledge of

Self, forever wishing the well-being of all devotees. It was our good fortune to witness these extraordinary qualities.

I remember that I was overawed by his powerful personality on the first day of our meeting. I noticed that he discouraged any kind of superficial talk and disliked any inconsistency between thought and word. His words of caution against cheap emotionality and verbosity unmatched by feeling hit the mark and affected me deeply. Gradually I learned to enjoy his company and I will never forget his limitless affection. I will try to portray these characteristics of Maharaj through certain anecdotes.

A nonresident Indian had come from Germany. He accompanied me to the Belur Math to see Chintaharan Maharaj. In replying to Maharaj's questions, this gentleman informed him, "Vedanta is studied in my town in Germany and many Indian and German devotees assemble in my house. After the study circle, they sit on the floor and eat *kichuri* [a rice and lentil dish] and *malpoa* [a homemade Bengali sweet]." After listening to all this Maharaj replied, "If you feed them *kichuri* and if they start wearing dhotis instead of trousers in your country, I can assure you that it will be a far cry from Vedanta." Maharaj's pointed comment gave me the insight that deliberate attempts to introduce alien ways of thinking and doing are of no value to either the propagator or receiver.

Cheap emotionality and exuberant sentimentality were sharply disciplined by Maharaj, and I will recount one such incident. I was out of Calcutta when my Gurudev, Swami Vireswarananda, passed away. Hearing this news I went to the Math with a heavy heart to see Chintaharan Maharaj. As I was about to enter the room I overheard his sarcastic remarks to a lady-devotee, "Alas, Prabhu Maharaj [Swami Vireswarananda] has gone away and emptied our lives, as if he was there before and has now ceased to be! His body was everything, so naturally when that goes away, nothing else remains...." These lashing words caused the lady to stop crying immediately, and I also received a wonderful lesson. I realized that one has to accept the separation of loved ones in proper philosophical perspective, rather than lose oneself in uncontrolled sorrow.

Beneath his apparently harsh exterior, there was always this feeling of loving concern for the devotees. Whenever my busy schedule permitted me to go to him, he showed great interest in my work and encouraged me to go ahead with whatever creative enterprise I was pursuing. His receptivity and analytical power were really wonderful. He never failed to comprehend the complicated technical or scientific aspects of the problem we were discussing, and would give valuable guidance on each occasion when I sought his help.

I will give an example of Maharaj's contribution to my character-building. A group of very influential but corrupt government officials was attempting to harm our organization by promising to give us a contract in exchange for a bribe. I consulted Maharaj with a great deal of anxiety, and I still remember his spirited reply as he raised his forefinger to warn me, "Beware! Do not give one paisa even if your whole work is totally burned to ashes." All my doubts and fears were dispelled by these strong words of caution, and I did not compromise. In course of time the work was executed without a hitch with the Grace of Sri Sri Thakur, but I will not elaborate on all that because it is irrelevant. The lesson I learned to adhere to the path of honesty has given me a lifelong example of Swamiji's Practical Vedanta.

One had a sense of timelessness while listening to Maharaj. I had gone to see him on a Sunday during the monsoon while he was staying in the monks' quarters at Gol Park. I found him in the lounge immersed in talk about Swamiji, the Upanishads, Vedanta, and other spiritual matters. I did not quite grasp all that he was saying due to my limited capacity, but his hallowed words were creating an atmosphere of joy, never before experienced by me, as they filled the air almost like the sounds of wondrous music. When Maharaj was talking like this the famous sarod player Ustad Ali Akbar Khan, then a guest at the Institute, came and joined us, but I was so entranced with Maharaj's talk that I didn't even notice when he got up and left, even though he had been sitting right next to me. It was raining very heavily and the streets of Calcutta were flooded, but for those few hours I had no connection with the outside world.

Chintaharan Maharaj has distributed divine nectar freely to all those who have come in close contact with him. He inspired me to strive for a pure life full of higher thoughts. His own polestar was Swami Vivekananda, which guided his entire life as he made untiring efforts for global unity based on religion and culture, a new world order calling upon the highest intellectual talent. I have not been able to absorb all his teachings, but whatever I have understood has been a source of endless personal enrichment.

KARAN SINGH

Swami Nitya-swarup-ananda was certainly one of the outstanding products of the Ramakrishna Mission in the twentieth century. I have known several swamis of the Mission but among the three who particularly stand out is Swami Nitya-swarup-ananda.

I recall that he had this tremendous vision of a centre of world civilization, the subject of a brochure which he wrote and gave me many years ago. He was very keen that I should take up this project in some way.

He was, of course, the founder and the moving spirit behind the Ramakrishna Mission Institute of Culture in Gol Park in Calcutta. So I kept asking him, "Swamiji, you already have this Institute, why do you not make it the corpus, as it were, the creative centre for your World Civilization Centre? Why are you trying to, as it were, reinvent the wheel, why are you moving away from that?" "No, no, that is something much bigger and it is on a much vaster scale," he replied. "Swamiji, I can appreciate that," I soon agreed, and I wrote to the Education Minister, Professor V. K. R. V. Rao, saying that here is the sort of project that the government of India should take up, to do the sort of global education that the Swami is considering.

Unfortunately nothing came of it, but we kept meeting every couple of years. Towards the end I found him a little disillusioned. It was such a fine and beautiful scheme to translate Swami Vivekananda's ideals into action, so why was it that it wasn't being taken up? I really think that it was too big physically and psychologically, too big an idea to be taken up by any one institution or even by the government.

Visionaries often have to face such disappointment. He was evidently a man who was far ahead of his time because it is only now, so much later, that the global society is beginning to emerge and we are still struggling with the birth pangs of a new civilization. I think Swami Nitya-swarup-ananda will be remembered as a visionary, as a savant, and as somebody who had this *grand* project. It was his dear, dearly beloved project, and I am sorry that he wasn't able to see it to its fruition during his lifetime.

SHUBHRA CHATTERJI

I first met Swami Nitya-swarup-ananda one April evening in 1983. He was sitting with Bharat Maharaj under the mango tree in front of Bharat Maharaj's room at the Belur Math. What first drew my attention to him was a *gerua*-coloured shirt, which was very unusual attire for a monk. My husband pointed out to me, "Don't you know who he is?—he is Chintaharan Maharaj, the Secretary of the Ramakrishna Mission Institute of Culture." Immediately he and my husband plunged into a deep conversation, the gist of which was that the preachings of Thakur and Swamiji have been dissipated within a hundred years of their advent. My husband commented that it took one hundred years after Christ to propagate His message, to which came the sharp retort from Maharaj, "But man has landed on the moon." Hitherto I had only been paying half attention to the conversation, but this incisive comment struck me immediately as highly original.

I started paying attention to the conversation and the next assault came soon after. There was some talk about the prevalence of *adharma* [immorality] in the world, and we gave a standard comment that it is time for the Divine Incarnation to come down and take care of it. Maharaj replied to this, "In that case you better put mustard oil in your nose [to sleep soundly] and go to sleep." I realized the fallacy, that we were shirking our own responsibility. I started giggling, and the anger in his tone changed to a twinkle in his eyes.

For the next few years, through continuous assaults of this type, he brought about a total change in my psyche. Although I must admit that at the time I found some of his remarks quite bizarre, in retrospect he was always correct and it was I who was not ready to receive them.

As an example of this, at one time Maharaj told me a greatly detailed story about two friends who had to cross a river. Both of them were tired and wanted to rest and smoke a hookah. But one of them decided to first cross the river, which he did, and after a few minutes the two friends could be seen sitting on opposite banks of the river smoking their hookahs and looking outwardly the same—but with what a difference! Not understanding the reason for this story at the time, I later discovered the relevance to my personal life—it is not the outward form that matters, but the inward process of being and becoming.

Another story, "the story of the cobbler," was actually a real-life incident. It left a very deep impression on my mind. Maharaj was on his way to Mayavati. Their car had broken down and they were forced to wait for a few hours. There was a cobbler sitting nearby and Maharaj decided to have his shoes shined. The cobbler did this with great respect and even refused to accept money. Maharaj's attention was drawn to the cobbler's shop which was unspeakably dirty and slovenly, and extended even to his lunch which consisted of two bananas. Maharaj started asking him why he didn't make any efforts to tidy up his shop and to take better care of his health. The cobbler's answer was "This body is made of dust and will return to dust." Maharaj told us, "I simply shuddered when I heard this answer from the cobbler. The loftiest of thoughts had been dragged down to the very mundane." He would then elaborate that this was an instance of pure *tamas* masquerading as *sattva*, a false philosophy—"and the whole country is full of this!" As a finale to this story, Maharaj would forcefully quote Swamiji's words about not dragging down the ideal to the real, but rather lifting the real to the ideal.

I was doing the Montessori course at that time at his insistence, and he had asked me to undertake it with total sincerity. A group of friends were making plans to take a trip to Jayrambati with Maharaj. Actually the whole thing was planned because I had mentioned that I had never been to Jayrambati. The day before the trip Maharaj seemed very surprised to hear that I was joining them and asked me, "How can you miss your classes?" I replied, "But Maharaj, it is no ordinary trip, it is a pilgrimage to Jayrambati and with you. So how does it matter if I miss one or two classes?" He became very serious and solemn and said, "Most of the time *preya* [pleasurable] comes to us in the garb of *shreya* [desirable]. You have to learn to discriminate." This was one of his teachings which has to a great extent altered my behaviour: discrimination as an actual practice in daily life.

Maharaj stressed perfection in every small act of life. In the Montessori course, we were asked to do a geometry file with great perfection. Maharaj was quite thrilled when he came to know that perfection was the criterion required and he was very pleased, almost like a child, when he saw the result. A few days later when he came to our house for breakfast, I served him green peas kachori and stuffed apples for dessert. Both were circles, and he drew my attention to the fact that none of the circles were perfect. He said, "What has happened to your geometry? The green peas should have been spread evenly, making a perfect circle within a circle. And the apples have not been cored in perfect circles." What struck me was the deep reverence in his voice—he was not joking.

Another incident occurred when we were accompanying him as he was going from Thakur's temple to Holy Mother's temple at the Belur Math. He was walking ahead down the cement pathway, and unthinkingly we took the shorter route over the grass to catch up with him. He was very put out, and said, "Why did you do that? Why didn't you take the regular route?" He then went on to elaborate that this attention to the proper way of doing things had been inculcated into him by Swami Atmananda (Shukul Maharaj). He gave the example of how he was once rebuked by Swami Atmananda for not closing a watch case the proper way, but rather with a loud snap.

A third incident that illustrates his reverence for detail was when he corrected me about my careless use of words. I had mentioned the word "perhaps" in some context, about which he was quite annoyed and said, "words like 'perhaps,' 'I think so,' and 'approximately' have no significance. They reflect clumsy thinking." These three instances of doing, walking, and talking in the wrong way were a wonderful lesson to me about how to practise perfection.

I also used to think that it is not always possible to implement ideals into practice, and that compromise is inevitable. But Maharaj used to reply, "You say that '*it* is not possible' when you should say that '*I* am not willing to do it.'" He taught me to perceive that it is *our* unwillingness and inability to do something as it should be done that promotes compromise. The problem of "dragging down the ideal to the real" happens often in my field of education. I use Maharaj's "cobbler story" in all my teacher-training programmes to illustrate the perils of self-delusion.

Maharaj often spoke of the highest ideals of education. He would quote Swamiji that the dawning of civilization will occur when each and every child born on this earth will be full of yogic powers. "You teach preschoolers," Maharaj used to say to me, "but education should begin when the child is still in its mother's womb! And from the moment of the child's birth, every mother, like Madalasa (the enlightened queen), should rock the cradle singing *Tvamasi niranjana* (Thou art Taintless)." The soothing voice of Maharaj repeating *Tvamasi niranjana*, as he made a gently rocking movement with his hands, still rings clearly in my mind. "Make the child's whole world reverberate with the singing of the glory of the Atman," he added for emphasis. "It is the only way to fight this onslaught of materialism."

Maharaj always insisted that I read Swami Vivekananda and Sister Nivedita with regard to everything that they had written about education. After Maharaj's passing, I came upon a quotation from Sister

Nivedita which moved me deeply: "Spirituality has many manifestations, religion is one and education is the other." The significance of
Maharaj's "obsession about education," as he used to say, suddenly
struck me in the totality of its spiritual context. And this became the
link to Maharaj's many teachings to me over the years. Education for
me now has become an act of reverence.

ARABINDA BASU

My initial meeting with Revered Swami Nitya-swarup-anandaji at the
Ramakrishna Mission Institute of Culture in Gol Park was a memorable
incident in my life. His features were nothing exceptional, but his loving,
piercing eyes could see through each soul. In simple words, he could
carry any person to the depth of his profound religious philosophy—
"One soul, One humanity, One world." His sense of wit and humour
with motherly affection impressed me from the first day.

Maharaj gave us a long discourse on religion as envisaged by Swami
Vivekananda as "Practical Vedanta." He stressed honesty, sincerity,
and perfection in day-to-day work, at home or elsewhere, however
small it might be. We need to earn our livelihood, but avarice is sin as it
deprives others. These maxims produce a change in one's outlook and
lead to the ideal of "work as worship."

"What can I do for you?" should be the key to all our interactions,
wherever we may be. We learned from Maharaj that this readiness and
eagerness to serve others will develop fellow feelings, leading us to
"service to humanity" which will culminate in the "service to God."
We will begin to see "Atman or Brahman" in each soul around and
within us. We are the children of the same God, call him Rama, Buddha, Jesus, or Allah. This motto will lead us to Universal Brotherhood:
"One world, one Religion—the Religion of all religions."

Once I asked Maharaj, "So many thoughts come into my mind during meditation, what should I do?" "Since you are a doctor," he replied,
"you are serving your patients and treating the poor patients free of
any consultation charge, even supplying them with medicines. This

service itself will lead to *chitta suddhi* [a purified mind]." It enlightened me to have faith in my work as the path and encouraged me to do better service.

In August 1985 Maharaj took a few of us by car to Jayrambati where we were introduced to Rammoy Maharaj [Swami Gauriswarananda] who had served the Holy Mother in her daily routine as a young boy. Much later, when Chintaharan Maharaj was hospitalized in July 1987, he and Rammoy Maharaj were in adjacent cabins. I went to Chintaharan Maharaj and his cabin was vacant. Then I took a chance to peek into the next cabin and I saw Chintaharan Maharaj whispering something into the ear of Rammoy Maharaj, who was probably breathing his last at that moment. I just turned quietly without disturbing the sanctity of that atmosphere.

Later that year, in November, Maharaj arranged another car trip to Jamshedpur, and from there we travelled to the Bishtupur Math to pay our respects to revered Swami Adinathananda. We witnessed a heavenly scene when these two seniormost monks, both the monastic disciples of the Holy Mother, attempted simultaneously to take the dust of each other's feet, obstructing each other time and again until ultimately they simply embraced. I was so overwhelmed at their love for each other that I forgot to record this rare scene in my camera.

Maharaj used to suffer acutely from bronchitis and bronchial asthma. Almost every year in the winter he would have to be admitted to the Ramakrishna Mission Seva Pratishthan for several months. Humidity and polluted air were responsible for the trouble. I, along with two of my friends who are also physicians, Dr. Murali Mitra and Dr. S. P. Bakshi, used to see him for his medical care at Udbodhan, Balaram Mandir, or the Belur Math.

In March 1986, he moved to New Delhi where the dry climate suited him. Before leaving for New Delhi, he casually mentioned about a trip to Mayavati Ashrama with us. Receiving a telephone call from New Delhi in May 1986, we about twelve in number rushed to join him. A meticulous programme was chalked out to reach Mayavati in a minibus, stopping at Naini Tal, Almora, Kaushani, and Chowkuri. Six of us took a side trip to Samlatal without his knowledge. On return, I heard that he had only commented that we should have informed him before leaving. I was so scared and ashamed, apprehending a scolding from Maharaj, but to my surprise he just ignored our folly. What an example of affection and indulgence! I am one of the very few who never had the blessings of scolding or harsh words from him.

For this pilgrimage to Mayavati, Dr. Mitra and myself took all possible precautions, carrying an oxygen cylinder and other materials, so that Maharaj could stand the long, strenuous journey in extreme cold. Passing this endurance test helped Maharaj later to get a "green signal" for his second tour abroad in 1987, which lasted for a long fourteen months. During our stay at Mayavati, after dinner we used to talk in the sitting room. Maharaj asked us to read out from *Atiter Smriti*, the reminiscences of Swami Virajananda, and particularly the chapter when he was taking Swamiji to Mayavati in December's bitter cold and in the dead of night through the forest, enduring hardships on the way. We felt that the hardship undergone by Swami Virajananda to collect the porters and make all the other arrangements for this arduous trek indicated his love and respect for Swamiji, which may have been the point he wished to impress upon us.

In December 1986, he invited all his friends to lunch at Balaram Mandir. He planned every minor detail days in advance—the menu, catering, cushions for seating, plates, everything delicately matching. A few of us presented a big decorated cake befitting the occasion. As nobody was bold enough to request our revered Maharaj to cut the cake, somehow I picked up the courage to request him to do so. He readily appreciated the gesture and cut the cake to our full enjoyment and joy. Later on, I could gather that he presented the cake to the caterer, as a token of his deep appreciation for his work. This wonderful luncheon in his loving holy company is a remembrance that is treasured by all who were present.

Revered Maharaj's health improved so much on his trip to the United

States in 1987 that he did not need to continue his routine medicines. He had cataract surgery (intra-ocular lens implantation) to his left eye, resulting in partial improvement of vision, as the right eye was also developing lenticular opacity. Glaucoma was detected in both eyes and treatment with drops initiated. After returning from the United States, reexposure to pollution aggravated his old trouble of bronchitis, and he was hospitalized in September 1988. When his condition improved considerably, he went to stay at the Institute of Culture, where he had an air-conditioned room to minimize his respiratory problem.

From early 1992, he was losing appetite gradually, and complaining of weakness in the lower limbs. He at one point developed an allergic skin eruption over the hands and forearms as well. In great respect to him, many leading consultants of Calcutta gave their valuable opinions and treated him. He was found on X-rays to have severe spinal collapse of almost all the vertebrae with protrusion of the discs, most of them herniated. This condition, due to his advanced age, contributed to both the weakness in his legs and back pain. Despite all these difficulties, Maharaj continued to selflessly receive the many visitors who came to see him and to ardently pursue the work at hand.

On his birthday, February 22, 1992, I went to visit him and saw a bouquet of roses in his room. He asked me casually, "Are you coming in the evening? You bring your daughter and son-in-law." We arrived together in the evening and sat in the lounge amidst his friends. Maharaj asked us to bring that bouquet, and he then presented it to my newly married daughter and son-in-law. He hadn't mentioned anything about his birthday (usually he didn't permit anyone to celebrate his birthday), but someone had brought a cake and we all managed to sing "Happy Birthday" to him on that happy occasion.

From May 1992 Maharaj also started having fever with rigour two to three times a month. Many diagnostic studies were performed but the cause could not be detected. He was working hard, even late at night and early in the morning, to complete a book, which he assigned as his last responsibility to fulfil. The fevers and chills, with the weakness of

the lower limbs, persisted and then restricted him to bed. Further inves-
tigations failed to reveal any clue to his fever. The latest antibiotics
failed, though corticosteroids (Decadron) relieved him to some extent.

He was again hospitalized at Seva Pratishthan. The service of attendants was somewhat irregular, specially at night. Our request for a bell
connection from his cabin to the duty room, and for the appointment
of a private attendant, could not be arranged as they did not fit in with
hospital rules. I was also suffering mentally thinking of my helpless-
ness. Some of Maharaj's friends approached him with proposals to
shift him to some nursing home for better service and treatment. But
Maharaj vehemently rejected the proposal by saying that he would
rather die than violate the discipline of the Sangha—so long as he was
in the Order, he was morally bound to obey the Sangha.

When he was able to sit in a wheelchair, he returned to the Institute
of Culture. From August 1992 he was moving in a wheelchair, receiving visitors as usual, reading with failing vision and making revisions
of his book in fulfilment of his last desire. In September, Dr. Shelley
Brown arrived anxiously to Calcutta and received instructions for the
final makeup of the book of Maharaj with her computer.

After his last hospitalization, Maharaj used to say that no restoration
of his health would be possible this time with the help of any treatment. But whenever he used to get relief from any ailment, I used to
receive a ring at 6:30 A.M.: "Arabinda Babu, you have done a miracle, I
am much better now. Oh, how I suffered yesterday!" It so happened
many a time. Revered Maharaj used to appreciate even the minor
achievements of any person, whosoever. Just to give me an opportunity to touch his divine body, two to three times daily, he suffered so
much physically, outwardly, for the last few years. Only his blessing,
his affection, his love, were my ecstasy.

On October 22, 1992, Maharaj anxiously requested me over the
phone at about 11:15 A.M. to arrange a night attendant, as the usual attendant did not turn up the previous night. I assured him not to worry. But
he reminded me again after fifteen minutes. He was concerned about

Rashbehari, his daytime attendant, who was serving him both day and night at the Institute when required. I appreciated Maharaj's concern for his attendant, and how lucky Rashbehari was, when I received a frantic phone call at 12:30 P.M. I rushed to the Institute within fifteen minutes, only to see that his room (No. 20) was full of saffron-clad sadhus. Dr. Shelley Brown was weeping like a child. Everything was over. Our Revered Maharaj was lying with his eyes closed, in peace and tranquillity, as if lying in the lap of the Holy Mother. Rashbehari's face was buried in sobs between the feet of Revered Maharaj.

At first, I could not believe that a person who talked to me an hour earlier could leave this world quietly, giving me no chance of rendering my last service to him. Only Rashbehari had been at his side. I was struck dumb. It was as if I lost my father a second time in my life. The only consolation for me was to see him beyond the realm of physical and mental suffering of this unhappy world. I was so stunned that not a drop of tears appeared in my eyes.

His body was placed in the foyer of the Institute, where endless streams of men and women paid their homage to him in tears before he was taken to the Belur Math for final ceremonies. After a week, on October 29, a few of us came to the Institute with garlands seeking entry into Room No. 20 where Revered Maharaj breathed his last. The whole room was totally ransacked—everything was in a mess. Quickly we put the room in presentable order, covering the bed with a saffron dhoti. Then I placed the garland in the form of the symbol for the sacred word *Om* on the bed, and another at the base of the photos of Sri Thakur, Holy Mother, and Swamiji. By that time, Dr. Shelley Brown and others entered the room with burning incense sticks. We sat on the floor around the bed, with closed eyes, remembering him with utmost respect. At last, yes, at last my accumulated sorrow broke loose into a flow of tears—I could not contain myself. My agony and my anguish knew no bounds for this divine soul who had dedicated his whole life for the Sangha and who had created solely on his own a vast work: spiritual instruction for the institution of education for human unity and world civilization, leading to "One Soul, One World, One Religion."

S. P. BAKSHI

It was a Sunday morning at Udbodhan house in Baghbazar on the northern fringe of the city of Calcutta. My intimate friends for the last forty years, Dr. Arabinda Basu and Dr. Murali Mitra and their wives, introduced my wife and me to Swami Nitya-swarup-ananda. Though an elderly man well into his eighties, he looked so bright and cheerful! The Swami's attention was immediately focused on the six of us, as we were so close-knit, like a family sharing our joys and sorrows. This sort of oneness, he remarked, he had rarely seen throughout his long life. And after that he always introduced us as a family to his acquaintances.

The six of us were led to a room on the first floor and after paying our respects, we started to listen to his deliberations. It was a wide-ranging discussion about our profession of medicine, the idealism to be practised according to the teachings of Swami Vivekananda, and even current affairs. He had a profound knowledge and was up-to-date on every subject. I recall that he even informed us that the meaning of the word "socialism" had been changed in recent editions of the English dictionary since the transfer of power from orthodox Communism in Russia to the more liberal Mikhail Gorbachev.

In November 1985 Swami Nitya-swarup-ananda went with us and a few other devotees to Jamshedpur by car. We put up at the Ramakrishna Mission Boys' Home, where Arabindo Maharaj was in charge. The hostel's residents were mostly poor tribal boys, and he lived, slept, and ate with them as well as imparting education, to instil confidence. Arabindo Maharaj also happened to be a good cook, and we ate to our hearts' content some sixteen to twenty courses for both lunch and dinner, with Swami Nitya-swarup-ananda suggesting the dishes to be prepared.

It was on this trip that I gained some insight into his vast progressive mind. One evening we went to the Bishtupur area where the Ramakrishna Mission Ashrama was situated. Kalidas Maharaj [Swami

Adinathananda] was in charge of the Ashrama. He was an elderly man, and like Chintaharan Maharaj, a disciple of Ma Sarada. During the discussion, Kalidas Maharaj introduced us to a boy with a first-class degree in Sanskrit who was performing all the pujas at the Ashram. Chintaharan Maharaj became a little annoyed and said, "Pujas can be performed by anybody. Instead have this boy study the Puranas and other scriptures so that he can expand his sphere of knowledge and so a real synthesis of religion can come out of his work." His mind dwelt on ideals more than rituals. Once at the Belur Math during the Durga Puja, we went to see him, and instead of taking us to the ceremonies, he led us to his room and discussed Swami Vivekananda's grand vision of education and the emancipation of women.

Once Chintaharan Maharaj went to Advaita Ashrama at Mayavati with some devotees, but unfortunately I could not join them. After the others came back to Calcutta, Maharaj stayed back in Delhi and remained for awhile at the Ramakrishna Mission Ashrama. I wrote him several letters there but received no reply. To my surprise, as soon as he returned to Calcutta he walked over to my residence one day at 7:00 in the morning, just to say that he had come personally to convey his feelings since he could not answer my letters. His charm and sense of purpose filled me with sudden joy.

When asked by my nephew about *diksha*, Chintaharan Maharaj told him that initiation was not a must for spiritual upliftment and that its absence doesn't make someone a nonentity. He said very forcefully that honesty of purpose and idealism as propounded by Swami Vivekananda were more important than so-called *diksha*.

In his later life he became ill and needed constant medical attention. Dr. Arabinda Basu looked after him like a son looking after his old ailing father, and did his best to ensure his every comfort till the time of his death. I examined him occasionally during this illness, and thus came to know him more intimately. He was pleased when I presented him with an electronic digital thermometer which he could read himself, and often mentioned this small gift before he passed away. It was a fateful day on October 22, 1992, and amidst the chanting of the hymns as his mortal remains were lying in the foyer of the Institute, I felt a terrible void at the thought that such a strong personality was no longer with us as a guide.

ARABINDA BHOSE*

Occasionally one comes across a great soul in this ephemeral world who transcends the ordinary human realm. By ignoring *anitya* [temporal] they become *nitya* [eternal] and thereby help us to understand God. Revered Swami Nitya-swarup-ananda Maharaj was such a rare soul, and I was fortunate in coming close to him.

I will give an example of his great affection for us. One morning towards the end of 1986 I got his phone call—"Arabinda, can you come and see me this evening?" His call was my command, so I reached Balaram Mandir by that evening. "I want to have Thakur's *prasad* with a few close friends (he always addressed his devotees as 'friends')," he announced, "and I need your help to make the necessary arrangements." Accordingly, Deb Babu (Debu Barik, the owner of the famous Bijoli Grill that was going to prepare the food) was asked to come and join in the discussions.

"Arabinda, what do you suggest?" Maharaj asked me. "Should we have Continental dishes? For example, some cold dishes like chicken salad and assorted cold meats, and baked items such as 'Chicken Princess,' 'Chicken Landlord,' or some fish dishes or 'sizzlers'?"

I replied, "Maharaj, we are mainly Bengalis and so I think this kind of menu will not be appreciated. We can have Mughlai dishes or very traditional Bengali dishes such as some prawn preparation or fried hilsa fish." He at once consented and selected prawns along with other Bengali items. The menu was finalized after days of discussion, during which time I gained an idea of his vast epicurean knowledge.

On the day of the feast we had the good fortune to take Thakur's *prasad* in Maharaj's company. One thought kept coming to my mind. We have all read in the *Kathamrita* the description of Thakur having *prasad* with his devotees. Although one can only imagine the ecstatic joy of such an event, nonetheless our lunch at Balaram Mandir gave me a sense of elation which is not easily expressed. It made me feel blessed.

KIREET JOSHI

The first time that I met Swami Nitya-swarup-ananda, I found in him a soul of universality. And I discovered that he had devoted his life and his work to concretize a dream which was also deep-seated in my own heart, for I am myself committed to education that would promote the unity of mankind. I saw that the Swami had given a concrete form to an ideal system of education in his writing and that his book aimed at the presentation of that concrete form. I thought it would be extremely useful for humanity to preserve it and to work on that presentation.

When Swamiji came to me in 1986 with the complaint that he was not receiving the needed help at the Ministry, I really felt one with his inner suffering and I sensed that if I had not been in the Ministry, I would have been myself in his position. I was fortunately at that time in charge of UNESCO affairs of the Ministry of Human Resource Development, and I was also Member Secretary of the Indian Council of Philosophical Research.

As soon as the matter came to my hands, I inquired into the relevant section of the Ministry and I found a ready response in my section; colleagues working with me were favourable to his proposition, and the needed funds were found by combining the allotments that could be utilized for this purpose in the Ministry of Education and in the Indian Council of Philosophical Research. In both the places there was a good response. A great deal of the credit belongs to Mr. Baldev Mahajan, an excellent colleague who was a Secretary for the Indian National Commission for Cooperation with UNESCO, and it was with his willing collaboration and supervision that the book was rescued from its previous difficulties and finally published.

I appreciated the Swami very deeply and the kind of labour that he was putting into his work stirred me to my depths. So it was not with a sense of helping him that this was accomplished. I met him not just once but several times in the Ministry of Education, and not merely as one who wanted to bring out his book but so we could share our common feelings, sentiments, and ideals. Our conversations were on the theme of human unity, an exchange of ideas about how to bring to fruition this great ideal of education. We found ourselves in full agreement.

After the book was ready we had a very pleasant meeting, a satisfied meeting. Here was a man who had laboured so much and ultimately his efforts were fulfilled. I think he felt very pleased, both of us were very happy, not a kind of a personal happiness but a happiness that comes out of one's sense of universality. It was not as if he did this work, or I did this work, it was a work for humanity—a work which humanity accomplished through some instruments which are found along the way. It was a work for the ideal.

Swami Nitya-swarup-ananda was a citizen of the world, having transcended all limiting ideologies and ideas of partisanship. His great vision of the unity of mankind and of the proper system of education was an extension of his universality. My own ideas on the philosophy of education, developed over three decades, were further enriched by our discussions. As a tribute to the Swami, let me present brief reflections on the three main objectives of education that we discussed which I feel were directly related to his theme of education for human unity. It explains some of the new demands that are being imposed on our contemporary teachers and the need for our Indian policy to accept the theme of education with a world view.

I. Education for Peace

In recent times, when high-pitched world tensions are endangering human survival to the utmost, there is a new imperative to generate and strengthen the forces of harmony, peace, and understanding. Peace is not just the absence of war, but a fundamentally positive concept. It is the active striving and rigorous pursuit of understanding on an international level. In education, this means instilling a global perspective. All cultures, civilizations, and values must be respected and understood, not as mere knowledge of other peoples but as a comprehensive commitment to the Family of Man.

II. Education for Development

One of the perennial objectives of education has been to develop man's capacity to change in relation to progress, increasingly a challenge since the pace has quickened with man's deliberate thrust into the future. "Education for development" has emerged as a major objective, not in the sense of a materialistic mind-set and excessive consumption but in order to promote productivity and social justice. It aims at the growth of an interrelationship between the individual and his whole society, while encouraging the right use of science and technology in solving society's major economic and cultural problems. In this process science and art should join hands: both involve the creative impulse and both require a fertile imagination to arrive at the truth by piercing veil after veil of appearances through rigorous discipline. Our system needs more opportunities for the blossoming of imagination and for its expression in literature, poetry, painting, music, dance, and drama.

III. Education for an Integral Personality

An integrated man, in possession of himself and with a durable meaning to his life, can be a potent instrument for harmonious relationships and peace. Contemporary education must play the crucial role in producing people of this calibre. The emergence of an integrated personality is a lifelong process requiring the progressive development of all parts of the human being—physical, rational, aesthetic, moral, and spiritual. Gradually comes an accrual of values which the personality then embodies, expresses, and fulfils. The teacher's role in this value-oriented education is most exciting, dealing not merely with subjects and books but with faculties and capacities. Above all, teachers must look upon their work objectively as a discipline for integrating their own personalities. It takes wisdom and courage to stick to impartial observation in pursuing the truth, but it is only through the combined efforts of teachers and students alike in practising these disciplines that their mutual growth can be achieved.

1987-88
(Second visit to the United States)

VIOLET AMORY EATON

It was still very dark that early winter morning. Swami Nitya-swarup-ananda had arrived the evening before at our SRV retreat house in New York State's northern farmlands. We wanted so much to make him comfortable and happy and ask him a thousand questions. He seemed so simple, so human, full of humor, and a loving challenge to become alert!

Early the next morning I hurried down the long stairs of the old Victorian mansion. It was cold, always chilly under those high ceilings, but I pushed the thermostat up as I ran along the corridor to the large and lovely shrine room, mentally going over my duties to light the candles and wave the incense before the Lord, and generally prepare the room for the morning's meditation. It was still only 5:10 in the morning—good, I thought, lots of time for the shrine to warm up. We had told Swami that we always met for meditation at 6:00. Questions flew through my mind: "Which cushion shall I put out for Swami? Where would he like to sit? Which incense should I offer? Rose, I think."

And so, fussing in mind, I opened the door from the hall into the back of the shrine, pulling the draft curtains gently apart. The shrine was already alight with one candle under Sri Ramakrishna's photograph. Just in front of it was a round mound swathed in *gerua* cloth. Swami was already up! It must be Swami, but where was his head? It must be there, bowed beneath his shoulders as he sat with crossed legs on top of his cushion.

I sat down feeling guilty at first, but all that left very quickly. Such silence! Such alive silence and beauty. I bowed my head in real sincerity.

Ramakrishna was here! Holy Mother was here! Oh God, Oh wonderful Holy Swami, thank you!

The orange mound never moved. Coming back from this experience, I felt an even deeper love for this extraordinary man.

RENEE LA PAN

When Swami Nitya-swarup-ananda emerged from Jack Kelly's spacious blue van in June 1987, he greeted us somewhat shyly. His stature reached approximately all the way up to a portly four foot ten. Or maybe it just seemed that way. He was about eighty-eight years old but could pass for twenty years younger. We had been told that as the former Head of the Ramakrishna Mission Institute of Culture he was accustomed to traveling in high-level circles, among the movers and shakers, so to speak, and to "giving orders." So we were not quite sure what to expect.

We three were living at and operating an independent retreat house under the ownership of the SRV (Sarada-Ramakrishna-Vivekananda) Association. Jack Kelly and Erik Johns were on the steering committee and kept in close contact with us. Hence this was the Swami's first visit to their pet project. He wanted to see everything: the furnace in the basement, the woodpiles waiting to go into the same, the tools, the tractor, the gardens, the temple, everything. He appreciated the meticulous care that had been taken in creating and maintaining every detail around the place, from the hand-finished woodwork to the flowers arranged colorfully in their beds; it matched his attitude of "whatever you do, do with whole-souled devotion."

It must have met with his approval because by September Swami began spending most weekends with us. This was partly because Jack and Erik needed some assistance in taking care of him. Although he was more than two decades their elder, he kept both of them hopping. We soon found out that he could keep all five of us hopping!

We had prepared a special two-and-a-half-foot-square overstuffed *gerua* pillow for him in the shrine. But, instead of the expected method of using it as a seat while the legs remain folded on the floor, Swami invariably sat squarely and completely in the middle of it, looking ever so much the spiritual potentate that he was. He would arrive early in the morning before some of us and usually leave after most of us had gone. We rationalized our short stay because of preparing breakfast for him and for whoever else happened to be orbiting around him that weekend. For he did indeed draw people.

But back to the orange cushion. He attacked his *japam* vigorously. From the persistent rattle emanating from under his shawl one would have expected his *mala* [rosary beads] to be of the jumbo variety. But indeed it was just normal sized, as we discovered when one of us had to do some emergency repairs on the thread. This *mala* had been given to him by Swami Arupananda in 1917 and Holy Mother herself had blessed it.

I was not prepared for the Swami's peppery Bengali personality. He called everything into question. "Why do you do that? Why not this?" Questions came like bullets. Thankfully, he did not impose solutions on us; his task was merely to try to make us "see."

The first couple of months were difficult and not without conflicts. We felt that we were already stretched to the maximum and he introduced a further exactingness into everything. Before he even arrived we did some painting in his room. After he arrived we needed to change his mattress. Then we had to put in a board to keep the bed firm, etc., etc. His presentation alternated between gruff and jovial, so he kept us rather confused. We wanted to accommodate, but two of us were still holding outside jobs and this made it even more difficult.

But then we would hear from his attendants that he would spend half the night in meditation, and we would feel strangely protected and honored to have him with us. After a while a story about him that I had heard previously came to mind. Every night before sleeping as he lay on his bed, he would take his pictures of the Master and Mother, hold them on his chest for a few minutes, and surrender everything to them.

During the afternoons, Nitya-swarup-anandaji would take up his place at the far end of the dining room table where he could see both

the northern Catskills framed by the big picture window and into the
kitchen where dinner was in preparation. Here he held court for the
many visitors who wanted to meet him. We heard the same ideas from
him over and over again as the trickle of new visitors became a steady
flow. He challenged the visitors to examine their preconceived notions.
The thing he hated to hear the most was that Swami so-and-so (usually
the speaker's guru or the current head of their center) was against
such-and-such an idea being put into action. Then, explosively, he
would brush all of that aside. "Oh, this 'ananda' and that 'ananda.' *You*
do what *you* know is best." He would launch into a recitation from one
of Swamiji's lectures which he had memorized in his youth. One of us
would run for a copy of the *Complete Works* to bolster his attempt. He
liked to hold onto it, whether he needed it or not. Or sometimes it
would be a poem, usually from "Kali the Mother":

> Who dares misery love,
>   And hugs the form of death
> Dance in destruction's dance.
>   To him the Mother comes.

He was extremely reluctant to talk about the Holy Mother with us,
probably out of immense reverence. He was all soft about her, like his
ideal man Vivekananda had been.

Between visitors, Swami would supervise the cook through the
dutch door separating the kitchen from the dining room. He inspired
and encouraged the cook to create ever more dishes, so that over the
course of the year the meals became much more elaborate. And he was
pleased when we prepared dishes from our own produce: apple desserts,
bean casseroles, and so on. His eyes would positively light up when we
brought steaming platters of asparagus to the table full of devotees and
admirers. "You think that you are eating," he would say, waving his
fork around. "You are not eating, you are *being eaten*. You think that
you are enjoying, but you are not enjoying. You are *being enjoyed*." He
appreciated the shock value of such statements and he frequently
demonstrated his feeling with startling body language. When anybody

said something particularly shocking, his whole body jolted, "Whaaaat?" Often, but not always, he was just having fun with us.

Even the cook would get pulled into joining his afternoon walk. We would start at the parking lot from the kitchen door, go around through the orchard, and pause under the trees, absorbing the green of the grass and the leaves. Then we would circle to the front of the house, past the flower beds to the temple. There he would survey the open horizon, the foothills and mountains that formed a horseshoe on three sides of our hill. I'm sure he could not help himself, for he would invariably lift his cane and slowly swing it in an arc of benediction encompassing the whole visible world, looking much like Yoda in Star Wars II. You limit yourselves with your fear, he seemed to say. Break out of it!

We developed little insider's jokes, as all groups do. For some reason, the Swami consistently confused muffins and waffles so that the word came out "muffles." And so they have remained for me to this day. We actually served him muffins. The large soft ones. They constituted one of the staples of his breakfast. When we didn't bake them ourselves, Jack would get them fresh from a bakery.

The seasons turned. Through the picture window he watched the landscape go bare, then white. He left us for a substantial part of the winter to go to the West Coast, and it was very quiet without him. For his age he showed a remarkable degree of adaptability. It was particularly noticeable when he returned in early spring; he had mellowed, was more relaxed, laughed more. When I say laugh, I mean with his whole body, like the statues of the laughing Buddha. It wasn't so much vocal as kinetic. Waves of laughter would undulate repeatedly from head to toe. Everyone joined in.

He followed the path of participation in the world process but his underlying nonduality unmistakably came to the fore. Here are some examples of that.

One day after dinner Jack brought out an anonymous letter from a devotee on the West Coast which laid blame on "the system" for creating passivity among the devotees. Swami Nitya-swarup-ananda said, "Now just see. This person has not yet become a Vedantin. He is allowing something to happen to him which he does not want, and then he blames the other for doing it." He wanted us to take responsibility for our own actions based on an unswerving conviction that we are the Atman (since there is only one Atman, therefore there are no differences) and then go forward with all the infinite power that knowledge awakens.

"Men bring down the teachings of Vedanta and Swamiji to their own level. We identify with our mind, body, and senses, take them to be real and adjust the truth, compromise it. We deceive ourselves into thinking that we are living the ideal. But spirit is not matter. Spirit is not nature."

One day Swami said with folded hands, "When you make pranam in the shrine you should say, 'I bow to Sat; I bow to Chit; I bow to Ananda; I bow to my own true Self.'" He wanted to see an American expression of that inspiration. He did not particularly want to hear us sing Indian devotional songs; he wanted original ones. He did not want us to serve him Indian food, but our own, and similarly in all categories. "You are veritable goddesses," he would say, much to our embarrassment.

He had been present at our first big gathering the previous fall. We had invited acquaintances with minimal exposure to Vedanta but who were open enough to listen. He wanted us to do the entire program, but afterwards he came out and joined us for refreshments.

The Swami found many positive features in Americans, but he also did not overrate present-day India. One day I heard him in a conversation with another swami: "India is no more. It exists only in idea form. India is therefore not a material place, but exists on a conceptual level."

When I was blathering on about something to do with interreligious activities (a subject in which he was normally interested), he curled back his upper lip in something very akin to a snarl and said slowly, "You are still interested in religion. I am not interested in religion." Now it was my turn to be shocked. But later I think I discovered what he meant. He was interested in realization, not religious forms. Swami was hard to understand and definitely not wishy-washy. His wonderful diversity and depth of character kept us fascinated.

To his joy the tulips came and went. Then the strawberries. He would sit on a lawn chair with or without visitors and come back inside with the warmth of the sun still on his face. He was like a young child seeing things for the first time, but knowing it was the last. After watching all of us so effortlessly mow the lawn, he decided to drive the tractor himself one day. He couldn't quite coordinate the steering with the accelerator, but he gave us all a tremendous laugh.

On July 23, 1988, we held a willow tree planting ceremony in honor of the Swami's visit. About twenty of us went down to the pond over the hill south of the house. The hole had already been dug, and he gave a heartfelt blessing as he poured a spadeful of earth back into the hole around the roots. We felt that something of him would be there always.

Earlier I had spoken with him about problems with a particular situation. He grasped it immediately and said, "You will have to use your wits and learn how to work around it." Essentially he was suggesting a substitute for confrontation. I tried, but never felt I could quite accomplish it.

He seemed to know that some of us had already lost our Camelot, but were nevertheless trying to carry on according to the Ideal. Though he never spoke of it directly, this is what I liked most about him. Swami was always encouraging and supportive, but said that we had to admit that we were trying to do the impossible. Nevertheless do it! "Pay attention to the means, the ends will come."

He also told me a story about a brahmachari who had served with him at the Institute of Culture. This young man served very faithfully and worked hard. After his duties were finished one day he went to the shrine to do some *japam* and meditation. The Swami suddenly had some urgent office business and called the young man out to attend to it. He said to the Swami, "All of this is killing me." And the Swami responded, "Yes, it is killing you. You came here to be killed." (We had heard that Nitya-swarup-ananda himself had been reassigned to another post after twenty-five years with the Institute of Culture. His detachment was such that he simply turned in his keys to his superior and went on.)

Swami's health improved overall during his stay in the United States. But concern over the possibility of illness made him decide to return to India. He wanted to prevent the devotees from having to pay for his medical care. We tried to convince him to stay, but he told us that we needed younger, more dynamic swamis to come. He said it took too much energy to adapt from his old ways.

A year after his arrival, amidst doubts of our ability to handle the additional responsibility, it was amazing how much I was affected by his leaving us. His last day at SRV, standing in the parking lot, he traced the horizon with his cane, enjoying the whole panorama. Then he left, sitting bolt upright in the passenger seat of the van.

He was one of those people whose desire for excellence exceeded human ability. He pushed, pushed hard, because he didn't know what else to do to get people to move. But, on a day-to-day basis, he simply came and shared himself with us—ALL of himself: his pleasure with the brilliant autumn foliage or the relaxing fire in the stove in the living room, his nervousness when he had to deliver a public address, his grin when we tied his bib across his ample frontage, his frustration with the mediocrity he found encroaching on his beloved Order.

He was fortunate to come within the sphere of Sri Ramakrishna's direct disciples at an early age. That was the light that he shared most with us: how they had changed his life and had given him a global perspective. I will always be grateful for the time he spent with us, his untiring energy in promoting the message of universality, and his willingness to try a new venture in Vedanta. May that spirit of Swami Nitya-swarup-ananda inspire the next century of Vedanta in America.

PHILIP STAPP AND JOHN BASS

Swami Nitya-swarup-ananda was not a cold, austere man. For anyone whose approach was sincere, he was comfortably accessible. He was gentle, lucid in the English language, and often humorous. We saw him from time to time quite informally at the farm of Erik Johns and Jack Kelly in New York State.

His most memorable characteristic seemed his passionate intensity to bring the light of Swami Vivekananda's teaching into a wider focus, especially in the United States. He was sympathetic to the viewpoint of many Americans toward openness to other's beliefs.

Once he came to lunch with Erik and Jack to our home in Connecticut. It was a warm spring day. We lunched outside under a wide grape arbor. After eating a few bites of his lunch Swami Nitya-swarup-ananda began to knead his food with his fingers as though the food was clay which he wanted to model into some perfect unspecified shape. He talked incessantly, seemingly unaware of what his hands were doing. His words reflected his intense desire that people in the West might come swiftly into the light of Swamiji's teaching. Between his words we sensed disappointment that this understanding was not happening more quickly. After a time Erik said gently, "Swami, perhaps you should eat your food."

On every chance occasion of our meeting the impression Swami Nitya-swarup-ananda left was that of a remarkable human being, driven to brighten the lives of the motley Americans he met with his spiritual happiness. It was easy to see that he was a disciple of Holy Mother, who looked upon the foibles and procrastination of fellow humans with sympathetic compassion.

We are blessed indeed that the path of Swami Nitya-swarup-ananda crossed ours, even in so tangential a manner. His memory will endure.

SHELLEY BROWN

Swami Nitya-swarup-ananda was bubbling over with amusing and lofty conversation as he sat in my medical consultation room one crisp September day in 1987, escorted by one of his hosts in the United States, Erik Johns, for a routine checkup. Perfectly natural and full of enthusiasm, the Swami impressed me by his utter lack of pretension. Despite his heady reputation as a disciple of the Holy Mother, Founder of the Institute of Culture in Calcutta, and a seniormost monk of the Ramakrishna Order, I felt immediately at ease.

Shortly after this meeting, he developed a high fever with bronchitis, and I went to check his condition every day at the Vedanta Society in New York, where he was staying during his illness. Even while convalescing, he could talk for hours from some inner reserves of energy. His stream of talk was always on the highest spiritual level. "Live and move and have your being in THEM and THEM alone," he would exhort, and then he would carry this theme into ever more detailed practical scenarios for one's own life. One day he became absolutely transported, sitting cross-legged on his bed, speaking of how going to the hospital is like going to the temple, each room a place of worship, each patient a Divinity. And then he *became* a temple priest making all the motions of doing the offering as he continued to talk. "Is it more important to offer a flower and some incense in the temple than to do a medical procedure or examine a patient?" he would exclaim, as if to say "What nonsense!"

The dynamic force of his words gave familiar Vedantic concepts fresh meaning. The idea that every task is worship equivalent to the worship performed in a temple immediately inspired a more intense commitment to one's routine work. And within the stream of his talk, this revelation of the power to spiritualize everyday tasks was fused with the concept of transcendence, of identification with the Spirit as the only goal. Such conversations with the Swami made an indelible impression. I was eager to continue the spiritual dialogue on the telephone, with periodic visits to Erik's home, Moss Hill Farms, where the Swami returned to stay once he had recovered.

He was easily persuaded to have a cataract operation in New York to improve his failing vision, which impaired his reading and other work. His gracious deportment and warmhearted manner quickly won over Dr. Barry Smith, who performed the surgery, as well as the nurses in the recovery room, and just about anyone else who came into contact with him. I was amazed at his fortitude at that advanced age as he underwent the surgery in the morning and went back to the Vedanta Society by noon that same day, walking out without assistance and inquiring about lunch!

Unfortunately, he didn't see as well out of that eye as he had hoped, since there were retinal difficulties behind the cataract that could not be remedied. We did the best we could with his spectacles, and the optometrist who adjusted them always remembered the experience with a smile, for the Swami was an absolute perfectionist with endless patience and perseverance, and the adjustments on his glasses also went on for some time until he was reasonably satisfied. Yet all this was conducted so sweetly and with such good humour that it seemed more like a special occasion than an effort to please an exacting customer. Everyone who had taken care of him continued to inquire after his health for years thereafter, asking, "How is the Swami?"

As part of his itinerary in the United States, Swami Nitya-swarup-ananda intended to visit the Vedanta centres on the West Coast. His health was a bit fragile, so it seemed natural for me to accompany him out to Portland, Oregon, in September 1987. The flight included a stop of several hours in Chicago, making the whole trip well over eight hours, but he took this all in stride, perfectly relaxed throughout, looking fresh and keenly interested in everything, and even enjoying the airline dinners. Swami Aseshananda came personally to the Portland airport to receive Swami Nitya-swarup-ananda. It was a sight, watching these two venerable elders of the Order, each a spiritual powerhouse with strong opinions, show each other the most exquisite respect.

Every evening at the Vedanta Society in Portland, the two swamis sat in the foyer with the devotees, answering questions and speaking extemporaneously. I received permission to tape these impromptu conversations and discovered many spiritual treasures when transcribing them, excerpts of which have been included in the present biography. I returned to New York at the end of my week's leave, while the Swami remained to complete his tour of the West Coast. Swami Nitya-swarup-ananda was still in California when I returned from a trip to India in March 1988, at which time our long telephone conversations were resumed and preserved in a journal.

In June and July 1988, Swami ventured twice to Ocean Grove, New Jersey, a historic seaside community which is still an active Methodist campground. Swami, Jack Kelly, and Erik Johns stayed in a small bed-and-breakfast inn down by the sea, and had their midday meals at Sri Sarada Kutir, a little Victorian cottage that I used as a retreat. Swami called the quiet community "Heaven on Earth" and took the whole experience in with great delight. The extraordinary scene which remains most vividly impressed upon my mind from this two-day visit occurred on the beach. The sun was very hot and we were all sitting on mats under a large protective umbrella when Swami suddenly decided to walk along the shore. He said that the place reminded him of the beach at Puri, a holy city in India. With remarkable strength, grace, and balance he started striding barefoot just by the edge of the water, and all the while speaking emphatically of the highest Vedantic philosophy with such conviction, with such a sense of reality, and with such inspiration that one lost all sense of time and place. I cannot look at the beach today without remembering the vigour of his stride and of his words, as this amazing sadhu went up and down the beach in his *gerua* apparel at the age of ninety with us in tow.

I believe that many a devotee in the West gained new appreciation and insight into Swami Vivekananda as a result of listening to Swami Nitya-swarup-ananda. He kept emphasizing the idea that Sri Rama-krishna could never be understood except through Swami Vivekananda, a concept that was at first difficult to grasp and to accept. It was not until I had the opportunity to type and review his manuscripts for his books *Back to Vivekananda* and later *Divine Rights of the Sangha* that I really began to get a glimpse into the veracity, force, and purity of Swamiji's ideals. It was then that I recognized in full measure our good fortune in having Swami Vivekananda as a bridge, as well as an exemplar.

This appreciation of Swami Vivekananda was reinforced by seeing how Swami Nitya-swarup-ananda himself lived Swamiji's ideals in every particular and in every moment. I shall never forget an experience with the Swami which has given me a lifelong lesson in truthfulness—

the strictest adherence to Truth, as Swami Vivekananda himself put it. In 1989, a large, beautifully hand-carved teak shrine had been made for me by the eminent Calcutta artist and designer, Mr. Raghunath Goswami, which Swami Nitya-swarup-ananda himself had commissioned. For shipping purposes, this four-foot-square shrine was enclosed in its own special wooden crate, but even so presented a tremendous challenge in that no one would take the responsibility for shipping it, nor was it deemed practical at that time for me to check it into the cargo hold of the airplane to take it back to New York.

After endless discussions, numerous telephone calls, and dozens of inquiries, the Swami himself accompanied me to a shipper who had said he might be willing to take care of it. At the conclusion of the whole discussion, the gentleman agreed and said he would take on the responsibility, but it would be necessary to put on the shipping label "For Exhibition Purposes Only" or words to that effect. I was vastly relieved, but the Swami sat there in dead silence. Then he looked up and said quietly, "But that isn't true, it is a shrine, it is not for exhibition purposes only." The shipping officer tried to cajole him into permitting this label, which he said was "just a technicality."

But the Swami was firm and we eventually walked calmly out of the office, "back to square one." For me, this was a new dimension of truth in action and it made me realize the slippage of truth that one rationalizes for oneself in order to get the job done conveniently. As the Swami would say so often, "We stand for the Truth, for strict adherence to the Truth. We stand for certain Principles!" As his own words were always truthful, they had that force of conviction. Thanks to the help of friends, it was possible for me to get the shrine back to New York on the plane without the slightest damage—and uncontaminated by any falsehood.

Although photographs of Sri Ramakrishna, Holy Mother, and Swamiji had been placed in the shrine in India, Swami Nitya-swarup-ananda in his great thoughtfulness wanted to go further. Knowing that I had a long-standing commitment to photography and was familiar with the best professional services in New York City, he informed me that he was having a most precious original photograph of Sri Ramakrishna hand-delivered to me by a monk of the Order who would soon be visiting the Vedanta Society in New York; I was to have a copy negative as well as prints made from this photograph and then hand-carry the original back to him in India. He said that doing this would also be of great service to the Order.

This particular photograph, one of the four original photographs of Sri Ramakrishna in existence, had initially been discovered among the pages of the *Encyclopaedia Britannica* in Varanasi at the house of Pramadadas Mitra, presented to him, it was felt, by Swami Vivekananda himself. It was subsequently acquired by Swami Shankarananda, the Assistant Sectretary of the Mission, who had in turn given it to Swami Nitya-swarup-ananda when the latter was preparing the *Sri Ramakrishna Centenary Souvenir* album in 1936. In the intervening years it had been kept by another monk of the Order, but Swami Nitya-swarup-ananda requested it back in order to transport it to New York.

It was certainly one of the most auspicious events in my life to have the opportunity to have this photograph copied. The master photographer made an 8-by-10-inch copy negative while I waited, as it was unthinkable to let the original photograph out of my hands for more than a few minutes, and a 6-by-7.5-inch photograph (the size of the original) was printed under his supervision from the copy negative. The image of Sri Ramakrishna was in superb condition, but the upper left-hand corner was bent and there was a vertical crack in the photograph on the left side, both of which were retouched on the copy print by delicate airbrushing. A second copy negative from the airbrushed print was then made for additional prints.

When I returned to India, I carried the original photograph along with negatives and copy prints which I presented to Swami Nitya-swarup-ananda. (One of the prints had been sent to the Sarada Convent in Santa Barbara, California, so that matching pictures of Holy Mother and Swamiji could be produced for the shrine, a difficult task accomplished superbly by Brahmacharini Bhavani, now Pravrajika Bhavaprana.)

Swami Nitya-swarup-ananda was satisfied and had a set of these same photographs framed for his room at the Institute of Culture.

Whenever I visited India I would stay at the Institute for the privilege and joy of his company. His conversation sparkled with hilarious comments but he always kept it tuned to the sublime. I had the opportunity to witness his mastery as a psychologist and benefactor to the friends he received in the foyer near his room during the late morning, afternoon, and evening. He knew the grandparents as well as the parents of many visitors—virtually their entire life story for generations. Tales of their distress elicited from him the exact words that would comfort or clarify.

One day a young man known to him since childhood arrived in the foyer and announced that he had been invited to become a political "team leader." He was speaking in English but it wasn't clear to me at the beginning how Swami was taking this news. He began with gentle questioning and it soon evolved from his probing that the young man might be doing this to please his relatives. Then Swami began chipping away at this idea of political activity, but so masterfully that the young man only very gradually began to feel the heat of his remarks, then became perplexed and started to defend his decision. "You do not know your own mind," Swami said to him suddenly, "people like you are a nuisance—leave now!" The young man responded tearfully before he left, "May I come back?" A few weeks later, I saw this same young man return, his face calm, telling Swami that he had decided not to participate in politics after all. In such ways did Swami Nitya-swarup-ananda strip away the temporary illusions of those who had the good fortune to come under his loving scrutiny.

I had many a painful lesson from Swami myself, which might be categorized under the heading "The Real Lessons Are Not Easy," for they remove entrenched attitudes and mental blinders that shield areas of ignorance. One such revelation involved the seemingly small matter of the sweets I would be offering in the shrines at Shyampukur and "M's" house. I had purchased very ornate sandesh in the shapes of lotuses with silver foil on the top, and moreover I was very proud that I had discovered this nice confectioner's shop on my own after a long walk around the Ballygunge Lake in Calcutta. When Swami saw those ornate sweets he became extremely upset, saying that I shouldn't buy any sweets without asking him, and "why had I bought those sweets in such a place," etc., going on with this tirade for some time. I explained hesitantly that I had done it because it was a "fancy" place, to which he replied abruptly, "All that glitters is not gold."

He then had a driver take me to a sweets shop of his choosing, giving him detailed directions about where the sandesh was to be bought as well as the garlands, which he told me must be "the best in Calcutta" for Thakur. This sandesh turned out to be perfectly plain, gentle soft mounds of the purest ingredients. He also lent me his copy of the *Gospel of Sri Ramakrishna* with the pages marked for me to read at Shyampukur. I was absolutely devastated by all this, both by his kindness and by his criticism—but most of all I was jolted by my misconception. But it was only in this state of misery that I came to understand that yes, of course, only the purest and most *sattvic* sweets must be offered to Sri Ramakrishna—how could one possibly offer anything *rajasic* to Thakur? Unthinkable, yet there was the inescapable conclusion that I hadn't perceived it before. In what other ways, it occurred to me, am I unknowingly insensitive? Swami Nitya-swarup-ananda's spiritual acuity was a mirror for self-reflection, just as his lessons in truth were a commandment for authenticity.

I missed our long conversations once I returned to New York so I kept in close touch by telephone. I also spoke with his physician, Dr. Arabinda Basu, for reports on his health, and my heart sank in June 1992 with the news that Swami was having fevers. As the summer passed it became increasingly clear that his health was failing. I decided to return to Calcutta as soon as my professional responsibilities would permit, arriving in September to find him almost totally incapacitated with severe back pain and still weak with fevers. Despite this sad state of affairs, he was intent on readying his book for publication (*Divine*

Rights of the Sangha, a March 1992 revision of Part I of *Back to Vive-kananda*). Always the perfectionist, he was editing it day and night, sitting painfully at his desk. I had the room directly beneath his at the Institute and I could hear the chair scraping at his desk in the wee hours of the morning—almost inconceivable considering his acute back discomfort and his weakened state of health.

Throughout this difficult period, he had what seemed to me to be guardian angels. The service of his attendant, Rashbehari Misra, became an inspiration to behold, especially since the Swami, frustrated by his physical incapacity, was increasingly impatient with the details of his daily existence. Every evening, Mr. Samiran Sarkar and Mr. S. B. Ghosh could be found sitting in his room as other friends stopped by regularly for his company and to inquire after his needs (among the ladies I saw almost daily were Mrs. Shubhra Chatterji, Mrs. Bhabani Goswami, and Mrs. Chhanda Bose, who was bringing his meals). He could barely take any food, and the matter of his digestion as well as all other practical details about his comfort were being discussed with Dr. Arabinda Basu, who was seeing him several times a day.

I would usually meet with Swami Nitya-swarup-ananda very early in the morning for a slow and painful stroll with his walker up and down the veranda outside his room, and again when Dr. Basu and other friends arrived. Those poignant last days of witnessing his determination despite great pain and infirmity remain enshrined in my memory as an exemplar of spiritual strength.

It was a final wish that *Divine Rights of the Sangha* must be widely distributed, and so it was heartbreaking to hear that it had been removed from the press and confiscated. By that time Swami Nitya-swarup-ananda had left his body, and it was left to his friends to try to honour his memory.

CARMEN FARMER

These events took place during Swami Nitya-swarup-ananda's visit to the Vedanta Society of Portland, Oregon, in the winter of 1987.

It was a very special blessing to have him present for the celebration of Holy Mother's birthday. He stayed for about a month, and during that time there were informal talks after the reading every evening. One night I voiced my concern about "spiritual amnesia" in the workplace. It seemed that during office hours I had a great deal of trouble remembering Sri Ramakrishna and Holy Mother, and treating work as worship. I expressed my frustration to Swami Nitya-swarup-ananda, who replied at length. The gist of his instruction was, "Your problem is that you think there are two things: spiritual life and secular life. There is only life." He went on to say that what we do is spiritual or not because of how we do it and what our motives are. The same action taken by the same person can be spiritual or not, depending on motives. Another important part of our work experience is to develop concentration of mind, whether typing a letter or doing any other task in the workplace. If we can gain a concentrated mind, we are then able to concentrate on anything; using that concentration to place the mind on the Chosen Ideal in meditation becomes much easier. While I can't say that I've developed a concentrated mind, his words about there being "only life" have stayed with me and helped me remember what's really important in many difficult situations.

Another vivid experience with the Swami was in the library of the Portland Society. He was sitting alone after a Sunday lecture and I gathered my courage to talk to him directly. He told me that there were three things about Americans that he liked and admired very much. After telling me what they were, he gave me a little quiz and asked me to repeat them back to him, which I did. I'm embarrassed to admit that today I can only remember two of them: independence and ambition. When questioned about admiring ambition, which seems to have a negative connotation in spiritual circles, he said it was important to be able to set a goal and achieve it. It was very refreshing to hear Americans described in positive terms. It's something we don't hear very often, and many of us tend to think of ourselves as "materialistic Americans," or "materialistic Westerners."

I will always be grateful to Swami Nitya-swarup-ananda for his gracious words of encouragement and inspiration. Just to spend time in his holy presence was a great blessing for all of us.

CLEO ANDERSON

VAG-VAGARTHA, word and its meaning. These great swamis of the Ramakrishna Order bring us Vedanta, the highest truth, and then manifest it in themselves.

For so many years I had treasured the thrilling words of freedom in my well-worn copy of *Ashtavakra Samhita.* So, in 1987 when the translator of that book, Swami Nitya-swarup-ananda, appeared here at our Sacramento center in "living color" my heart was filled with love. I was overjoyed. Almost immediately the Swami became my friend. Since I worked in the office he enlisted my help in running the copy machine as he worked at the task of revising some of his writings. Almost every morning during his five-week stay with us I would eagerly wait for him to come to the office with his cheery greeting, "Hallo, good morning, Cleo! Good morning, good morning, good morning!"—while making straight for his desk with incredible energy and intensity of purpose.

Swami Shraddhananda had let me arrange my other work so as to keep myself free to serve the Swami in whatever way I could. So as Swami Nitya-swarup-ananda would sit at his desk writing and rewriting and making ever and ever finer corrections, my job was to type and retype, cut, paste, and xerox. From one to two hours every morning we would go on working. It was wonderful to see such worship of perfection as he would rewrite again and again to bring a single thought into expression in the written word. If his body was in pain or discomfort, I'm sure he barely knew it or knew it not at all.

On Sunday, January 24, 1988, he was to read a paper from the lectern in the auditorium at 11:00 A.M. But his eyesight was poor and the paper to be read was very, very long. After it was all typed we realized that he would not be able to do it. So I suggested that I take the work to a xerox copy shop and have the print greatly enlarged. He was so happy with that solution to the problem that he insisted on going with me. He went directly to his room and got his hat and coat, and we left. It was then about 3:30 P.M. on Saturday afternoon.

The young people working at the copy shop were at first somewhat annoyed at what they considered needless fussiness as the Swami continued to make demands on their time and attention (it was a very big and busy shop). He was working to achieve a particular ideal result he had in mind as to the correct size of the print and paper and color and binding, etc., and this shop was a wonderland of endless possibilities in the world of print! Before they closed at 5:00 P.M., however, I noticed that they too had become "enslaved" in the effort and completely charmed. It is unlikely that any of them had ever been exposed to real selfless service, where nothing or no one is present—no one except the Ideal.

As it was now closing time, they gave us directions to their main shop, which stayed open twenty-four hours a day. That shop was located about fifteen miles away in a neighboring suburb. The sun had gone down. It was dark. As we were driving to that place I said, "Maharaj, I am going to stop at the center and let them know where we are. They must already have discovered your absence and will be wondering where you are, and they will begin to worry." "No, no. Keep going," he shouted, "we have no time for that." I tried to reason with him that it was only a half block off from our route and we should stop there for a minute. He became very angry and again shouted, "No time for such foolishness. Keep going!" As soon as we reached our destination, however, he let me call the center. He was able to have the work completed to his satisfaction by a new crew at this second shop, and we returned to the center at about 8:00 P.M.

The temple was filled when he presented his paper the following morning. We were all totally inspired and he seemed happy.

A few days later he left our center to go to San Francisco for a few days and then to move on to other centers. I felt I would see him again but I couldn't think how since he was on his way to the East Coast and from there to India. Yet I knew that there was a sort of subtle knowing in the hearts of numberless devotees in all the centers that this Swami somehow belongs to us in the West and we must keep him here.

In the last phone call I made to him at Erik Johns's farm, I again said goodbye to him. But it was only words. I knew I would see him again. And I did! I saw him many, many times at the Institute of Culture in Calcutta from October 1989 to April 1990. Then again I had to say goodbye. But the goodbye was only words, for we kept him in our hearts. His presence and inspiration are very much with all who loved him. His love for Sri Ramakrishna, Holy Mother, Swamiji, the Ramakrishna Order, and the highest truths of Vedanta shine through his form in the mind's eye.

He scolded, criticized, exhorted, pushed, demanded, and all the while he loved us and praised us. He wanted us to live Vedanta. He would tell us, "Do something!" And we will and even now are doing. He wanted us to express ourselves Vedantically as Americans. He told us, "Don't say 'Pranam, Maharaj,' say 'Hi, Swami,'" and he would raise his hand and wiggle his fingers.

RAY BERRY

For years I had heard about Swami Nitya-swarup-ananda, his fiery spirit, his outspokenness, and his love of Americans and their independent nature. So I looked forward to seeing him when he came to Olema on his last visit to the United States.

The Swami was staying in Sacramento with Swami Shraddhananda, and I decided to drive up one day to meet him. One of the first things he said to me was, "I want to take a meal at your house and eat only what you raise on your own place." I guessed that someone had told him that we raised almost all our own food: vegetables, eggs, chickens, goats, and so forth. I told him we would be delighted to have him for lunch. The day he came we had several guests, and there was a veritable feast including all kinds of fresh garden vegetables, roast chicken with stuffing and gravy, and strawberries for dessert. The Swami was so busy talking enthusiastically with the guests that I had to put a stop to the conversation so that he could eat. Once involved with the meal, he noticed that we hadn't served him any stuffing. He asked, "What's that?" I told him it was corn bread stuffing but not grown in the garden. He said, "Give it anyway." He ate with great delight that day, and we all had a grand time in his company.

The Olema Retreat consists of over two thousand acres of open fields, pristine forests, and running streams; wild game also abounds, including several large herds of deer. The Swami asked me, "Do you take a deer occasionally?" I looked at him a little puzzled, but I knew what he was asking, and he went on to explain, "In the early days of Mayavati, sometimes food was very scarce in the winter, and we would shoot a deer, and it would feed us for several days." And then he named the participants: Swamis Vireswarananda, Madhavananda, Ashokananda, and several others. One day at lunch in the monastery he turned to Swami Prabuddhananda, who has always been a strict vegetarian, and said to him, "You are in America, eat as the Americans do, take meat!" Everyone at the table had a good laugh at that one.

After he left Olema for San Francisco, there was a reception for him at the New Temple. He was speaking about his ideas for a peaceful, harmonious, and spiritually aware world. When I ventured to bring up Sri Ramakrishna's analogy of the dog's curly tail to suggest that while his ideas were fantastic, he immediately caught my gist [that they were too idealistic] and thundered at me, "Fantastic, fantastic, fantastic!" And then he proceeded to dress me down (and everyone else too) for not wanting to jump in and do any work to improve the world and raise man's consciousness. Interestingly enough, later on that evening, he confided to me in very serious tones, "I see no hope for this world other than America—you Americans will be the hope for keeping these Vedanta ideals alive!"

FATHER JOHN MILLS

I had heard of Swami Nitya-swarup-ananda for a long time from Jack Kelly and Erik Johns, especially how his generous and loving spirit had

guided both of them. I heard of his gentle perceptions and his broad compassion for all persons, his desire to bring all faiths into harmony even as
Vivekananda had held up this ideal. Such a warm and unifying spirit
touched my heart and enlarged my vision. All this was my preparation.

Then one day, I heard from Jack that Swami was coming to America for a long stay. My heart gladdened, for I knew then that he would
spend some time at Moss Hill Farms where Jack and Erik had their
welcoming foyer for all believers and all seekers. Our first meeting was
at a restaurant in nearby Fishkill, and I saw Swami Nitya-swarup-
ananda climb out of Jack's van. I thought, "What will he ever eat in
this place?" but the practical overcame the esoteric, and there we were
at breakfast eating pancakes and sharing table fellowship with thanks.

Swami was so quiet and easy to be with. He just seemed to go with the
flow—and yet from time to time he would inject penetrating questions:

—"Where have we come from?"
—"Where are we going?"
—"Are we led by the Spirit?"
—"How can we better understand each other?"
—"What does your church do?"
—"What are the special opportunities of your state of life—your
personal ambience?"

I felt my mind and soul responding to these little inquiries, not with
information but with sharing something of myself in a new openness.

Then there were the times at the Vihar, the SRV retreat center in
Greenville, New York, when Swami was gathering all of us into his
mode of thinking and into his peace and quiet of mind. In the shrine he
was self-effacing—a participant, a devotee. In the temple with its great
clear windows looking out into clouds, blue sky, and mountains,
Swami stood for the unity of world religions and the one Spirit of God
blowing like the wind through all of them. Like the exclamation of
Pope John XXIII: "Away with the cobwebs!"

Then came that glorious Easter morning at St. Mary's Church in the
Highlands, Cold Spring, where I was at the altar for the festival Mass. At

the time of the Gospel I looked down into the congregation in the dim light of the candles in the nave and I saw Erik Johns. I looked again at the figure beside him. Was it an orthodox priest, dark and mysterious? I looked hard—and my heart leapt up. It was Swami! I cannot express my joy as I recall that moment. His being there affirmed all that I had learned and experienced from him, his humble compassionate outreach. Then I thought, "What will he do at Communion? I don't want him to feel left out." I need not have wondered. There with the others was Swami Nitya-swarup-ananda at the altar rail, receiving the consecrated bread of God, sharing with us in the eucharistic fellowship, the table of the Lord. Surely there is a Reality higher than any of us: a Truth that beckons, a God, Yahweh, Brahman, Allah who calls, and we respond by the path we have learned, understanding each other better and caring.

This is Swami to me, as I recall that Easter morning when new life had a special manifestation in the person of this great and loving man. How the people gathered round him after church to greet and welcome him to our parish! And now that he has gone to the Paradise of God, I think of the "rush of happy greetings—on heaven's blissful shore."

KRISHNA SESHAN AND PATRICIA JIMINEZ

We had the privilege of spending a great deal of the summer of 1988 with Swami Nitya-swarup-ananda when he was staying nearby in upstate New York as the guest of Jack Kelly and Erik Johns at Moss Hill Farms.

Swami always delighted in everything. He urged us to develop a Universal Attitude. He would speak of this constantly without any provocation. He spoke at length about his interest in a "World University," a university without walls where scholars could meet pupils with a free exchange of knowledge. Swami was never tired of talking about this. For him "knowledge" meant something deep, wonderful, and mysterious, not just in the sense of "information" as we call it. He spoke of his attempts to start such a "World University" with the help of the United Nations.

He wanted those of us who are Indians in the United States to start such an effort, to give back something to India. He once told me, "Mother India has given you all you wanted; now it is time that you gave something back to Mother India," and he shook his finger at me like an old schoolmaster, laughed, and continued. Those words will haunt me all of my life. It is a question that haunts many Indian-Americans. Swami was of the opinion that we, the first generation, were in a special place and had a special opportunity for doing such service.

Swami was curious about everything. We had a small portable computer so we could type whatever would be useful to him. He, of course, wanted to use the computer himself and was not daunted about learning to make it work. And was he fastidious! We stapled several copies of a letter he had written, but he wanted all the copies to be stapled in exactly the same spot. He made us realize that paying attention to minute details made for greatness. We had read how Sri Ramakrishna was fussy that way.

Another fond memory is of Swami Nitya-swarup-ananda planting a sapling at the Vivekananda Vihar. Many people congregated for this joyous occasion. We now treasure the photographs that we took of the tree-planting ceremony and are delighted that our friend Erik Johns has made a painting of it. Whenever we go to the Vihar, we do not miss the opportunity to visit Swami's tree.

Another time we met Swami Nitya-swarup-ananda at Thousand Island Park. We had access to a motorboat and took him for a ride. He even wanted to drive the boat. In a sudden burst of wind his hat blew into the water. It was a warm day so I had no trouble diving into the water and rescuing the hat, but he did everything he could to convince me that I had done something heroic. Later Jack Kelly showed him how to broil a lobster. Swami seemed to enjoy every minute of this trip. It seemed so easy to amuse him. Today both Swami and Jack Kelly have shed their mortal coils, are free, yet when we think of the summer of 1988 we can still hear their laughter.

1989–91
(Final years in India)

I first saw Chintaharan Maharaj at the Foundation Day celebration of the Institute of Culture, probably in the late 1970s or early 1980s. I was eager to meet the Founder of the Institute (where I am employed). Swami Lokeswaranandaji, the Secretary of the Institute, mentioned in his inaugural address, "It is a happy day for the Institute because today we have its Founder present among us." I was also keen to make my pranam to him because he was a direct disciple of Holy Mother. I have had the good fortune to meet only a few of the direct disciples of Holy Mother, but I have been struck with one endearing quality which is common to all of them: the appearance of a naughty child seated quietly on the lap of the Mother! This was evident in all their actions and in the way they spoke, moved, and behaved. Chintaharan Maharaj was no exception. This had an irresistible appeal for me.

After that day I met Chintaharan Maharaj a number of times but never really had a chance to be close to him until after his return from the United States in 1988, when he began staying at the Institute of Culture. While in New York City, Maharaj had given a talk called "How I Came to the Feet of Sri Ramakrishna," which his devoted friends were now keen to get published. As I worked in the Publications Department of the Institute of Culture, this manuscript gave me the opportunity to know him more closely, despite my usual shyness. One day one of the brahmacharis of our department came and told me, "Chintaharan Maharaj has sent for you." My reaction to this message was peculiar, a combination of fear and delight; delight, because at last I could approach this great personality, and fear, because I had heard that he was extremely fastidious about work and quite severe in his criticism.

But when I entered his room all my fears vanished. "A venerated monk," "a great worker," "an erudite scholar"—all the epithets crowding my mind and inhibiting my movements suddenly just dropped away. I felt I was in the presence of a playful and mischievous elder brother. This again is something very strange, that my enormous regard and awe for him coexisted side by side with a reassuring undercurrent which I always felt in his presence.

He had this special capacity of making everyone his own. I wore my hair long at that time. He asked me, "Why have you worn your hair that long, like a Baul? Are you a singer?" I answered in the negative. Later on whenever he sent for me he used to say, "Call that boy with the Baul-like long hair."

The book was on its way to the press. It was almost complete. Yet his drive for perfection was so immense that he never missed an opportunity to further refine any work he had done up till the very last moment. One morning he handed me the book and told me, "I want it back by one o'clock this afternoon." I pleaded for some more time and said, "If I rush it like this I might overlook the errors." He extended the time till evening. I did the proofreading and found a few mistakes. When I sat down to discuss the discrepancies with him, it was then I realized that he was as superb a listener as he was a teacher. He would undergo ordeals, hours of sheer backbreaking hard work just to modify one expression or a particular turn of phrase. He would humbly seek the opinion of others: "I think this expression needs to be modified a bit, what do you suggest?" He would think over it deeply, sometimes for one whole night!

I have heard a little anecdote from his attendant, Rashbehari. One night Rashbehari had left him working at his table. He took leave before going, "Maharaj, I am now going to sleep." Next morning he came back and found him seated in the same position. Rashbehari thought that perhaps Maharaj had woken up early that morning. Imagine his surprise when Maharaj asked him, "What happened, Rashbehari? Why did you come back? Won't you go to sleep?" He had not even realized that a whole night had slipped away while he was absorbed in his work.

Let me now come back to the incident I was narrating. Maharaj went through my corrections meticulously and inquired in great detail about each and every doubt raised by me. He accepted a few of my suggestions and rejected the rest, but not without ascribing very definite reasons for the latter. There was not a trace of pride in him. He was quick to accept suggestions and change his mind whenever he felt a change was needed. He would never impose his views. If he felt that I was wrong, he would ask me to consult a particular book, and I would later come to realize that he was correct.

He was always interested in the latest rules of printing. Once he called me to his room. This was a few months before his passing away. There were other people in the room. The point at stake was with a punctuation rule regarding "full stop" [period]. We put a full stop to mark the end of a sentence. If something is said after that within brackets, should the full stop be placed after the bracket, or not? To some this would have been a minor consideration, but not to Chintaharan Maharaj. He wanted to know what the latest *Editor's Guide Book* had to say about it. He even told us that he had asked someone to get him the latest edition of the *Editor's Guide Book* from the United States.

Nowadays students complain about their teachers, that they are averse to learning or exploring anything new, and keep teaching them the same hackneyed material from their moth-eaten notebooks. Such teachers should take cognizance of this ever-learning mind who was well into his nineties!

Swami Nitya-swarup-ananda disliked irrelevant questions, superficial curiosity, or improper planning before embarking on a course of action. He also disliked emotionality. I think this is why many people misunderstood him. I was forewarned by many of my colleagues about his lashing tongue, but my experience turned out to be otherwise. He was always so patient about things of which I was ignorant, always extremely helpful and encouraging. He taught me a great deal, even once personally instructing me on how to plan and design the cover of a book. The editorial guidance I received from him has been invaluable.

He was concerned about everybody. He gave equal importance to everyone who came to him—academicians and scholars, industrialists, actors and actresses—people from all walks of life. They discussed their problems with him and talked freely, regardless of position. All received the same type of affection (and scolding if necessary). A driver was equally welcome. Once a driver was sent to take Maharaj to some location. As expected, Maharaj asked him searching questions about himself and about the route, and so forth. The driver perhaps got nervous and fumbled, which irritated Maharaj no end, and he said, "You seem to know nothing about the roads. You'll cause an accident." By then the driver had regained his composure and replied, "Do not worry, I can take you safely." Maharaj liked people to be forthright. He then had a long conversation with this driver during the trip. It was election time and the city was full of posters. Maharaj asked him who he was going to vote for and why the opposition candidates were not chosen, and numerous other considerations. The conversation was held in a manner that the driver felt his opinion was valued.

It was impossible to get away with careless work with him. He was truly a hard taskmaster. Anyone who has worked for him has gained immensely because he would teach all the details so beautifully! His attendant, Rashbehari, was a living example of this. Rashbehari kept all Maharaj's papers perfectly in order, though this was something he had never done before. It was not easy. Maharaj had first, second, third, fourth, or even more versions of his various manuscripts. They were all kept in order and Rashbehari had mastered the art of handing over the right copy whenever needed.

I have heard from the old employees of the Institute that when the building was being constructed, he would meticulously supervise everything, right from the watering of bricks which were to be laid out, to the putting up of the symbol of the Order at the entrance. Nothing was insignificant. Every single job had to be executed with equal care and attention.

What fascinated me most about Chintaharan Maharaj was the sheer force of his energy, both mental and physical, and at an age when the tired body and mind usually take their toll. I wonder how illustrious his youthful days of vigour and *élan* must have been!

He stayed on the second floor of the International Guest House of the Institute, which was opposite my room in the office. I could see him from my table. He was usually at his desk, either reading or writing. I and my colleague, Arun Adhikari, never stopped admiring his unwavering devotion to studies, and his strict discipline regarding this, which continued unabated till the very last, in spite of his failing health.

One very small incident: Once I failed to staple a thick pile of paper. I complained that the stapler was too small. He took the papers from me, applied the stapler, and stapled the sheets together with a hard thump. I remembered his age and felt like "hiding my face in shame," as Swami Vivekananda had once told someone in another context.

Although he declined to discuss anything about the Holy Mother, once I had managed to overcome my shyness and blurted out a few things I felt, he was very indulgent. After reading what he had to say about Holy Mother in his book *How I Came to the Feet of Sri Ramakrishna,* I told him, "Maharaj, I am aware that you do not usually talk about Holy Mother. But now I have got to know from your book what you feel about her. You have written how you came to Holy Mother, which to you was the same as coming to Thakur. So you regard both of them as One." He was quiet, looking at me affectionately, then said, "You see, I have no personal memories. Mother was always in a veil. I have gone to her, taken initiation and made pranam. But I never had a chance to be near her or watch her closely. Only a few among us, such as Swami Gauriswarananda and Swami Saradeshananda, have been so fortunate, and they have all recorded their experiences."

One very touching incident: Once I went to him on my birthday to make pranam. Usually my shyness never permitted me to go to him without some specific work. He must have noticed it because he asked, "What is the matter today? Why suddenly this advent just to make pranam?" He probed till he found out the reason and then wished me

"Happy Birthday" very cheerfully. He brought out a packet of biscuits and handed it over to me with great affection.

Once I was sent to the press regarding the book. The work took longer than expected and I was held back at the press till evening. After my return I was told, "Maharaj was so anxious about your delay. He has gone out just now to bring you back personally." This is how his affection was showered on me. He made me feel that my tiny contribution to the work was so important—like the little squirrel who had offered his help to Lord Ramachandra when he was building the bridge across the ocean. Maharaj told my mother, "Your son helps me out a great deal."

In this ephemeral world, nothing is permanent, nothing stays. The blessed company of this great soul that I have enjoyed was also short-lived. The end came...he was talking on the telephone. He put the receiver down and fell asleep, forever. We all rushed to his room. The room was filled with chanting of "Hari Om Ramakrishna." It seemed he was just resting, that any moment he would get up and ask for Rashbehari. Rashbehari, who had served with total devotion in his last few years, lay prostrate on the floor with grief. Devotees came to have a last darshan. Swami Lokeswarananda was seated beside, totally silent and absorbed in thought. Someone suggested that a photograph ought to be taken of him in his room. Luckily, I had a loaded camera at home and therefore managed to take the photograph. He was then taken to the foyer. Streams of people from all walks of life came in to pay their last homage.

Even today I keep looking at the closed door of his room. Yes, that door is now closed, the door leading to the path of divinity which was opened to me for a short while through the company of this great soul.

SUMANA GHOSH

It was some time in August 1989. I had gone to see Swami Nitya-swarup-ananda after my return from San Francisco, where I had gone for a holi-day after completing high school. "So you have just returned?" he asked me, "Sit down and tell me all about your trip, all your experiences of

America." I was pleasantly surprised that my experiences could be of any interest to a widely travelled person like Maharaj.

I began by saying, "I reached San Francisco Airport at 5:00 in the evening, San Francisco time. My aunt and her family took me home..." Here my narration was interrupted by his question, "How far is the airport from their house?" I started fumbling. Desperately I tried to figure out the distance in terms of miles and kilometres when his voice cut short my frantic calculations, "Don't try to answer in terms of miles and kilometres. Americans measure distance in terms of driving hours—tell me how long did it take you to reach the house?" I heaved a sigh of relief. This was simple and I gave him the answer. "Now describe the house," he said. This was also something quite easy, or so I thought. I began enthusiastically, only to be cut short with the remark, "First of all, tell me whether the house is east-facing, or north or south?" I told him I had no idea! He was visibly irritated, replying, "How can you say you have no idea. You stayed in that house for two whole months and you did not even observe this fundamental thing? All right, proceed, tell me about the rooms." This time I was very tentative, wondering what the next assault would be, and sure enough, it came: "Tell me the size of the rooms in terms of square feet." I again had to tell him I had no idea. I could tell that he was quite annoyed when he said, "Can't you even tell me approximately?"

So we continued our strange dialogue for over an hour. I had to tell him in detail about my routine there, the places I visited, the people I met, and so forth. My narration was often interrupted with little questions like "Did you have pancakes for breakfast, or cereal?" and "What kind of a schedule do your aunt and her family have?" To everything he listened with deep attention.

To be quite frank, at that time I had found some of his questions quite awkward and amusing, but later I realized that they were actually an indication of his penetrating mind, a mind which was capable of probing the depth of any subject matter, however trivial and insignificant, if his attention happened to be focused on it at that particular moment. Perhaps this is what they call a "truly disciplined mind." I don't know, but the experience made me realize that most of the time we are very superficial in our observations.

His attention to details was something which was evident to all who came in touch with him. One of my aunts was working at the Institute while the new building was being constructed in Gol Park. She recalled that Swami Nitya-swarup-ananda's supervision and his attention to the minutest detail of the construction work was a marvel. Even the brand of detergents and room fresheners to be used did not escape his attention.

I was always vastly amused at how Maharaj scolded grown-ups as if they were errant children. He spared no one when he felt a talking-to was necessary, and this he did in his inimitable style. I remember one such incident. We had the rare privilege of having Maharaj come to our house one day for lunch. He sat at the head of the table talking and laughing from time to time, and, as always, actively interested in what was being offered to him. I remember my aunts and my mother anxiously trying to serve in the best possible manner, "Shall we give dal, Maharaj? Will you try some of this soup?" and so on. His response to their overzealous solicitude was quite unexpected: "You do not know how to serve!" he exploded. The elders were thoroughly taken aback. He resumed, "Look, when you are serving a guest, the best way to make him feel comfortable is to tell him the entire menu at the beginning. Then let him decide what he would like to have, and serve accordingly."

He was always very interested in whatever went on around him. His mind was open and alive to everything. I have never seen anyone so encouraging and appreciative of others. If you were a student and you told him what you were studying, he would immediately respond with "Good, very good. Do your best. Keep moving forward." I have always received tremendous encouragement from him regarding my academics, although I was doing nothing remarkably different from what thousands of other young people around me were doing.

There is one very lovely memory. I used to visit Maharaj every year on my birthday to offer my pranam to him. I used to wait in the foyer on the second floor of the Institute for him to come out from his room. Every year without fail, Maharaj, clad in his warm plaid coat, used to emerge with a beaming face, flowers in one hand and sweets in the other, singing "Happy Birthday to You" loudly and confidently off-key! Then we would sit and he would ask me to eat some of the sweets in his presence, all the while wishing me the "very best" (he would always get annoyed if you asked for his blessings).

I cannot think of any other person from whom I have received such unlimited, selfless love.

ROSTISLAV B. RYBAKOV

I never saw him, I never heard his name except casually as "the old Swami" though I had been coming to Calcutta every year for more than a decade and always stayed in the International Guest House of the Ramakrishna Mission Institute of Culture. Once I was even staying in the room next to his, and I remember how in the tropical darkness of the night, somewhere around four in the morning, the yellow electric light was suddenly switched on in the next room, pushing and conquering the darkness; it was the old Swami who was awake—by some necessity? to take a medicine? Maybe, but much, much more probably, to pray.

Then the day came when he sent a boy and with aristocratic politeness, he summoned me to his room. He was sitting on his bed but it was not at all a variation on the theme "an old man sitting on his bed." The man sitting cross-legged in front of me was full of energy, his movements were tigerlike (the combination of slowed motion and mighty emotion), his mind was extremely quick, his bubbling speech enthusiastic.

I was really shocked by his directness. Just a few words of introduction (and I found to my surprise that he needed no introduction, no explanations, he already knew everything about me) and then he immediately went up, up to the global problems.

It was so poignant that he tried to say so much in a very short time. He had much to say, very important and deep things, but he wanted to save his visitor's time as if he was not sure how many minutes the visitor could spend. The words were coming fast, and he himself jumped up and took some books, and his fingers quickly went through these books, and words were coming ever faster. I think he was very lonely. I don't know whether I have the right to say such things but still I think the same.

It is not the time to repeat what he was trying to convey at that meeting and many others afterwards. It was not merely polite talk, it was the Message. He was in a hurry to give the Message and he wanted to see whether it reached the other's heart and mind. I can say here only that he was talking about nations and cultures, and above all about education. He was quoting and memorizing, but at the same time his talk was not about the past but all about the Future. He was not teaching, he spoke from heart to heart involving you in the discussion, helping you to formulate your ideas and destroying them without pity the next moment only to open your eyes to wider horizons the moment after. He was extremely alive, full of humour and even sarcasm. He was reading my soul as an open book and he spoke to my soul directly with tremendous energy, not forgetting to punish me immediately if my words were not correct (in the philosophical sense, of course, not the linguistic). And he was not theorizing, he was absolutely concrete—in his plans, in his explanations, in his expectations. I left him with my head aching. The vibrations were too strong, too dominating, too demanding…

It was just a beginning because I found myself completely conquered by his manner of speech, by his ideas, by his personality. That day he gave me his book *Education for Human Unity and World Civilization*. He wrote some very kind words for me beneath the dedication and then said with a smile: "When I was in your country, in Russia, nobody could repeat my name, so I said to the officer in the customs, 'Look, it is so simple, you just divide it into three parts,'" and saying this he concluded his inscription with not so steady a pen "Nityaswarup-ananda, Calcutta, 5 March 1990." Only later I came to know that this was his usual practice.

After that meeting we met again several times. Sometimes I saw him from a distance. I can close my eyes now and see so vividly the morning picture: I am standing on the balcony of the International Guest House and across the inner courtyard, across the beautiful flowers always in full blossom, on the opposite balcony I see the small old man in a warm shawl (in Calcutta!) slowly moving with a stick step by step, slowly, with physical difficulty but spiritual determination, step by step—moving towards the stairs and up to the meditation room. Every morning with the same determination—step by step. And always I felt some pain in my heart, looking from the distance, watching him go.

Sometimes we met on his way back from the meditation room. We used to stay on the balcony and talk for about half an hour. Here he was even more energetic than in the quietness of his room—he shouted at me, he made faces, protruding his tongue and winking and smiling, he gestured with fist and stick, he jumped while talking—and always he was taking me so high, to such highest worlds from where you can see past, future, and Eternal. And he was absolutely not in the least self-centred, he was fatherly, attentive to whatever you tried to say, and you could not just stay there and nod to him, that was not the response he wanted. Talking with him was not easy but it was a truly thought-provoking and eye-opening experience. After even a short encounter with Swami you never were the same man, the meetings with him made you grow. Of course we met in his room many times, there he was not in a hurry and talked at length, always surprising me, the young spirit in an old body, the eternal fire transformed into light for the benefit of others.

Once he surprised me even more: he came to the Belur Math all the way from Calcutta to attend my lecture on Sri Ramakrishna's birthday. He was seldom seen outside his small room in Calcutta's Institute of Culture, and some brahmacharins in the Belur Math had never even seen him before. He was sitting in the first row and senior swamis were coming up to him to pay their respects. It was quite an ordeal for me, I have to confess. Even without his presence it would have been a great honour for me as a foreigner to speak at that spot on that day to such an illustrious gathering, as well as a very great responsibility. His coming made the task even more difficult. I knew that he would miss nothing and I knew that his reaction would be straight and undiplomatic.

It was one of the most important examinations of my life. And till the end of my life I will remain happy and proud because he did not disapprove of me that evening. Again he was very straightforward. Two minutes after my return to a tiny room in the International Guest House my telephone rang. It was Swami Nitya-swarup-ananda himself calling to inform me about his impression. Amazing—he had returned much earlier and was watching from his room, so that immediately after my coming back he called me!

I remember how I came back to Calcutta from Moscow, a Moscow this time full of "perestroika," violence, corruption, hopes, betrayals, and so on. I knocked at the door next to my room. He was with a visitor on the balcony. I went there. He was sitting in an armchair talking to a middle-aged lady. He had become older, I thought for a moment, but he jumped from the armchair and embraced me and shouted at me in his energetic manner: "Come to me later, I will explain to you everything about your Russia. We must talk, come to me later!"

I never saw him again. I saw doctors coming in and out. I saw Swami Lokeswarananda running to his room. I saw tears on the face of his boy-attendant, but I never saw Swami Nitya-swarup-ananda again. And who will explain to me now everything—about Russia, about the world, about myself?

RUPCHAND LOHIA

I had been an admirer of the Ramakrishna Math and Mission right from childhood, and I was initiated by Swami Vishuddhanandaji Maharaj when he was Vice-President of the Order. After hearing about Chinta-haran Maharaj from one of my close relatives who was his ardent fol-lower, I ventured at last to visit the Institute of Culture, accompanied by my wife and two grown sons, to offer our pranam to Maharaj.

The very first sight of Chintaharan Maharaj filled me with a divine feeling which I cannot express in words. We were all pleasantly surprised to find that he was quite knowledgeable about ordinary worldly concerns in spite of being a sannyasin of the highest order. All of us were fascinated by his deliberations and listened with rapt attention to every word he uttered. Even my elder son, who by that time had completed three years as a student in the United States, was highly impressed. Maharaj spoke on varied subjects with due stress on the teachings of Sri Sri Ramakrishna Paramahamsadev and Swamiji and the relevance of their teachings to the present-day world. His manner of expression was so elevating, yet so objective, that it made me realize for the first time the meaning of the true ideals of the Ramakrishna Mission. After returning home I went through the writings of Swami Vivekananda and my impression was reinforced, as well as my respect for Maharaj's high standards.

Thereafter I visited Maharaj several times at the Institute of Culture, and when he was ill at Seva Pratishthan. It was always a highly rewarding experience to be on the receiving end of his wisdom. Swami Nitya-swarup-anandaji's sudden departure from this world was a great shock to me, and I shall miss his highly educated company.

RABBI JONATHAN KLIGLER

I had the pleasure and privilege of a brief meeting with Swami Nitya-swarup-ananda in late February 1991. I was a tourist in India for a month. Fortunately, I had contacted the Lahiri family through mutual American friends and was paying them a visit. Mr. Lahiri insisted that I come meet the Swami, who had been for many, many years an inspirational teacher to Mr. Lahiri. I had very little knowledge about Ramakrishna's work and was simply coming along in a mood of openness and curiosity.

The Swami agreed to meet with me for a few minutes. He put his writing aside, turned toward me, and looked at my T-shirt. It had a picture of the Milky Way galaxy on it, with the words "You are here" next to an arrow pointing to the approximate location of our solar system within the vast nebula. Swami Nitya-swarup-ananda beamed at me and read my shirt.

"You... are... here," he recited, and then addressed me with this glorious interpretation of those words. "You are here," he said, and he pointed to his own heart. "You see, there is no separation between me and you. That is an illusion. You are truly here. You are me and I am you...." The Swami continued to speak, reiterating his theme. Sometimes I had difficulty understanding him over the drone of the air conditioner, or when his words would jumble together a bit, but the connection of love he was offering to me was crystal clear. I had been feeling isolated and lonely, as long-range tourists often will. I felt my loneliness lift, and my heart open to this delightful presence. What a gift!

I floated out of his room and the Mission into the streets of Calcutta. I was amazed and full of gratitude as I drifted along, so relieved to have dropped for the moment the defenses I had erected over the previous weeks against the assault of India's street life. It was late, but my feet directed me to the Kali temple. Some boys approached me, eager to sell their services to me as guides around the temple. I didn't respond by shooing them away as I had grown accustomed to do, or even by silence. Without making any conversation, I allowed them to lead me all around, spent much more money than I felt was appropriate buying flower wreaths, and followed their instructions in the proper series of activities in worshipping the Goddess at her temple. For a short while, I wasn't afraid of being cheated or taken, I simply allowed myself to be with these boys on their own terms. I was silent, and smiling, thinking over and over to myself, "You are here."

P.S.: I am not in any way a practicing Hindu. I am, in fact, a liberal American Jewish rabbi. But I told this story to a friend of mine who has followed Ramakrishna for many years, and she suggested I write it down. I do so with pleasure, to honor the memory of Swami Nitya-swarup-ananda.

JOHN SCARBOROUGH

For three weeks in August 1991, I stayed at the Ramakrishna Mission Institute of Culture in an air-conditioned room just a few doors down the hall from Swami Nitya-swarup-ananda's quarters. I was delighted. I saw Swami Nitya-swarup-ananda many times. We would talk for an hour or two, sometimes longer. His words were fresh in my mind when I returned to my room to record them. In this selection from my journal, I hope I have captured some of his extraordinary vigor, humor, wisdom, and joy. I did not see him again; he died the following year.

In August 1991, Swami Nitya-swarup-ananda was ninety-two years old. He had a deep, jolting cough, and he wore a back brace. If these spoke of physical decline, his eyes denied it. They charged into the room. Set in great sockets, held in check above and below by eyelids like venetian blinds, they laughed, they reposed, they probed, they puzzled, they interrogated.

When I first inquired about him, I was led into the foyer near his room, a large sunny area at the end of the hall equipped with couches and chairs. Seated in an armchair, he was talking in Bengali to a woman about thirty-five years old. After a few sentences, he turned to me and asked where I was from, and he motioned for me to sit down. When his visitor left, he sat for several minutes with his eyes closed, then asked me to come to his room after I had shut off the foyer's fan and lights.

In his room, curtains drawn against the late afternoon's intense sun, he sat still for a few minutes on his bed, one foot placed on the other thigh, head back slightly, eyes closed, rocking gently. He stopped rocking and opened his right eye only.

"Knowledge," he said. He adjusted his position, coughed, and again sat still for a while. "That is the question: What is knowledge? Everything depends on that. Do you think anyone would want to live in darkness?" he asked. "No," he answered. "Everyone wants to know, and to know more. We live on that knowledge. Without knowledge, no one could live for a moment. No one would want to."

The air conditioner's noise made hearing difficult, so I moved to the floor near his bed. He pointed to a chair, then to where I sat. I brought over the chair and sat down, facing him.

"You came on that knowledge. In a huge, multiton aircraft that flew thirty thousand feet above the earth, from Seattle to India in a day. It is incredible. It is knowledge. And people want more. Always more! It is our nature, we want always to learn more. At that level it is endless.

"And there is higher knowledge, and higher still, and the highest knowledge of all, the knowledge of the knower itself. We want to know because it gives us joy, and satisfaction." He paused, closing his eyes. "That knowledge brings infinite peace," he said, his face growing broader as it relaxed into a peaceful expression. "Infinite joy, supreme happiness..." He opened his eyes, and looked at me.

"What is your name?" he asked.

"John Scarborough."

"Johns?"

"John, no 's.'"

"John, no 's.' Carborough," he chuckled, playing with my name. "O-u-g-h?"

"Yes."

"John Scarborough. What is your occupation?"

"I am a software-testing engineer for Microsoft."

"Microsoft?"

"Yes, Microsoft. It's computers."

"Oh, computers! Microsoft! I know nothing about all that. That's new."

"Yes," I said, "it is a sort of madness."

"It is all madness," he said. "Everything is madness. It is because we want to know. Have you had your dinner?"

"No."

"Then you . . ." He looked at his watch.

"Yes, I'll go eat now," I said. "May I come again?"

"Yes, any time you like." I took the dust of his feet and went out the door. He called me back: "John. John. Very good. There are many famous Johns in the world." He chuckled and raised his hand in farewell.

The next day he asked about my experiences in Vedanta. I told him about meeting my teacher, Swami Vividishananda; I named a handful of books that had been very important for me; I recalled learning to do *puja;* and I spoke of several monks of the Order whom I had met. His smile slowly faded when I mentioned having learned *puja.* When I stopped talking, he said, "Your first instruction was the exact opposite of what a swami should teach at the very beginning. Devotee, separation—it is hard to remove."

"No," I corrected. "No, his first instruction, his first instruction to me was 'Atman and Brahman are one.' And his last words, his very last words to me, were just five words: 'Atman alone is the goal.' He gave me the same message, first and last."

Swami Nitya-swarup-ananda looked at me searchingly, his eyes huge and dark. "Yes," he said. Looking down, rocking slightly, he continued thoughtfully, a line between his eyebrows growing prominent and deep. "Yes, yes, Atman alone...the Self alone abides...the Self alone. Yes, he is correct. Good, good. You are very fortunate to have had the opportunity to contact such a great swami."

I asked, "Did Sri Ma [Sri Sarada Devi] ever talk about jnana?"

He grimaced. "What? What is jnana? Why talk about jnana? Why should she talk about jnana? She IS jnana. She is the world. She is the universe. She is who jnana is, who is jnana itself, who is the giver of jnana. She, seeing whom one sees God, sees the Absolute, she will talk about jnana. Eh!"

A few minutes passed in silence. He pointed to the picture of Sri Ramakrishna hanging on the wall behind me, and asked me, "What do you see represented there?" I began, "As a devotee—" but I got no further. "What? What is a devotee? Why are you using that word? What is meant by that word? It is a wrong notion! It separates you from truth! A seeker of truth, yes, a devotee, no. An emotional state, perhaps, but it separates us from the truth. Why do you say this, this 'as a devotee'?" he asked, screwing up his mouth as though he had just taken a drink of soured milk.

"I see Sri Ramakrishna in more than one way," I replied. "When I meditate, I think of him in one way. When I think of what he said in the light of the teachings of other traditions, I think of him somewhat differently, especially when talking to people who know nothing of him."

"No," he said. "Tell them what it is. If they can take it, good. If not, let them hear it and later they will understand it. Truth is one. The rest is delusion, *maya*. Hear it, meditate on it, realize it." His eyes rested on the picture of Sri Ramakrishna for a few moments, and then he said, "Thakur, Ma, Swamiji—this is the only ideal for the world. To prevent destruction of the world.

"Swamiji's letter from Almora to a Muslim in Naini Tal, you know it? He says, I want to leave the world a place where the Veda, the Bible, and the Koran are seen as different aspects of One. *That* is harmony. Yes. Six billion people are six billion radii converging on and emerging from a common center. As many radii, so many paths." His attendant arrived. "We will have many such talks," Swami Nitya-swarup-ananda said. "You and I agree on many things." He laughed. "Maybe we will disagree. We shall see! You have met many swamis, it is a great advantage."

The next morning, I knocked hesitantly on his door. When I received no response, I let myself in. He was sitting up in bed. Whether he was meditating or asleep I could not tell. I moved quietly—silently, I hoped—across the room. I was about to sit down when his eyes flashed open, and he roared:

"You are the sun! Never forget it!"

His eyes blazed and the force of his voice blasted my entire body. As a child I had experienced a recurring dream in which I watched a man's head, as large as the sun itself, rise at dawn over a distant mountain range, filling the universe with light, and me with love. After seeking for years the owner of the sun-man's face, as an adult I came to understand that I had been filled with love and freed from fear by watching the dawn of the Self. Swami Nitya-swarup-ananda's few words welded my dream and my understanding.

"Each soul is divine! Each soul is the sun!" he continued. "Each soul is the sun covered over by so many clouds. The only difference between soul and soul is owing to clouds. Some have more, some have less—this is the truth. You may teach it to the Muslim, and he will not understand, you may teach it to the Hindu, and he will not understand, you may teach it to the Christian, and he will not understand. It doesn't matter. It is the *truth*, whether one realizes it now or later. If no one hears it, who will know?" He recited a verse in Sanskrit, then translated: "Rare is the soul who, turning from body, mind, and senses, discovers the truth dwelling within."

Again Sanskrit and a translation: "'Arise, awake, and stop not till the goal is reached!' This was said one hundred years ago by Swamiji in America. It should have been renewed by every swami in America since then, but look what has happened. We have made a mess of it, creating a crowd of (he winced) *devotees*, weak and passive. Devotees! They separate themselves from the truth, and we have encouraged them. We have created a cult and lost sight of truth. Truth is One! Unity!"

When I returned after breakfast, he was reading the newspaper. "Formerly there were two superpowers. Now there is only one. If we had done what Swamiji envisioned, think what could have been done now. Vedanta—not India, not dhotis, not cooking—but the oneness and unity that is Vedanta, the essence of the Veda, could now be spread throughout the entire world. But this superpower will not do it. Did you read today? The United States ambassador to Pakistan has said that Kashmir must be Muslim. That is their way! Divide, divide, divide, on the basis of the one thing—religion—that should unite all people. They want only power, not peace." He spoke about the responsibilities of a superpower for some time, and then said he was very much enjoying our conversations and looked forward to more. I eagerly accepted his invitation to come for tea.

"Freedom is renunciation!" he exclaimed when we had each eaten a cookie and sipped our tea. "Not an orange cloth, or a shaven head, or giving away all possessions; not saying goodbye to mother and father and family. That is not renunciation. Renunciation means seeing your-self in every human being, seeing yourself in plants, trees, the sky, in *all* people—friends, family, strangers, the poor and the sick. They are your Self! One's Self is the universe, and the universe is your Self. One! Each person is a spoke on the wheel of existence, all beings are so many spokes in the same wheel, having a common center and reaching out in so many different rays. Each radius, each spoke is its own path, there are as many paths as there are people. There is not one path, rather there is one truth, with infinite paths to the realization of that truth, oneness.

"But America, the land of the free, is practicing a perverted free-dom. It is the freedom of bondage: you are free to be bound by your senses, your instincts, and your desires. You will not question, 'Where will this lead me?' No, you will do what you want to do because you want to do it. It will give you nothing, you will have less than what you started with. But still you will do it. Enjoyments are not bad, they are not evil, but if you do not rise above them, they continue on and on and on. Yes, everyone must realize the truth, it is one's own nature, one's very being in itself. But when? This searching and searching for greater enjoyment, for any enjoyment, it is endless.... There is *no* enjoyer, *no* object of enjoyment, *no* enjoyment: there is only *one*."

The next day, sitting next to him over early morning tea, I was won-dering to myself what simple formulation could summarize all he had said in the last few days. Just then he said, with great intensity, "*There is no knower, no object known, no knowledge—no knower-object relationship.*" He abruptly raised his right index finger a few inches away from my nose. "*One!*" he said. He sipped his tea. I repeated internally what he had just said until I could feel it, literally taking it to heart.

"You know that poem with the line about embracing Death?" he asked me. "That is real strength, that is real devotion. I am the Self in all. Have you come, Death? Welcome, you are my own Self! I embrace you. Is such a man conquered by death? No, he has conquered death itself by seeing himself in all. I am the universe, the universe is in me, I am all, I am one. Will I be afraid of death? 'Welcome, brother Death! Pleased to meet you.' What will die? What will be replaced? I am the Self of all! How can I disappear, how die? One! One! We are one, we are one, not two."

He pointed to Richard Lannoy's book *The Speaking Tree,* which I had brought along for him to see, and he remarked that Lannoy quoted Gandhi approvingly: "Our greatest strength is our weakness." "That was Saint Paul's cherished notion as well," I interjected. "This is a *wrong* notion!" he stormed. "What strength is there in weakness? There is strength in strength, not in weakness. That is your Christianity, that is your devotee. Such a person can be controlled! Where is strength there? What will you say? Will you say that it is impossible?"

He did not wait for my reply. "Swamiji said that his goal is that one day every infant will be born into this world with this knowledge. It is impossible? If even one man or woman has this knowledge, it is possible for many, it is possible for all. But not just one has had this knowledge! There is Sri Ramakrishna, Sri Sarada Devi, and Swamiji. There have been and will be many more such. It is one's birthright, how is it impossible? And then you push it away from you and worship it and say, 'Oh, I am nothing.' No! Real faith gives strength!

"The whole universe is here, here (thumping his chest with his fore-finger). Mind, senses, sense objects, world, people—nothing. All one. It is here. I am the universe. You are divine—the universe is in you, and you are the universe."

A few days later I stopped in to see him at 9:45 in the morning. "What time is it?" he asked. He was sitting on his bed at a writing table. "I am feeling a little tired," he said. "Can you come here in half an hour?" "Yes, Maharaj. Actually, I have banking to do. Will 11:15 be all right?" "Yes, yes," he said; "I want to talk to you some more. I like you very much." "I like you very much, too, Maharaj," I said in a tone better suited for stating a preference for coffee as opposed to tea. "Ore baba!" he cried, and burst into laughter. As I was closing the door behind me, he called me back. "You will come then?" "Yes," I replied. "All right. Please remove this table."

At 11:30, after my traveler's checks had been reviewed and approved by five bank employees in three lines on two floors of the bank, I went to Swami Nitya-swarup-ananda's room. I entered without knocking, sat down, and waited. After a few minutes he looked up.

"There is a wonderful painting by Abanindranath Tagore. Parvati is seated, and he has shown that she has become Shiva. Above her, coming out of her and in her, is Lord Shiva, with flying hair, *damaru* (a drum held in one hand whose attached beaded cords strike its two heads), like that—husband and wife in *unison*. He is in her, and she in him. She sees him as her Self. And he sees her as his own Self. The purpose of life is to realize the Self in all beings. Yajnavalkya tells his wife Maitreyi that the husband is dear to the wife, not for the sake of the husband, but for the sake of the Self in him. The wife is dear to the husband, not for the sake of the wife, but for the sake of the Self in her, which is also his own Self. Sri Ramakrishna and Sri Sarada Devi—how did they regard each other? Each of them on separate occasions confided that he and she were the same. To know one is to know the other as well. They realized the Self in all beings, and that is how they regarded each other.

"That is the purpose of life. When you work, you are offering that work to the Lord of the universe, who is your Self. Don't think it is for you, that you are doing this." By gestures he showed work being offered to another, and then, cupping his hands together, he brought them in a sweeping motion to his heart.

"If that thought comes—'I,' 'I'—do not let it take hold. You are a shadow, that little 'I' is but a shadow. Work wholeheartedly, with full concentration, but know that it is not done by or for you, constantly remember that. Otherwise when you sit for meditation what will you meditate? Only those thoughts of your work. Half an hour in the

morning and evening is not enough! The whole life must be transformed. That is the way. Every moment: One! Not two. The apparent
'I' is only a shadow. Ah, I am so glad to talk to you."

On my last day, I went to Swami Nitya-swarup-ananda's room to
take leave of him.

"I came to your room earlier," I said, "but you were asleep." "Yes,
yes, I know. I was asleep but I sensed that you were here. I am very
happy to have met you and talked to you. It is too bad you cannot stay
longer, we would have many more talks. I find that you appreciate and
understand these ideas."

We talked for a couple of hours about projects that he and I hoped to
work on together in the future. "I may go home before this is realized,
do you understand?" "Yes," I said. "Back to the source. How much
longer will you live, Maharaj?" "I do not know. I may live up to…" He
stopped, and gestured toward the picture of Sri Ramakrishna. "I do
not control that."

"Stick around for a while, Maharaj," I said. "I want to see you again."
"Yes," he said. "And I would like to see you. It is an ocean! All souls
reach their fulfillment when they are dropped into the ocean, so many
streams all pouring into that sea of consciousness. You must write that
book," he said, referring to a book I had been thinking of writing for
several years.

"But it will do no good," he said of the projected book, "if it just
enshrines the memory of a particular individual. That is the whole problem all over again. Lift up, expand, bring together. And it is not just an
idea—it must be realized, that is the thing. It has been lost! That wonderful vision of Swamiji's, lost! All souls are divine. *Each* soul. We are that
One. Oneness! Let every nation discover what its greatness is, how it has
contributed to the culture of the world, and how it can benefit by learning from every other nation what their greatness is. Each has its own perspective. They must acknowledge their own and that of others.

"You know Mayavati?" I said that I did. "Do you know what
Swamiji's plan was for it? That people from all over the world would

go there and, with the backdrop of the Himalayas soaring skyward, listen to one another and discover that Oneness. Always strive for that Oneness. You are that One! See it in every living being.

"Well, let us part on that note." He raised his hands, parted, above his head, slapped them together, and brought them, joined, to his forehead. "May all blessings be on you and your wife," he said.

As I was leaving, he called me back and said, "I am very happy to have met you. It was a rare, a rare opportunity that you had contact with so great a soul as Swami Vividishananda. Write me soon, and often, and I will call you. Now you may go."

SUHAS CHANDRA SEN

I met Swami Nitya-swarup-ananda for the first time in September 1991. I had heard that he was one of the few disciples of the Holy Mother who were still alive and I was very keen to meet him.

My first meeting with him was without any appointment or introduction. I had gone to the Ramakrishna Mission Institute of Culture to purchase a book. When I inquired about Swami Nitya-swarup-ananda, I was told that I could go up to his room. A sannyasin standing near the counter very kindly escorted me there. The Swami asked several other persons sitting in his room to come back later, so I had the opportunity to talk to him without interruption, and our conversation lasted more than two hours. I was very pleasantly surprised to find that although he was more than ninety, his intellect was razor sharp and he was fully aware of what was happening all around. In fact he had cut out two pages from a recent issue of *Time* magazine showing a sketch plan of the lineup of the two opposing forces in the Gulf War, and had hung it up on his wall. He told me that this looked like the lineup at the battle of Kurukshetra. He asked several questions to find out about me. I also asked him a number of questions which he answered frankly.

I went to see him again after a month. This meeting lasted more than three hours. Although he was not keeping very good health he would not allow me to come away and we discussed any number of subjects, agreeing on some and disagreeing on a few as well. He was emphatic in his views in very forceful language. When I was leaving his room he said, "I can discuss a large variety of topics with you, please come again."

On my part, I was amazed to see his dedication and total commitment to the Ramakrishna Math and Mission and to the ideals of Swami Vivekananda. He could quote ad lib from the works of Swamiji. He told me repeatedly that the ideas of Vivekananda must be followed at any cost.

After the second meeting, I didn't meet him again for several months. Then one day I rang him up to find out if he was free to see me. He asked me straightaway whether I had forgotten him altogether. I went to see him at once. Several other persons were present that day, and he discussed the importance of leading an active life. The famous letter written by Swami Premananda to Swami Abhedananda about the last day of Swami Vivekananda's life was read out, and Swami Nitya-swarup-ananda's comment was "See how very active Swamiji was! No time was wasted even on the last day of his life."

Swami Nitya-swarup-ananda was also fully active till the last day of his life. His intellectual curiosity was amazing. He had read an article on Sri Ramakrishna written by Sri Aurobindo in Bengali. He felt puzzled by a particular phrase used by Aurobindo, and kept asking everybody about the exact meaning of the phrase, but no one could give him a satisfactory answer. Then one day he told me that he had found the meaning at two o'clock that morning. I asked him what he was doing at 2:00 in the morning. He answered that this was a habit acquired from his days at the Belur Math. He was accustomed to get up at 2:00 A.M. or so and note the time in his diary. On that particular early morning he had thought of consulting Monier-William's *Dictionary*, and there he had discovered the proper meaning of the phrase. I found such energy and intellectual avidity at the age of ninety-two truly amazing.

When he was lying ill at the Ramakrishna Mission Seva Pratishthan hospital, I went to see him on several occasions. He did not waste much time discussing his physical problems, but went straight to his favourite subject: the ideals of Swami Vivekananda and how to implement them.

He was a very simple and outspoken man. I knew him but briefly, but came to love and respect him. I could talk with him frankly on any topic, including personal matters. He was always positive in words and action. When I heard the news of his death, I felt it as a great personal loss. If only I had gone to see him more often!

J. CHAKRAVARTY

I had the opportunity to meet Swami Nitya-swarup-ananda as a consultant dermatologist. I was called in by his personal physician, Dr. Arabinda Basu, to treat a skin condition which had erupted from one of his medications. He asked me to visit him frequently, and one time when there was a long gap in my visits, he became very upset and rang me up to find out the reason. I felt that he loved me very much, and on many occasions he would give me a good luncheon. Apart from his treatment, we held discussions on a variety of other interesting topics, including the modern trends of various therapies since he was interested in medicine. He called me a "magician" when his skin problems were cured!

During my brief acquaintance with him, Swami Nitya-swarup-ananda inspired me with the need to fulfil in modern life Swami Vivekananda's ideal that service to man is service to God, irrespective of race, colour, or creed.

CHHANDA BOSE

[The following narrative was written by Mrs. Chhanda Bose, based on the oral reminiscences of Rashbehari Misra, who was Swami Nitya-swarup-ananda's personal attendant at the Institute of Culture. The grief-stricken Rashbehari poured out his story to a few of Swami Nitya-swarup-ananda's close friends shortly after the Swami passed away.]

Rashbehari

He doesn't stand too tall off the ground. Like so many millions from rural Bengal, he is polished ebony of skin, with a head full of crisp black curls. And also like so many millions of Indians he has a mouthful of gleaming white teeth which he flashes in a smile that is warm and yet shy, no matter how well he knows you. But his eyes are what rivets one's glance to his face. Thick eyelashes rise in a wave, lazily and soundlessly, to reveal a pair of eyes that seem to dive in an unending subterranean path to somewhere few are permitted to go, or have the gumption to go.

These are some of the things he told us about Maharaj's "going away"... those last moments.

He had bathed Maharaj. He had noticed that Maharaj was having a lot of difficulty in breathing. Dr. Basu had told Maharaj that he had congestion and was not to exert himself (why, Rashbehari wondered, had he told Maharaj what was wrong on that day, as he had never done so before). Then Dr. Basu had told Rashbehari that Maharaj must be allowed to rest undisturbed and that he should not be moved at all.

Rashbehari had deboned the fish and prepared Maharaj's lunch. He asked another elderly attendant to go and get the medicine he was to give Maharaj before his meal. Maharaj had his face turned away from Rashbehari. When he went to call him he realized that Maharaj was having difficulty trying to cough up some phlegm. He put his hand into his mouth to try and ease out the phlegm, but, he said, "His mouth was dry. Even his lower denture which I took out was dry." He kept changing Maharaj's soiled linen. He said he felt that Maharaj wanted to be lifted up, but he couldn't do it, his hands were full. He kept rubbing Maharaj's chest. Rashbehari continued, "Then he said to me in almost a whisper, 'Don't, I have gone beyond you all now.'" Rashbehari gently turned him.

Then he said: "I saw his face was absolutely white and glowing. Then I knew I could not keep him any longer. I had been with him through

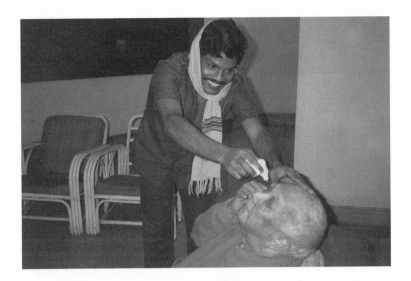

many crises. But this time, when I saw his face, I knew." Then everybody arrived.

Rashbehari, who had been sobbing in the telling of all this, suddenly became calmer. I cannot report the exact order in which all the words he said came, but these were the things I recall:

"I knew him for God's true representative. That is why I forgot all my family, my mother and father, everyone. He was Thakur's true sadhu. There will never be another like him."

"He was the Prana of my Prana." (I don't know how one can translate this. In English, one would say "heart of my heart" or "soul of my soul," but it is much more than that—the expression in Bengali would be "Heart of my Heart," "Soul of my Soul," "Breath of my Breath," "Life of my Life"... I can hear Maharaj's voice sounding in my ears: "*raison d'être*," my very reason for existence.)

Rashbehari cried and spoke. His eyes were riveted upon the photograph of Maharaj [taken in 1991] in the room. He said, "I want a copy of that picture. Look at his face. He is transported. In direct communion with Them."

Then Rashbehari broke down again. He said, "What was the need to finish the book in such a hurry? He told me that he would go when his work was finished. Why did you all have to hurry? If you had delayed, I would have had him with me for a little while longer."

(A few stray thoughts: the day before, since it was raining, Rashbehari had told Maharaj, "Don't ask me for your warm clothes tomorrow, I have sent them to the laundry," to which Maharaj had replied, "There will be no winter. Oh, winter will come, but I won't be here!" On another occasion, Rashbehari said he had asked Maharaj: "Dr. Brown has come twice this year. Will she be able to come again in January?" Maharaj had said: "If it is necessary she will come. Otherwise she will not.")

Rashbehari was then told gently that it was Maharaj's wish that the book must be finished; he had felt he could not hold on much longer. When we spoke the words "He was tired, his body could take no more. He wanted to be free," Rashbehari broke out in tones of an aggrieved mother lioness defending her cub: "I do not accept it. He was fine. He was ninety-three years old, and yet he could walk and talk. His head was clear. He ate his food. He was fine!"

Then he turned on us with anger born of an unbearable pain: "He was such a great being, and you left his welfare in my hands—me, an illiterate sweeper. Don't you know who he was? And I trembled at the enormity of the responsibility. There was no one to share the burden of looking after someone like him. He took me, a mere sweeper, and he gave me a status (and the Bengali here is very beautiful, "*maathar oporay*"). I was brought back from death at the age of fourteen to do this." He told us how, when he was fourteen years old, a sharpened bamboo had entered his skull. He had lain unconscious for fourteen hours. The villagers had wanted to bury him. His mother clung on. And he recovered. He had studied up to Class VIII and then the need to earn money for his family had brought him to Calcutta.

Rashbehari was a natural storyteller, and my words lack the sheer lilt and rhythm of his words. Also the very wry, dry sense of humour that is encountered so often by us in the villages. He next had us laughing as he told us how he had come to Maharaj's service.

He had worked in the kitchen at the Institute. But some illness forced the authorities to move him to the Guest House as a sweeper. One day there was turmoil and tension. Where was the fire? Chinta-haran Maharaj was coming back!!! Hustle and bustle, and much fear and trembling. Rush off to Bombay Dyeing. New sheets. Bedspreads and towels. Not a cobweb must lurk in a corner. Not a speck of dust must evade a careless broom. And Rashbehari was in charge.

Rashbehari continued, "He was such a disciplined man. Exactly every day at 7:25 A.M. Maharaj would leave his room Number 20 and go for breakfast. On the way he would stop at the Mandir. Then EXACTLY at 7:30 A.M. he would enter the Refectory. If he was a minute early, then he would wait till the clock hand moved to 7:30 A.M. He would eat his breakfast and converse with the other swamis. In that time I would have to get his room ready. Everything must be JUST SO! Everything must be EXACTLY in place." (Here, with typical Rashbehari style, he pointed to the clock in Dr. Brown's room, slightly askew: "Nothing could be left like that! Is that any way to keep a clock!")

After a few days, the Manager of the Mission called Rashbehari and informed him: "Chintaharan Maharaj has sent for you." No sooner had he heard this than Rashbehari was all set to go back to his village. Rashbehari described it thus: "My knees couldn't hold me up. I insisted the Manager come with me. He did. But as soon as the door opened, he disappeared (the word he used in Bengali means 'fled'). I entered the room. My tongue was stuck to my palate. There was no saliva in my mouth. Without looking at him I went down in a full sastanga pranam. (Here he gave an aside, 'My knees couldn't hold me up in any case!') Then Maharaj asked me to stand up. He looked me up and down. Then he asked me: 'Are you the person who cleans my room?'
I nodded.

Then I said: 'If I have done something wrong, I'll put it right just now.'

'What is your name?'

I answered: 'Sri Rashbehari.'

'What kind of boy are you?'

I said: 'How can I answer that myself?'

'How far have you studied?'

'Till Class Eight.'

'Do you know how old I am?'

I said nothing, merely shook my head.

Then he said: 'Ninety.'

(Rashbehari said to us: 'By this time, my fear had evaporated.')

Maharaj went on:

'I am ninety. In all these years I have never seen such work. I am totally enamoured of your work.'"

Then Rashbehari said he saw Maharaj more often. One day Maharaj said to him: "Will you put the eyedrops in for me? Every evening at 7:30." From then on Rashbehari was giving Maharaj his medicine.

Gradually, imperceptibly, Rashbehari was drawn into doing more and more work for Maharaj. All this happened in October 1988. In April 1990, Rashbehari decided to go home. When he told Maharaj, he said that Maharaj at first had not wanted him to go, but on hearing that Rashbehari still had some duties to perform for his parents and also to see to the marriage of his sister, he had agreed.

Rashbehari was away for three weeks. When he returned, he found Maharaj had suffered his first attack of gout. Two brahmacharis had been in charge of looking after Maharaj. No sooner had Rashbehari returned than they exclaimed, "Now, Maharaj does not say 'Ramakrishna' as often as he says 'Rashbehari.' He does not like our *seva* [service]."

At 6:30 the next morning, Swami Lokeswarananda called Rashbehari and told him as of that day he was released from all other duties and was solely in charge of Maharaj's needs.

Rashbehari recounted to us many experiences with Maharaj over the years, how Maharaj had told him about his visit abroad, and how he had made him a part of many other events. But, Rashbehari said: "In all these years, I have never heard him talk about anything other than Thakur and Ma. One day, I asked him, 'Maharaj, don't you have anything else to talk about?' He smiled."

Once again Rashbehari began talking grievously about the last days. He felt that if he had been trained and educated, he might have saved Maharaj: "I would have known how to rub his heart and keep him alive. You left such a priceless being in my unlettered hands—how could you? Don't you know what he was?"

"You were all there at the pyre at the end? I couldn't have seen it. Had I been there, they would have had to build a second pyre near his."

There was much else that he said. How nothing about Maharaj's bodily functions or anything else ever made him feel repulsed. When a replacement was sent to give Rashbehari some rest, Rashbehari was appalled that he would not clear out Maharaj's phlegm stuck in his throat. Rashbehari had told that attendant: "Go do some other work. You are not fit to be a *sevak*."

One day Maharaj had said to him: "I'm killing you, Rashbehari. You are not getting any rest because of me." And then Rashbehari turned to us in agony, "I think he went away to give me rest."

When Rashbehari's food started to be sent up to Maharaj's room, because neither Maharaj nor Rashbehari was happy with the temporary attendant during mealtimes, Maharaj would stay awake until the food arrived. Then he would say, "Rashbehari, now that your food has come, I shall sleep."

Rashbehari felt that he had been harsh with Maharaj at times, and he said: "I cry now remembering the times I lost my temper with him. That is what burns me, Didi. But what could I do? I was all alone."

That is Maharaj's Rashbehari—a man who taught us so much, a man way above millions of others, a man who has been blessed and privileged. He has shown us what selfless devotion can do. He is a living testament of how Maharaj could touch the humblest man and make him reach depths and heights he did not know he possessed. And is that not the measure, the true hallmark, of a great soul?

PROFILES OF CONTRIBUTORS

SWAMI ABJAJANANDA

The late Swami Abjajananda was the noted author of treatises on the Upanishads and Vedanta philosophy, and also published works on the lives of Sri Ramakrishna, the Holy Mother, Swami Vivekananda, and other saints. Formerly, he was the editor of *Udbodhan* magazine, the Head of the Saradapitha at the Belur Math, the President of the Ramakrishna Math at Bhubaneswar in Orissa, the Secretary of the Ramakrishna Mission of Shillong (Meghalaya), and a member of the Advisory Board of the Ramakrishna Mission at the Belur Math. In his later years, independent of the Order, he was the Head of Udayan Ashrama at Simultala in Bihar.

CLEO ANDERSON

Miss Anderson was associated with the Vedanta Society of Sacramento, California, from its inception in 1964, and was the late Swami Shraddhananda's secretary at the Society beginning in 1972. She graduated from the University of Denver, Colorado, with a B.A. in Psychology, followed by a career as a teacher and as a social worker in child welfare. She made several prolonged pilgrimages to India before moving there permanently. She now resides in Calcutta.

S. P. BAKSHI, M.B.B.S.

Born in 1929 at Coochbehar in West Bengal, Dr. S. P. Bakshi was educated in Calcutta, receiving his undergraduate degree from St. Xavier's College in 1946 and his M.B.B.S. degree from the R. G. Kar Medical College in 1952. Since then he has been practising medicine in Ballygunge, South Calcutta.

RAMANANDA BANDYOPADHYAY

 Born in 1936, Mr. Bandyopadhyay is a renowned artist, widely exhibited throughout India, whose philosophical approach is rooted in Indian culture. He studied art at the Kala Bhavan in Santiniketan from 1953 to 1959 under the tutelage of Nandalal Bose, and later was Head of Fine Arts in the Ramakrishna Mission at Purulia. From 1975 to 1996 he served as Director of the Museum and Art Gallery of the

377

Ramakrishna Mission Institute of Culture, Calcutta. His paintings reflect a spiritual practice in which purity of form combines with grace, beauty, and a fluid simplicity. "Painting as a vocation improves the quality of life," Mr. Bandyopadhyay believes. "It brings one closer to God."

PRABHAT KUMAR BANERJEE

The late Prabhat Kumar Banerjee was born in 1923 and studied at both Calcutta University and St. Paul's College, graduating in 1942 with honours in Economics. He was also awarded the Nirmalendu Ghosh Medal in Sanskrit, English, and Economics. Mr. Banerjee's articles were published in *Udbodhan* and other magazines. His treatise on the letters of Swami Vivekananda was dedicated to Swami Nitya-swarup-ananda.

ARABINDA BASU, M.B.B.S.

Dr. Basu completed his medical studies at R. G. Kar Medical College, and has been practising as a general physician in South Calcutta since 1955. He became Swami Nitya-swarup-ananda's personal physician after meeting him in April 1985 and also accompanied him on various pilgrimages. Dr. Basu and his wife, Tapati, have two daughters, Arundhati and Anuradha, both of whom have chosen the medical profession.

SANKARI PRASAD BASU

Professor Basu began his distinguished career in writing and editing as the co-editor, with Sunil Bihari Ghosh, of the acclaimed *Vivekananda in Indian Newspapers* (1969). Further contributions to the Ramakrishna-Vivekananda literature include his seven-volume classic, *Vivekananda O Samakaleen Bharatvarsha* (1975–87), which received both the National Sahitya Akademi Award, and the Vivekananda Award from the Ramakrishna Mission Institute of Culture. Additional research materials are currently being published serially in English as *Swami Vivekananda in Contemporary Indian News, 1893–1902*, beginning with Volume 1 in 1997. His diverse writings include works on Sister Nivedita (*Nivedita Lokmata*, Volumes 1–4, 1968–94, and the *Letters of Sister Nivedita*, Volumes 1–2, 1982), writings on Subhas Chandra Bose, a fictionalized biography of Emma Calvé, books on literary criticism, and books that introduced cricket literature in Bengali. With thirty-seven books to his credit, he has been widely recognized for his scholarship, with seven prestigious awards for outstanding literary achievement. Professor Basu was formerly Ramtanu Lahiri Professor, Calcutta University, and is currently Director of the Swami Vivekananda Archives, Ramakrishna Mission Institute of Culture, Calcutta.

CHINMOY BASU THAKUR

The late Chinmoy Basu Thakur (b. 1918) recounts in his reminiscence his close association with Swami Nitya-swarup-ananda, as well as the many ties of affection with which Swami Nitya-swarup-ananda held his brothers Sukumar and Sunil. Mr. Basu Thakur was formerly the Labour Officer of the Fort William Jute Mill in Shibpur, and Labour Officer, then Personnel Officer, of the Titagarh Paper Mill.

ROOMA BASU THAKUR

 A graduate of Calcutta University in Library Science, Miss Basu Thakur joined the library staff of the Ramakrishna Mission Institute of Culture, Calcutta, on August 8, 1958, while it was at Russa Road, and until her recent retirement, was Assistant Librarian at Gol Park looking after the Children's Library. She was instrumental in collecting the reminiscences of the Basu Thakur family included in the present volume.

SAMARENDRA NATH BASU THAKUR

The late Samarendra Nath Basu Thakur, who lived well into his nineties, was a renowned freedom fighter for India's independence. He was devoted to public service throughout his life, and served as the president of many benevolent organizations, such as the Sarvodaya Organization in West Bengal, the Purba Kalikata Gandhi Smarak Samiti, the Birth Centenary Committee of Dr. Prafulla Chandra Ghosh (first Chief Minister of West Bengal), the Biplabi Niketan, the Nagri Lipi Parisad, and the Dr. Suresh Chandra Banerjee Memorial Committee. He was on the original committee that founded the Ramakrishna Mission Seva Pratishthan hospital in Calcutta.

SUJATA BASU THAKUR

The late Sujata Basu Thakur, the wife of Chinmoy Basu Thakur, was Headmistress of the Kamkinara Rathtala Rajlakshmi Balika Vidyamandir in 24-Parganas, West Bengal.

RAY BERRY

Mr. Berry is a carpenter, cabinetmaker, and mason in the little Northern California town of Olema. He became interested in Vedantic teachings in his early twenties while travelling in Europe when he discovered a copy of the Bhagavad Gita in Spain, which made a profound impression. He is the author of *The Spiritual Athlete: A Primer for the Inner Life,* a collection of biographical sketches of mystics from the major faiths. It was selected for recording by the U.S. Library of Congress and in British Columbia.

DINESH CHANDRA BHATTACHARYA SHASTRI

Pandit Dinesh Chandra Bhattacharya began his schooling in the National School started by the National Council of Education in 1909, and later the Bangabasi College. At his father's behest, he began studying Nyaya and Vedanta philosophy under illustrious pandits, winning scholarships and gold medals and securing the titles of "Shastri," "Tarkatirtha," and "Vedantatirtha" in acknowledgement of his high achievements. He served as Professor of Vedanta in the Ramakrishna Math at Bhubaneswar, and from 1940 to 1950 was Professor of Sanskrit and Indian Philosophy at Haraganga College in Munshiganj (East Bengal). He began teaching at the Ramakrishna Mission Institute of Culture, Calcutta, in 1950 at Russa Road, where he was in charge of its Sanskrit Chatuspathi, and in 1961, he became the Director of its new School of Sanskritic Studies at Gol Park; his service at the Institute continues today in various teaching and research capacities. He has authored twelve philosophical books, one of which received the Rabindra Puraskar Award from Varanasi in 1976. He was also appointed "Sastrachudamani Scholar" by the government of India (1988–90), and was honoured by the National Council of Education in April 1994.

JAYANTA BHATTACHARYA

Mr. Bhattacharya is a filmmaker whose work has been acclaimed in India and abroad. As a member of the group called "Agragami," he scripted films based on stories of the great writers of Bengal, such as Rabindranath Tagore (*Nishithey*), Tarashankar Bandopadhya (*Dak-Harkara*), Narendra Nath Mitra (*Head Master, Bilombita Loy*), and Moti Nandi (*Kony*). Several of his films have won national awards, including the Swarna Kamal (Golden Lotus), the highest national award of India, and have been featured at international film festivals. His documentaries include a much-extolled film on Swami Vivekananda (*Bhavadhara*), made in association with the late Raghunath Goswami.

NANDITA BHATTACHARYA

Mrs. Bhattacharya had her early schooling at the Sri Saradesari Ashrama, followed by an M.A. in English and advanced training ("Gita Bharathi") in Music. Her husband was the late Ram Kumar Bhattacharya, who was closely associated with the

Ramakrishna Math and Mission and who established the "Sri Ramakrishna Sarada Samsad" at their residence in Calcutta. Swami Nitya-swarup-ananda was a frequent visitor to their home whenever he was staying at the nearby Udbodhan Office. Mrs. Bhattacharya's daughter (Mrs. Padma Mukherjee) has also written a reminiscence.

ARABINDA BHOSE

Mr. Bhose was born in 1933 in the renowned Sutanuti family of Calcutta. Following his education, he worked with social and welfare organizations, such as the R.W.A.C., Civil Defence, and St. John's Ambulance. He also served as a Special Police Officer (Honorary) in Calcutta.

CHHANDA BOSE

 After graduating with History honours from Lady Brabourne College in Calcutta, Mrs. Bose did postgraduate work at St. Hugh's College at Oxford and took her B.Ed. at St. Xavier's College, Calcutta. In 1987, she founded the Vikramshila Education Resource Society. She developed a reputation as an innovative educator with a social conscience, and was awarded an Ashoka Fellowship (from Washington, D.C.) for outstanding public service. Mrs. Bose has been an executive at the International Labour Organization as Coordinator for Education, Training, and Communication, with a dedication to the issue of children's rights and the abolishment of child labour, and an Adviser for GTZ (German Development Corp.) in Nepal and Delhi, among other prestigious consultantships. Mrs. Bose is also a gifted writer of children's stories and plays.

SHELLEY BROWN, M.D.

See "About the Author."

EULA BRUCE

Mrs. Bruce worked as an office manager for over twenty years in the San Diego area, where her husband, Dr. Ellsworth Bruce, practised as an oral surgeon. They joined the Vedanta Society of Southern California in Hollywood after a chance visit there in 1959, and travelled the 125 miles back and forth, twice weekly, to attend its meetings. Several prolonged trips to India ensued. In 1974, they retired and moved to the desert country in Utah, becoming interested in Native American art and sculpture, and opening a shop for fine Indian crafts. Mrs. Bruce has managed the shop since her husband passed away in 1988, and moved it in 1990 to a much larger establishment at the scenic entrance to Zion National Park.

DARSHAN KUMAR BUBBAR, G.D. ARCH., FIIA

Mr. D.K. Bubbar is the proprietor of The Angles Architects in Bombay, a distinguished firm that has executed housing, office buildings, and campus planning, as well as interior projects for such clients as the Methodist Church, Citibank, Lipton, and the Vivekananda Kendra. His work has been featured in reputed journals, magazines, and newspapers. Mr. Bubbar was felicitated in February 1994 by the Alumni of the Academy of Architecture for his outstanding accomplishments. He has written a three-volume treatise, *Spirit of Indian Architecture*, a modern classic on the architecture of harmony based on ancient principles that foster the well-being of the indweller.

JAGADISH CHAKRAVARTY, M.B.B.S.

Dr. Chakravarty received his M.B.B.S. with honours in 1960, and later became the first medical doctor in Dermatology, Venerology, and Leprology from Calcutta University. He was awarded the title of Binodini Gold Medalist in Leprology at the School of Tropical Medicine, Calcutta, and he has authored over twenty-five publications in his specialty. He is a Professor in Dermatology at the RKM Seva Pratishthan, and a Consultant Dermatologist at other establishments.

SATYAPRIYA CHAKRAVORTY

Mr. Chakravorty is Assistant Secretary to the Ramakrishna Vivekananda Mission in Barrackpore, District of 24-Parganas.

GAUTAM CHATTERJI

Mr. Chatterji received his degree in the first class from the Regional Engineering College, Durgapur. Initially he worked as a Sales Executive with Das Reprographics, and later was chosen as one of three Management Trainees at HMT (Hindusthan Machine Tools) International to prepare their first comprehensive market survey of the Indian machine tools industry; this was followed by a successful career as a Sales Engineer and Export Manager in charge of the HMT International office in New Delhi. He was also Marketing Manager (All India) of Bengal Ingot Company, and Assistant General Manager of Sales for Usha Atlas Company, prior to founding his own engineering agency house in Calcutta, Omni Tech India, which markets a broad range of industrial products. He has been associated with the Ramakrishna Math and Mission since his early childhood.

SHUBHRA CHATTERJI

 Mrs. Chatterji is the Director of the Vikramshila Education Resource Society, a nongovernmental organization that has a long-standing commitment to educating the poor in villages and urban slums. Under Mrs. Chatterji's leadership since June 1993, Vikramshila has spread its activities throughout eight states of India, until it is now one of the country's foremost organizations in the field of nonformal and primary education, providing teacher training combined with creative teaching materials at the grassroots level. Prior to joining Vikramshila, Mrs. Chatterji was a pioneering educator in the Montessori tradition. After her honours work in undergraduate English, she received her diploma in Montessori Education and a master's degree in English, both in the first class, then spent seven years starting Montessori environments and providing teacher training. She founded the Montessori Association of Eastern India in 1986. Mrs. Chatterji has become a frequent speaker at state- and national-level workshops in education, and is in demand as an organizer for events that help to raise the self-esteem of poor children through sports and other activities.

SUMITRA CHAUDHURI

Mrs. Chaudhuri is the youngest of the four children of the renowned historian, the late Dr. Ramesh Chandra Majumdar, and his wife, Priyabala Majumdar. She passed the B.A. examination with honours in History from Calcutta University, and married Sri Hirendra Chaudhuri, Solicitor, in 1947.

WILLIAM CONRAD

Mr. Conrad is a biophysicist and a World War II veteran. He has been an active member of the Vedanta Society of New York since 1955, and was one of the organizers for its Centennial celebrations. He has written articles on Vedanta for the journal *Vedanta Free Press* (and its successor, *American Vedantist*), and he served as one of Swami Nitya-swarup-ananda's attendants at the Vedanta Society during the latter's visit to New York in 1987–88.

ANADI DAS, PH.D.

Dr. Das is a resident of British Columbia, where he is a Professor of Mathematics at Simon Fraser University in Burnaby, B.C. He received his doctorate in Mathematical Physics at the National University of Ireland in 1960, and his Doctor of Science (D.Sc.) from Calcutta University in 1964. Dr. Das is the Founder-President of the

Vivekananda Vedanta Society in British Columbia, and is also the Vice-Chairman of the Vedanta Society of Western Washington, Seattle. His father, a disciple of Swami Brahmananda, was a college classmate and close friend of Swami Nitya-swarup-ananda.

ABHAYA DAS GUPTA

 Miss Das Gupta headed the internationally renowned Library at the Ramakrishna Mission Institute of Culture from 1988 until her retirement in May 1996, with over thirty years' experience in library work and library administration. She studied Library Science in Calcutta, and also as a Spalding-Trust Scholar in Oxford and Cambridge, following which she became the Assistant Librarian and then the Librarian of the National Library in Calcutta. She was a student of its Director, Mr. B.S. Kesavan, and was trained by him. A prolific contributor of articles to magazines and volumes in English and Bengali, she published her first book, *Sri Sri Sarada Devi: Atmakatha* (Sri Sri Sarada Devi on Herself) in 1979, a recognized source book for research on the Holy Mother. Currently, she is writing a book on Sri Ramakrishna. Miss Das Gupta and her family had a lifelong association with Swami Nitya-swarup-ananda.

SANTWANA DASGUPTA

 The late Professor Santwana Dasgupta (d. November 20, 1999), formerly the Head of the Department of Economics, Bethune College, Calcutta, spent most of her busy academic life as a scholar of Swami Vivekananda's social philosophy. She was introduced to the Rama-krishna-Vivekananda literature by her parents, both disciples of Sri Sarada Devi. Professor Dasgupta later carried out her lifelong research on Swami Vivekananda, inspired by her teacher, Professor Benoy Kumar Sarkar, and contributed a stream of original articles on Swamiji and his social philosophy starting in the 1940s, the first being "Vivekanander Samyavad," followed by various articles in *Udbodhan*, the Bengali magazine of the Ramakrishna Order. These culminated in her first book, *Vivekanander Samai-Darshan*, published in 1963. Professor Dasgupta was a Research Fellow at the Ramakrishna Mission Institute of Culture, Calcutta, as well as the Nivedita Lecturer of Calcutta University. She was awarded the coveted Nivedita Prize in honour of her pioneering contributions to the Vivekananda literature.

BHABATOSH DATTA, PH.D.

The late Dr. Bhabatosh Datta was born February 11, 1911, in Patna, India. Revered as a teacher (many of his former students became illustrious economists, including the 1998 Nobel laureate, Amartya Sen), Dr. Datta spent his final years as Emeritus Professor of Economics at Presidency College, and Visiting Professor of the Centre for Studies in Social Sciences, in Calcutta. He was widely published on economics as well as other subjects. During the 1960s, he was a member of the Governing Body of the Ramakrishna Mission Institute of Culture. Among his many honours, Dr. Datta was invited by Calcutta University in 1981 to deliver the first set of the newly endowed Professor Manmohan Sen Memorial Lectures.

NANDITA DATTA

Mrs. Datta received her master's degree in Modern History from Delhi University before she began studying and teaching in England for some time. She has written short stories for radio and television, and has published stories and articles in magazines. Since 1990, she has edited and published a magazine entitled *Divya-Jyotir Pathé*. She gives concerts of devotional music, has issued cassettes, and has also published a book on Swami Vivekananda. Her husband, Dr. Anutosh Datta, an eminent ophthalmologist, was Sheriff of Calcutta. Their only son, Dr. Vivek Datta, is also a prominent ophthalmologist.

SATCHIDANANDA DHAR, PH.D.

Dr. Dhar is a renowned scholar in Oriental Studies, as well as a distinguished linguist with a command of Sanskrit, Pali, Bengali, Japanese, and Tibetan. He was a research scholar of Calcutta University in Sino-Tibetan Culture from 1948 to 1950, and subsequently attended the Tokyo University of Foreign Languages as a Government of India Scholar in 1956–57. His doctoral work on Mahayana Buddhism, and numerous treatises on Indian culture as well as Buddhism, have received academic acclaim. Currently he is a Fellow at the Netaji Institute for Asian Studies and is the officiating editor of its journal, *Asian Studies*. Dr. Dhar was an editor of the recently published *A Portrait of Sri Ramakrishna* (the first English translation of *Sri Sri Ramakrishna Punthi*), issued by the Ramakrishna Mission Institute of Culture in 1998.

VIOLET AMORY EATON

Mrs. Eaton was married with three children when she first encountered Vedanta through meeting Swami Prabhavananda in California in 1965. She subsequently became an active member of the Vedanta Society of Southern California, and after her first trip to India in 1977, she requested Swami Swahananda, then Head of the Society, to expand her service to it. With his encouragement, she moved to Del Mar, California, and helped to start the Society's branch centre in San Diego. Mrs. Eaton also donated the Retreat House for Women to the Vedanta Society in Seattle, thus extending her largesse to Washington State. On the East Coast, she became cofounder of the SRV retreat house in Greenville, New York, and has also remained close to the Ramakrishna Vedanta Society in Boston, where she has long been a member.

CARMEN FARMER

Miss Farmer received her B.S. degree in Radio-TV-Film at the University of Texas in Austin, and has worked ever since in broadcasting and advertising. She was introduced to Vedanta in 1979 and moved to Portland in 1982 to be more closely associated with Swami Aseshananda and the Vedanta Society of Portland, where she lived for eight years at Sarada House, one of the two residences established by Swami Aseshananda for women spiritual seekers.

JOAN FOX

Miss Fox is a native Canadian who was introduced to Vedanta in 1959 when she moved to Portland, Oregon, and came into contact with Swami Aseshananda. She became closely associated with the Vedanta Society of Portland, and lived for many years in "Holy Mother's House," one of the residences established by Swami Aseshananda for women devotees who were interested in leading a more concentrated spiritual life under his direction. Before her retirement, Miss Fox held administrative positions in the legal and safety areas of the corporate sector and in the director's offices of a retirement community. She is now retired and has returned to Alberta, Canada.

PRADYUT KUMAR GANGULY

Mr. Ganguly, born in 1952, has a master's degree in Modern History from Jadavpur University. For the past twenty years, he has been working in the Publications Department of the Ramakrishna Mission Institute of Culture. He became close to Swami Nitya-swarup-ananda while assisting him with the preparation for publication of his book *How I Came to the Feet of Sri Ramakrishna*.

MARGARET GARLAND, R.N.

Miss Garland was an actress in the theatre and television in New York and London for fourteen years (1938–52). Following a sojourn in France, she returned to the United States, where she graduated from nursing school in 1962. She worked as a nurse at the Psychiatric Institute at Columbia-Presbyterian Hospital in New York City and then as a private psychotherapist until 1993, when she retired from professional practice. Miss Garland has been a student of Vedanta since 1950, when she started attending the Ramakrishna-Vivekananda Center in New York City. Between

1955 and 1980, she made several long pilgrimages to India, during which she visited with Swami Nitya-swarup-ananda.

SUMANA GHOSH

Miss Ghosh graduated with English honours in 1992, and went on to complete her postgraduate education in English at Jadavpur University. She is a freelance designer with a particular interest in books and the field of publication. Her other talents include music, and she spends her free time forming amateur singing groups with friends.

RAGHUNATH GOSWAMI

The late Raghunath Goswami (1931–95) was a celebrated artist, designer, puppeteer, and filmmaker. In 1961, he established R. Goswami and Associates, an independent team of designers and production specialists, now an established resource for advertising, public relations, communications, theatre and film productions, festivals, and convention exhibitions. His design projects spanned India and beyond, to include permanent museums at the Belur Math ("Ramakrishna Darshan"), Santiniketan ("Rabindra Bhavana"), and Kanyakumari ("Arise and Awake") as well as a proposed "Craft Village" in the Salt Lake area of Calcutta for the Bengal Chamber of Commerce. Mr. Goswami, a Consultant for the National Institute of Design, was also the designer for innumerable events and projects, such as the Ramakrishna Mission Convention Exhibition in 1980, the RKM Youth Convention Exhibition in 1985, the Commonwealth Institute in London, the Festival of India in France (1985) and the USSR (1987), and the museum "The Wandering Monk" on Swami Vivekananda in Kanyakumari (1991), to mention only a few. Renowned in the world of puppetry, he founded The Puppets, a noncommercial puppet theatre, produced puppet film festivals and workshops, and was the recipient of the Academy Award of 1993 for his lifetime achievements in this art. Mrs. Bhabani Goswami worked alongside her husband in puppetry and design, and continues their tradition of excellence; their son, Mangal, earned a Ph.D./A.B.D. in Economics from Kansas State University before pursuing his career in finance.

PHULRENU GUHA, PH.D.

Dr. Guha, an eminent social worker, was born August 13, 1911, in Calcutta. She received her M.A. from Calcutta University and her doctorate (D.Litt.) from the Sorbonne in France. By the age of thirteen, she had joined the Jugantar Party. She was a member of Rajya Sabha from 1964 to 1970, and served as Minister of State and Social Welfare for the government of India from 1967 to 1970. From 1984 to 1989, she was a member of the Lok Sabha. During her long and accomplished career, Dr. Guha received the Padma Bhushan Award from the government of India, as well as the Netaji Award and the Tagore Literacy Award. She has presided over many organizations, and her publications include seven books and innumerable articles. Dr. Guha's husband was a prominent scientist, the late Dr. Biresh Chandra Guha.

SUNILAVA GUHA

Professor Guha taught economics for many years at City College, Calcutta. He came under the influence of the Ramakrishna Mission at an early age as a student of the Ramakrishna Mission Vidyapith, Deogher. He was a member of the Basu Thakur family, to whom Swami Nitya-swarup-ananda was a friend, philosopher, and guide.

NAMITA GUPTA

Mrs. Gupta has written, "I was born on March 7, 1919, in Hazaribagh (Bihar). I was the youngest daughter of the late Surat Gupta and Jayabati Gupta. Both my school background (at the Mission School, Hazaribagh, and at Loreto House, Calcutta) and my family heritage imbibed in me a sense of responsibility and discipline. My husband, Arunaday, inherited his father's tea plantation at Cacher. Ever since his death in 1982, I have tried to advance the family business. Swami Madhavananda initiated me into the [family] of Sri Ramakrishna. Spiritual assistance of Swami Nitya-swarup-ananda strengthened my will power."

ARUNA HALDAR, PH.D.

Dr. Haldar received her doctorate in Philosophy at Calcutta University before teaching at Patna University, eventually as a Reader in Philosophy and as the Head of the Department of Philosophy at the Women's College. Now retired, she was also formerly a Visiting Professor of Indian Philosophy, Sanskrit and Bengali Languages, on the Oriental Faculty at Leningrad University, USSR.

ERIK JOHNS

Mr. Johns first attended the Hollywood Vedanta Center in 1946. He later joined the Vedanta Society of New York in 1955 as a student of Swami Pavitrananda, where he now serves on the board of directors. He is also President of the Sarada-Rama-krishna-Vivekananda Association of America at Greenville, New York. Mr. Johns is a respected artist whose design career has included major social functions, such as the inaugural dinner of President John F. Kennedy, other presidential galas, and interiors in the New York City area. He is also a published librettist, writer, and the co-editor of *American Vedantist*. Mr. Johns, with the late Jack Kelly, arranged and hosted Swami Nitya-swarup-ananda's trip to the United States in 1987–88. Mr. Johns also hosts the annual Fourth of July celebration in honour of Swami Vivekananda at his home, Moss Hill Farms, in association with the Vedanta Society of New York.

KIREET JOSHI

Mr. Joshi studied Philosophy and Law at Bombay University, receiving the Gold Medal and Vedanta Prize when he stood "first class first" in the M.A. examination. He resigned from the Indian Administrative Service in 1956 in order to devote his life to the study and practice of Sri Aurobindo's Yoga at Pondicherry, India. From 1958 to 1975 he taught at Sri Aurobindo's International Centre of Education, where he also established an International Institute on Educational Research. In 1976, Mr. Joshi became an Adviser to the Indian Ministry of Education, and later served as its Special Secretary in Human Resources. He chaired the government of India committee for Teachers' Training and the UNESCO Committee on International Education, to cite a few of his prestigious positions. His publications include *A Philosophy of Education for the Contemporary Youth* and *A Philosophy of the Role of the Contemporary Teacher*, among others. Mr. Joshi is currently Chairman of the Value Education Centre in New Delhi, established in 1992.

PARIMAL KAR

Professor Kar was a College Lecturer in Economics for over forty years. With Swami Nitya-swarup-ananda's encouragement, he dedicated himself to voluntary rural community service, publishing in this field for more than a decade. The pilot project that he organized on Youth and Social Service on behalf of Asutosh College was recognized in 1957 as one of the five UNESCO Associated Youth Enterprises in Southeast Asia. In 1958, he was the Chairman of Education for youth at the Eleventh UNESCO Conference of Organizers of International Voluntary Work Camps. Professor Kar was closely associated with Swami Nitya-swarup-ananda from 1945, and served as an Assistant Secretary to the Ramakrishna Mission Institute of Culture, as well as the Secretary to the General Editor of *The Cultural Heritage of India*. Continuing his lifelong commitment to the youth of India, Professor Kar is presently Coordinator of the Asutosh College Training Centre. In June

1996, he became the Honorary Director of the Bengal Social Service League, which runs the State Resource Centre for Adult Education in West Bengal. He is the author of five books on sociology, three in English and two in Bengali, the first of which was a pioneering work on sociology in Bengali, now in its seventh edition and with a new translation into Hindi published in 1997. On August 15, 1997, Professor Kar was honoured by Calcutta University as an "Eminent Teacher for 1996" for his outstanding contribution to teaching and research for over two decades.

PREM KIRPAL, HON. PH.D.

 Dr. Kirpal was educated at Government College and University Law College in Lahore, and Balliol College, Oxford. He became an international figure in the fields of education and culture, holding prominent positions in India and abroad: Professor of History and Political Science at the Punjab College in Lahore, Educational Adviser to the Indian High Commissioner in London, Secretary to the Government of India in the Ministry of Education and Culture, Director of the National Council of Educational Research and Training, Member of the Indian Education Commission, Director of UNESCO's Department of Cultural Activities in Paris, Chairman of the Executive Board of UNESCO, Chairman of the Indian Council on Peace Research, Senior Specialist in the East-West Centre at Honolulu in Hawaii, and so forth. Dr. Kirpal is the author of several works on education and culture, in addition to nine books of poetry. He received honorary doctorates from Temple University (Philadelphia, U.S.A.), Leningrad University (in the former USSR), and the University of Punjab, as well as several national and international honours, including the UNESCO Gold Medal in 1972 and the Order of the Republic of Egypt and the U.A.E. At present, he lives in New Delhi, where he pursues his educational and cultural work as the President of the Delhi Public School Society and as the Life President of the International Educational Consortium, in addition to his personal interests in poetry, painting, and meditation.

RABBI JONATHAN KLIGLER

Rabbi Kligler graduated from Reconstructionist Rabbinical College in Philadelphia in 1989, and subsequently became the first rabbinical director of the Woodstock Jewish Congregation in Woodstock, New York—a new, progressive, and liberal spiritual congregation. Rabbi Kligler serves as a cantor, but is also an experienced guitarist, folk music singer, and dancer, who has taught improvisational dance. His services at the Woodstock Jewish Congregation are filled with the arts of music and dance as a form of worship.

RENEE LA PAN

Miss La Pan was born in Michigan, and received her B.A. and master's degrees in Business Administration from the University of Michigan in the mid-1970s. She has been closely associated with Vedanta in various centres in the United States since 1978, and has been a monastic member of the Vedanta Society of Southern California since 1991.

PRAKASH LOHIA

Mr. Lohia is the Manager of a business and industry belonging to his joint family. He received his Bachelor of Technology (Chemical) degree at the Indian Institute of Technology in New Delhi.

RUPCHAND LOHIA

Mr. Lohia is noted as one of the promoters of the Merino Group of Industries in India, with responsibilities in the Corporate Head Office in Calcutta. He attended Calcutta University and took a degree in Mechanical Engineering from Jadavpur University before joining the family business (cold storage, plywood manufacturing, decorative laminate manufacturing, farming, floriculture, horticulture, etc.); his two sons have also joined him in the business. Mr. Lohia took *diksha* from the late Swami Vishuddhananda Maharaj, and knew Swami Nitya-swarup-ananda during the last five years of his life.

AMIYA KUMAR MAJUMDAR

The late Professor Amiya Kumar Majumdar (1917–98) had a brilliant career, both as a student and in his professional life as an eminent scholar and educationalist. He was educated in Calcutta at the Rani Bhabani School, Scottish Church College, and Calcutta University, graduating with a first class degree, both in honours and M.A. examinations. He taught Philosophy at Presidency College, Calcutta, and was the Principal of the Hooghly Mohsin College before he became Deputy Director of Public Education for West Bengal. He was also a valued member of the Public Service Committee, the General Secretary of the Indian Philosophical Congress, a member of the Editorial Board of the *Marhatti Encyclopaedia of Philosophy and Religion*, and a member of the Indian National Commission for Co-operation with UNESCO, representing India at international seminars in 1960 and 1988. He became a regular lecturer at the Ramakrishna Mission Institute of Culture, Calcutta, in the early 1950s, and later its Assistant Secretary. He published widely, including contributions to *The Cultural Heritage of India*, *A Seminar of Saints*, *Prabuddha Bharata*, *The Calcutta Review*, and the *Viswabharati Journal of Philosophy*. Among his books, mention may be made of *Understanding Vivekananda* and *Vivekananda as a Vedantist*, in addition to the books he edited, such as the *Sister Nivedita Commemorative Volume* and, jointly with Swami Prajnananda, *The Bases of Indian Culture*. In later years, his many eminent positions reflected his stature as a respected scholar and the breadth and depth of his learning, such as Senior Research Fellow, The Asiatic Society, Calcutta; Chairman of the Vivekananda Kendra; Executive Committee of the Indian Academy of Philosophy; and Honorary Research Director of the Ramakrishna Mission Institute of Culture, Calcutta, to name but a few. An ardent admirer of Swami Nitya-swarup-ananda, Professor Majumdar played the key role in organizing the Memorial Lecture Programmes of 1993 and 1994, which he also chaired.

SUHRID MAJUMDAR

The late Suhrid Majumdar (d. 1993) was the Gol Park Site Supervisor of Messrs. Martin Burn Ltd., the well-known construction company in charge of building the permanent facility of the Ramakrishna Mission Institute of Culture.

SHYAMA PRASAD MANDAL, M.B.B.S., M.S., M.CH. (ORTH.)

Dr. S.P. Mandal is a prestigious orthopaedic surgeon in New Delhi, where he is Chairman of the Department of Orthopaedics at the Sri Ganga Ram Hospital. He has also been President of the Indian Orthopaedic Society and a pioneer in India of arthroscopic surgery. Dr. Mandal devotes considerable time to the less fortunate members of society, operating on thousands of children with polio free of cost and treating the poor at Ramakrishna Mission hospitals and elsewhere. He was awarded the Aman-e-Hind for his work with slum dwellers in Delhi and is the President and Founding Member of the Amar Jyoti Charitable Trust for the Handicapped (National Award for best institution in the field of rehabilitation). Dr. Mandal's wife, Dr. Anindita Mandal, is Director of the Govind Ballar Pant Hospital in New Delhi.

FATHER JOHN MILLS

Reverend Mills is an Episcopal priest who graduated with honours in French and Latin before attending the General Theological Episcopal Seminary in New York City in 1949. He served as the Curate of several churches and taught English at Wisconsin State College before he became Rector at St. Mary's Episcopal Church in

Cold Spring Harbor, New York, a position that he held from 1961 until his recent retirement. During his rectorship, Father Mills did graduate work in English and Theology and conducted serenity retreats. Currently involved in Patristic studies at Fordham University, he is studying Saint Irenaeus of Lyon. He has had an interest in Eastern religion since 1956.

SOMEN MITRA

Mr. Mitra, B.E.C.E., M.I.E., is a Chartered Engineer who graduated in Civil Engineering (B.E.) from Bengal Engineering College, Howrah, West Bengal, in 1957, and became a member of the Institute of Engineers, Calcutta, in 1981. He is a Director of Neo-Parisrutan Private Limited, Calcutta, and has been engaged in the design, construction, and supply of equipment, and commissioning of water and effluent treatment plants all over India for the last thirty-six years. He has been associated with various philanthropic activities of the Ramakrishna Math and Mission for many years, such as its Rotary International, and is also a longtime member of the Rotary Club of East Calcutta, and a member of the Rotary District Committee.

GOVINDA GOPAL MUKHERJEE, PH.D.

Dr. Mukherjee is a renowned Sanskrit scholar, teacher, and lecturer. He was formerly Professor of Sanskrit at the Sanskrit College of Calcutta (1954–63) and Banaras Hindu University (1946–48); Professor and Head of the Department of Sanskrit at Burdwan University (1963–83) as well as Dean of its Faculty of Arts (1965–67); Visiting Professor of Sanskrit at Rabindra Bharati University (1970–75); and Research Professor of Sanskrit at the Ramakrishna Mission Institute of Culture (1984–94). His numerous associations include membership with Bharatiya Vidya Bhavan in Bombay and Calcutta, and his many books include the *Studies in the Upanishads* (Calcutta Sanskrit College Research Series), as well as many other titles both in English (including *Sangita Damodara, Trilingual Dictionary, A Great Savant,* and *Pearls of Wisdom*) and Bengali (including *Gitar Katha, Bhagavat Katha,* and *Mahajan Samvada*). He became associated with the Ramakrishna Mission Institute of Culture in 1960 when Swami Nitya-swarup-ananda engaged him to give weekly discourses on the major Indian scriptures, which he continued for more than thirty years until his official retirement in 1994. He also helped edit *The Cultural Heritage of India,* Volume 5, and was associated with both the School of Humanistic and Intercultural Studies and the School of Sanskritic Studies started at the Institute by Swami Nitya-swarup-ananda. Dr. Mukherjee gave the Invocation at the Swami Nitya-swarup-ananda Memorial Lecture Programmes in 1993 and 1994, and his recent course of Upanishad classes at the Institute has been welcomed with fresh acclaim.

394 CENTRED IN TRUTH

PADMA MUKHERJEE

Mrs. Mukherjee had her first schooling at the Nivedita Girls' School, graduating with honours in Bengali, followed by an M.A. from Calcutta University. Early in life, she imbibed the spiritual ideals of her parents, Mrs. Nandita Bhattacharya and the late Ram Kumar Bhattacharya. She also trained as a musician, and is an accomplished singer. After her marriage, she formed a Ladies' Circle ("Mangalik") at her father-in-law's house at Bhowanipur, as encouraged by Swami Nitya-swarup-ananda. "Mangalik" has since blossomed into a large assembly of devotees with weekly classes, bhajans (devotional songs), and readings as regular activities, and with special lectures by the monks of the Ramakrishna Mission and the nuns of Sri Sarada Math.

SREELA DEVI NAKACHI

Mrs. Nakachi and her family have been devotees of the Ramakrishna Math and Mission for many years. She and her husband live in Tokyo, and were well known to Swami Nitya-swarup-ananda.

SWAMI NITYANANDA

Swami Nityananda, a disciple of Swami Virajananda, is the Founder-President and Secretary of the Vivekananda Math and the Ramakrishna Vivekananda Mission, respectively, in Barrackpore. He received his M.A. in Philosophy from Calcutta University, and was a member of the Ramakrishna Order from 1956 until 1976, during which time he was the Secretary of the Ramakrishna Mission Boys' Home at Rahara, Principal of the Vivekananda Centenary College, and also Headmaster of the Mission's School. Subsequently, he separated from the main organization and established the Barrackpore Math and Mission.

BETTY ROBINSON, PH.D.

Dr. Robinson, a retired teacher, received her master's degree in History from Vanderbilt University and her Ph.D. in South Asian History from Columbia University, with her doctoral thesis on the Ramakrishna-Sarada Math in West Bengal. She has been a Vedantist since 1951 when she read *The Gospel of Sri Ramakrishna* and became a student of Swami Nikhilananda at the Ramakrishna-Vivekananda Center in New York City. She has made several long pilgrimages to India and now resides in Ocean Grove, New Jersey, where her house serves as a summer retreat for devotees of the Vedanta Society of New York.

ROSTISLAV B. RYBAKOV, PH.D.

Dr. Rybakov is the Director of the Institute of Oriental Studies of the Russian Academy of Sciences in Moscow, and is a well-known Russian Indologist and scholar of Hinduism, Indian culture, and cross-cultural contacts. He is the author of about seventy works on Hinduism, the Ramakrishna-Vivekananda movement, and Indian-Russian cultural contacts. He is also the Chancellor of Oriental University and the President of the Institute of Buddhism. Dr. Rybakov first met Swami Nitya-swarup-ananda in 1990, and is a frequent visitor to India.

AMRITA SALM, PH.D.

Dr. Salm has been active in Vedanta for over twenty-five years. She is currently the Secretary of the Vedanta Society of Southern California, and the Vice-President of the Vivekananda Retreat, Ridgely, in New York State. She received her Ph.D. in Higher Education in 1979 from the University of California, Berkeley. Dr. Salm has been involved in editing and indexing books for Advaita Ashrama in Calcutta, most recently editing and publishing *A Portrait of Sri Ramakrishna* (the first English translation of *Sri Sri Ramakrishna Punthi*), issued by the Ramakrishna Mission Institute of Culture in 1998. She has also been a grant writer and fund-raiser for nonprofit organizations in Santa Barbara, an Associate Professor of Elementary Education at California State University, Los Angeles, and a Senior Administrative Analyst for the University of California, Los Angeles.

KESHAB CHANDRA SARKAR

Born in 1925, Mr. Sarkar participated in the Quit India movement in 1942 prior to matriculating in 1943. After two years of college studies, he worked in several governmental departments before joining the Ramakrishna Mission Institute of Culture at Gol Park, Calcutta, in December 1960. Mr. Sarkar has also been an actor in Bengali dramas and was associated for nine years with Sri Mohitlal Majumdar, the Bengali poet and critic, from whom he received a liberal education. He retired from the Institute of Culture in 1997, but continues to teach Bengali to foreign scholars, as he has since 1923.

JOHN SCARBOROUGH

Mr. Scarborough interrupted his college education to serve as a monastic in the Ramakrishna Order for ten years, during which he attended Swami Vividishananda throughout the four years of his final illness. He completed his undergraduate degree at the University of Washington in Philosophy, which included the study of Shankara's commentary on the Brihadaranyaka Upanishad in Sanskrit with Professor

Karl Potter. Intrigued by systems development, he worked for ten years as a software engineer at Microsoft. He has recently retired and lives in Ashland, Oregon, with his wife, Margaret.

JOHN SCHLENCK

Mr. Schlenck is the Music Director, Secretary, and Librarian of the Vedanta Society of New York, where he has been a member since 1958 and a resident member since 1960. He graduated from the Eastman School of Music, University of Rochester, in 1957, and worked as a musician with leading dance schools for many years. Mr. Schlenck is a composer whose work "Seek the Eternal: An Interfaith Cantata Celebrating the Spiritual Life" was performed at the Parliament of the World's Religions in Chicago, 1993. A 1994 concert of his music premiered at Alice Tully Hall at Lincoln Center in New York City. He is also the Secretary/Treasurer of Vedanta West Communications, which he cofounded in 1996 to communicate Vedantic idealism through Western cultural forms; its music subsidiary is Vedantic Arts Recordings, and it publishes the journal *American Vedantist*.

RABINDRA NATH SEN

The late Rabindra Nath Sen (1907–94) was educated at Calcutta University, and at London University in the U.K. In 1939, he became a Chartered Accountant and joined the famous international auditing firm of Price, Waterhouse, Peat and Company in Calcutta, becoming a senior partner in 1961. Following his retirement from the firm, he was widely respected as a public figure, becoming the Sheriff of Calcutta in 1963, and the Chairman or the Director of several public and private sector companies. From his boyhood, Mr. Sen was closely associated with the Ramakrishna Sangha, and was beloved of many senior monks, especially Bharat Maharaj and Chintaharan Maharaj. Encouraged by the latter, Mr. Sen was an active participant during the formative years of the Ramakrishna Mission Institute of Culture, as well as a long-standing committee member of the Institute.

JUSTICE SUHAS CHANDRA SEN

 The Honourable Justice Suhas Chandra Sen (b. 1932) was educated in Calcutta and had his M.A. and LL.B. degrees from Calcutta University. He became a Barrister-at-Law of Inner Temple, London, in 1959, and practised as an Advocate in Calcutta High Court. He was elevated to the bench of the Calcutta High Court in 1981, and became a Judge of the Supreme Court in June 1994. Since January 1998 he has been Chairman of Authority for Advanced Rulings. He has also been President of the National Consumer Disputes Redressal Commission since March 1998.

TRIGUNA SEN, PH.D.

The late Dr. Triguna Sen (1904–98) was renowned for his erudition and his advancement of education in India. Following a doctorate in Mechanical Engineering from Germany, he joined the Indian National Council of Education, and later became Rector of Jadavpur Engineering College; owing to his untiring efforts, the College finally emerged as a full-fledged university. Dr. Sen held many other posts, including Vice-Chancellor of Banaras Hindu University, Union Education Minister, and Mayor of the Calcutta Corporation, during which he made a mark on the educational and cultural life of Calcutta. An international figure, Dr. Sen participated regularly in conferences abroad, and published widely during his long career. In the face of these legendary accomplishments, Dr. Sen's personal humility was the mark of his lifelong spiritual discipline.

MOTHER SERAPHIMA

Mother Seraphima is a nun of the Orthodox Christian Church in America. She met Swami Nitya-swarup-ananda when she was a student at the Vedanta Society in New York City, and subsequently saw him in India on pilgrimage.

KRISHNA SESHAN AND PATRICIA JIMINEZ

Mr. Seshan is an Engineer (Berkeley, 1975) who taught metallurgy at the University of Arizona and worked at IBM in New York and for the Intel Corporation in San Jose, California. Growing up in India, he attended the Ramakrishna Mission in New Delhi with his father. He met Swami Swahananda in Berkeley in 1969, and subsequently he and his wife, Patricia Jiminez, both attended the Berkeley Vedanta Society. Patricia has a master's degree in Journalism from the University of Arizona (1983) and a Master of Divinity degree (1993) from Andover Newton Theological School in Massachusetts.

KARAN SINGH, PH.D.

Dr. Singh is respected in India and abroad as an eminent scholar whose academic achievements have been complemented by both a distinguished political career and a dedication to global concerns. After receiving his doctorate from Delhi University with his thesis "The Political Thought of Sri Aurobindo," Dr. Singh was for many years Chancellor of Jammu and Kashmir University as well as of Banaras Hindu University. His numerous scholarly books and articles have disseminated his enlightened views on a broad range of religious, philosophical, social, educational, political, and cultural subjects. Born heir apparent to the Maharaja and Maharani of Jammu and Kashmir in 1931, he ruled as Regent from 1949 until 1967, when (at age thirty-six) he became the youngest Central Cabinet Minister in India. He was subsequently reelected in 1971, 1977, and 1980, and also held at various times the prominent positions of Minister for Health and Family Planning, Minister for Education and Culture, and Indian Ambassador to the United States. Dr. Singh currently serves as a member of the Rajya Sabha (the Upper House of Parliament). Dr. Singh has a unique multifaceted global perspective. His active espousal of interfaith harmony, education, the environment, and wildlife preservation are but a few examples of his dynamic leadership in solving some of our most pressing planetary problems. Readers are referred to Dr. Singh's Web site for the fascinating story of his life, his family, and his commitments (http://www.karansingh.com).

PHILIP STAPP AND JOHN BASS

Mr. Stapp, a Guggenheim Fellow, made animated educational films for the Marshall Plan in Paris, the United Nations in New York, and the World Health Organization in Geneva. He is now designing handscrolls based on analogies between visual patterns and the structure of musical counterpoint. John Bass, now retired, was a Captain in the British Army, and later a Production Manager for Funk and Wagnalls, and for the division of Reader's Digest General and Condensed Books. Both Mr. Stapp and Mr. Bass were drawn to Vedantic teachings by Swami Pavitrananda in New York.

SWAMI YOGESHANANDA

Swami Yogeshananda is an American monk of the Ramakrishna Order who became a monastic member of the Vedanta Society of Northern California in 1945. His introduction to Vedanta came from the revered Swami Yatiswarananda in Philadelphia. After training in the California monasteries, he took final vows in India. He served for some years as the Assistant Minister of the London Vedanta Centre and then transferred to the Chicago Center. At present, Swami Yogeshananda is the resident minister in the Vedanta Center of Atlanta, which has its own facility in Tucker, Georgia. Originally incorporated as "The Eternal Quest," it has its own Web site (www.vedanta-atlanta.org). His publications include *The Visions of Sri Ramakrishna* (1973) and *Six Lighted Windows: Memories of Swamis in the West* (1995).

Memorial Lecture Programmes

INTRODUCTION

IMMEDIATELY AFTER the passing away of Swami Nitya-swarup-ananda on October 22, 1992, a group of his close friends and admirers, the author included, gathered in grief. A great light had gone out of our lives. As we found comfort in each other, the idea naturally arose of organizing a public event to honour the Swami's memory, by which to share the legacy of his life and work that had so illumined our own lives.

The initial commemorative activities were planned and executed under the banner of the "Friends of Swami Nitya-swarup-ananda." Full- and half-page obituary notices were placed in the Calcutta newspapers on November 3, 1992. These imposing tributes, which included a large photograph of Swami Nitya-swarup-ananda, made quite a stir at the time.

Four months later, on February 22, 1993 (the Swami's birth anniversary), the first "Swami Nitya-swarup-ananda Memorial Lecture Programme" was held in Calcutta. His many friends, as well as the general public, were invited to hear renowned scholars discuss one of his major ideas: "Human Unity and Global Civilization: Swami Vivekananda's Vision." A second Memorial Lecture Programme was held the following year, on February 22, 1994, at which distinguished speakers and musicians from the various religious faiths gathered to celebrate another global theme in his honour: "Beyond Tolerance."

Myriad tasks were involved in preparing for these events: coordinating the speakers for the programme, booking the auditorium, placing the press notices, hand-delivering the printed invitations, arranging for the refreshments, and organizing the transportation of guests, to mention only a few. The "Friends of Swami Nitya-swarup-ananda" worked hard on these commemorative projects with dedication and goodwill. Our group included Dr. Arabinda Basu, Mrs. Tapati Basu,

A gathering of the "Friends of Swami Nitya-swarup-ananda" in February 1993.
Standing, left to right: Mr. Gautam Chatterji, Mr. Raghunath Goswami,
Mr. S. B. Ghosh, Dr. Shelley Brown, Mrs. Bhabani Goswami,
Mrs. Shubhra Chatterji, Dr. Arabinda Basu, and Mr. Samiran Sarkar.

Mrs. Chhanda Bose, Mr. Salil Bose, Mr. Gautam Chatterji, Mrs. Shubhra Chatterji, Mr. S. B. Ghosh, Miss Sumana Ghosh, Mr. Raghunath Goswami, Mrs. Bhabani Goswami, Mr. Prakash Lohia and his family, Mr. Satya Brata Mukherjee, Mrs. Barsha Mukherjee, and Mr. Samiran Sarkar. We were fortunate in having the leadership and support of Professor Amiya Kumar Majumdar, an eminent scholar and speaker, who had been a friend of Swami Nitya-swarup-ananda for forty years. Professor Majumdar presided as Chairman of the symposia, lending his considerable experience and prestige.

The venue for the memorial lectures was the G. D. Birla Sabhaghar, an elegant auditorium with a marble entryway, which could accommodate an audience of about six hundred in comfortable plush seats. Mr. Raghunath Goswami directed all aspects of the artistic production, and created a special ambience with his designs for the stage and the programme guide.

For the inaugural event, a starkly beautiful thick rope of white flowers, which had been handcrafted before our eyes backstage, was laid across the entire front of the platform as an opened garland. At mid-

Mr. and Mrs. Raghunath Goswami at
the first programme

Preparing the rope of flowers for the stage

stage, a lectern and long table, draped with *gerua* cloth, accommodated the speakers and panelists. The focal point was a large banner ("Swami Nitya-swarup-ananda Memorial Lecture Programme") suspended aloft a towering vertical backdrop bearing photographs of Sri Ramakrishna, the Holy Mother, and Swami Vivekananda, as well as the honouree. The programme guide, handed to members of the audience as they arrived, included in its two inside pockets a copy of the keynote address, a reprint of Swami Nitya-swarup-ananda's monograph *India's Message to Herself and to the World*, and profiles of the speakers.

A gala atmosphere took hold as the auditorium began to fill with the intelligentsia who gathered to pay tribute to Swami Nitya-swarup-ananda's memory (politely escorted to their seats by the volunteers organized by the "Friends"). Attendees included the Swami's vast circle of distinguished friends—scholars and professors from academic life, high court justices, artists, writers, educationalists, scientists, and, of course, those drawn to him for their commitment to a spiritual life. Heads turned as the keynote speaker, Dr. Triguna Sen, slowly walked down the auditorium aisle to take his seat in the speakers' area in the front row. The sight of this venerable and beloved teacher (now ninety years of age) was an emotional moment for many in the audience, who rushed to pay him their respects or request his autograph at intermission.

A view of the audience

Dr. Triguna Sen and Dr. Govinda Gopal Mukherjee at intermission

Dr. Sen's presence uniquely honoured the occasion. His pioneering work in education was legendary in India, and especially in Calcutta, where he had established one of the city's finest universities. He was also revered as a man of serious spiritual discipline. The audience suddenly became hushed as Dr. Sen took his place at the podium. Everyone was eager to hear this intellectual and spiritual giant, who was so humble and loving that his refined personal qualities were as impressive as his temporal accomplishments. Indeed, it was a rare treat for a Calcutta audience to hear him speak—as noted in one newspaper review of the first Swami Nitya-swarup-ananda Memorial Lecture Programme ("Calcutta Notebook," *Statesman*, April 12, 1993):

VISIONARY SWAMI

When was the last time we heard the redoubtable Dr. Triguna Sen from a public platform? Memory fails, but old-timers recall the educationalist with awe and admiration. He could, apart from anything else, captivate an audience by the sheer magic of his words. He still does. This was more than evident last week when he delivered the keynote address to pay tribute to Swami Nitya-swarup-ananda, founder of the Ramakrishna Mission Institute of Culture.

Many of Calcutta's leading lights were present at the Birla Sabhaghar to remember the man who built what is now often described as the "miniature UNESCO." The spiritual insight blending with a global viewpoint, making the Swami not an idle visionary but a practical idealist, were the qualities that came through in the tributes from Dr. Shelley Brown, Dr. Sushil Kumar Mukherjee, Dr. Kalyan Dasgupta, Dr. Hossainur Rahaman and Professor Santwana Dasgupta.

What did Swami Nitya-swarup-ananda actually have in mind when he established the Ramakrishna Mission Institute of Culture in 1938 as a memorial to Sri Ramakrishna, whose birth centenary had been observed in 1936? At a basic level it was the potential divinity of man, the development of a world community and the unity of all religions. Does that ring a bell in today's India? The speakers didn't have to overemphasize the point.

This enthusiastic response to our initial venture filled the "Friends" with relief and gratitude. It had been well attended and well received, though longer than expected with three successive panels, each comprising several speakers and a moderator. The second Swami Nitya-swarup-ananda Memorial Lecture Programme in 1994 had a simpler format, but was equally ambitious: an interreligious symposium that featured religious speakers, a single panel discussion by prominent scholars, and interludes of sacred music and chanting. An eloquent summation by Professor Majumdar, and the fervour of Baul songs, brought the evening to a stirring close.

After a second successful programme, spectators looked forward to an annual function. But the devastating deaths of Mr. Raghunath Goswami in January 1995 and of Mr. Samiran Sarkar the following month, as well as the ill health of several other friends who had contributed their time and talents, dealt an unexpected blow to the continuation of the memorial lecture series after 1994. Even so, many observers felt that a genuine service had been rendered by the "Friends of Swami Nitya-swarup-ananda" in the years immediately following the Swami's passing—a labour of love that had provided the only opportunity to render him public homage by participating in, or attending, two star-studded commemorative events.

This section is devoted to a brief review of the two Memorial Lecture Programmes. It includes highlights from the talks, which offer a glimpse of the speakers' sensitive appreciation of Swami Nitya-swarup-ananda's life and ideas, and of their distinctive insights drawn from their vast personal experiences in a variety of religious and academic disciplines.

First Swami Nitya-swarup-ananda
Memorial Lecture Programme
February 22, 1993

Professor Amiya Kumar Majumdar
Chairman

Invocation: Vedic Hymn   Dr. Govinda Gopal Mukherjee,
                             Ex-Principal, Sanskrit College, Calcutta

Swami Nitya-swarup-ananda: Professor Amiya Kumar Majumdar,
A Short Biography   Ex-Vice-Chancellor, Rabindra
                             Bharati University, Calcutta

Audio recording of excerpts from Swami Nitya-swarup-ananda's lectures

KEYNOTE ADDRESS:
HUMAN UNITY AND GLOBAL CIVILIZATION:
SWAMI VIVEKANANDA'S VISION

Dr. Triguna Sen, Ex-Rector, Jadavpur University, Calcutta

-Interval-

PANEL I: INDIA'S MESSAGE TO HERSELF

Speakers:

Prof. Santwana Dasgupta, Head of Dept. of Economics, Bethune
College, Calcutta

Prof. Hossainur Rahaman, Head of Dept. of History, Hooghly
Mohsin College, Chinsurah

Prof. Dipak Kumar Barua, Head of Dept. of Pali Literature, Calcutta
University

Moderator: Rev. Dr. Somen Das, Principal of Bishops College,
Calcutta

PANEL II: INDIA'S MESSAGE TO THE WORLD

Speakers:

Dr. Sushil Kumar Mukherjee, Ex-Vice-Chancellor, Calcutta
    University

Dr. Kalyan Dasgupta, Bageswari Professor of Indian Art, Calcutta
    University

Moderator: Srimat Swami Yuktananda, Founder-Chairman,
    Vivekananda Nidhi, Calcutta

PANEL III:

GLOBAL SOCIETY: THE EMERGING SCENARIO

Speakers:

Dr. Shelley M. Brown, Senior Attending Physician and Blood Bank
    Director, New York

Srimat Swami Yuktananda

Moderator: Dr. Abdul Subhan, Head of Dept. of Comparative
    Islamic Literature, Maulana Azad College, Calcutta

CONCLUDING ADDRESS: Professor Amiya Kumar Majumdar

———————

*Twelve distinguished participants assembled for the First Swami Nitya-
swarup-ananda Memorial Lecture Programme. Following the welcome by
Mrs. Chhanda Bose, and the Invocation hymn chanted by Dr. Govinda
Gopal Mukherjee, the Chairman paid the first tribute to Swami Nitya-
swarup-ananda in his opening remarks (this and the other addresses in this
section were excerpted from the tape recordings of the event).*

A SHORT BIOGRAPHY
Professor Amiya Kumar Majumdar

It is a rare privilege to be called upon to say something about Swami Nitya-swarup-ananda, whom I had known since I was a student in Scottish Church College in 1936. We have assembled here to pay our humble tribute to the Swami, but I was wondering whether any tribute can be paid to him, because in my opinion, he is beyond all tributes.

Swami Nitya-swarup-ananda was, indeed, a monk of the Rama-krishna Order, but he was a monk with a difference. I have seen him from very close quarters, and I can say that here was a monk, a very rare soul, who combined in himself erudition with humility; a scientific bent of mind with spiritual insight; and a respect for traditional values with an awareness of contemporary reality. Above all, he combined in himself contemplation with action—Swami Nitya-swarup-ananda was a dynamic personality, always more interested in action than in abstract ideologies. To present before you a short biography will be touching only the fringe of the matter, because biography, after all, is something external that does not touch the inner core of a man, especially such a unique personality as Swami Nitya-swarup-ananda. Nevertheless, since it is custom to introduce the person about whom we shall be talking today, I bow down to the wishes of the organizers and will say a few words about his life sketch.

... Swami Nitya-swarup-ananda was a rare combination of vision-ary and practical idealist. He struggled long and hard to work out the plans for the Ramakrishna Mission Institute of Culture. That was in 1934 when he was put in sole charge of the Institute—its planning, development, administration, academic work—he was in charge of everything. Formally, in 1938, on January 29, this Institute was founded physically. That was a red-letter day in the life of Swami Nitya-swarup-ananda. He didn't know sleep—at dead of night he would come up with an idea, put it into writing, and then say, "This is

Professor Amiya Kumar Majumdar delivering
the chairman's address

how this should be done, not otherwise." And as you know, he was a
hard taskmaster. He never liked anything shoddy, slipshod, unclean,
imperfect, or anything fragmented. The history behind the Institute
was also very arduous and painstaking.

One day he said to us, "Look, the United Nations and UNESCO
were founded in 1945. But this Institute was founded in 1938, and we
foreshadowed all the principles which were incorporated in the
Charter of the United Nations." In that sense, the Institute was a pre-
cursor, a forerunner of the United Nations. That was the grand contribution, the permanent contribution, of Swami Nitya-swarup-ananda.

Even so, humble as he was, he would never say, "I have founded
this." The sense of "I" and "mine" was wiped out from his mind. He
was always the torchbearer of Swami Vivekananda, and he knew nothing about anybody else except Vivekananda. I should say, he was full
of Vivekananda. When he was inhaling or exhaling, when he was talking to his visitors, always Vivekananda was the refrain of his song.
That is how he adored him, and he deeply felt that the message of
Vivekananda is not only for India but for the entire world.

When he founded the Ramakrishna Mission Institute of Culture, he
enunciated the principles on which the Institute should be founded.
These were three: Every man is potentially divine; Religion is One;
Humanity is One. This sense of interdependence we call today "global,"

or "holistic." Swami Nitya-swarup-ananda seized upon this idea, and he translated it into action in the Institute of Culture.

The solidarity of mankind-as-a-whole became the song of his soul. This was the Grand Dream which Swami Nitya-swarup-ananda nurtured. He wanted the Institute of Culture to become the international meeting place where all researchers could meet and exchange ideas, where they could study other cultures while preserving the identity of their own. This would lead to an appreciation of "world culture," of which individual cultures are but diverse manifestations, and ultimately to the recognition of human unity, his Grand Dream.

I do not know to what extent this idea is being fulfilled today, but if we have any responsibility, if we are really devotees, friends, and admirers of Swami Nitya-swarup-ananda, this responsibility revolves on each one of us to carry this programme into action. He was himself a man of action, a dynamic personality, and he would not rest till he found that his idea or dream was realized or fulfilled.

I will close my talk with a line from Rabindranath Tagore: "All the days of my life will be illumined by the radiance of your being, and all the nights of my life will be graced by the beauty of your personality." Swami Nitya-swarup-ananda entered into mahasamadhi on October 22 of last year, but his spirit is still there, and his spirit will remain so long as India will remain, so long as its cultural identity will remain— so long as India will say that not out of hatred but out of peace and love she will stretch her hands to all human beings all over the world. This is the grand dream that has to be fulfilled.

THE KEYNOTE ADDRESS
Human Unity and Global Civilization:
Swami Vivekananda's Vision
Dr. Triguna Sen

I feel very happy and privileged to be here as the keynote speaker on this auspicious occasion of the First Swami Nitya-swarup-ananda

Memorial Lecture. I will be speaking to you on a topic that was very dear to the Swami's heart: education for human unity and world civilization. It was the centrepiece of the Swami's life's work, and thus, I feel, a befitting subject for the keynote address in his honour.

In addressing you, I will discuss firstly, Swami Vivekananda's vision that inspired Swami Nitya-swarup-ananda to dedicate his lifelong energies to this work; secondly, the practical educational programmes that Swami Nitya-swarup-ananda himself envisioned in his many publications on the development of a world civilization, or global civilization, to use the current phrase. This, of course, includes his founding and development of the unique Ramakrishna Mission Institute of Culture in Gol Park, which he conceived of specially as a world civilization centre for education in human unity. And thirdly, I will conclude with a discussion of Swami Nitya-swarup-ananda's brilliant vision of the fulfilment of mankind's spiritual destiny as the ultimate goal of world civilization, and of India's role in world spiritualization.

Swami Nitya-swarup-ananda regarded this particular quotation of Swamiji as expressing the basic viewpoint [of human unity]:

> One atom in this universe cannot move without dragging the whole world along with it. There cannot be any progress without the whole world following in the wake, and it is becoming every day clearer that the solution of any problem can never be attained on racial, or national, or narrow grounds. Every idea has to become broad till it covers the whole of this world, every aspiration must go on increasing till it has engulfed the whole of humanity, nay, the whole of life, within its scope.

Swami Nitya-swarup-ananda's conclusion was that education alone could bring about the new world order envisioned by Swami Vivekananda. I will attempt to summarize for you Swami Nitya-swarup-ananda's key points on why we need a new type of education to move us into the new world order.

1: It is a fact of reality that the world as a whole is interrelated and interdependent. Progress must be progress for all. What happens in one place affects everyone everywhere else. This is increasingly recog-

Dr. Triguna Sen delivering the keynote address

nized on the material plane, but has yet to be recognized as having a spiritual basis. As Swami Vivekananda said, "Wherever there has been expansion in love or progress in well-being, of individuals or of numbers, it has been through the perception, realization, and practicalisation of the eternal truth—the oneness of all beings." We get a glimpse of this spiritual unity in our daily relations with those whom we deeply love, whose hopes we share, and whom we cherish regardless of any momentary clashes of opinion. But Swamiji is calling us to a deeper and broader love of mankind itself, a cherishing that goes beyond the family, beyond national boundaries, and beyond any form of self-interest, to embrace the whole human race.

2: Science and technology are closing the distances between people on the physical plane, but unity in the political, social, and economic spheres lags behind. What is missing in these spheres is the consciousness that mankind itself is the community; what is needed in these spheres is the consciousness that we must all live peacefully together as cohabitants of this planet Earth—that we must work together, struggle together, and support each other as a totality, even to survive. But are we ready for this? Or do we ourselves need education for the future unity of mankind? An honest answer to this question readily reveals that we are not ready for this. The fact is that we, as well as the rest of mankind, are in a great dilemma. The vast majority of humanity is not yet psychologically prepared or equipped to take a global stance or to accept a world view, much less to implement the concept of "one world, one people, one soul." The spectre of dreaded change is more apt to provoke reactionary conservatism in the human mind.

3: One of the main necessities of this new education envisioned by Swami Nitya-swarup-ananda is that the idea of "one world, one people, one soul" must be accepted within the diversity of various cultures— diverse, yes, but impelled by the same goal for the good of all. There is no dichotomy between this ultimate altruism and self-interest, for once it is realized that one is oneself a part of the greater consciousness, and that one is dependent upon the integrity of this consciousness for one's own well-being, the whole must be accepted as the sum of its diverse parts.

In pursuit of this all-embracing perspective, Swami Nitya-swarup-ananda called for worldwide human enrichment and human progress, to foster worldwide happiness and human fulfilment. His blueprint for "Education for World Civilization" involves a planned educational programme of cultural interaction and multicultural enrichment to eradicate ingrained separatism, without sacrificing the wisdom of one's own cultural tradition. Can we honestly deny that this concept of wel-coming other cultures as an enrichment to our own, however essential to the future global community, is severely lacking at the present moment? There are too many chauvinistic cultural hackles. It is only natural to say, "My culture is best, and what do I need to learn from any other culture?" We cling out of comfortable habit to our old ways of thought and behaviour. We must have the courage to examine our own culture critically.

We lay the blame for our discomfort on science and technology, but science and technology are not to blame for making these realities [of multicultural proximity] self-evident. Science and technology, rather than being the problem, provide the material framework for global unity, and are constructive in moving forward the interdependence of life. Instead of decrying the global influence of science and technology, this powerful technological network should be put to proper use to communicate to the whole world the facts and the remedies of our global interdependence. We must use all the tools of modern science to further these ends, as well as all the insights and wisdom of the world's varied cultures. Science and technology are not the problem, our outmoded attitudes are the problem—and the solution also lies in our hands.

Let us as individuals be part of the solution instead of part of the problem. Each of us, as Swami Nitya-swarup-ananda said, must find within ourselves and the world around us a profound sense of unity; each of us must come to realize that in spite of outward appearances, we as individuals are interrelated and interdependent. Then we will be able to accept differences in thought and ideas, and different ways of life, as but different expressions of the same basic reality and as enriching experiences. It is then that we will acquire a sense of human community and release ourselves from the old, narrow attitudes and feelings.

Now let us examine, at least briefly, the innovative concept in Swami Nitya-swarup-ananda's educational process of a thorough grounding in one's own culture, followed by a confrontation between cultures as a source of enrichment for ourselves as well as for the world community. As he put it, the birth of a global point of view can take place only when each and every nation of the world finds its own cultural identity. It is only by utilizing our own distinctive cultural riches that we can enrich the global community and make a distinctive contribution to the new world order. In a world already unified by modern science and technology, this new type of education calls for a carefully planned confrontation of cultures. This confrontation will take the form of an educational programme in which scholars and students from all parts of the world will participate. The outcome will not be skin-deep knowledge, but a living experience for teachers and students alike. Through an active process in which everyone is engaged, each individual will enter into ways of thinking and living different from his or her own.

Swami Nitya-swarup-ananda had all this in mind when he envisioned the prototype of an educational institution. It led, inevitably, to his founding of the Institute of Culture as a centre of world culture and civilization. It is a testament to the success of the Swami's personal achievement that UNESCO in 1961 acclaimed the Institute of Culture as its prototype for international, intercultural, and interracial understanding. Under the Swami's guidance, it became not only the first, but the only, such institution in the whole world. Even so, given the far-reaching and lofty goals that the Swami envisioned for the ultimate education for world civilization, he was not satisfied that these conditions had been fulfilled during his lifetime, and he was never complacent with the accomplishment. He was ever exploring new realms to bring Swami Vivekananda's vision of human unity and mankind's divine Oneness into our present-day life.

4: Finally, there is a need for the new education because mankind has an ultimate spiritual destiny to fulfil. There is a continuity in the traditions of human civilization. The past has brought us to the present, and the present will influence the future. Swami Nitya-swarup-ananda believed that India has a critical role to play in this future spiritual destiny. On the surface, the situation does not look much better as regards India. Our own country is now facing the same terrible problems at each level of its existence—political, social, cultural, economic, and religious. If we go to the root of this malaise, we will find that we as a nation are moving away from our own cultural identity. As Swami Nitya-swarup-ananda said, only by a thorough grounding in one's own distinctive cultural genius can any contribution to the world view be made.

In our heart of hearts, I think many recognize that India's spiritual heritage and ideals are, indeed, the essence of her unique national genius, and the source of her life-force. Swami Vivekananda commented on this when he said that economic improvements, education, social reform—all such things will have to be introduced through religion in India. We must return to our consciousness of the eternal truth of spiritual unity and human solidarity in our civilization. It is only after becoming conscious of this life-force that India will awaken to a wider sense of responsibility and to the contribution she can make to world thought, this spiritualization of the human race.

Our assurance comes in the words of our great prophet of the new age, Swami Vivekananda, who said that mankind's destiny is ultimately a spiritual destiny. Shall we dispute the words of our prophet, or shall we as individuals who are privileged to be aware of Swamiji's vision do whatever we can in our own lives to carry this great destiny forward on a spiritual level, as well as human level? We need not be overwhelmed by the apparent hopelessness of our problems and situations. I quote Swami Vivekananda again:

> We believe that every human being is divine, is God. Every soul is a sun covered over with clouds of ignorance; the difference between soul and soul is due to the difference in density of these layers of clouds. We believe that this is the conscious or unconscious basis of all religions, and that this is the explanation of the whole history of human progress either in the material, intellectual, or spiritual plane—the same spirit is manifesting through different planes.

And this is Swami Vivekananda's declaration of the culmination of harmony:

> We want to lead mankind to the place where there is neither the Vedas, nor the Bible, nor the Koran; yet this has to be done by harmonising the Vedas, the Bible, and the Koran. Mankind ought to be taught that religions are but the varied expressions of THE RELIGION which is Oneness, so that each may choose the path that suits him best.

The spiritualization of the human race was Swamiji's ultimate sacred trust, and Swami Nitya-swarup-ananda devoted *Divine Rights of the Sangha*, his final book, to this sacred trust. He concludes his inspired analysis in *Divine Rights of the Sangha* with Swamiji's statement of hope to all of us: "The day of Sri Ramakrishna's divine descent heralded the dawn of the Satya-Yuga, the Age of Divine Enlightenment." Let us be worthy, not only of a new world of human unity and global civilization, but also of our sacred inheritance of a new Age of Divine Enlightenment. Swami Nitya-swarup-ananda devoted his entire life in this cause. Let us try to emulate his example in our own life, to our own capacity. That would be the only proper homage to this great and dedicated child of Sri Ramakrishna, Holy Mother, and Swami Vivekananda.

A word about my personal relationship with Swami Nitya-swarup-ananda. From the day when he first acquired that plot of land where you see Gol Park, the President of the Ramakrishna Mission Institute of Culture requested that I should be the Vice-President while Swami Nitya-swarup-ananda was the Secretary. I was busy at the time, working in a small institution, Jadavpur, trying in a humble way to develop it into a university, but in spite of it, I spent most of the time with Swami Nitya-swarup-ananda in the Institute, thinking and planning with him. I cannot forget those years of my life that I had the benefit of his association. I remember him with respect and honour.

HIGHLIGHTS FROM THE PANEL DISCUSSIONS

PANEL I: INDIA'S MESSAGE TO HERSELF

Professor Santwana Dasgupta: India's ancient truths are of immense importance at this moment of the worst national crisis in India's history, a crisis of national identity in which divisive forces seek to destroy national unity. In India's holy past, the first and foremost distinctive ideas are the divinity of all beings, the spirituality of life, and the universality of any true religion. These ancient truths are not meant to be taken on blind faith, but as directly realized experience that culminates in complete identification with all that exists in the universe, as in Sri Ramakrishna's supreme identification with the suffering of all beings. There is no room for persecution, dogmatism, or intolerance in the light of such experience. The salvation of India today does not lie in the pseudosecularism of the West being preached by our denationalized

Panel I participants. *Seated, left to right:* Professor Dipak Kumar Barua, Professor Santwana Dasgupta, Swami Yuktananda, Professor Amiya Kumar Majumdar, Dr. Somen Das, and Professor Hossainur Rahaman.

intellectuals, but in the great ideal of universal religion as preached by India from time immemorial. The modern prophets, Ramakrishna and Vivekananda, proved that this great ideal is still living.

Far from being allied with fanaticism, bigotry, and sectarianism, authentic religious experience validates the unity of all beings, and is the basis for India's national unity as called for by Swami Vivekananda. We Hindus know that all religions are but so many attempts of the human soul to realize the infinite.

Professor Hossainur Rahaman: I have had the privilege to know Swami Nitya-swarup-ananda, this great monk of the Ramakrishna Order. What I gathered from him in his last days was this: that India's message is "live and learn, live and love, live and sacrifice." There is a need to sacrifice for suffering humanity, including the sacrifice of one's exclusiveness. We want humanity, but we do not want compartmentalization of that humanity.

In India, we want liberation from the yoke of mental stagnation. An ideological straitjacket does not work. India has no religion in the ordinary sense of the term, for religion in India is a whole-time preoccupation that every Indian has to live in every moment.

The new national identity that India has been trying to develop since 1947 has been broadly based, not on political unity in the sense that the West uses political unity, but on social harmony through spiritualization. We have been trying to do this through a kind of inner voice coming out from the inner depth of consciousness. This is India's vital message to the rest of the world, and probably to herself doubly, that we must raise our inner voice in order to solve the conflict. We have to raise the dimension of our consciousness to understand the harmonious social instinct of the human being. In our country, religion means ultimately socialization, spiritualization, of the human being.

Professor Dipak Kumar Barua: Buddha's teachings of peace, compassion, and tolerance are as relevant today as they were many centuries ago. The Buddhist code of ethics is universal in nature. It is a framework wherein people can learn and respect the fundamentals of one another's dharma. It brings diverse people together.

The sacred utterances of Lord Buddha aim to maintain social integration and communal harmony among people of various faiths. As emphasized by Swami Nitya-swarup-ananda, there is a fundamental right to freedom of religion, and a need for continuous give and take between religions for mutual enrichment. The harmony of religions is the basis of universal peace and development.

Each panel concluded with an open discussion, based on written questions submitted to the speakers from the audience. After the first panel, one questioner wrote: "Why is there the apparent dichotomy between India's spiritual heritage and current divisiveness? If ours is such a rich heritage, why are riots happening today?" On the same theme, another questioner asked, "The message of India down the ages has been dignity of man and universality, peace, and harmony—or is it otherwise in view of all the

Professor Hossainur Rahaman and Professor Santwana Dasgupta,
replying to questions from the audience

current troubles?" The panelists replied to these and other questions
about the troubling gap between India's ideals and her present reality as
follows:

Professor Hossainur Rahaman: Too much politicization and too much
insistence on economics has done this disservice to India's heritage.
Heritage is not a commodity, but is something to be practised by the
people of a country.

Professor Santwana Dasgupta: Throughout the ages India has been one
nation. It was never divided. It has embraced every new idea that has
come from outside. This catholicity of attitude we have forgotten
today. We have forgotten to practise it. We must learn to coexist, we
must "live to learn, live to love," as Professor Rahaman has said—and,
I must add, we must live to serve, to serve others, to serve humanity.

Reverend Dr. Somen Das (Moderator): I believe that we are meeting at a
very critical juncture in the history of humanity, in the history of this

great nation. We have a glorious heritage, and it seems that we are betraying our own heritage. It is at that point that we must remind ourselves of
the message of Swami Vivekananda and Swami Nitya-swarup-ananda,
and it is a matter of joy that we can do this together this evening. As Dr.
Triguna Sen has reminded us in the memorable words of Swami
Vivekananda, the discoveries of spiritual science make it incumbent on
every religion to lead humankind to the place where there is neither the
Vedas, nor the Bible, nor the Koran, yet this has to be done by harmonizing the Vedas, the Bible, and the Koran. I believe that remains our message, and it must persist.

PANEL II: INDIA'S MESSAGE TO THE WORLD

Dr. Sushil Kumar Mukherjee: From the scientific viewpoint, we need a
synthesis of ancient ideals with the technology of the West. In the
course of the last two hundred years, India has been increasingly under
the influence of a technological civilization that has helped her to take
care of material needs and to acquire mastery over nature. But gradually it has been realized that material and physical achievements are
nothing if they are not strengthened by spiritual values.

Recognition that the tyranny of the material world is taking its toll
has prompted a new trend to look back and try to recapture spiritual
values, but the problem remains of how to do so. Sri Ramakrishna and
Swami Vivekananda are the brightest examples of the recent past, the
embodiments of India's message to the world. They demonstrated
unequivocally in their lives and teaching how spiritual values could be
made the basis of modern life in order that the nations of the world
could live together in peaceful coexistence.

Swami Vivekananda wanted the integration of the ancient faith of
India with modern humanism, in order to synthesize the ideals of India
with the West. Through the worship of the common man, who lives,
works, and suffers in all men, Swami Vivekananda tried to harmonize,
for India as well as for the world, the enormous potentialities of Indian
religion and ethics for a social, egalitarian movement. This was echoed

Dr. Sushil Kumar Mukherjee and Swami Yuktananda (on Panel II)

in Swami Nitya-swarup-ananda's plea for "consecration in the service of the universal man."

The spectacular achievements of science and technology stand in contrast to the wanton degradation of the environment, an alarming situation viewed by many scientists as the possible end of *Homo sapiens*, and by others as the mere replacement of the biosphere with a techno-sphere capable of satisfying all human needs. The sensible approach of teaching men to coexist with nature and with themselves is the scheme Indian ancients followed in all their daily activities of life; this is also a source of wisdom for our troubled planet today.

India must develop herself, to establish unity, equality, and har-mony at home, and to rise again to a great height; only then would she make her rightful spiritual contribution to the progress and civilization of the world.

Dr. Kalyan Dasgupta: Examples from India's long history illustrate her commitment to interreligious understanding. Since the Rig Veda, which anticipated the doctrine of nondualism later associated with Shankara-charya, India has been a land of diverse religions, a land of assimilation.

In spite of their elaborate pantheon, Hindus can see in their multiple divinities this great One, the Supreme Reality.

Coupled with this ideal of unity, India's unbounded love for mankind, and the perennial belief in the greatness of man, have created a spirit of tolerance. Great men of India through the ages have worked to pro-mote religious understanding for the good of humanity. India's history abounds in the practical results of a faith in monism, from Ashoka to Gandhi, who said, "I believe in Advaita. I believe in the essential unity of man, for that matter all that lives. I believe that if one man gains spiritually, the whole world gains with him, and if one man falls, the whole world falls to that extent."

There are many lesser-known examples of this universal view, such as the folk monism of the Baul poet-singers of Bengal. Sophisticated and folk levels share a sense of cultural oneness, and the feeling of a universal spirit.

Such cultural values are rooted in Indian "dharma," a word of deeper import than "religion." In dharma there is no dry ritualism, no superiority complex, and no ill feeling. Its essence lies in nonviolence and universal goodwill. These are the two basic principles of our dharma and our culture, practised for millennia by the best souls of India, whether celebrated or anonymous.

Swami Nitya-swarup-ananda's world view is in perfect consonance with the spirit of our age-old culture. His concept of a World Civilization Centre is a means to enable man to recognize the truth of world unity.

Srimat Swami Yuktananda (Moderator): Dr. Mukherjee indicated that power over nature has become dominant in advanced countries instead of spiritual values. In contrast, our Indian heritage views power in terms of how little one needs to live a contented life—the idea of "simple sufficiency." This is eco-friendly. In his submission, Dr. Das-gupta pointed out that without emotional integration, what have we achieved through science and technology by fostering one world for one mankind to live in? In a situation like this, if we remain emotionally isolated and divided, and our actions are divisive and destructive, then everything will be lost.

PANEL III: GLOBAL SOCIETY: THE EMERGING SCENARIO

Dr. Shelley Brown: Swami Nitya-swarup-ananda was our role model for a global citizen in the West—a true master in the art of cultural assimilation.

We learned by his living example of what he referred to in his books as "cultural confrontation." By this he meant the deep assimilation of other cultural values, not the adoption of foreign cultural ideas and forms at the expense of one's own, but rather an integration of both value systems to produce a reconfiguration of one's mind and psyche. He knew that this integrative process would create inner tension, but he also knew that it was the only way to replace narrow attitudes and prejudices with a world view.

In our dynamic encounter with the Swami, we began to learn new ways of incorporating spiritual values into our own cultural assets. The stage was set for our education by the Swami's candid interaction with us. This was a mind-to-mind and soul-to-soul spiritual dialogue, not mere friendliness, but we quickly felt that the Swami made us his very own. He conveyed to us in a perfectly natural, loving, often humorous way, the truths of our own culture and our own lives, both that which he appreciated and that which he felt was harmful or irrelevant to our spiritual life. The deep, focused concern of the Swami for our welfare, the authenticity and sensitivity and insight of his every word, his expressiveness, and his constant absorption in another, spiritual world (without the slightest conceit or pretense) deeply touched our hearts. And so practical were his suggestions, so strength-giving were his words, so confidence-building was his encouragement as we struggled to incorporate his penetrating insights into the very fabric of our lives!

This was truly a living transmission to us of India's living spiritual tradition. At the same time, it was a deeper grounding in the essentials of our own culture, and a challenge to some of our most cherished

Panel III participants. *Seated, left to right:* Dr. Shelley Brown, Swami Yuktananda,
Professor Amiya Kumar Majumdar, and Dr. Abdul Subhan.

misconceptions—all seen through the prism of the Swami's vast
understanding and appreciation for all cultures worldwide.

I will describe four concrete examples, using his own words of
advice to us, to illustrate this ongoing educational process of cultural
confrontation and assimilation:

First, he was opposed to the idea that the superficial engraftment of
another culture's external forms had any relevance whatsoever to our
spiritual life. This had nothing to do with authentic cultural confrontation. While in India, he preferred us to wear Western dress, except in
certain ceremonial settings, to sit on chairs as we are accustomed to do
(and which he always insisted upon in his presence), and to eat with
our usual utensils, forks and knives, unless the situation was made
more graceful otherwise. He would seldom permit us to make pranam
to him, as that is not our custom, and when we did occasionally man-
age to do so, he would immediately quote in the most amusing way
from the *Ashtavakra Samhita,* telling us, "Before making pranam to
anyone, first think 'How wonderful am I!' You are bowing to your own
self by bowing to all—don't lose confidence in the indwelling spirit. If
you don't recognize it there, you won't find it anywhere."

Secondly, he praised ambition. In America, a land of immigrants
who have sacrificed much and worked hard to give their children a better life, it is considered a cultural asset to be ambitious and to take
responsibility for one's own self-fulfilment. Devotees are, therefore,

sometimes confused about ambition in terms of a spiritual life of self-abnegation. Swami Nitya-swarup-ananda would immediately say to this, "But ambition is *good*." Ambition, he urged, is necessary to raise the mind from inertia. What one wishes to become, one *can* become. Life itself is being and becoming. Life itself is spiritual practice. Live and move and have your being in God and God alone. Be ambitious to become established in that consciousness in every moment of your life.

Thirdly, regarding self-surrender, he would say, "God-dependence means to *challenge* the Mother, this is faith." He always gave the example of the time he heard Swami Premananda's soul-enthralling rendition in a *fighting* spirit of the song "Mother, am I thine eighth month child" from the *Kathamrita*. He emphasized, "Faith makes the child invincible. If one feels Grace, one becomes immediately invincible.This is the sign of real Grace. You are a child of the Mother—all Her strength you have inherited. *This* is faith." Then there is courage to stand for the Truth, and to fight this battle of life and all the circumstances which try to crush you down. Be an instrument, and fight for Truth. *This* is self-surrender.

Fourthly, regarding power, he would say, "Without developing power, nothing can be achieved, either spiritual or intellectual. Without power you cannot control the mind or get rid of the conditioning of the mind. It takes tremendous strength and power of mind to harness the power of the ego and restrain it: *sattva* is not meekness, it is ego-power spiritualized, it is *power restrained*. And it takes inconceivable power to transcend the body and mind.

On hearing such forceful words from the Swami, we would find our own cultural values reinforced as a spiritual *sadhana* at the same time we were relieved that it was not necessary to adopt an Eastern cultural mode for the sake of a devoted life. On the contrary, he conveyed to us the idea that this emphasis on ambition and power in our own culture could be a contribution from the West in the form of a dynamic empowerment of a sense of individuality for those who lack faith in themselves and who are in the grip of a helpless *tamasic* fatalism, masquerading as self-surrender to the divine will.

On the other hand he warned us against what he called the American idea of freedom which he termed the idea of "Do as you please." He was adamantly opposed to the identification with body and mind which permitted one to "roam freely in the forest like a beast," and in which instinct replaces discrimination. True freedom, he told us, comes only through perfect control of the mind so that one is no longer bound by its demands. This is spiritual freedom. And it was precisely in this type of context that Swami Nitya-swarup-ananda would introduce to us the theme of renunciation as the precious spiritual heritage from India which we very much need in the West. He would quote Swami Vivekananda that India has found the solution in unworldliness and renunciation, and that this is the theme of India's lifework—the spiritualization of the human race.

The Swami led us to a new appreciation for this special genius of your culture. Many of us had already been tenderized by pilgrimages to India, and had already grown to love the quality of your lives, the exquisite sensitivity and delicacy of your relationships, and your all-pervading sense of reverence. This, too, became a part of our education in cultural confrontation.

It is not possible to do justice to the profound impact of this process of spiritual cultural integration on our personal lives, but Swami Nitya-swarup-ananda showed us that this is not mere idealism; it can be implemented in our own lives, and, indeed, it must be implemented on a large scale for the development of global citizens with a consciousness of the human race as a whole. Education for world civilization is the new global imperative.... If we do not change our attitudes to embrace all that is holy and worthy of our respect throughout the world and from every culture, and from every nation, surely we have missed Swami Nitya-swarup-ananda's point.

Srimat Swami Yuktananda: The global society is Truth Absolute. Its emergence is already palpable. This was predicted when Swami Vivekananda proclaimed, "I shall inspire men everywhere until the world shall know that it is one with God." Swami Nitya-swarup-ananda liked this sentence very much, and in the last conversation I had with him over the telephone, two or three days before he passed away, he told me to remember always that proclamation of Swamiji through all actions. I will discuss it now from several viewpoints.

In the systems view of the social development of a newborn, initial awareness of identity—a sense of "I-ness"—enlarges gradually to include the mother, the family, the neighbourhood, the nation. This expansion of consciousness towards unity is the story of human civilization. Civilization expands from small fighting tribes, to larger groups, nations, and federal states. Without relinquishing the narrowness of the individual ego, man is always trying to feel oneness with the universe through communication. Within our self-centredness, there is an inherent human inspiration to be unified with cosmic existence. We are progressing to one world not only physically but emotionally as well.

From the spiritual viewpoint, each individual is a pilgrim from ignorance to sainthood. This transfigurative journey to egolessness and enlightenment is a process of deification. The emergence of global society as a deified humanity is caused by the transformation of individuals. Only when this spiritual awakening occurs on a large scale will justice, fellow-feeling, sharing, and other refined qualities develop. Humankind is progressing towards that. Suffering is for purification. The voices of Sri Ramakrishna and Swami Vivekananda are being heard through their followers, such as Swami Nitya-swarup-ananda, who are the agents of change for a new society which is not to be achieved overnight.

Dr. Abdul Subhan (Moderator): I happen to be a Muslim, not a theologian. The physical unity and spiritual unity of mankind have been proven in the Koran, and by the great Sufi mystics that India has produced. And mankind is exalted in the Koran as unsurpassed in the divine hierarchy of creation—higher than the angels, which are invisible to us. All that has been created is for man only, and only man has the capacity to bring all that God has wrought under his control. Mankind is the key element in the emerging global scenario.

CONCLUDING ADDRESS
Professor Amiya Kumar Majumdar

The speakers in the first panel, "India's Message to Herself," pointed out that India's message rests not on blind faith but on realization. It is not speculation but the sages' intuitive experience of truth which reminds Indians of their soul, of their central message in life. Religion is not reserved for a particular time or date but is coeval with life; it is life-permeating, life-transforming. India's message to herself includes the concept of sacrifice, the sacrifice of one's own self for the betterment of suffering humanity, and of submission, not to authority but to conscience, to intuitive insight. Finally there is liberation from the erroneous, partial, fragmentary view of humanity as a whole.

When we come to the second panel, "India's Message to the World," it is a question of emphasis. Swami Vivekananda used to say that when I go to foreign countries, I speak of spirituality, but when I speak to my Indian brethren, I speak of material progress and prosperity. Those who have had the opportunity to go through the "Rules and Regulations of the Belur Math framed by Swamiji in 1898" must have seen that he says that this Math will in course of time be transformed into a university and that emphasis should be laid on technical education. He is saying that it is the prime duty of a monk to give hungry millions of people food.

Swami Nitya-swarup-ananda was such a brilliant doctor in diagnosing these ills of human society! He foresaw that we are heading towards a catastrophe of unimaginable magnitude as we enter into the threshold of the twenty-first century. He said that there will be four thousand million starving people confronting one thousand million affluent, well-fed people—but that fight will not be worthwhile for the underprivileged because the affluent society is armed with deadly weapons, whereas the poor are not armed with any weapons whatsoever. This is why Swami Vivekananda emphasized that the poor must be fed, cared for, and educated. No politics will be of any avail.

The speakers on the second panel also rightly pointed out that science and technology have paved the way for physical intercourse between one nation and another. Space and time have been conquered and the world has shrunk into a very small unit. Yet scientific advancements have not wiped out the evils of hatred, oppression, and violence in the hearts of peoples; the scientific achievements in the outer world are out of balance with the achievements of man in his inner world, which has created chaos and confusion in human society. That is why the speakers have emphasized that what Swami Vivekananda said is very relevant: Vedanta and science should be harmonized.

The ecological problem is really a spiritual problem. Swami Vivekananda, and following him Swami Nitya-swarup-ananda, time and again reminded us that the spiritual and the material are not mutually antagonistic. Rather, the material serves as the foundation on which spiritual values flourish and can be promoted. Therefore, Swami Nitya-swarup-ananda never condemned science and technology. He never made a dichotomy between sensate civilization and ideational civilization. He said one is a stepping-stone to the other. We must develop a sense of friendship with nature. Nature and man are really two aspects of the same unity. There is a kinship between the two. But we must curb our consumerism (materialism of the worst type) and reduce our wants to the maximum.

In the third panel, "The Emerging Global Scenario," it was pleaded that the time has come to discard isolationism, divisionism, and rootless secularism, and to develop emotional integration. What is needed is an integral education in which the body, the mind, the psychic being, and the spiritual will be developed and coordinated into a whole. For this, a very practical scheme has been formulated by Swami Nitya-swarup-ananda in his book *Education for Human Unity and World*

Civilization. And this is found in his own life, for he was an integrated personality, a global citizen, whom both East and West could relate to and appreciate.

On the theme of the expansion of the individual from self-centredness to self-transcendence, Swami Nitya-swarup-ananda was fond of saying, "Hinduism is not a proselytizing religion—still there is a kind of conversion in Hinduism." Anxiously we looked up and asked, "What is it, Swamiji?" and he replied, "It is a conversion from the 'I'-centred egotistical existence to the 'all'-centred universal existence."

All the speakers in the three panels have focused on the main point, that is humanism. Man has a central position in the universe. The message of India, both to herself and to the world, is recognition of human excellence, the dignity of human life, and the spiritual solidarity of humankind.

Second Swami Nitya-swarup-ananda
Memorial Lecture Programme
February 22, 1994

Professor Amiya Kumar Majumdar
Chairman

FIRST SESSION: 6:00 P.M.

Welcoming Remarks

Mrs. Shubhra Chatterji, for Friends of Swami Nitya-swarup-ananda

Vedic Invocation

Dr. Govinda Gopal Mukherjee

Theme Address

Dr. Shelley M. Brown

Religious Speakers

Islam:	Dr. Md Shahidullah
	Principal, Calcutta Madrassah College
Christianity:	Reverend Sujoy Bannerji
	Bishop's College
Hinduism:	Srimat Swami Yuktananda
	Vivekananda Nidhi

Buddhist Chanting

Monks from the Mahavodhi Society of India

SECOND SESSION: 7:30 P.M.

Sufi Chanting

Panelists

Justice Sishir Kumar Mukherji
Judge, Calcutta High Court (Ret'd)

Professor Hiranmoy Bannerji
Professor of Philosophy, Jadavpur University

Dr. Sushil Kumar Mukherjee
Ex-Vice-Chancellor, Calcutta University

Summation

Professor Amiya Kumar Majumdar

Baul Song

Vishwanath Baul - Bolepur

———

A bold theme was chosen for the Second Swami Nitya-swarup-ananda Memorial Lecture Programme, held on February 22, 1994. The idea of going "beyond tolerance" added a new dimension to the usual interfaith discussions in a world where peaceful religious coexistence contends with communal strife. The programme guide for the occasion outlined the reasons for the theme:

BACKGROUND AND OBJECTIVE

With a lifelong dedication to the implementation of Swami Viveka-nanda's vision of human unity, Swami Nitya-swarup-ananda often wrote on the theme of "Religion is Oneness" as the universal per-spective which must be imparted to an ever-shrinking, yet increas-ingly fragmented and strife-torn world. In *India's Message to Herself and to the World*, he described this non-dualistic consciousness of spiritual unity to be India's cultural genius, her life-force, her contri-bution to mankind's wisdom, and her mission in the spiritualization of the human race. He stressed the fundamental right to freedom of religion, and the harmony of religions as the basis of universal peace.

A complementary theme in Swami Nitya-swarup-ananda's publi-cations was his emphasis on the value of diversity in contributing to the richness of mankind's store of wisdom: as all religions are the varied expressions of Ultimate Truth, spiritual wisdom is a common heritage from which all can benefit, and not the exclusive property of any individual or culture. For the same reason, no particular religion can claim any special privilege, an illogical limitation to only one aspect of the universal self.

An acceptance of the world's great faiths on their own merits, and in the light of their unity in Ultimate Truth, is a far loftier goal than the attitude of special privilege which results in either intolerance or tolerance, two sides of the same coin. It also goes far beyond a super-ficial appreciation, for as Swami Vivekananda said, "We must become many-sided, indeed we must become protean in character, so as not only to tolerate, but to do what is much more difficult, to sympathize, to enter into another's path, and feel with him in his aspirations and seeking after God."

The objective of the Second Memorial Lecture Programme is to explore the various aspects of the challenging task of going beyond tolerance to profound acceptance, based on the highest truths of India's perennial philosophy: the awareness of unity in diversity and the universal religion of God-consciousness.

Several meetings were held with the speakers in preparation for the symposium. Professor Amiya Kumar Majumdar chaired these meetings and set a high philosophical tone as he explored common ground for interreligious understanding. An "Approach Paper" by the author, distributed at the meetings, helped focus the discussion on the transcendental aspects of religion, such as the universal experience of God-consciousness. The decision to include musical chanting from the various faiths made the venture doubly challenging, and the "Friends of Swami Nitya-swarup-ananda" laboured to pull everything together in time. Early in the evening on February 22, the speakers and musicians gathered in the wings as the audience took their seats. The curtain rose to the strains of music composed by the twelfth-century saint Hildegard von Bingen, the liturgical prelude to the event.

The brief review of the programme in this section, excerpted from a selective tape recording of the event, presents a few highlights from the author's theme address, the talks of the three religious speakers, and the Chairman's summation.

THE THEME ADDRESS
Beyond Tolerance
Dr. Shelley Brown

"We must become many-sided... so as not only to tolerate but to do what is much more difficult...." These words of Swami Vivekananda inspired our theme: the need to go beyond tolerance to a genuine acceptance of other faiths *as equal to our own*. Swamiji was relentless in exposing the attitude of the conceited person who tolerates others from a sense of superiority. Tolerance is still bigotry, he warned in a forceful letter to his brother-disciple, Swami Ramakrishnananda:

> Remember this specially, that universality—perfect acceptance, not tolerance only—we preach and perform. Take care how you trample on the rights of others.... Remember, perfect devotion minus bigotry—that is what we have got to show.

THE SECOND MEMORIAL LECTURE PROGRAMME

Mrs. Shubhra Chatterji delivering the welcome

Professor Amiya Kumar Majumdar presiding

Monks from the Mahavodhi Society

Baul singers from Bolepur

And it was perfect acceptance, not tolerance, that Swami Viveka-nanda proclaimed at the Parliament of Religions in 1893. Sitting among hundreds of representatives from the great religious traditions, he alone had the scope to embrace all their faiths and say to them, "Accept and understand one another"—which is still the best motto for religious harmony more than a century later.

"Accept and understand one another" are the words of a rishi, a world teacher, whose personal experience confirmed for modern times the eter-nal verities of India's perennial philosophy—the nonduality of the God-head, the divinity of the soul, and the unity of existence. Through his illu-mined eyes, Swamiji made others see that these ancient truths are living principles; they embody a nonsectarian credo that does not destroy any belief or demand any allegiance, but rather supports and strengthens the transcendental values of religion as a whole. He preached these universal principles to East and West alike, yet he knew that such vast concepts are not easily assimilated, since the human mind is conditioned to think in small, ordinary ways. "This great idea of the real and basic solidarity of the whole universe has frightened many, even in this country," Swamiji said to an audience in India, then added, "I tell you, nevertheless, that it is the one great life-giving idea which the world wants from us today."

... Swami Nitya-swarup-ananda took up this great life-giving idea of spiritual unity as one of his main themes. In *India's Message to Herself and to the World*, he defined religion as "the consciousness of the eternal truth of the spiritual solidarity of humankind," a clear echo of Swamiji. Yet the human challenge is to live harmoniously in the midst of diversity, to accept the universal spirit in its infinite phenomenal forms. To meet this practical challenge, Swami Nitya-swarup-ananda called for the cultivation of inter-religious enrichment, a profound give-and-take of spiritual ideas. There is much to share among the various faiths (a belief in God, the existence of the soul, reverence for holiness, and an ethical code of conduct), and much to learn (unfamiliar rituals, philosophies, and mythologies). As the learn-ing process deepens, understanding deepens, and the inner spiritual unity becomes revealed.

... In conclusion, I refer to the symbol before you on the dais, which Swami Nitya-swarup-ananda conceived to illustrate the concept of Religion is Oneness, and which signifies that all paths lead to the same goal. The radii represent different religions, and the centre is God. In God we all meet, as in a circle with many radii, all radii meet at the centre. The closer we come to God, the closer we shall feel to other religions. By devotedly following the deep spirit of our own faith, we shall approach the deep spirit of other faiths. At the centre we are One, where there is no longer any question of tolerance, but we need the wisdom to "accept and understand one another," until we finally reach that goal.

RELIGIOUS SPEAKERS

ISLAM

Dr. Mohammed Shahidullah (translated from the Bengali)
India is a land of many religions. I want to state to the representatives of different religions present in this hall, as well as to those worldwide, that the main aim of different faiths is to look for the Eternal Truth, and to surrender oneself to the Creator of this Universe. Sadly, in spite of this underlying unity of thought, what we observe today is that various religions are indulging ever more in fighting and dissent.

The Chairman of this meeting is a distinguished philosopher and I am like his student, so I am emboldened when I say that the meaning of religion according to Indian philosophy is something that holds us—a guiding force that protects us from all evil and injustice and takes us to all that is good, true, and beautiful. Our message is *Satyam-Shivam-Sundaram* [Truth-Goodness-Beauty]. To reach this goal we need to be broad-minded, patient, and aware; in short, we have to be accepting.

Swami Vivekananda has said that mankind ought to be taught that religions are but varied expressions of THE RELIGION which is ONE-NESS, so that each may choose the path that suits him best. The founder of Islam, Hasarat Mohammed, has said in the Koran, "Your religion is for you and my religion is for me," which means that we have the freedom to follow our own religion.... Hasarat Mohammed demonstrated throughout his life and work a liberal attitude towards all religions. This is one of the basic tenets of Islam.

...In the spiritual democracy of Islam, there is no difference between one person and another. The decree that Hasarat Mohammed gave to the priest of St. Catherine's Church can be cited as a shining example of religious freedom. The gist of the decree was as follows: Muslims would protect the homes and properties of the priests, no unjust taxes would be levied on them, no priest would be driven out from his church, no Christian would be forced to give up his religion, no Christian woman marrying a Muslim would be denied the freedom to practise her own religion, and no Christian church would be destroyed to build a mosque. Observing the liberal practices of Islam, Swami Vivekananda remarked [in a letter that referred to the equality of Advaitism as "the only position from which one can look upon all religions and sects with love"]: "On the other hand, my experience is that if ever any religion approached to this equality in an appreciable manner, it is Islam and Islam alone."

CHRISTIANITY

Reverend Sujoy Bannerji
...In its long and arduous journey in the path of ecumenism, the Christian faith has come to recognize and affirm the liberating role of all religions, and has stated boldly that the gospel requires us to assume that God's grace is offered to all. Through the experience of grace...and the love of God, one is enabled to recognize, respect, welcome, and embrace the authentic spiritual experiences that underlie all forms of religion. Absolutist, exclusivist, and fanatic positions are a denial of the Christian concept of God, whose nature is interrelational and dialogical.

It is true that each faith has its own particularity, its own limitation also. The limitations are built in by the historical development of a faith in its own social and cultural context.... Each religion must, therefore, recognize its particularity and its limitations, and search for fullness by transcending itself. Christianity shares with all religions its need to be complemented, its need to grow out of itself.... We have to discover where our egotistic, reactionary, hidebound self-consciousness has bridled the liberative power of our religions. It calls for people of every religion to strive together.... We have to learn to enter a meaningful, creative, and constructive relationship with peoples of other faiths, and even of no faith.

...The concept of tolerance in religion has undertones of superiority and condescension. It has the same egotistic element that has led to the isolation and indifference between religions today—a defense mechanism that stores religions in safe places, and a sure step towards sterility and fossilization. But in accepting other religions, we turn from our stoic indifference to a dynamic encounter with living faiths. Such an encounter cannot take place only at the intellectual or theoretical level; rather, it calls for a daring faith-sharing, even an immersion into the faith-experience of other religions.... Such an acceptance of people of other faiths, and of their profound aspirations, enables us to hear the cry of our world today for justice, peace, and integrity of creation.... Each religious tradition must contribute to our search for a meaningful community as God's family.

HINDUISM

Srimat Swami Yuktananda
Hinduism is not the creation of a single founder, and for this reason it has always welcomed and assimilated all faiths. Hinduism has had its basic tenets retested, reassessed, and reaffirmed by seers and saints down through the ages. The secret of its resilience and adaptability lies in the eternal principles that form the basis of its perennial faith.

...The question today is, can Hinduism hold its own when society is changing so rapidly? Manu, the ancient lawmaker who has been so often condemned as reactionary, made a very catholic statement. He said that any maxim or injunction of the shastras will be accepted or admitted only when it is found to be conducive to the good of humanity at large; if an ancient scriptural injunction does not fit in today and goes against human welfare, reject it as poison; if it contributes to human good, accept it as wholesome—that is the test. Likewise, "whatever endures for the good of humanity" is one of the meanings of *Satya* [Truth] at the heart of Hinduism, which acts as a strong pillar in withstanding and adapting to the circumstances of societal change.

...From the ancient Upanishads we learn that all things originate from Brahman [the Supreme Reality], and having been born in Brahman, all beings are sustained by bliss (ananda), which can never be taken away or lost. In Hinduism, therefore, since Supreme Reality is all-pervading, there is no consideration of evil or original sin. In Hinduism the Supreme Truth absorbs everything, good and bad. Truth, or bliss, is every person's innermost nature; our destiny is to be in bliss, to be fully identified with that bliss. It is a vast concept. In Hinduism, religion is only a tool to be used and then abandoned, for one must go beyond.

SUMMATION
Professor Amiya Kumar Majumdar

...Taking a very common-sense point of view of "tolerance," we often say, "I have to tolerate something which I cannot stop." Perhaps your neighbour is a nasty person, a ruffian who does not allow you to live peacefully, but you cannot stop him because he is stronger physically, politically, socially, or economically. Well, you have to tolerate him because you have no option, you cannot find another dwelling. Likewise, toleration may mean cowardly submission to an aggressor whom you cannot rectify or stop. On the other hand, toleration may mean allowing another's point of view to exist side by side with your own in coexistence and fellowship.

Dr. S. Radhakrishnan used the word "toleration" in a special sense. He was very fond of figures of speech. He said, "Toleration is a homage made by the finite mind to the inexhaustibility of the Infinite." Now, whatever meaning you take for a working definition, I should like to say that toleration means allowing another's religion to flourish in the same way as I would wish my own religion to flourish. So I should not make any distinction between my religion and another's religion. Why? Because I have to stand on that fundamental basis, namely, "Truth is One, but its expressions are many."

In his inimitable language, Swami Vivekananda said, "Religion is One, religions are many." It is difficult to comprehend the significance and inner meaning of this statement. Anthropologists and sociologists will not accept that "Religion is One but religions are many." But Swami Vivekananda has a special sense which means that there is unity of existence throughout the universe—man, lower animals, insects, vegetable kingdom—all are interrelated.

Dr. Sushil Kumar Mukherjee is here, an eminent scientist; I do not have the courage when he is present to speak before him, but students of science know that modern science is speaking of a stage of consciousness where Vedanta has already taken us. Modern science is taking us to that place where there is One Consciousness, One Cosmic Energy, and the universe is not to be looked upon as a collection of bricks, but as music, as a symphony or a poem—as something where parts are not isolated and then aggregated, but one enters into the other, as it were. As Bergson, the French philosopher, used to say, "The past enters into the present, and the present gnaws into the future."

So this interrelation is there, and when Swami Vivekananda spoke of Oneness, this is what he meant. He predicted that the day would come when science would confirm the Vedantic Truths regarding religion. By religion he did not mean muttering of beads or taking a dip in the Ganges, not going to temples or mosques, not doctrines and not talk— he meant realization. Of what? Of the potential divinity of man.

Is this acceptable to the Christians? In 1968, the seventy-fifth-year

Platinum Jubilee of the original Parliament of Religions was held in Chicago. A Christian representative there said that we have not yet heeded Swami Vivekananda's teaching to realize the potential divinity of man through the four Yogas—Bhakti, Jnana, Raja, and Karma. This is the most important thing. As Sri Aurobindo said in recent times, "All life is Yoga." This discipline is necessary, talk will not do! You can have a seminar or a symposium, but these will not give you religious harmony. It is Yoga which will create harmony. William James, despite his pluralistic universe, says, "Sometimes I catch a glimpse of the monastic music of Swami Vivekananda." He was a pluralist but was leaning to nondualism when he came in contact with Swami Vivekananda during his time. In his book *Varieties of Religious Experience,* he quoted profusely from Swami Vivekananda's *Jnana Yoga* and other works. James said, "I am wavering between pluralism on one hand and nondualism on the other," and added that he didn't know which way he would go.

I thank you for responding to our call for participating in this fruitful seminar, for paying respect to that savant and seer, Swami Nitya-swarup-ananda, who breathed religion, who lived religion in the sense in which Swami Vivekananda said, "Religion is Oneness."

We shall leave this hall with the refrain of that song "Religion is One," and it is our duty to make religion effective in our lives—not pseudoreligion, not fanaticism, not fundamentalism, but religion in its essence, which means spiritual solidarity of "mankind-as-a-whole," to use Swami Nitya-swarup-ananda's phrase. Every man is our brother because all of us have a common Father.

ILLUSTRATIONS

All photographs in Volume 2 are by the author unless otherwise noted.

Frontispiece: Commemorative portrait of Swami Nitya-swarup-ananda by Ramananda Bandyopadhyay, 2000.

Memorial Lecture Programmes

THE SECOND MEMORIAL LECTURE PROGRAMME
(Photographs by Dr. Arabinda Basu)

Photograph of the author by Gale G. Brown, M.D.

INDEX

Page numbers in italics indicate illustrations.

ABOUT THE AUTHOR

Dr. Shelley Brown began her study of Vedanta philosophy at the age of sixteen with Swami Nikhilananda, the founder of the Ramakrishna-Vivekananda Center in New York. With his encouragement, she left the world of classical ballet to attend Barnard College, where she completed her premedical courses while majoring in English literature.

Dr. Brown received her medical degree in 1963, and opened her clinical practice as a consultant Hematologist and Oncologist after seven years of postdoctoral training. She became a senior attending physician and the Director of the Blood Bank at Lenox Hill Hospital, with a teaching professorship at the New York University School of Medicine. She published widely, lectured internationally, and was asked to speak on philosophical as well as medical subjects during her annual visits to India after 1984.

The author's study of Vedanta philosophy came full circle in 1987 when she became engaged in a spiritual dialogue with Swami Nitya-swarup-ananda that went on unabated until he passed away. It galvanized her contemplative life, led to her early retirement, and inspired her to write the present opus, her first book.